Independence and Impartiality in International Commercial Arbitration

Independence and Impartiality in International Commercial Arbitration

An Analysis with Comparative References to English, French, German, Swiss, and United States Law

Ilka Hanna Beimel

eleven

Published, sold and distributed by Eleven
P.O. Box 85576
2508 CG The Hague
The Netherlands
Tel.: +31 70 33 070 33
Fax: +31 70 33 070 30
email: sales@elevenpub.nl
www.elevenpub.com

Sold and distributed in USA and Canada
Independent Publishers Group
814 N. Franklin Street
Chicago, IL 60610, USA
Order Placement: +1 800 888 4741
Fax: +1 312 337 5985
orders@ipgbook.com
www.ipgbook.com

Eleven is an imprint of Boom uitgevers Den Haag.

ISBN 978-94-6236-207-9
ISBN 978-90-8974-542-2 (e-book)

It "is of fundamental importance that justice should not only be done, but should manifestly and undoubtedly be seen to be done".

Lord Hewart, in *R v. Sussex Justices, Ex p. McCarthy*, England and Wales High Court of Justice, 9 November 1923 [1924] 1 KB 256, 259.

Table of Contents

List of Abbreviations

AAA	American Arbitration Association
AAA Rules	AAA Commercial Arbitration Rules, 2013
ABA	American Bar Association
AC	Appeal Cases
ALF	Association of Litigation Funders (in England and Wales)
ALI	American Law Institute
Am. Rev. Int'l Arb.	American Review of International Arbitration
Arb. Int.	Arbitration International – The Official Journal of the LCIA
ARIAS U.S. Rules	AIDA (Association Internationale de Droits des Assurances) Reinsurance and Insurance Arbitration Society Rules
Art.	Article
ASA Bull.	Swiss Arbitration Association Bulletin
Austrian YB Int'l Arb.	Austrian Yearbook on International Arbitration
Bd.	Board
BeckOK	Beck'scher Online-Kommentar
BeckRS	Beck-online Rechtsprechung
BezGer	Bezirksgericht (Swiss District Court)
BGBl.	Bundesgesetzblatt (Federal Law Gazette)
BGE	Entscheidungen des Schweizerischen Bundesgerichts (Official compilation of decisions by the Federal Supreme Court of Switzerland)
BGer	Bundesgericht (Federal Supreme Court of Switzerland)
BGH	Bundesgerichtshof (German Federal Court of Justice)
BIT	Bilateral Investment Treaty
BLR	Building Law Report
BSK	Basler Kommentar
BT-Drucks.	Deutscher Bundestag Drucksache
BTE	Before the event (insurances)
Bus. Horiz.	Business Horizons
Bus. L. Int'l	Business Law International
BVerfG	Bundesverfassungsgericht (German Federal Constitutional Court)
CA	Cour d'appel (French Court of Appeal)
Calif. Judges Ass'n	California Judges Association

Cap.	Capture
CAS	Court of Arbitration for Sports
Cass civ 1ère	Cour de Cassation, Première Chambre Civile (First Civil Chamber of the French Court of Cassation)
Cass civ 2ème	Cour de Cassation, Deuxième Chambre Civile (Second Civil Chamber of the French Court of Cassation)
Cass com	Cour de Cassation, Chambre Civile, Section Commerciale (Commercial Chamber of the French Court of Cassation)
Cf.	Compare
Chap.	Chapter
CIArb	Chartered Institute of Arbitrators
CIETAC	China International Economic and Trade Arbitration Commission
CIETAC Rules	CIETAC Arbitration Rules, 2015
Cir.	Circuit, Federal Court of Appeals (United States)
CLC	Commercial Law Cases
Co.	Company
Corp.	Corporation
Croatian Arb. YB	Croatian Arbitration Yearbook
DAC	Departmental Advisory Committee on Arbitration Law
D.C.	District of Columbia
Def. Coun. J.	Defense Counsel Journal
DIS	Deutsche Institution für Schiedsgerichtsbarkeit (German Arbitration Institute)
DIS Rules	DIS Arbitration Rules, 2018
Disp. Res. J.	Dispute Resolution Journal
Disp. Resol. Int'l	Dispute Resolution International
Div.	Division
EAA	English Arbitration Act
ECHR	European Convention on Human Rights
ECT	European Community Treaty
ECtHR	European Court of Human Rights
ECJ	European Court of Justice
E.D.	Eastern District
E.g.	Exempli gratia (for example)
Emph. add.	Emphasis added
Et al.	Et alia (and others)
Etc.	Et cetera (and so forth)
Et seq.	Et sequentes (and the following)

EWCA	England and Wales Court of Appeal
EWHC	England and Wales High Court of Justice
F.2d	Federal Reporter, Second Series 1988-1993/West's Federal Reporter, Second Series
F.3d	West's Federal Reporter, Third Series
F.Supp.	Federal Supplement
F.Supp.2d	Federal Supplement, Second Series
F.Supp.3d	Federal Supplement, Third Series
FAA	U.S. Federal Arbitration Act
Fed.Appx.	Federal Appendix Reporter
Fla. S. Ct.	Florida Supreme Court
French COJ	French Code de l'Organisation Judiciare (Code of Judicial Organisation)
French CPC	French Code de Procédure Civile (Code of Civil Procedure)
French RIN	French Règlement Intérieur National de la profession d'avocat (National Regulations of the legal profession)
FS	Festschrift/Liber Amicorum
GAR	Global Arbitration Review
German BGB	German Bürgerliches Gesetzbuch (Civil Code)
German BRAO	German Bundesrechtsanwaltsordnung (Federal Lawyers' Act)
German GG	German Grundgesetz (Basic Law, i.e., the Constitution)
German RiG	German Richtergesetz (German Judiciary Act)
German ZPO	German Zivilprozessordnung (Code of Civil Procedure)
Harvard L. Rev.	Harvard Law Review
HKIAC	Hong Kong International Arbitration Centre
HKIAC Rules	HKIAC Administered Arbitration Rules, 2018
HL	House of Lords
Hong Kong AO	Hong Kong Arbitration Ordinance, L.N. 38, 2011
IBA	International Bar Association
IBA Arb. News	IBA Arbitration News
ICC	International Chamber of Commerce
ICC Int. Ct. Arb. Bull.	ICC International Court of Arbitration Bulletin
ICC Rules	ICC Arbitration Rules, 2021
ICDR	International Centre for Dispute Resolution
ICDR Rules	ICDR Arbitration Rules, 2014
ICJ	International Court of Justice
ICSID	International Centre for Solution of Investment Disputes
ICSID Convention	ICSID Convention, 1966

ICSID Rules	ICSID Rules of Procedure for Arbitration Proceedings, 2006
I.e.	Id est (that is)
IJAL	Indian Journal of Arbitration Law
Inc.	Incorporated
Ins.	Insurance
Int'l Arb. L. Rev.	International Arbitration Law Review
Int'l & Comp. L.Q.	International Comparative Law Quarterly
IOC	International Olympic Committee
JAMS	Judicial Arbitration and Mediation Services
JAMS Rules	JAMS International Arbitration Rules & Procedure, 2021
J. Disp. Resol.	Journal of Dispute Resolution
J. Int'l Arb.	Journal of International Arbitration
J. Int'l Disp. Settlement	Journal of International Dispute Settlement
Jud.	Judicial
Juridical Trib.	Juridical Tribune
KB	King's Bench Division
KG	Kammergericht (Court of Appeal in Berlin, Germany)
KGer	Kantonsgericht (Swiss Court of Appeal)
L. & Prac. Int'l Cts. & Trib.	The Law and Practice of International Courts and Tribunals
LCIA	London Court of International Arbitration
LCIA Rules	LCIA Arbitration Rules, 2020
LG	Landgericht (German Regional Court)
Lit.	Littera (letter)
Litig.	Litigation
Ltd.	Limited
Loyola L.A. Int'l & Comp. L. Rev.	Loyola of Los Angeles International and Comparative Law Review
M.D.	Middle District
McGill J. Disp. Res.	McGill Journal of Dispute Resolution
MünchKomm	Münchener Kommentar
N.	Note/Footnote
N.Y. Int'l Rev.	New York International Review
N.Y. L.J.	New York Law Journal
NASD	National Association of Securities Dealers

New York Convention	Convention on the Recognition and Enforcement of Foreign Arbitral Awards, 1958
NGFA	National Grain and Feed Association
NJ	Neue Justiz
NJOZ	Neue Juristische Online-Zeitschrift
NJW	Neue Juristische Wochenschrift
NJW-RR	Neue Juristische Wochenschrift Rechtsprechungsreport Zivilrecht
NStZ	Neue Zeitschrift für Strafrecht
NZM	Neue Zeitschrift für Miet- und Wohnungsrecht
Ohio Sup. Ct. Bd. of Comm'rs	Ohio Supreme Court Board of Commissioners
OLG	Oberlandesgericht (German Higher Regional Court)
OLGR	OLG Report
Op.	Opinion
P./pp.	Page/pages
Para.	Paragraph
PCA	Permanent Court of Arbitration
PIABA Bar J.	Public Investors Arbitration Bar Association Bar Journal
PK	Praxiskommentar (commentary)
Prague Rules	Rules on the Efficient Conduct of Proceedings in International Arbitration, 2018
QB	Queen's Bench Division
QMUL	Queen Mary University London
RB	Arrondissementsrechtbank (Netherlands Regional Court)
Rev. Brasileira Arb.	Revista Brasileira de Arbitragem
Rev. de l'Arb.	Revue de l'Arbitrage
S. African L. J.	South African Law Journal
S. Illinois U. L. J.	South Illinois University Law Journal
San Diego L. Rev.	San Diego Law Review
SCAI	Swiss Chambers' Arbitration Institution
SCC	Stockholm Chamber of Commerce
SCC Rules	SCC Arbitration Rules, 2017
SchiedsVZ	Zeitschrift für Schiedsverfahren
S.C. Advisory Comm.	Southern California Advisory Committee
S.Ct.	Supreme Court Reporter
S.D.	Southern District

Sec.	Section
SIAC	Singapore International Arbitration Centre
SIAC Rules	SIAC Arbitration Rules, 2016
SRA	Solicitors Regulation Authority
Stanford J. Int'l L.	Stanford Journal of International Law
Stockholm Arb. YB	Stockholm Arbitration Yearbook
Swiss BGFA	Swiss Bundesgesetz über die Freizügigkeit der Anwältinnen und Anwälte (Federal Act on Free Movement of Lawyers)
Swiss BGG	Swiss Bundesgerichtsgesetz (Federal Supreme Court Act)
Swiss BV	Swiss Bundesverfassung (Constitution)
Swiss IPRG	Swiss Bundesgesetz über das Internationale Privatrecht (Private International Law Act)
Swiss Rules	Swiss Rules of International Arbitration, 2017
Swiss ZPO	Swiss Zivilprozessordnung (Code of Civil Procedure)
TCLR	Trade and Competition Law Reports
TDM	Transnational Dispute Management Journal
TGI	French Tribunal de Grande Instance
Tr. Cog. Sc.	Trends in Cognitive Science
UAA	United States Uniform Arbitration Act
U. Dayton L. Rev.	University of Dayton Law Review
UKPC	United Kingdom Privy Council
UKSC	United Kingdom Supreme Court
UNCITRAL	United Nations Commission on International Trade Law
UNCITRAL Arbitration Rules	UNCITRAL Arbitration Rules, 2013
UNCITRAL Model Law	UNCITRAL Model Law on International Commercial Arbitration with amendments, 2006
USA/U.S.	United States of America/United States
v.	versus
WL	Westlaw Database
YB Arb. & Med.	Yearbook on Arbitration and Mediation
YB Com. Arb.	Yearbook on Commercial Arbitration
YB Int'l Arb.	Yearbook of International Arbitration
ZIP	Zeitschrift für Wirtschaftsrecht
ZK	Zürcher Kommentar

Acknowledgements

First and foremost, I am deeply grateful to my mentor Professor Dr. iur. Ingeborg Schwenzer, LL.M., for constantly supporting, guiding, and inspiring me. Her encouragement on so many projects, including writing this book, is invaluable to me. She made the time I spent at her Chair as student, and later research and teaching assistant, a truly educational and rewarding experience. Furthermore, I am deeply indebted to Professor Dr. iur. Ulrich G. Schroeter for his helpful comments on this book and for providing an excellent working environment during the time I could work at his Chair. I would also like to express my deep gratitude to Dr. iur. Florian Mohs, LL.M., for sharing with me his knowledge and practical experience in international arbitration, which substantially augmented the content of this book.

In addition, I would like to thank the *Freiwillige Akademische Gesellschaft* Basel for funding my stay as a Visiting Scholar at Columbia Law School in New York. During that inspirational time, I had the fortune of being supervised by Professor George A. Berman, who provided invaluable advice, insights, and ideas. I am deeply grateful for this experience.

I would also like to cordially thank my colleagues and friends, in particular Victoria Jennett, Ph.D., Dr. Philipp H. Hofmann-Klingler, and Matthias Hausdorf, LL.M., for proofreading this book; Dr. Alissa Palumbo Högger for editing; and Claudio Marti Whitebread for sharing his ideas with me.

Lastly, my parents and Florian deserve a very special thank you for their precious and unconditional support for all my projects, including this book.

Düsseldorf, March 2021

Introduction

Users' trust in the independence and impartiality of any judicial process is of paramount importance. Without trust and confidence in the decision makers, decisions risk not being respected by users. Independence and impartiality bring about confidence and trust. Generally, this cycle of trust applies to arbitral proceedings. Yet, slight differences in the perception of arbitration in different legal systems induce divergent applications and interpretations of independence and impartiality. The applicable standard, the application of individual grounds for finding dependence and partiality, and the consequences attached to these grounds vary. Different laws, rules, and guidelines try to abolish these differences and harmonise the approaches to independence and impartiality in international arbitration. Against this backdrop, this book will analyse the state of play of independence and impartiality in international commercial arbitration. It will not try to explain and develop independence and impartiality on any theoretical basis, and shall not be another attempt to define independence and impartiality in general. Rather, it will provide an overview of the current status of independence and impartiality applied in international commercial arbitration, focusing on case law from France, Germany, Switzerland, the United Kingdom, and the United States.

To contextualise independence and impartiality in international commercial arbitration, **chapter 1** provides a short introduction to international commercial arbitration and its particular dual nature. **Chapter 2** addresses some applicable laws, rules, and guidelines, to be used later in the overviews and analyses, while **chapter 3** provides a short overview of the legal systems compared. **Chapters 4** and **5** paint the picture of current tendencies in the application of independence and impartiality. They address possible grounds for finding dependence and partiality, which will be streamlined in theoretical standards of independence and impartiality, in **chapter 6**. Thereafter, **chapter 7** lays out some consequences of independence and impartiality: the obligation to disclose, the need to object and the possibility to waive, and the possibility to circumvent the arbitrator's challenge. Finally, **chapter 8** provides a brief outlook and suggests some practical guidance.

Within all chapters of this book, the purposes of independence and impartiality and the attached principles guide the argumentation. The outcome of any such argumentation heavily relies on balancing the different purposes and may change accordingly. The guiding principles, the terminology of independence and impartiality, and the personal scope are to be explained in the following section.

Independence and Impartiality as a Fundamental Principle

Arbitrators solve disputes outside the courtroom. At first sight, one may question whether they need to be independent and impartial, characteristics that apply inside the courtroom. However, in order to bring arbitration and state court proceedings on an equal footing, fundamental principles must be adhered to. States can only accept arbitration as an alternative dispute resolution mechanism if independence and impartiality are secured.[1] Independence and impartiality guarantee that no external facts and circumstances affect the decision-making process.[2] The role of any decision maker requires "neutrality and distance" towards the parties in the proceedings.[3] Arbitrators accede to the "status of a judge" through the parties' designation,[4] i.e., the arbitration agreement, and are decision makers. Thus, they need to be independent and impartial.

Generally, independence and impartiality are part of the *ordre public* of many legal systems, and procedurally guarantee the parties' right to be heard and their equal treatment.[5] Through neutrality and objectivity, the arbitrator, as a decision maker, preserves both parties' rights.[6] He or she is open towards both parties' arguments and has no connection to either party that would affect the evaluation to the detriment of the other party. In France,[7] Germany,[8] and Switzerland,[9] statutes accept this paramount role of independence and impartiality as applying in arbitration as in state court proceedings. In the United Kingdom, statutes and case law provide for these particular aspects,[10] and in the United States, primarily case law concretises this role of independence and impartiality.[11] In the

1 Stein/Jonas/P. Schlosser, § 1036 para. 9.

2 BGer, 20 May 2014, BGE 140 III 221.

3 BVerfG, 8 February 1967, 2 BvR 235/64, NJW 1967, 1123-1124, referring to judges.

4 CA Paris, 12 January 1999, Rev. de l'Arb. 1999, 381-384, 383.

5 Cf. C. Armbrüster/V. Wächter, *Ablehnung von Schiedsrichtern wegen Befangenheit im Verfahren*, SchiedsVZ 2017, 213-223, 214-215, stating that arbitration is part of the "material judiciary". Hence, independence and impartiality constitute a guaranteed minimum standard, and are part of the procedural *ordre public* in Sect. 1059(2)(2)(b) German ZPO.

6 OLG Frankfurt a.M., 24 January 2019, 26 SchH 2/18, BeckRS 2019, 848.

7 E.g., through Art. 6(1) ECHR, applicable to arbitrators, C. Seraglini/J. Ortscheidt, *Droit de l'arbitrage interne et international*, para. 770. See below chapter 2.6, for more details on the application of Art. 6(1) ECHR.

8 E.g., §§ 1025(1), 1036(2) sentence 1 German ZPO, § 1059(2)(2)(b) German ZPO.

9 E.g., Arts. 180(1)(c), 179(6) Swiss IPRG. Before the revision of the Swiss IPRG, courts and commentators referred to Arts. 29, 30(1) Swiss BV, Art. 6(1) ECHR, and Art. 47 Swiss ZPO concretising Art. 30 Swiss BV, BGer, 16 October 2019, 4A_292/2019, para. E 3.1; BGer, 24 November 2017, 4A_236/2017, para. E 3.1.2; BGer, 17 February 2000, 4P.168/1999, ASA Bull. 2001, 781-786; N. Voser/E. Fischer, *The Arbitral Tribunal*, pp. 63-64. See also, D. Girsberger/N. Voser, *International Arbitration*, para. 697 et seq.

10 E.g., Art. 33(1) EAA; *Halliburton Co. v. Chubb Bermuda Ins. Ltd.*, [2018] EWCA Civ 817, upheld by *Halliburton Co. v. Chubb Bermuda Ins. Ltd.*, [2020] UKSC 48.

11 E.g., *Transmarine Seaways Corp. of Monrovia v. Marc Rich & Co. AG*, 480 F.Supp. 352 (S.D. New York 1979). The court states that a partial arbitrator violates *ordre public*. However, critical whether independence

words of the U.K. Supreme Court, "it is axiomatic that a judge or an arbitrator must be impartial; he or she must not be biased in favour of or against any party in a litigation or reference. A judge or arbitrator, who is not in fact subject to any bias, must also not give the appearance of bias: justice must be seen to be done".[12] Therefore, independence and impartiality are "of the essence" for the arbitrator's jurisdictional mission.[13]

DIFFERENTIATION BETWEEN INDEPENDENCE AND IMPARTIALITY

Some scholars and some statutes differentiate between independence and impartiality. The former can be understood to include objective elements,[14] as it encompasses institutional and organisational independence. The latter can be understood to include subjective elements.[15] In other words,

> impartiality is primarily about an attitude of mind which as an abstract concept is difficult to measure, whereas independence is a necessary external manifestation of what is required as a prerequisite of that attitude and is an objective examination into the relationship between the parties and appointed arbitrator.[16]

In this sense, independence may be described as referring to "relationships"[17] and impartiality to conduct. However, these definitions are far from set. Both terms are also used interchangeably and, in fact, both terms may refer to an inner state of mind.[18]

---

and impartiality are part of *ordre public*, D. Branson, *American Party-Appointed Arbitrators - Not the Three Monkeys*, U. Dayton L. Rev. 30 (2004), 1-62, 5.

12 *Halliburton Co. v. Chubb Bermuda Ins. Ltd.*, [2020] UKSC 48, Lord Hodge, para. 1.

13 CA Paris, 12 January 1999, Rev. de l'Arb. 1999, 381-384, 383; CA Paris, 29 June 1991, cited in *Laker Airways Inc. v. FLS Aerospace Ltd. & Anor*, [1999] CLC 1124, 1130.

14 G. Halleringer/P. Ayton, *Bias, Vested Interests and Self-Deception in Judgment and Decision-Making: Challenges to Arbitrator Impartiality*, p. 25; P. Egger, *Die Konstituierung Internationaler Wirtschaftsschiedsgerichte*, p. 155.

15 See A. Redfern, *The Importance of Being Independent, Laws of Arbitration, Rules, Guidelines - and a Disastrous Award*, IJAL 6 (2017), 9-23, 12; P. Egger, *Die Konstituierung Internationaler Wirtschaftsschiedsgerichte*, p. 154, both favouring the clear differentiation between subjective and objective elements.

16 H.-L. Yu/L. Shore, *Independence, Impartiality, and Immunity of Arbitrators: US and English Perspectives*, Int'l & Comp. L.Q. 52 (2003), 935-967, 936.

17 D. Lawson, *Impartiality and Independence of International Arbitrators, Commentary on the 2004 IBA Guidelines on Conflicts of Interest in International Arbitration*, ASA Bull. 2005, 22-45, 39 et seq.; M. Donahey, *The Independence and Neutrality of Arbitrators*, J. Int'l Arb. 9 (1992), 31-42, 31.

18 See, e.g., BGer, 24 November 2017, 4A_236/2017, para. E 3.1.2 and BGer, 29 October 2010, BGE 136 III 605, 608, on the objective and subjective elements of independence. See also, CA Paris, 10 June 2004, YB Com. Arb. XXX (2005), 499-504, 503; BSK BV/J. Reich, Art. 30 paras. 24-25; and C. Rogers, *Ethics in*

Additionally, the interconnection of independence and impartiality has been described in varying ways, with some authors using independence as a proxy for the requirement of being impartial.[19] Independence and impartiality are part of due process and guarantee the right to be heard and equal treatment of parties on the individual level. It is, thus, not surprising that there is a tendency in statutes, rules, guidelines, and case law to either refer to both terms or include the meaning of both terms.[20]

For example, the EAA requires arbitrators to be impartial and is silent on independence.[21] One may assume that this silence is to be interpreted to exclude independence completely. However, the approach taken by English courts is that this wording includes "non-partiality" independence, i.e., the lack of independence giving rise to justifiable doubts of impartiality is included.[22] The courts follow the DAC Report, noting that the "inclusion of independence would give rise to endless arguments, as it has, for example, in Sweden and the United States, where almost any connection (however remote) has been put forward to challenge the 'independence' of an arbitrator".[23] Thus, the English standard includes independence in the frame of impartiality. One may conclude that English courts apply, to some extent, a unified standard of both independence and impartiality.[24] Like the EAA, Swiss arbitration law formerly referred to only one term. However, contrary to the EAA, the Swiss IPRG omitted impartiality and not independence.[25] Since 1 January 2021, Article 180(1)(c) Swiss IPRG includes independence and impartiality.[26] With this update, the Swiss legislator

---

International Arbitration, p. 91, clarifying that "in practical terms it appears to be largely a distinction without a difference".

19 G. Helleringer/P. Ayton, *Bias, Vested Interests and Self-Deception in Judgment and Decision-Making: Challenges to Arbitrator Impartiality*, p. 25, who also state that "requiring independence is an indirect strategy to achieve impartiality". Similarly, Hascher argues that independence is a guarantee of impartiality, D. Hascher, *A Comparison between the Independence of State Justice and the Independence of Arbitration*, ICC Int. Ct. Arb. Bull., 2007 Special Supplement, 77-89, 83.

20 But see, K. El Chazli, *L'impartialité de l'arbitre*, para. 13 et seq.

21 According to Art. 24(1)(a) EAA, an arbitrator can be challenged if "circumstances exist that give rise to justifiable doubts as to his impartiality". According to Art. 33(1)(a) EAA, the arbitrators shall "act fairly and impartially", and according to Art. 68 EAA, an award may be annulled if it does not comply with Art. 33 EAA.

22 *Laker Airways Inc. v. FLS Aerospace Ltd.*, [1999] CLC 1124, on the term "non-partial"; *Halliburton Co. v. Chubb Bermuda Ins. Ltd.*, [2018] EWCA Civ 817, on impartiality, upheld by *Halliburton Co. v. Chubb Bermuda Ins. Ltd.*, [2020] UKSC 48. Also, the LCIA Court follows this approach, e.g., LCIA Reference No. 81160, LCIA Court, 28 August 2009, Arb. Int'l 27 (2011), 442-454. See also, N. Andrews/J. Landbrecht, *Schiedsverfahren und Mediation in England*, para. 88.

23 DAC Report, in particular, para. 102.

24 This is in particular the case where the applicable arbitration rules refer to both terms. See, e.g., *Laker Airways Inc. v. FLS Aerospace Ltd.*, [1999] CLC 1124.

25 Art. 180(1)(c) Swiss IPRG previous version.

26 It reads in German: "*Ein Mitglied des Schiedsgerichts kann abgelehnt werden: [...] wenn Umstände vorliegen, die Anlass zu berechtigten Zweifeln an seiner Unabhängigkeit oder seiner Unparteilichkeit geben.*" Translation:

turned a cause into law that was already applied by Swiss courts.[27] The Swiss Bundesgericht consistently interpreted Article 30 Swiss BV and Article 6(1) ECHR to place a tribunal established by law with jurisdiction and being independent and impartial.[28] Case law on Article 30 Swiss BV does not differentiate precisely between impartiality, independence, and bias.[29] The FAA refers only to partiality. Article 10(a)(2) FAA reads as follows:

> In any of the following cases the United States court in and for the district wherein the award was made may make an order vacating the award upon the application of any party to the arbitration [...] where there was evident partiality or corruption in the arbitrators, or either of them.

Case law defining "evident partiality" refers, inter alia, to "relationships",[30] "bias or misconduct".[31] Neither of these terms is exclusively covered by independence or impartiality. French arbitration law refers to both independence and impartiality.[32] The conclusion by French authors[33] and courts[34] that arbitrators need to be both independent and impartial, is not surprising. Occasionally, French case law differentiates between objective independence, i.e., "*independence de situation*," and subjective independence, i.e., "*independence d'esprit*".[35] Similar to French law, the German ZPO refers to both terms.[36] German case law and scholars occasionally refer to the unified standard of independence

"A member of the arbitral tribunal may be challenged if circumstances exist which give rise to justifiable doubts as to his independence or impartiality."

27 BGer, 4 July 2018, 4A_505/2017, para. E 4.2.1; BGer, 24 November 2017, 4A_236/2017, para. E 3.1.1. et seq.

28 BGer, 7 November 2006, BGE 133 I 89, para. E 3.2. See also, BGer, 30 June 1994, 4P.292/1993, ASA Bull. 1997, 99-107, 104, and B. Berger/F. Kellerhals, *International and Domestic Arbitration in Switzerland*, para. 794.

29 BSK BV/J. Reich, Art. 30 para. 24. According to Reich, other authors often consider impartiality as a generic term, i.e., a court or tribunal is impartial if it is independent and unbiased.

30 *International Produce, Inc. v. A/S Rosshavet*, 504 F.Supp. 736 (S.D. New York 1980).

31 *Washburn v. McManus*, 895 F.Supp. 392 (D. Connecticut 1994).

32 Art. 1456(2) French CPC requires disclosure of circumstances that might affect the independence or impartiality. This differs from the provision applied to judges, Art. L 111-5 French COJ. According to the wording of this provision, judges are only required to be impartial.

33 C. Seraglini/J. Ortscheidt, *Droit de l'arbitrage interne et international*, para. 729. The authors argue that independence is a precondition of impartiality. They define independence as the absence of material or intellectual links characterising a situation of affecting the judgment of the arbitrator and constituting a risk of partiality to one of the parties. Impartiality is the absence of prejudgments. See also, for more details, C. Seraglini/J. Ortscheidt, *Droit de l'arbitrage interne et international*, paras. 222-227.

34 Cass civ 1ère, 4 May 2017, 15-29 158, Rev. de l'Arb. 2017, 770; Cass civ 1ére, 10 October 2012, 11-20.299, Rev. de l'Arb. 2013, 129-130.

35 E.g., CA Paris, 10 June 2004, YB Com. Arb. XXX (2005), 499-504.

36 § 1036(1) and (2) German ZPO. Interestingly, § 42(2) German ZPO only requests judges to be impartial, whereas § 25 German RiG demands independence.

and impartiality as the principle of neutrality.[37] In the context of arbitration, the terminology of "neutrality" may bring some confusion since neutrality is often used in a political and cultural sense. For example, neutrality may demand the arbitrators to be of a different nationality than the parties.[38] Therefore, the terms independence and impartiality are preferable.[39]

Most remarkable, institutional rules and guidelines often refer to both terms.[40] Similarly, the UNCITRAL Model Law and UNCITRAL Arbitration Rules require arbitrators to be both independent and impartial.[41] Under the premise that international institutions and UNCITRAL usually tend to apply an international and harmonised approach, their preference to refer to a unified standard of independence and impartiality can be seen as leading.[42] Additionally, the distinction between independence and impartiality is rather unpractical in international arbitration. The case law analysis in chapters 4 and 5 demonstrates that similar scenarios are covered by different terminologies. Thus, even if both terms can be defined differently, their usage clarifies that it is more useful to refer to both terms collectively and require a "unified" standard of independence and impartiality. To conclude with Born, the general distinction between independence and impartiality should be abolished.

> [T]he two concepts are inextricably linked, and neither can be properly understood or applied without reference to the other. [... B]oth formulae address different aspects of the same inquiry and must be considered together.

---

37 BVerfG, 8 February 1967, 2 BvR 235/64, NJW 1967, 1123-1124, referring to judges and arguing that the need for neutrality and distance of judges is based on Art. 101(1) sentence 2 German GG; OLG Frankfurt a.M., 24 January 2019, 26 SchH 2/18, BeckRS 2019, 848, para. 74; A. Rojahn/C. Jerger, *Richterliche Unparteilichkeit und Unabhängigkeit im Zeitalter sozialer Netzwerke*, NJW 2014, 1147-1150, 1147; Musielak/Voit/W. Voit, § 1036 para. 1.

38 M. Donahey, *The Independence and Neutrality of Arbitrators*, J. Int'l Arb. 9 (1992), 31-42, 32. For the arbitrator's nationality, language or cultural affiliations as a ground for dependence and partiality, see below chapter 4.2.5.

39 See also, D. Lawson, *Impartiality and Independence of International Arbitrators, Commentary on the 2004 IBA Guidelines on Conflicts of Interest in International Arbitration*, ASA Bull. 2005, 22-45, 25, for the understanding that neutrality encompasses independence and impartiality.

40 E.g., General Standard 1 IBA Guidelines 2014; R-18(a) AAA Rules; Art. 9.1 DIS Rules; Art. 32 CIETAC Rules; Art. 13 ICDR Rules; Art. 9.1 JAMS Rules; Art. 5.3 LCIA Rules; Art. 18(1) SCC Rules; Art. 13.1 SIAC Rules. Interestingly, the ICC Rules 1998 required arbitrators to be "independent" but did not expressly refer to "impartiality". This was changed in 2012.

41 Art. 12 UNCITRAL Model Law and Arts. 11 and 12(1) UNCITRAL Arbitration Rules.

42 This is also in line with the ECtHR's approach to Art. 6(1) ECHR, ECtHR, Guide on Art. 6 ECHR, paras. 149, 217 et seq.

> [... P]recisely the same analysis and results should apply even where only one of the formulae is used.[43]

Personal Scope of Independence and Impartiality

This book applies a broad concept of independence and impartiality. Generally, this covers not only active decision makers, but also parties passively involved in decision-making. A broad concept is not limited to decision-making, but also includes institutional and judicial independence (and impartiality). Thus, the question arises of who needs to be independent and impartial in the arbitral proceedings.

Primarily, the arbitral tribunal is at the centre of arbitral decision-making and is, hence, covered by the personal scope of independence and impartiality. Most institutional rules and arbitration laws regulate its independence and impartiality.[44] Within this primary category, the focus lies on the arbitrators' relationships and conduct. Additionally, counsels' relationships and conduct may impair the independence and impartiality of the arbitral tribunal. Some ethical rules and guidelines dealing with the code of conduct of counsel – either in arbitration or litigation – include provisions concerning the counsel's independence. Often, these provisions only refer to independence and not impartiality,[45] since counsels represent their parties and act within their interest. However, where a party is funded by a third-party funder, the risk arises that the counsel is not acting solely in the interest of the client.[46] Conflicts of interest may arise here as well. Third-party funders themselves, like parties, do not need to be independent and impartial. Where the arbitral tribunal relies on experts or uses secretaries, independence and impartiality of these groups may be at issue as well. The exact standard of independence and impartiality applied to experts or tribunal secretaries may differ from that for arbitrators as decision makers.[47]

Finally, it is questionable whether arbitral institutions need to be independent and impartial. They are service providers[48] serving both parties and the arbitrators. One could argue that

43 G. Born, *International Commercial Arbitration*, p. 1910.

44 E.g., Art. 12 UNCITRAL Model Law; Art. 9.1 DIS Rules; Art. 5.3 LCIA Rules; Art. 9(1) Swiss Rules.

45 E.g., Art. 4.1 French RIN; § 3(1) German BRAO.

46 BGer, 10 December 2004, BGE 131 I 223, 236. For more details on third-party funding, see below chapters 4.1.1.1.10, 4.1.4.2. Also, on the counsel's requirement to remain solely obliged to the party, T. Scholl, *Rechtsschutzversicherung und Prozessfinanzierung*, pp. 250-252.

47 For a detailed analysis of grounds for finding dependence and partiality in case of experts, see below chapters 4.1.1.3 and 4.1.5. For the standard of independence and impartiality applicable to experts, see below chapter 6.6.

48 F. Schäfer, *Institutionelle Schiedsgerichtsbarkeit*, para. 107.

arbitral institutions are not obliged to treat parties fairly and equally outside their contractual relationships with the parties. However, this fails to recognise that institutions may indirectly influence the award to be rendered: they appoint the arbitrators,[49] may decide on challenges,[50] and may scrutinise the award.[51] Also, institutions aspire to being chosen again by the parties. The likelihood of being chosen again is higher where institutions provide a fair and equal procedure.[52] Thus, it is at least within their own interest to act independent and impartial.

This book will focus on the arbitrator's independence and impartiality and addresses issues of independence and impartiality of other actors in the arbitral proceedings less extensively. Using a broad understanding of independence and impartiality, these other actors will be addressed within the arbitrator's independence and impartiality.

---

49 E.g., Art. 13.1 DIS Rules; Art. 13 ICC Rules; Art. 5.6 LCIA Rules; Art. 9.3 SIAC Rules – all usually after nomination by the parties.

50 E.g., Art. 14(3) ICC Rules, Art. 10 LCIA Rules; Art. 16 SIAC Rules.

51 E.g., Art. 34 ICC Rules; Art. 32.2 SIAC Rules. The LCIA Court does not scrutinise awards but is "happy to review a draft award when asked to do so by an Arbitral Tribunal", Sect. 6.7, para. 50, LCIA Note for Arbitrators.

52 Users of institutional arbitration are confident about an institution if it treats the parties fairly and equally. In the QMUL/White & Case, *2018 International Arbitration Survey*, "neutrality/internationalism" was among the top four reasons given by respondents explaining their favoured choice of arbitral institutions, pp. 13-14.

1 Introduction to International Commercial Arbitration

In international arbitration, different mechanisms have evolved from common and civil law principles, and it is impossible to draw a clear distinction between them.[1] Arbitration may be seen as a "globalisation of fundamental legal concepts".[2] Under this premise, it is questionable how the concepts of "independence" and "impartiality" are articulated and applied in international arbitration.

The following introduction to arbitration in general, and independence and impartiality in particular, will outline the roles of the arbitration agreement and the *lex loci arbitri* (1.1). Additionally, differences between ad hoc and institutional arbitration (1.2), and the dualistic nature of arbitration (1.3) will be illuminated with regard to independence and impartiality, before concluding with final remarks (1.4).

1.1 The Arbitration Agreement and the *lex loci arbitri*

The arbitration agreement is the "foundation stone" of international commercial arbitration.[3] The arbitrator's jurisdiction derives from this agreement,[4] and it is the primary source for the applicable standard of independence and impartiality. Besides choosing the applicable laws and rules within the arbitration agreement, parties may wish to derogate from otherwise applicable provisions. They may provide a detailed challenge procedure,[5] agree on one particular appointment mechanism[6] or, as an application of the parties' right

1 Cf. BSK IPRG/D. Hochstrasser/S. Burlet, Einleitung zum Zwölften Kapitel para. 130.

2 Cf. BSK IPRG/D. Hochstrasser/S. Burlet, Einleitung zum Zwölften Kapitel para. 133.

3 H.-L. Yu/L. Shore, *Independence, Impartiality, and Immunity of Arbitrators: US and English Perspectives*, Int'l & Comp. L.Q. 52 (2003), 935-967, 962.

4 *ASM Shipping Ltd. of India v. TTMI Ltd. of England*, [2007] EWHC 927. Or, in the words of Justice Crane in the dissenting opinion in *American Eagle Fire Ins. Co. v. New Jersey Ins. Co.*, 240 N.Y. 398 (Ct. App. 1925): "The Arbitration Law is based on contract. There can be no arbitration enforced upon the parties by the courts in the absence of contract."

5 E.g., that the challenged arbitrator is deemed successfully challenged under the law applicable as soon as the opposing party consents, or that a concrete third party is named to decide the challenge.

6 The agreement on a particular appointment mechanism risks resulting in a partial tribunal. But see, *Anderson, Inc. v. Horton Farms, Inc.*, 166 F.3d 308 (6th Cir. 1998). The U.S. Court of Appeals concluded that the arbitration agreement calling for arbitration with a grain association (NGFA) did not automatically result in a partial tribunal where only one party was a member of NGFA. The NGFA Rules request arbitrators to be and act impartial. In a different scenario, the German *Bundesgerichtshof* did not enforce an award

to appoint, the parties may choose specific characteristics and features of the future arbitrator or even already name the arbitrator. The significant role of the arbitration agreement and party autonomy determines the different nature of arbitration compared to state court proceedings. The parties' freedom to opt out of litigation and into a more private mechanism of dispute resolution brings changes to procedural principles. Independence and impartiality in the decision-making are fundamental procedural principles and the role of the arbitration agreement, i.e., the role of party autonomy, needs to be balanced with the traditional judicial understanding of these procedural principles.

The *lex loci arbitri* is the arbitration law of the seat of arbitration. Usually, the *lex loci arbitri* names the most fundamental principles to safeguard due process, which are also part of the *ordre public*. Some states base their arbitration laws on the UNCITRAL Model Law.[7] The triumvirate of the *lex loci arbitri*, the arbitration agreement, and applicable institutional rules determine the parties' rights and obligations during the arbitral proceedings, including the arbitrators' obligations, and the standard of independence and impartiality.

During enforcement proceedings, both the *lex loci arbitri* and national laws of the enforcement state may determine the standard of independence and impartiality, often via Articles V(1)(d) and V(2)(b) New York Convention.[8]

1.2 Differences between Institutional and Ad Hoc Arbitration

There are many differences between institutional and ad hoc arbitration.[9] Institutional arbitration supplies the institution's structure, assistance, and personnel.[10] On the matter of independence and impartiality, institutions may have a substantive task and act as an additional filter. First, arbitral institutions may provide for concrete disclosure obligations using statements of independence and impartiality, and second, some institutions have established an organ to decide on challenges of arbitrators.[11] Thus, institutional rules and

---

that was based on an arbitration agreement where the parties appointed current members of the parties' advisory board to the tribunal, BGH, 11 October 2017, I ZB 12/17, SchiedsVZ 2018, 271-275.

7 See chapter 2.8, on the UNCITRAL Model Law.

8 If the *lex loci arbitri* and the arbitration law of the enforcement state should deviate in their standard of independence and impartiality, it is questionable which one prevails. In BGH, 1 February 2001, III ZR 332/99, NJW-RR 2001, 1059-1061, the German *Bundesgerichtshof* concluded that the applicable standard is that of the *lex loci arbitri*. However, the court did not examine whether both standards deviated. See chapter 2.7, for more details on the New York Convention.

9 See generally, F. Schäfer, *Institutionelle Schiedsgerichtsbarkeit*, paras. 107-121.

10 Institutional arbitration adds another actor, the institution, to the contractual relationship between parties and arbitrators, F. Schäfer, *Institutionelle Schiedsgerichtsbarkeit*, paras. 114-117.

11 E.g., such organs are the ICC Court of Arbitration and the LCIA Court.

institutional decisions influence the interpretation and application of independence and impartiality.[12]

Ad hoc arbitration usually provides more flexibility to the parties. Their choice of any individual procedure must, however, be within the mandatory limits of the applicable *lex loci arbitri*. The presence of previous institutional decisions on arbitrator's challenges[13] and a full set of institutional rules may result in more legal security for the parties in institutional arbitration. However, the mere absence of these factors and the added filter that an institution might provide does not render ad hoc arbitration generally more susceptible to partiality.[14]

1.3 THE DUALISTIC NATURE OF ARBITRATION

The legal nature of arbitration is dualistic or hybrid in that it encompasses both contractual and judicial approaches.[15] It is based on the parties' agreement to arbitrate, i.e., the contractual nature, and the arbitrators render an award that may have the same effects as a court decision, i.e., the judicial nature.

1.3.1 The Judicial Nature of Arbitration

The judicial nature of arbitration includes, first of all, those elements that allow the direct comparison of arbitration to state court proceedings. The arbitrator is a decision maker,

---

12 G. Born, *International Commercial Arbitration*, p. 1961 et seq.; H.-L. Yu/L. Shore, *Independence, Impartiality, and Immunity of Arbitrators: US and English Perspectives*, Int'l & Comp. L.Q. 52 (2003), 935-967, 938 et seq. See chapter 6.1.2.4, for more details on the standard of "justifiable doubts".

13 Unfortunately, they are often not publicly available. The LCIA and the SCC publish summaries of decisions on the arbitrator's challenge. The ICC announced to publish their awards as a default from 2019 onwards, B. Jolley/O. Cook, *Revised ICC Note to Parties and Tribunals*. A database providing for challenge decisions "could be useful in providing a broader range of evidence against which [...] arguments might be judged" and ultimately lead to similar results, J. Carter, *Reaching Consensus on Arbitrator Conflicts*, Disp. Resol. Int'l 17 (2012), 17-35, 28 et seq.

14 Probably contrary, F. Gélinas, *The Independence of International Arbitrators and Judges: Tampered With or Well Tempered?*, N.Y. Int'l Rev. 24 (2011), 1-48, 8, stating more generally on international adjudication that ad hoc tribunals often comprise adjudicators appointed and remunerated by the parties, or on their behalf, for the purpose of a particular case. This would lead to a competition for appointments of adjudicators "as fiercely as lawyers compete for clients".

15 The dualistic or hybrid nature is the current modern view, M. Henry, *Le devoir d'independance de l'arbitre*, paras. 36-37. Some authors criticise the classification in favour of the contractual or judicial approach since it hinders the full powers of the arbitrator to be effective. They prefer the simple classification of an "autonomous" nature, see for references M. Henry, *Le devoir d'independance de l'arbitre*, para. 18. Henry prefers to classify arbitration as plainly original, M. Henry, *Le devoir d'independance de l'arbitre*, para. 55.

similar to a judge. It is an inherent principle of most judicial systems that no judge should be judge in his or her own cause. The different grounds for finding dependence and partiality in arbitral proceedings are examples of the judicial nature of arbitration, including the parties' right to assure the presence of independence and impartiality, e.g., by challenging the arbitrators. Independence and impartiality are, in their core function, part of the judicial nature of arbitration. To this extent, independence and impartiality are often part of *ordre public.*[16]

In difference to state court judges, arbitrators may freely decide whether to accept or decline an appointment. However, once appointed, the arbitrator is likewise obliged to render a decision. The U.K. Supreme Court clarified that

> an arbitrator when deciding to accept a reference is not under the same obligation as a judge to hear a case but, having taken up the reference, the arbitrator may reasonably feel under an obligation to carry out the remit unless there are substantial grounds for self-disqualification.[17]

This feeling of an obligation to carry out the remit may be more than the arbitrator's contractual obligation to render a decision in accordance with the contract between the arbitrator and the parties.

Additionally, there is a presumption that the arbitrator will act professionally, and this presumption potentially includes being independent and impartial,[18] until proof to the contrary. Such a rule of presumption could be similar to that applied to judges.[19] Presuming independence and impartiality of judges is a mechanism of institutional independence. Institutional independence, inter alia, safeguards the parties' rights for a statutory judge.[20] Concerning arbitrators, such a rule of presumption protects the parties' right to appoint their arbitrator – a contractual right opposed to the judicial right for a statutory judge. It remains to be seen what the effects of this presumption are, especially in regard to the applicable standard of independence and impartiality.[21]

---

16 See above Introduction, on the fundamental principle of independence and impartiality.

17 *Halliburton Co. v. Chubb Bermuda Ins. Ltd.*, [2020] UKSC 48, Lord Hodge, para. 68.

18 Cf. BGer, 27 May 2003, BGE 129 III 445, 449-465; BGer, 30 June 1994, 4P.292/1993, ASA Bull. 1997, 99-107; M. Hwang, *Arbitrators and Barristers in the Same Chambers*, Bus. L. Int'l 6 (2005), 236-257, 243, referring to *Nye Saunders and Partners v. Alan E Bristow*, (1987) 37 BLR 92; Zöller/R. Geimer, § 1036 para. 3; M. Smith, *Impartiality of the Party-Appointed Arbitrator*, Arb. Int'l 6 (1990), 320-342, 339, citing M. Bedjaoui, *The Arbitrator: One Man – Three Roles*, J. Int'l Arb. 5 (1988), 7-20; T. Clay, *L'arbitre*, p. 332.

19 BGer, 30 October 2008, 9C_836/2008, para. E 4.3, on state court and part-time judges.

20 BGer, 30 October 2008, 9C_836/2008.

21 See below chapter 6.

1.3.2 *The Contractual Nature of Arbitration*

One of the lodestar examples of a contractual characteristic in arbitration is the parties' right to appoint their chosen arbitrator.[22] The understanding of independence and impartiality in international commercial arbitration is driven by the parties' right to appoint an arbitrator. When applying the principles of independence and impartiality, the parties' right to appoint needs to be borne in mind. A few voices in arbitration criticise the unilateral appointment of arbitrators, and rather favour requiring that all three arbitrators are either nominated bilaterally or by a third party.[23] In particular, Paulsson developed the argument that the party-appointed arbitrator system is a moral hazard for international dispute resolution, and denied any fundamental right of the parties to appoint their arbitrator.[24] According to him, party-appointed arbitrators open the door for parties to appoint arbitrators who "will help them win the case" and, in turn, arbitrators will feel obliged to support the claims of the party that appointed them. In line with this, the Netherlands proposed to change their Model BIT and abandon unilateral party appointments in investor-state arbitration, in 2018.[25] Without going into too much detail of the differences between investment and commercial arbitration, it is questionable whether such a "radical" proposal is useful for international commercial arbitration. Considering some arbitration surveys, the predominant role of party appointments in practice may reasonably be questioned.[26]

However, there are good reasons not to diminish the parties' right to appoint their chosen arbitrator. First, and foremost, the parties' right to appoint ensures the parties' trust and confidence in the proceedings and the judgment.[27] The parties' trust is one of the key

---

22 Or, in other words, "selecting the tribunal is the most important decision to be made in any international arbitration (apart from the rendering of the actual award)", G. Aksen, *The Tribunal's Appointment*, p. 333.

23 J. Paulsson, *Are Unilateral Appointments Defensible?* See reference to Paulsson, in A. Battisson/C. Teo, *The Call to Remove Unilateral Appointments, Seven Years On*. But see, A. Mourre, *Are Unilateral Appointments Defensible? On Jan Paulsson's Moral Hazard in International Arbitration.*

24 J. Paulsson, *Are Unilateral Appointments Defensible?* See also, reference to Paulsson in A. Perry/J. Valencia, *Draft Model BIT Abandons Party-Appointed Arbitrators.*

25 A. Ross, *Radical Proposals in Draft Netherlands Model BIT.*

26 Only 39% of the respondents named the ability of parties to select their arbitrators as one of the three most valuable characteristics of international arbitration, QMUL/White & Case, *2018 International Arbitration Survey*, Chart 3, p. 7. The first three characteristics are enforceability of awards (64%), avoiding specific legal systems/national courts (60%), and flexibility (40%). On the other hand, the closeness of the right to appoint to flexibility reveals that it is indeed for many respondents one of the three most valuable characteristics.

27 D. McLaren, *Party-Appointed vs List-Appointed Arbitrators: A Comparison*, J. Int'l Arb. 20 (2003), 233-245, 234.

elements of the parties' initial choice for arbitration.[28] The tripartite arbitral tribunal can be justified with the assumption that "parties fear that one person will get the result wrong".[29] In fact, the parties' inclusion in the creation of the arbitral tribunal legitimises the decision-making process.[30]

Second, the party-appointed arbitrator is a tool to guarantee in an international dispute that each party is properly heard. Party-appointed arbitrators usually speak

> the party's native tongue, understand the cultural, economic and political environment in which that party acted, appreciate the procedural expectations (and misconceptions) that the party may have, and otherwise are likely to seek to understand and fully appreciate the nuances of that party's case.[31]

Third, party autonomy is implemented and potentially strengthened by the system of party nominations. Party nominations bring the expertise required by the parties to the arbitral tribunal, for example, technical skills and knowledge. Additionally, arbitrators are practitioners who "care deeply about the respect of their colleagues, for reasons both personal and professional".[32] Thus, it is far from set that arbitrators "will help their party win the case".[33] Finally, the contractual character of arbitration and party nomination may enhance the likelihood of cooperation by the parties with the arbitral process and their voluntary compliance with the ultimate award.[34] Therefore, the concept of party appointments is not outdated.

Respecting the parties' right to appoint and the contractual nature of arbitration introduces some leeway when applying grounds for finding dependence and partiality, e.g., the leeway in reappointments or the remuneration of the arbitrators can be explained with the

28 Cf. K. Schwab/G. Walter, *Schiedsgerichtsbarkeit*, Chap. 14 para. 1. In addition, the principle of trust is the key to the solution of the issues of conflicts of interest, C. Castres Saint-Martin, *Les conflits d'intérêts en arbitrage commercial international*, p. 415.

29 D. Branson, *American Party-Appointed Arbitrators – Not the Three Monkeys*, U. Dayton L. Rev. 30 (2004), 1-62, 39. Branson later postulates that parties additionally fear the unknown. "They are naturally nationalistic and may fear the unknown cultural and legal traditions of foreign arbitrators from the neutral venue." The tripartite system "augurs some ability to alleviate that fear", 43.

30 A. Battisson/C. Teo, *The Call to Remove Unilateral Appointments, Seven Years On.*

31 G. Born, *International Commercial Arbitration*, p. 1942.

32 W. Park, *Arbitrator Integrity: The Transit and the Permanent*, San Diego L. Rev. 46 (2009), 629-704, 653.

33 J. Paulsson, *Are Unilateral Appointments Defensible?.*

34 G. Born, *International Commercial Arbitration*, p. 1944.

contractual nature.[35] Also, characterising the arbitrator's obligations as a "mandate"[36] flags the contractual nature.

Moreover, there are good arguments to place the obligation to disclose primarily in the contractual category, although this obligation is difficult to categorise.[37] It is in itself no precondition of justice.[38] It originates from the legitimate expectations of the parties and their will, since the parties may excuse the arbitrators from their obligation to disclose, but not from their obligation to be independent and impartial.[39] Also, the obligation to disclose contributes to the parties' confidence in the arbitrator they appoint – they can only be confident if they know all the facts about their "chosen judge", since "information is a guarantee of confidence".[40]

1.4 Concluding Remarks

To conclude this short introduction to international commercial arbitration from the viewpoint of independence and impartiality, the importance of the dualistic nature of arbitration shall be highlighted. The dualistic nature, inter alia, causes the presence of different sources for the standard of independence and impartiality. Primarily, the arbitration agreement may directly or through the choice of institutional rules and the seat foresee a standard to be applied. In addition, other chosen laws, rules, and guidelines may apply besides the *lex loci arbitri*. Although the parties enjoy party autonomy, their freedom of contract is not unlimited as arbitration is nevertheless substantive jurisprudence, and must, thus, be in line with the fundamental judicial prerequisites.[41]

---

35 See below chapters 4.1.1.1.2, and 4.1.1.1.5.

36 C. Partasides, *The Fourth Arbitrator?*, Arb. Int'l 18 (2002), 147-161, 147.

37 See below chapter 7.1.

38 M. Henry, *Note – Cour d'appel de Paris, 14 octobre 2014, SA Auto Guadeloupe Investissements v. société Columbus Acquisitions Inc. et autres*, Rev. de l'Arb. 2015, 156-182, 159.

39 M. Henry, *Note – Cour d'appel de Paris, 14 octobre 2014, SA Auto Guadeloupe Investissements v. société Columbus Acquisitions Inc. et autres*, Rev. de l'Arb. 2015, 156-182, 164.

40 M. Henry, *Note – Cour d'appel de Paris, 14 octobre 2014, SA Auto Guadeloupe Investissements v. société Columbus Acquisitions Inc. et autres*, Rev. de l'Arb. 2015, 156-182, 164.

41 BGH, 3 July 1975, III ZR 78/73, NJW 1976, 109-111.

2 Applicable Laws, Rules, and Guidelines

The examination of independence and impartiality in international commercial arbitration can include a vast number of different statutes, rules, guidelines, and other regulations. Some of these regulations play an important role in harmonisation of the applicable standard of independence and impartiality in international arbitration.

The following outlines those provisions that will be addressed within this book. This includes the IBA Guidelines on Conflicts of Interest (2.1), the IBA Rules on the Taking of Evidence (2.2), the IBA Guidelines on Party Representation (2.3), the IBA Rules of Ethics for International Arbitrators (2.4), different institutional rules, guidelines, and codes (2.5), a short reference to European Law (2.6), the New York Convention (2.7), and the UNCITRAL Model Law (2.8).

2.1 IBA Guidelines on Conflicts of Interest in International Arbitration (IBA Guidelines 2014)

The IBA Guidelines 2014 are the most popular soft law instrument on the matter of independence and impartiality. They "offer advice on how to analyse conflicts and when to investigate or disclose conflicts".[1] The Guidelines set forth seven General Standards in the area of conflicts of interest, in Part I, and add non-exhaustive "Application Lists" with possible practical scenarios in Part II. These scenarios are categorised into a Non-Waivable Red List, and Waivable Red, Orange, and Green Lists, according to their potential influence on independence and impartiality. The introduction to Part II states that the colouring guides the likelihood of constituting a conflict of interest and the need for disclosure.

The Guidelines "are not legal provisions and do not override any applicable national law or arbitral rules chosen by the parties".[2] In line with this restrictive description by the Guidelines themselves, authors and courts often note that the Guidelines have no "independent legal effect",[3] or "binding authority [... or] the force of law".[4] However, if the parties explicitly agree on the Guidelines to apply, they should be directly binding.

---

1 B. Fuller, *Arbitrary Standards for Arbitrator Conflicts of Interest: Understanding the "Evident Partiality" Standard*, PIABA Bar J. 20 (2013), 59-66, 62.

2 Part I, Introduction, para. 6 IBA Guidelines 2014.

3 G. Born, *International Commercial Arbitration*, p. 1971.

4 LCIA Reference No. 81160, LCIA Court, 28 August 2009, Arb. Int'l 27 (2011), 442-454, 449.

The response to the IBA Guidelines 2014 is split. Some courts laud the Guidelines as a "valuable working tool"[5]; others describe in detail their difficulties in applying them, particularly the Orange List.[6] The criticism and difficulties root in the Guidelines' purpose to guide the likelihood of constituting a conflict of interest and the need for disclosure in the same, coloured list in Part II. In *H v. L and M*, the England and Wales High Court of Justice interpreted the Orange List to primarily purport the need for disclosure. However, that need does not import any suggestion or presumption of doubt as to the arbitrator's impartiality.[7] Before that decision, the High Court already outlined the Guidelines' failure to clarify the impact of the Application Lists on the standard of independence and impartiality in *W Ltd. v. M Sdn Bhd.*[8] Indeed, the standard of disclosure and the standard of independence and impartiality need to be distinguished. Although both standards have similarities and interact with each other, they are different concepts.[9]

In the same manner, scholars and practitioners criticise the Guidelines for being too broad[10] and fostering the divergent application of the different applicable standards of disclosure, and independence and impartiality, resulting in "confusion" and "uncertainty".[11] English courts' criticism of the Orange List is particularly salient as this list is the most important one. It entails borderline scenarios, i.e., those that will often lead to challenges.[12]

Even though the IBA Guidelines 2014 are criticised, their ability to streamline an international standard to be applied in international arbitration is apparent. They "reflect actual practice in significant parts of the international arbitration community".[13] They are not often incorporated by the parties, but nevertheless may assist appointing authorities, arbitral institutions, and national courts when they are faced with conflicts of interest.[14]

5 BGer, 10 June 2010, 4A_458/2009 ASA Bull. 2010, 520-539, 529. In French: "*un instrument de travail précieux*".

6 *H v. L and M*, [2017] EWHC 137 (Comm).

7 *H v. L and M*, [2017] EWHC 137 (Comm).

8 *W Ltd. v. M Sdn Bhd.*, [2016] 1 CLC 437. The High Court of Justice criticised the compendious treatment of "(a) the arbitrator and his or her firm, and (b) a party and any affiliate of the party". It concluded that although the case was equal to para. 1.4 of the Non-Waivable Red List, the award was not to be annulled since the applicable (international) standard of independence and impartiality was met.

9 See, inter alia, below chapter 7.1.4.1.

10 D. Lawson, *Impartiality and Independence of International Arbitrators, Commentary on the 2004 IBA Guidelines on Conflicts of Interest in International Arbitration*, ASA Bull. 2005, 22-45, 38 et seq., criticising the previous version.

11 G. Born, *International Commercial Arbitration*, p. 1972.

12 G. Born, *International Commercial Arbitration*, p. 1981.

13 LCIA Reference No. 81160, LCIA Court, 28 August 2009, Arb. Int'l 27 (2011), 442-454, 449.

14 G. Born, *International Commercial Arbitration*, p. 1984.

Their consistent application may lead to more predictability, and, as a result, may lead to the reduction in actions to annul awards on the basis of alleged partiality.[15]

2.2 IBA Rules on the Taking of Evidence in International Arbitration (IBA Rules 2020)

The IBA Rules 2020 aim to provide a resource to parties and arbitrators for an efficient, economical, and fair process for the taking of evidence in international arbitration.[16] Similar to the IBA Guidelines 2014, they intend to streamline an international standard and bridge procedures used in different legal systems.

Regarding independence and impartiality in international commercial arbitration, the Rules include procedures for party-appointed and tribunal-appointed experts. Both experts shall submit a "statement of [...] independence from the Parties, their legal advisors and the Arbitral Tribunal",[17] and the tribunal-appointed expert is additionally required to be "independent".[18] Under Article 9 IBA Rules 2020, the arbitral tribunal has the power to determine the admissibility, relevance, materiality and weight of evidence, and to "exclude from evidence or production any Document, statement, oral testimony or inspection", inter alia, for "considerations of procedural economy, proportionality, fairness or equality of the Parties that the Arbitral Tribunal determines to be compelling".[19] Article 9 IBA Rules 2020 may, thus, be a useful tool to circumvent the arbitrator's challenges for issues of conflicts of interest with any piece of evidence.[20]

2.3 IBA Guidelines on Party Representation in International Arbitration (IBA Guidelines 2013)

The IBA Guidelines 2013 address the multifaceted issue of a counsel's ethics in international dispute resolution. They are

> inspired by the principle that party representatives should act with integrity and honesty and should not engage in activities designed to produce

15 B. Fuller, *Arbitrary Standards for Arbitrator Conflicts of Interest: Understanding the "Evident Partiality" Standard*, PIABA Bar J. 20 (2013), 59-66, 59-60.

16 IBA Rules 2020, Foreword, p. 5.

17 Arts. 5(2)(c), 6(2) IBA Rules 2020.

18 Art. 6(1) IBA Rules 2020.

19 Art. 9(2)(g) IBA Rules 2020.

20 See below chapter 7.3.

unnecessary delay or expense, including tactics aimed at obstructing the arbitration proceedings.[21]

With this aim, they may be used to circumvent issues of dependence and partiality due to conflicts of interest between an arbitrator and counsel. Guideline 5 IBA Guidelines 2013 provides that no person should accept "representation of a Party in the arbitration when a relationship exists between the person and an Arbitrator that would create a conflict of interest". And according to Guideline 6, "[t]he Arbitral Tribunal may, in case of breach of Guideline 5, take measures appropriate to safeguard the integrity of the proceedings, including the exclusion of the new Party Representative". Although this may be criticised as "unusual" and doubtfully reflecting "either customary practice or the professional obligations of counsel under most national codes of conduct",[22] the Guidelines may "encourage a meaningful dialogue between the tribunal and the parties regarding ethical obligations that go beyond those dealt with in the Guidelines".[23] Additionally, the Guidelines may "inspire institutional action to embrace the issue and adopt institutional rules that give the tribunal authority to enforce rules that foster a fair process undisturbed by obstructionist tactics".[24]

The IBA Guidelines 2013 do not, however, address the issue of conflicts of interest.

2.4 IBA Rules of Ethics for International Arbitrators (IBA Rules 1987)

The IBA Rules 1987 partially precede the IBA Guidelines 2014.[25] The nine Rules rest on the "Fundamental Rule" that "[a]rbitrators shall proceed diligently and efficiently to provide the parties with a just and effective resolution of their disputes, and shall be and shall remain free from bias".[26] They include rather general provisions regarding substantive standards of impartiality and independence, disclosure, communications with parties, and fees.[27] Their focus is to provide general ethical principles concerning topics not addressed by national arbitration laws.[28]

21 IBA Guidelines 2013, Preamble, p. 2.
22 G. Born, *International Commercial Arbitration*, p. 3100.
23 E. Sussman, *Can Counsel Ethics Beat Guerrilla Tactics?*, Rev. Brasileira Arb. 10 (2013), 98-105, 105.
24 E. Sussman, *Can Counsel Ethics Beat Guerrilla Tactics?*, Rev. Brasileira Arb. 10 (2013), 98-105, 105.
25 Cf. IBA Rules 1987, Introductory Note and Part I, Introduction, para. 8 IBA Guidelines 2014.
26 Rule 1 IBA Rules 1987.
27 G. Born, *International Commercial Arbitration*, p. 1972.
28 G. Born, *International Commercial Arbitration*, p. 1972. Another set of principles partly overlapping with the IBA Guidelines 2014 are the Burgh House Principles, drafted by the International Law Association

2.5 Institutional Guidelines and Codes

Besides these rules and guidelines provided by the IBA, other institutions have established rules, guidelines, and codes applicable to arbitrators, parties' counsels, and other actors in international arbitration. These institutional rules, guidelines, and codes may provide guidance at different stages in the arbitration proceedings. For example, an arbitrator may consult the applicable set of rules when faced with the question of what to disclose at the outset of the arbitration proceedings, or an arbitral institution may refer to them when acting as appointing authority or deciding challenges.

The AAA and the ABA jointly prepared a Code of Ethics that aims at providing ethical standards for arbitrators when they are sitting on an arbitral tribunal. It reflects the general American practice in the field of ethics for arbitrators,[29] including the American peculiarity in domestic arbitration to agree on non-neutral party-nominated arbitrators.[30] Mandatory provisions of the applicable arbitration law limit the scope of application of the Code.[31] Even though the AAA/ABA Code of Ethics focuses on domestic arbitration and is, hence, not faced with as many cultural difficulties in shaping ethical guidelines as the IBA,[32] a similar criticism has been raised against the AAA/ABA Code of Ethics: it "falls short of providing a comprehensive means of evaluating when conflicts require disclosure, and when conflicts rise to the level of evident partiality".[33] The precise interplay of disclosure and the standard of independence and impartiality is uncertain. Besides, Born criticises

Study Group on the Practice and Procedure of International Courts and Tribunals in association with the Project on International Courts and Tribunals, F. Gélinas, *The Independence of International Arbitrators and Judges: Tampered With or Well Tempered?*, N.Y. Int'l Rev. 24 (2011), 1-48, 11-14. The Burgh House Principles were presented at the Berlin Congress of the International Law Association in 2004 and released shortly thereafter. They take full-time members of standing international courts "as the ideal type of an international adjudicator". F. Gélinas, *The Independence of International Arbitrators and Judges: Tampered With or Well Tempered?*, N.Y. Int'l Rev. 24 (2011), 1-48, 13. Their practical relevance in arbitration is, however, questionable as they do not clarify whether and to what extent they apply at all in arbitration. With regard to their view on full-time members of standing international courts, the Principles' target deviates substantively from commercial arbitration.

29 J. Fellas, *Evident Partiality and the Party-Appointed Arbitrator*, N.Y. L.J. 2018.

30 This particularity will be elaborated on and analysed below in chapter 6.3.

31 See J. Carter, *Improving Life With the Party-Appointed Arbitrator: Clearer Conduct Guidelines for "Nonneutrals"*, Am. Rev. Int'l Arb. 11 (2000), 295-305, 298, on the legal nature of the Code.

32 The Preamble reads as follows: "In those instances where this Code has been approved and recommended by organizations that provide, coordinate, or administer services of arbitrators, it provides ethical standards for the members of their respective panels of arbitrators. However, this Code does not form a part of the arbitration rules of any such organization unless its rules so provide."

33 B. Fuller, *Arbitrary Standards for Arbitrator Conflicts of Interest: Understanding the "Evident Partiality" Standard*, PIABA Bar J. 20 (2013), 59-66, 62.

the use of the Code in annulment procedures before courts. According to him, the use is inappropriate since the standards for annulment and challenge differ.[34]

Arbitrators may also be members of certain associations implementing guidelines and principles. One of these associations is CIArb, which publishes Guidelines, inter alia, on expert witnesses[35] and on interviews with prospective arbitrators.[36] With regard to disclosure, CIArb provides the CIArb Code of Conduct, addressing the member's work when acting for the institute in Part I, and the member's work in dispute resolution, in Part II. Part II establishes rules on, inter alia, behaviour, integrity, conflicts of interest, and competence. The purpose of these rules is to serve not only as a guide, but also as a point of reference for users of the process, and to promote public confidence in dispute resolution techniques.[37]

CIETAC provides for two additional sets of guidelines: the CIETAC Code of Conduct and the CIETAC Rules for Evaluating the Behavior of Arbitrators. The CIETAC Code of Conduct describes in fifteen provisions the arbitrator's rights and duties regarding due process, efficiency, and confidentiality of the proceedings. The CIETAC Rules for Evaluating the Behavior of Arbitrators consist of sixteen articles describing in detail circumstances that could lead to the arbitrator's challenge, withdrawal, or replacement. Article 10 CIETAC Rules for Evaluating the Behavior of Arbitrators states that where a violation of the rules

> might affect the parties' confidence in the Arbitration Commission or damage the image of the Commission, but the violation does not warrant withdrawal, replacement or dismissal of the arbitrator, the Commission shall issue a warning to the arbitrator.

This "warning" is rather unique in arbitration rules and it demonstrates an intense interaction of the arbitral institution.

The DIS does not provide additional rules or guidelines concerning ethics. The DIS does, however, provide Integrity Principles for its personnel, ensuring institutional independence. According to the DIS Integrity Principles, members of the DIS Appointing Committee

34 G. Born, *International Commercial Arbitration*, p. 1996.
35 CIArb Guideline on Experts.
36 CIArb Guideline on Interviews.
37 CIArb Code of Conduct, Introduction.

shall not accept mandates as arbitrators under the DIS Rules.[38] These members may, however, act as external counsel in arbitration proceedings under the DIS Rules.[39]

HKIAC publishes on its website a Code of Ethical Conduct comprising six rules concretely on the arbitrator's duties to act impartially.[40] In addition, the Code clarifies that the mere failure to disclose may create an appearance of bias and may constitute a ground for a challenge. It also forbids ex parte communication and actively soliciting appointments. The clear position on a failure to disclose deviates from the approach applied under other laws and rules.[41] The HKIAC also publishes additional information on the Removal of Arbitrators[42] on its website and offers additional Guidelines on the Use of a Secretary to the Arbitral Tribunal.[43]

The ICC provides the detailed ICC Note, applicable to parties and arbitral tribunals. The ICC Note covers several potential issues the tribunal and parties may encounter during an arbitration proceeding. It aims to provide "practical guidance concerning the conduct of the arbitrations under the ICC Rules" and the practices of the ICC Court of Arbitration.[44] Its detailed explanations contain guidance on the use of tribunal secretaries, arbitrator's disclosure, and fees and expenses. One of the particularities of the ICC Note is its explanation of Article 17(2) ICC Rules, the tribunal's power to exclude counsel and ex parte conduct.[45]

A similar note applies in proceedings with the LCIA. However, the LCIA has two separate notes: the LCIA Notes for Parties and the LCIA Notes for Arbitrators. The LCIA also addresses the use of tribunal secretaries within its note.[46]

---

38 Para. (3)(iv) DIS-Integrity Principles. This restriction also applies to members of the Secretariat and other employees, para. (4)(i), and executive members of the DIS Board of Directors, para. (5)(i).

39 Para. (3) al. 2. DIS-Integrity Principles. Members of the Secretariat and other employees, and executive members of the DIS Board of Directors may not act as external counsel in an arbitration under the DIS Rules, paras. (4)(ii), (5)(ii) DIS-Integrity Principles.

40 The Code explicitly states that besides applicable arbitration laws and rules the arbitrator's membership in certain associations or chambers, for example, CIArb, may provide for obligations on independence and impartiality.

41 See below chapters 4.2.1.6, and 7.1.4, for more details on consequences of non-disclosure.

42 The HKIAC underlines the application of the Code of Ethical Conduct when removing an arbitrator, and clarifies that the Code is based closely on the CIArb's Guidelines of Good Practice and Code of Ethical Conduct for Arbitrators.

43 For more details on the involvement and the status of tribunal secretaries, see below chapter 4.1.3.

44 Part I, General Information, ICC Note.

45 ICC Note, para. 15 on the exclusion of counsel and para. 68 on ex parte conduct.

46 LCIA Notes for Arbitrators, para. 8.

The use of tribunal secretaries is also described in some detail in the SCAI Guidelines for Arbitrators, stressing the importance of independence and impartiality of any tribunal secretary and the parties' discretion to object.[47] Additionally, the Guidelines address the accounting of expenses and payments.

Similarly to the ICC and LCIA notes, the SCC Arbitrator's Guidelines advise, inter alia, concretely on the arbitrator's conduct on case management, costs, and drafting the award. Within advising on case management, they refer to the independence and impartiality of tribunal secretaries.[48] The SCC provides a written SCC Appointment Policy, similar to the DIS Integrity Principles, demanding institutional independence and impartiality for the SCC itself.[49]

Finally, SIAC offers its users the SIAC Code of Ethics, and additionally Practice Notes on the appointment of tribunal secretaries, SIAC, Practice Note, PN – 01/17, and on the arbitrator's conduct in case of external funding, SIAC, Practice Note, PN – 01/15. The SIAC Code of Ethics explains, inter alia, the obligation to disclose and its scope in more detail, and defines independence and impartiality. The Code aims to supplement the SIAC Rules but, according to Article 7.2 SIAC Code of Ethics, shall not provide grounds for setting aside an award. As a preliminary remark, SIAC provides a rather articulated frame of rules for the participants in an arbitration proceeding.

2.6 European Law

European Law can be a source of applicable law in arbitral proceedings. The impact of European Law on international arbitration, in general, is complex and has recently been tested.[50] The decisions of European courts may have a significant influence on arbitration proceedings.[51] Concerning issues of independence and impartiality, the ECHR, in particular,

47 SCAI Guidelines for Arbitrators, paras. A.1., A.3.

48 SCC Guidelines, p. 8.

49 Para. I, SCC Appointment Policy.

50 E.g., in *Slovak Republic v. Achmea BV*, ECJ, 6 March 2018, C-284/16. For a general overview on the application of human rights in arbitration, see M. Benedettelli, *Human Rights as a Litigation Tool in International Arbitration, Reflecting on the ECHR Experience*, Arb. Int'l 31 (2015), 631-659; W. Habscheid, *FS Henckel*, pp. 341-352.

51 Even if, on first sight, the European Law in question is not applicable to arbitration, see e.g., in *Allianz SpA, Generali Assicurazioni Generali SpA v. West Tankers Inc.*, ECJ, 10 February 2009, C-185/07, on the role of European Law.

may influence decisions. English,[52] French,[53] and Swiss courts[54] tend to cite Article 6(1) ECHR[55] as a source for requiring the arbitrators' independence and impartiality in annulment or enforcement proceedings, as well as in appointment proceedings.[56]

Article 6 ECHR applies to disputes that relate to "rights and obligations" that are civil.[57] Materially, the article embodies the "right to a court", of which the right of access, i.e., the right to institute proceedings before courts in civil matters, constitutes one aspect. Guarantees laid down in Article 6(1) ECHR cover both the conduct of the proceedings and the organisation and composition of the court or tribunal. In sum, Article 6 ECHR constitutes the right to a "fair hearing".[58] Since the scope of Article 6 ECHR resembles that of many arbitration laws, there are few violations of Article 6(1) ECHR in practice. Scenarios where Article 6(1) ECHR may be violated are the failure to treat all parties equally in the appointment of arbitrators in multiparty proceedings;[59] the lack of judicial remedies against decisions of arbitral institutions on arbitrators' challenges;[60] or adjudication of the merits

---

52 E.g., *Locabail (U.K.) Ltd. v. Bayfield Properties Ltd.*, [2000] QB 451. See also, *Stretford v. Football Association Ltd.*, [2007] EWCA Civ 238, not on independence and impartiality, and *Primary Health Investment Properties Ltd., Primary Health Properties PLC, Dr N.B. Turnbull, Dr V.L. Beveridge, Dr R.A. Elder, Dr I.M. Wheatley v. The Secretary of State for Health & others, The National Health Service Litigation Authority Family Health Services Appeal Unit,* [2009] EWHC 519 (Admin), on domestic arbitration.

53 E.g, Cass com, 3 November 1992, 90-16751. In France, also the *juge d'appui* is bound by Art. 6 ECHR when appointing an arbitral tribunal in default of the parties, C. Seraglini/J. Ortscheidt, *Droit de l'arbitrage interne et international,* para. 756.

54 E.g., BGer, 30 June 1994, 4P.292/1993, ASA Bull. 1997, 99-107.

55 Art. 6(1) sentence 1 ECHR reads as follows: "In the determination of his civil rights and obligations or of any criminal charge against him, everyone is entitled to a fair and public hearing within a reasonable time by an independent and impartial tribunal established by law."

56 It is questionable whether arbitral institutions are bound by Art. 6 ECHR when acting as appointing authority. One may argue that there is a certain need for institutions, as a service provider, to safeguard as much as possible the enforceability of the arbitral award and, therefore, to adhere to Art. 6 ECHR. An obligation to safeguard the enforceability of the award is often allocated to arbitral tribunals. Institutions have only limited control on the proceedings and, in particular, on the award. Therefore, such an obligation should not be presumed for institutions, F. Schäfer, *Institutionelle Schiedsgerichtsbarkeit,* paras. 113-114. However, according to some authors, arbitral institutions may violate Art. 6(1) ECHR, e.g., by "overstepping [...] its merely administrative role through the exercise of judicial or quasi-judicial functions, e.g., when reviewing draft awards", M. Benedettelli, *Human Rights as a Litigation Tool in International Arbitration, Reflecting on the ECHR Experience,* Arb. Int'l 31 (2015), 631-659, 648.

57 ECtHR, Guide on Art. 6 ECHR, para. 3 et seq.

58 ECtHR, Guide on Art. 6 ECHR, para. 75.

59 Cf. Cass com, 7 January 1992, YB Com. Arb. XVIII (1993), 140-142. For the same example, see M. Benedettelli, *Human Rights as a Litigation Tool in International Arbitration, Reflecting on the ECHR Experience,* Arb. Int'l 31 (2015), 631-659, 647.

60 M. Benedettelli, *Human Rights as a Litigation Tool in International Arbitration, Reflecting on the ECHR Experience,* Arb. Int'l 31 (2015), 631-659, 648.

of the dispute by the same arbitral tribunal that issued an interim measure of a summary nature.[61]

The exact role of Article 6 ECHR in implementing independence and impartiality in international commercial arbitration is less direct. The ECtHR considers the national legislative framework for arbitral proceedings and, especially, the principle to respect the "considerable discretion" that Contracting Sates enjoy in regulating arbitration.[62] In case of voluntary arbitration, parties may waive certain rights under Article 6 ECHR.[63] Thus, the contractual nature of arbitration must be considered when applying Article 6 ECHR. However, the application of Article 6 ECHR in arbitration can advance harmonisation and internationalisation of the standard for independence and impartiality.[64] Furthermore, case law by the ECtHR supplies an additional source to exemplify and concretise the standard of independence and impartiality.[65]

2.7 New York Convention

International conventions applicable in arbitration also advance harmonisation and internationalisation of the standard for independence and impartiality. The most prominent example is the New York Convention,[66] which regulates the recognition and enforcement of foreign arbitral awards. Regarding independence and impartiality, the New York Convention provides two grounds that may prevent recognition and enforcement:[67]

---

61 M. Benedettelli, *Human Rights as a Litigation Tool in International Arbitration, Reflecting on the ECHR Experience*, Arb. Int'l 31 (2015), 631-659, 648.

62 *Suovaniemi and others v. Finland*, ECtHR, 23 February 1999, No. 31737/96.

63 D. Kozlowska-Rautiainen, *The Right to a Public Hearing in Arbitration in Light of ECtHR Judgments*, Stockholm Arb. YB 2020, 137-166, 142 et seq.

64 But see, G. Born, *International Commercial Arbitration*, p. 1792, generally arguing against the use of protections under national constitutions since these "are directed towards national courts and governmental institutions, not towards consensual dispute resolution mechanisms, between commercial parties".

65 See, e.g., *Mutu/Pechstein v. Switzerland*, ECtHR, 2 October 2018, Nos. 40575/10 and 67474/10; *Bramelid and Malmström v. Sweden*, ECtHR, 12 October 1982, Nos. 8588/79 and 8589/79, as an example of applying Art. 6(1) ECHR to arbitrators. See also, *McGonnell v. United Kingdom*, ECtHR, 8 February 2000, 28488/95, on independence and impartiality of judges.

66 The New York Convention applies in 168 states, as of March 2021. Another regional convention is the Panama Convention, i.e., the Inter-American Convention on international commercial arbitration, applicable in Argentina, Brazil, Chile, Colombia, Costa Rica, Ecuador, El Salvador, Guatemala, Honduras, Mexico, Panama, Paraguay, Peru, the United States, Uruguay and Venezuela, and additionally signed by Bolivia, Dominican Republic and Nicaragua. The Panama Convention regulates the conduct of international commercial arbitration and the enforcement of arbitral awards.

67 Whether Art. V(1)(d) or V(2)(b) New York Convention is more suitable to apply to the standard of independence and impartiality depends primarily on the facts of the case. See on Art. V(2)(b), *Kolel Beth Yechiel Mechil of Tartikov, Inc. v. YLL Irrevocable Trust*, 878 F.Supp.2d 459 (S.D. New York 2012), on alleged misconduct; F. Gélinas, *The Independence of International Arbitrators and Judges: Tampered With or Well*

Article V(1)(d), i.e., lack of proper composition of the arbitral tribunal,[68] and Article V(2)(b), violation of the *ordre public* of the enforcing country.[69]

Depending on the inclusion of the New York Convention in the national legal system,[70] and the interplay of national arbitration law and the New York Convention, the Convention may influence the standard applied for independence and impartiality in the recognition and enforcement stages.[71] Also, the New York Convention secures in Contracting States full acceptance of arbitration as an alternative dispute resolution mechanism to litigation.[72]

2.8 UNCITRAL Model Law

Finally, the UNCITRAL Model Law, and in particular its Articles 12, 18, 36(1)(a)(iv) and 36(1)(b)(ii), may influence the applicable standard of independence and impartiality, and the obligation to disclose. The UNCITRAL Model Law applies where incorporated by states. In that case, its commentaries and other case law from other UNCITRAL Model Law jurisdictions may provide guidance.

Article 12 UNCITRAL Model Law provides the following:

Tempered?, N.Y. Int'l Rev. 24 (2011), 1-48, 32-33; D. Branson, *American Party-Appointed Arbitrators – Not the Three Monkeys*, U. Dayton L. Rev. 30 (2004), 1-62, 26. See on Art. V(1)(d), E. Fontanelli, *The Disclosure Dilemma: Dealing with Arbitrator Issue Conflicts in International Arbitration*, IBA Arb. News 22 (2017), 68-71, 68. The term *ordre public* is generally construed narrowly, and often applied subsidiarily to other grounds of refusing recognition and enforcement. It should not be used to circumvent other grounds.

68 Art. V(1)(d) New York Convention reads as follows: "Recognition and enforcement of the award may be refused, at the request of the party against whom it is invoked, only if that party furnishes to the competent authority where the recognition and enforcement is sought, proof that: [...] The composition of the arbitral authority or the arbitral procedure was not in accordance with the agreement of the parties, or, failing such agreement, was not in accordance with the law of the country where the arbitration took place."

69 Art. V(2)(b) New York Convention reads as follows: "Recognition and enforcement of an arbitral award may also be refused if the competent authority in the country where recognition and enforcement is sought finds that: [...] The recognition or enforcement of the award would be contrary to the public policy of that country."

70 English law: Sect. 100 et seq. EAA; German law: § 1061(1) German ZPO refers directly to the New York Convention; Swiss law: Art. 194 Swiss IPRG refers also directly to the New York Convention; United States law: Sects. 201 et seq. FAA. Although France has signed and ratified the New York Convention, it does not refer to it in its arbitration law. It is the French understanding that French arbitration law is generally more favourable to recognition and enforcement, and applies, hence, due to Art. VII(1) New York Convention. See in more detail on this issue, D. Hascher, *Les perspectives françaises sur le contrôle de la sentence internationale ou étrangère*, McGill J. Disp. Res. 2 (2015), 1-15.

71 G. Born, *International Commercial Arbitration*, p. 1956, clarifying, however, that the standard for annulment must be different.

72 See Art. III New York Convention.

1. When a person is approached in connection with his possible appointment as an arbitrator, he shall disclose any circumstances likely to give rise to justifiable doubts as to his impartiality or independence. An arbitrator, from the time of his appointment and throughout the arbitral proceedings, shall without delay disclose any such circumstances to the parties unless they have already been informed of them by him.
2. An arbitrator may be challenged only if circumstances exist that give rise to justifiable doubts as to his impartiality or independence, or if he does not possess qualifications agreed to by the parties. A party may challenge an arbitrator appointed by him, or in whose appointment he has participated, only for reasons of which he becomes aware after the appointment has been made.

Commentators have highlighted that Article 12 UNCITRAL Model Law implements the principles of independence and impartiality in two ways: through the obligation to disclose and the grounds for challenge.[73] The obligation to disclose is "designed to inform and alert the person approaching the arbitrator at an early stage about possible doubts and, thus, helps to prevent the appointment of an unacceptable candidate".[74] Additionally, the ongoing obligation to disclose aims at providing

> the information to any party who did not obtain it before the arbitrator's appointment [...] and securing information about any circumstances which only arise at a later stage of the arbitral proceedings (e.g. new business affiliation or share acquisitions).[75]

Finally, grounds for challenge, i.e., "circumstances" include relationships and "instances of biased behaviour and misconduct".[76]

Aside from Article 12 UNCITRAL Model Law, the equal treatment of the parties, i.e., Article 18 UNCITRAL Model Law, may be decisive when considering the arbitral tribunal's ability to exclude a counsel or evidence to circumvent challenges.

In general, when interpreting the UNCITRAL Model Law, its international character and desire to harmonise national laws should be borne in mind. It was established "in view of the desirability of uniformity of the law of arbitral procedures and the specific needs of

73 UNCITRAL Model Law, Analytical Commentary, Art. 12 para. 1.
74 UNCITRAL Model Law, Analytical Commentary, Art. 12 para. 2.
75 UNCITRAL Model Law, Analytical Commentary, Art. 12 para. 3.
76 UNCITRAL Model Law, Analytical Commentary, Art. 12 para. 5. See also, A. Okekeifere, *Appointment and Challenge of Arbitrators Under the UNCITRAL Model Law: Part 2: Challenge*, Int'l Arb. L. Rev. 3 (2000), 13-18, for an overview on grounds for challenge applying Art. 12 UNCITRAL Model Law.

international commercial arbitration practice".[77] It bridges gaps between "considerable disparities in national laws on arbitration" and is – according to its description – "acceptable to States of all regions and the different legal or economic systems of the world".[78]

77 General Assembly, Resolution 40/72 of 11 December 1985, cited in UNCITRAL Model Law, Explanatory Note, para. 1, p. 23.

78 UNCITRAL Model Law Explanatory Note, paras. 2, 5, p. 23 et seq.

3 Overview of the Compared Legal Systems

This book features comparative references to statutes and case law from France (3.1), Germany (3.2), Switzerland (3.3), the United Kingdom (3.4), and the United States (3.5). The following short overview introduces these jurisdictions with a focus on their arbitration laws.

3.1 France

France is an originary civil law system. The legal system in France is based on statutory law. The judge's role is primarily to "mechanically" apply the law.[1] The judge usually does not go beyond general unwritten principles of law and may not be "creative".[2] The French CC is a mixture of Germanic and Roman laws and had a significant influence on many other jurisdictions.[3] Although the French system, as an originary civil law system, has no doctrine of precedent, lower courts generally rely on decisions of higher courts.[4]

The current French arbitration law was enacted in 2011 after a lengthy process of revision.[5] The French CPC includes the French arbitration law. It is not equivalent to the UNCITRAL Model Law and is described as "substantially more liberal" than the Model Law.[6] Special in French arbitration law is the role of courts through the *juge d'appui*. This "helping hand" is limited in its power to cases provided for by the French CPC, primarily referring to the

1 K. Zweigert/H. Kötz, *Einführung in die Rechtsvergleichung*, p. 88.
2 K. Zweigert/H. Kötz, *Einführung in die Rechtsvergleichung*, p. 125.
3 Including, inter alia, Belgium, Germany, Italy, Netherlands, Spain, Switzerland, cf. K. Zweigert/H. Kötz, *Einführung in die Rechtsvergleichung*, pp. 99-105.
4 N. Bouchardie/C. Tran, *Arbitration in France*, Practice Note 4-536-9585 (2018). In general, the traditional divide of common and civil law is not as present in practice as in theory. Regarding procedural law, J. Zekoll, *Comparative Civil Procedure*, p. 1329.
5 Changes to the previous arbitration law include a general definition of the arbitration agreement without differentiating between agreements concluded before and after the dispute arose, Art. 1442 French CPC; the exclusion of formal requirements for arbitration agreements in international disputes, Art. 1507 French CPC; a legal definition of the commencement of the arbitration, Art. 1456 French CPC; the introduction of the principle of estoppel, Art. 1466 French CPC; and others. For a detailed overview of the new French arbitration law, cf. D. Kühner, *Das neue französische Schiedsrecht*, SchiedsVZ 2011, 125-131, and Clay/Cadiet/T. Clay, Introduction générale.
6 N. Bouchardie/C. Tran, *Arbitration in France*, Practice Note 4-536-9585 (2018).

composition of the tribunal and prolongation of deadlines.[7] Further, the *juge d'appui* has to respect the parties' arbitration agreement.[8]

Regarding independence and impartiality, the French CPC provides in Article 1456(2) for the arbitrators' obligation to disclose any circumstances that may affect their independence or impartiality.[9] Before 2011, independence and impartiality had only been ordered negatively by constituting grounds for a challenge. By positively stating the requirement of independence and impartiality, Article 1456 French CPC considerably reinforced the fundamental guarantee.[10] Outside the obligation to disclose, however, independence and impartiality are not addressed within the French CPC.[11]

French case law on arbitration rarely compares the standard of independence and impartiality applied to state court judges with that applied in arbitration. Some authors doubt that the grounds used to challenge and recuse a judge apply to arbitrators since they are much more restrictive.[12] However, even if not directly applicable, the comprehensive catalogue in Article L. 111-6 French COJ, naming grounds for challenging a judge, can serve as a guideline of grounds of dependence and partiality applied in arbitration.[13]

3.2 Germany

Germany, like France, is traditionally a civil law system. Formalistically, it does not apply the doctrine of precedent. In practice, however, judges take decisions of other courts – especially higher ones – into consideration.[14] Contrary to French arbitration laws, German arbitration law relies on the UNCITRAL Model Law.[15] German arbitration law has a long

7 See, e.g., CA Paris, 24 May 2016, Rev. de l'Arb. 2017, 533-538.

8 C. Seraglini/J. Ortscheidt, *Droit de l'arbitrage interne et international*, paras. 776-778.

9 Art. 1456(2) French CPC reads: "*Il appartient à l'arbitre, avant d'accepter sa mission, de révéler toute circonstance susceptible d'affecter son indépendance ou son impartialité. Il lui est également fait obligation de révéler sans délai toute circonstance de même nature qui pourrait naître après l'acceptation de sa mission.*"

10 Clay/Cadiet/T. Clay, Art. 1456 para. 68.

11 French case law on arbitrators' and judges' independence and impartiality often refers to Art. 6(1) ECHR as an additional source for the requirement of being independent and impartial. See above chapter 2.6.

12 C. Seraglini/J. Ortscheidt, *Droit de l'arbitrage interne et international*, para. 732.

13 See below chapter 6.1.3.2, on the issue of comparing the standards for judges and arbitrators. Following the argument that the grounds applied to judges are more restrictive, these grounds could be applied as a minimum to arbitrators. It should be noted that the French *cour de cassation* states that the grounds for challenge applied to judges need to be interpreted inclusively, Cass civ 1ère, 28 April 1998, 96-11637, on Art. 341 French CPC referring to Art. L. 111-6 COJ.

14 S. Wilske/T. Fox/C. Krapfl, *Arbitration in Germany*, Practice Note 6-523-9833 (2018).

15 Without distinguishing between domestic and international arbitration, K.-H. Böckstiegel/S. Kröll/P. Nacimiento, *Arbitration in Germany*, p. 4.

history, especially of ad hoc arbitration with the first codification of general arbitration laws in 1879.[16] The current arbitration laws, contained in the German ZPO, came into force in 1998 and were amended in 2001.

§§ 1035(5) and 1036(2) German ZPO imply the necessity of independence and impartiality. If the seat of arbitration is in Germany, it is primarily the arbitral tribunal that decides on a challenged arbitrator. If the challenge is not successful, parties can request state courts to decide on the challenge within one month after receiving notice.[17] Apart from this challenge procedure, independence and impartiality may be a ground for annulment, under §§ 1059(2)(1)(b), (d), (2)(b) German ZPO, i.e., insufficient notice on the composition of the tribunal, irregular composition of the tribunal, or *ordre public*. It is questionable whether the same standard of independence and impartiality applies in challenge and annulment procedures.[18]

Some German case law on arbitration compares the applicable standard of independence and impartiality with the standard applied to judges or refers to it.[19] According to § 42(1) German ZPO,

> [a] judge may be recused from a case both in those cases in which he is disqualified by law from exercising a judicial office, and in those cases in which there is a fear of bias.

§ 42(2) German ZPO clarifies that "[a] judge will be recused for fear of bias if sound reasons justify a lack of confidence in his impartiality".[20]

---

16 K.-H. Böckstiegel/S. Kröll/P. Nacimiento, *Arbitration in Germany*, p. 4.

17 § 1037(3) German ZPO and S. Wilske/T. Fox/C. Krapfl, *Arbitration in Germany*, Practice Note 6-523-9833 (2018).

18 See MünnchKomm ZPO/J. Münch, § 1036 para. 27. See also, below chapter 6.2.3, on the issue of applying different standards.

19 E.g., OLG Frankfurt a.M., 24 January 2019, 26 SchH 2/18, BeckRS 2019, 848, 72; KG Berlin, 12 February 2018, 13 SchH 2/17, NJ 2018, 206-208, 207; OLG München, 10 July 2013, 34 SchH 8/12, NJOZ 2014, 1779-1782; OLG München, 3 January 2014, 34 SchH 7/13, SchiedsVZ 2014, 45-48, 48.

20 Additionally, some authors debate whether Art. 97 German GG applies to arbitrators. It reads: "(1) Judges shall be independent and subject only to the law. (2) Judges appointed permanently to full-time positions may be involuntarily dismissed, permanently or temporarily suspended, transferred or retired before the expiration of their term of office only by virtue of judicial decision and only for the reasons and in the manner specified by the laws. The legislature may set age limits for the retirement of judges appointed for life. In the event of changes in the structure of courts or in their districts, judges may be transferred to another court or removed from office, provided they retain their full salary." See on this debate, D. Effer-Uhe, *Schiedsgerichtliche Unabhängigkeit bei wissenschaftlichen Äußerungen*, SchiedsVZ 2018, 75-80, 76. Effer-Uhe disputes the applicability, arguing that a judge in the sense of the German GG refers exclusively to an organ of the state and covers only the judge's independence from a state, i.e., institutional independence.

3.3 Switzerland

Like Germany and France, Switzerland is a civil law system. It has a long tradition of arbitration, commencing in 1872 with the Alabama Claims.[21] The first unification of Swiss arbitration law for domestic and international disputes was the Concordat in 1969. Beforehand, the cantons regulated arbitral proceedings individually. The Concordat proved to be too rigid and unfit for international disputes in light of the first UNCITRAL harmonisations of rules.[22] In 1989, chapter 12 of the Swiss IPRG modernised the Swiss arbitration law for international arbitration. The most important innovations of the Swiss IPRG were the establishment of the subsidiary jurisdiction of courts in challenge procedures in Article 180 Swiss IPRG, deviating from Article 21 Concordat, and the priority of parties' agreements. As of 1 January 2021, the revised version of the Swiss IPRG is effective. The most recent revision clarifies the priority of the parties' agreement on the procedure for challenge and removal.[23] Article 180a(2) Swiss IPRG provides for interlocutory challenges before state courts, and it is a subject of dispute among scholars whether this challenge procedure is excluded completely in case of institutional decisions.[24] With regard to independence and partiality, it should be highlighted that the revision also clarified that arbitrators have to be "independent and impartial", Article 180(1)(c) Swiss IPRG.

Apart from the challenge procedure in Article 180 Swiss IPRG et seq., an award may be annulled for lack of independence and impartiality under Article 190(2)(a) or Article 190(2(e) Swiss IPRG: irregularities in the appointment or constitution, or *ordre public*. Whether the standard of independence and impartiality for annulment is to be differentiated is not settled in case law. In 2013, the Swiss *Bundesgericht* explicitly excluded the question of whether minor mistakes in the constitution of the tribunal justify annulment.[25]

Finally, some Swiss case law in arbitration also refers to the standard of independence and impartiality applied to judges.[26] Article 47 Swiss ZPO enumerates grounds for challenging a judge.[27] This enumeration is a useful illustration of potential grounds also for challenging arbitrators.

---

21 S. Hofbauer, *History of Arbitration*, p. 3.

22 S. Hofbauer, *History of Arbitration*, p. 4.

23 Arts. 180a(2), 180b(2) Swiss IPRG.

24 See BSK IPRG/W. Peter/C. Brunner, Art. 180 para. 34 et seq.

25 BGer, 13 November 2013, BGE 139 III 511, 515.

26 E.g., BGer, 19 February 2009, 4A_539/2008, para. C 3.2; BGer, 27 May 2003, BGE 129 III 445, 449; BGer, 15 March 1993, BGE 119 II 271, 275.

27 These include, e.g., personal interest in the case; having acted in the same case in another capacity, in particular as member of an authority, legal agent, expert witness, witness or mediator; being or having been

3.4 United Kingdom

The legal system in the United Kingdom is based on statutory legislation and common law, i.e., law made by sitting judges who apply statutory law and established principles. Acting lawyers are divided into barristers and solicitors, a distinction which is also relevant for arbitration and the issue of independence and impartiality.[28] Barristers traditionally represent the client in court, especially higher courts, whereas the solicitor was traditionally the intermediary between the barrister and the client, having direct contact and receiving instructions. This clear division of tasks has been blurred in recent years.

The EAA mirrors the UNCITRAL Model Law only in parts. Explicit differences include the standard for challenging an arbitrator, i.e., Section 24 EAA.[29] Section 24 EAA sets the standard as "circumstances exist that give rise to justifiable doubts as to his impartiality" and omits independence. In line with this wording, Article 33(1)(a) EAA requires arbitrators to "act fairly and impartially". A party's unsuccessful pursuit of an institutional challenge does not preclude English courts from deciding on the challenge of an arbitrator on the grounds of finding either dependence and partiality or misconduct.[30] On issues of independence and impartiality, English case law in arbitration often refers to case law rendered in court litigation. This case law compares the standard applied to judges with the standard used in arbitration.[31] Even though this case law differentiates arbitration and state court proceedings, it clarifies that state court decisions may provide guidance on issues of independence and impartiality.[32]

Apart from challenge procedures, the EAA provides for the annulment of awards, inter alia, in case of serious irregularities, e.g., if the arbitral tribunal failed to comply with

married to, or living or having lived in a registered partnership or cohabiting with a party or his or her representative or a person who has acted in the same case as a member of the lower court.

28 See below chapter 4.1.1.1.9, for more details on barristers.

29 Additionally, some crucial procedural aspects differ: Sect. 12 EAA and Sect. 45 EAA provide great influences of the courts, first, to intervene in the commencement of the arbitral proceeding by ordering extension of time and, second, to determine preliminary points of law.

30 *AT & T Corp. & Anor v. Saudi Cable Co.*, [2000] CLC 220.

31 E.g., in *Halliburton Co. v. Chubb Bermuda Ins. Ltd.*, [2018] EWCA Civ 817, upheld by *Halliburton Co. v. Chubb Bermuda Ins. Ltd.*, [2020] UKSC 48; *Dera Commercial Estate v. Derya Inc.*, [2018] EWHC 1673 (Comm). On the standard of "bias" the Court of Appeal referred, inter alia, to *Taylor v. Lawrence*, [2002] EWCA Civ 90.

32 But see, J. Steyn, *England: The Independence and/or Impartiality of Arbitrators in International Commercial Arbitration*, ICC Int. Ct. Arb. Bull. (2007) Special Supplement, 91-100, 95.

Article 33 EAA.[33] An application under Article 68(2)(a) EAA will usually be granted only if the irregularity caused or will cause substantial injustice to the applicant.[34]

3.5 United States

The legal system of the United States is, like the English legal system, a traditional common law system. Although it is based on the English legal system, its appearance today is different.[35] The most striking difference is the organisation of the United States into federal states and the derivative legislative powers of the federal states. The United States has a complex dualistic system of federal and state law with a similar complexity in the organisation of the judiciary.[36]

The FAA, enacted in 1925, governs arbitration in the United States. Its purpose was

> to reverse the longstanding judicial hostility to arbitration agreements that [...] had been adopted by American courts and to place arbitration agreements upon the same footing as other contracts.[37]

It does not rely on the UNCITRAL Model Law. Within the FAA "evident partiality" is a ground for annulling arbitral awards. However, there are no provisions for interlocutory judicial challenges to an arbitrator or disclosure. Hence, usually, there are no interlocutory challenges of arbitrators. Judicial review is streamlined in the review of arbitral awards. The FAA does not address impartiality and independence in any more detail. Hence, the FAA is described as addressing independence and impartiality less "directly" and "effectively".[38] Additional difficulties may result from diverse interpretations of the FAA in federal and state courts. In particular, the seminal case on evident partiality, i.e., *Commonwealth Coatings Corp. v. Continental Casualty Co. et al.*, has inspired diverse interpretations.[39] The case also addresses the comparison of the arbitrator's standard of

33 Art. 68(2)(a) EAA.

34 D. Sutton/J. Gill/M. Gearing, *Russel on Arbitration*, Chap. 8, Sect. 6(a).

35 K. Zweigert/H. Kötz, *Einführung in die Rechtsvergleichung*, pp. 235-236.

36 K. Zweigert/H. Kötz, *Einführung in die Rechtsvergleichung*, p. 244.

37 C. Palo, *Bias of Arbitrator as Ground for Vacatur of Arbitration Award*, Sect. 1. The FAA is based on the New York Arbitration Act, and both intended to allow arbitration outside the trades, unions, and the bilateral contracts using estimators and appraisers, D. Branson, *American Party-Appointed Arbitrators – Not the Three Monkeys*, U. Dayton L. Rev. 30 (2004), 1-62, 12.

38 G. Born, *International Commercial Arbitration*, p. 1895.

39 *Commonwealth Coatings Co. v. Continental Casualty Co. et al.*, 89 S.Ct. 337 (1968).

independence and impartiality with standards applied to state court judges.[40] Regarding judges, the Code of Conduct for United States Judges refers in more detail to (judicial) independence and impartiality.[41]

40 The Supreme Court, in its majority opinion, commenced its analysis of the standard of independence and impartiality by comparing it to the standard of judges and concluded that the same standard applies to arbitrators, if not a higher standard, due to the lack of appellate review in arbitration. It should be noted that courts have interpreted the decision very divergently. The position favouring a higher standard of independence and impartiality, i.e., a lower standard of partiality and dependence, for arbitrators is not applied any more. For more details on the question of comparing the standard applied to arbitrators with that applied to judges, see below chapter 6.1.3.2.

41 The Code is effective as of 12 March 2019. Canon 3 C. (1) Code of Conduct for United States Judges enumerates grounds for disqualifying a judge on grounds of partiality. Although the Code does not directly refer to the personal independence of the judge (it refers to independence of the judiciary), Canon 2 could be interpreted in this regard, i.e., "A Judge Should Avoid Impropriety and the Appearance of Impropriety in All Activities".

4 Conflicts of Interest

Case law and literature reveal an unlimited number of scenarios exposing potential dependence and partiality in arbitration.[1] The following chapter describes grounds that have been held to demonstrate dependence and partiality as well as scenarios in which one party alleges such grounds exist. The chapter also includes case law on judges, to present the full possible range of different grounds for dependence and partiality.[2] Faced with a challenge or annulment request on arbitral proceedings, many courts compare grounds for dependence and partiality of arbitrators to those of judges. Some courts apply case law on judges positively, others differentiate arbitration.

In a broad sense, a conflict of interest encompasses scenarios not guaranteeing independence and impartiality. More concretely, a conflict of interest includes a direct and present internal conflict between personal and third interests of which the affected person is in charge and where the personal interest of the affected person prevails.[3] Conflicts of interest pose a risk to independence and impartiality, parts of the general principle of due process, inter alia, requiring objective and fair decision-making. According to the principle of due process, no one should be a judge in his or her own cause.[4] This principle is at the centre of conflicts of interest. An abstract interest in the cause is, however, not enough to create a conflict of interest.[5] Different scenarios may constitute a conflict of interest, including "economic dependence, emotional ties, […] prior involvement in or knowledge about the matter, personal interests in common with a party and prior position taken as to the particular issue in dispute",[6] and more. Independence and impartiality are at risk in all of these scenarios.

---

1 E.g., all material or intellectual links between an arbitrator and a party that affect the arbitrator's judgment and cause a risk of partiality towards one party, C. Seraglini/J. Ortscheidt, *Droit de l'arbitrage interne et international*, para. 732.

2 Whether the standard of independence and impartiality applied in arbitration should be compared to that applied in state court proceedings will be addressed below, in chapter 6.1.3.2. It will be noted in the footnote whether cases deal with litigation. Not all grounds can be applied directly.

3 C. Castres Saint-Martin, *Les conflits d'intérêts en arbitrage commercial international*, p. 148.

4 Where an arbitrator is challenged, the question arises whether he or she may be involved in the challenge decision. Cf. *Pitta v. Hotel Ass'n of New York City, Inc.*, 806 F.2d 419 (2d Cir. 1986), where the award was annulled and additionally referred to another arbitrator. The case deals with domestic arbitration.

5 Cf. BSK BV/J. Reich, Art. 30 para. 28.

6 E. Fontanelli, *The Disclosure Dilemma: Dealing with Arbitrator Issue Conflicts in International Arbitration*, IBA Arb. News 22 (2017), 68-71, 68.

The burden of proof is a perennial procedural difficulty in addressing allegations of dependence and partiality. Generally, the burden of proof lies with the party requesting the cause of action.[7] However, it is often difficult for a party to supply convincing evidence to meet the threshold of lacking independence and impartiality, since independence and impartiality refer to an inner state of mind. The presence of solid relationships is typically used to prove dependence and partiality. Supplying proof for the allegation of dependence and partiality on the conduct of the arbitrator can be more difficult. The diverse cultural backgrounds of arbitrators can lead to diverging interpretations of different conduct. The conduct of the arbitrator as a ground for dependence and partiality is, hence, much more controversial and less effective.[8]

The following overview of conflicts of interest refers to the relationships (4.1) and conduct (4.2) of the arbitrator and other actors, potentially creating a ground for finding dependence and partiality. In addition, the arbitrator's nationality, language or cultural affiliations entail a potential conflict of interest (4.3). Finally, short concluding remarks summarise the key findings (4.4).

4.1 Relationships

Generally, any relation that deviates in intensity and quality from what is usual in social contacts may lead to a conflict of interest.[9] Analysing the term "relationship" under the category of conflicts of interest, the mere wording of the latter suggests that there need to be conflicting interests attached to the relationship.[10] Broadly, relationships are either social or professional. Social relationships may create enmity or friendship, while professional relationships may create either financial interest or situations of hierarchy and subordination.[11]

---

7 C. Palo, *Bias of Arbitrator as Ground for Vacatur of Arbitration Award*, Sect. 24.

8 Even though there is much case law on the interpretation of certain relationships constituting a ground for dependence and partiality, some relationships trigger controversial discussions on their interpretation as well. One of the aspects in discussions is the potential "trade-off" in arbitration, between independence and impartiality and the expertise of the arbitrator, E. Fontanelli, *The Disclosure Dilemma: Dealing with Arbitrator Issue Conflicts in International Arbitration*, IBA Arb. News 22 (2017), 68-71, 68. Additionally, the cultural background of parties and unconscious bias involved may cause a diverse understanding of the relationship in question. In fact, these questions affect any analysis whether a conflict of interest constitutes a positive ground for finding dependence and partiality.

9 Cf. BSK BV/J. Reich, Art. 30 para. 30. The author refers to judges and arbitrators.

10 Cf. C. Castres Saint-Martin, *Les conflits d'intérêts en arbitrage commercial international*, p. 149.

11 On hierarchy and subordination, see BSK IPRG/W. Peter/C. Brunner, Art. 180 para. 15. An additional categorisation by United States courts is the triviality of the relationship. Only the non-trivial relationship may constitute a conflict of interest, e.g., *Washburn v. McManus*, 895 F.Supp. 392 (D. Connecticut 1994).

When evaluating whether a relationship encompasses a conflict of interest within it, different factors are to be taken into consideration: the interest the party has in the proceedings, the directness of the relationship, the connection of the relationship to the dispute, and the proximity in time between the relationship and the arbitration proceeding.[12] A relationship constitutes a "material conflict of interest" if it reveals that the person in question is predisposed in favour of one of the parties to the dispute.[13]

Even though there is much case law and literature on the issue of relationships constituting a conflict of interest, many scenarios are not clear-cut. Any list of relationships that will "result in a per se [annulment] of an arbitration award" would be rather short.[14] In the end, the decision whether a conflict of interest results in dependence and partiality remains a case-by-case decision.

The point in time is an important parameter within the analysis of all relationships potentially constituting a ground for dependence and partiality.[15] Possible points in time are the nomination, the appointment of the individual arbitrator (or counsel, expert, or witness), the appointment of the whole tribunal, the hearing-phase, deliberations, or the award. Most case law suggests that the point in time of the appointment is the critical moment.[16] This approach is practical and in line with the needs of independence and impartiality. At the point in time of appointment, all parties are aware of any disclosures provided by the chosen person and may consciously decide whether or not they wish the arbitrator to decide their case. The appointment marks the beginning of the judicial function of the arbitrator. An earlier point in time cannot be relevant for the examination. The nomination is not final and may, hence, not serve as a relevant point in time. If a relationship is formed at a later point in time, that point will be decisive.[17]

---

12 C. Palo, *Bias of Arbitrator as Ground for Vacatur of Arbitration Award*, Sect. 23. See also, *Blackwell v. Merrill Lynch, Pierce, Fenner & Smith Inc.*, 22 F.Supp.3d 565 (W.D. North Carolina 2014).

13 *Scandinavian Reinsurance Co. Ltd. v. Saint Paul Fire and Marine Ins. Co.*, 668 F.3d 60 (2d Cir. 2012), 73-74.

14 *Morelite Construction Co. v. New York City District Council Carpenters Benefit Funds*, 748 F.2d 79 (2d Cir. 1984), 85.

15 E.g., in which period of time the arbitrator had been appointed how often, how long the arbitrator and counsel have known each other, etc.

16 *Certain Underwriting Members of Lloyds of London v. Florida*, 2018 WL 2727492 (2d Cir.), concluding that no conflict of interest could arise where the relationship ended before the appointment. See generally, C. Castres Saint-Martin, *Les conflits d'intérêts en arbitrage commercial international*, p. 177 et seq. On the appointment of counsels: Art. 4.2 French RIN.

17 But see, *Peoples Sec. Life Ins. Co. v. Monumental Life Ins. Co.*, 991 F.2d 141 (4th Cir. 1993). The court denied evident partiality, inter alia, with the argument that the relationship commenced after the appointment. At the point in time of the appointment, the relationship was not present. Even though the approach to focus at the point in time of appointment is to be welcomed, the argumentation cannot be followed: independence and impartiality are not only required at the stage of appointment but throughout the proceedings. If a

As an alternative to the appointment being the relevant point in time, some decisions favour the written award to be the relevant point in time.[18] This approach should be understood as an additional point in time for assessment. Independence and impartiality as fundamental procedural guarantees cannot be limited to only exist at either the appointment or the written award. They have to be respected throughout the arbitral proceedings.

4.1.1 *Arbitrator's Relationship*

Usually, arbitrators have a "business background" when they become arbitrators.[19] They are chosen from among those who are deeply involved with the subject matter in the dispute.[20] Hence, "relationships in arbitration are more frequent and narrower due to economic and professional necessities with regard to the persons active in the field".[21] Even if relations in arbitration are more frequent and narrower, arbitrators are professionals and should know how to remain independent and to favour independence to a friendly relationship.[22]

A relationship may exist between the arbitrator and all different actors in the arbitration. A conflict of interest rising to a ground for finding dependence and partiality may exist only where the relationship is intense. Independence and impartiality can be endangered by close relationships between the arbitrator and one party and by close relationships between the arbitrator and one party's counsel. This second group is more indirect and, hence, less likely to lead to partiality.[23] In addition, the arbitrator's relationship with a witness, expert, another arbitrator, or even with the appointing authority or institution can be an issue.

---

material relationship evolved within the proceedings, there can be a conflict of interest. However, in the domestic arbitration at hand, the circumstances were themselves not material. See also, BGer, 11 May 1992, ASA Bull. 1992, 381-401, 390. The Swiss *Bundesgericht* clarifies that independence and impartiality have to be guaranteed at the moment of appointment and during the whole proceedings until the notification of the final award.

18 *Republic of Argentina v. AWG Group Ltd.*, 211 F.Supp.3d 335 (D. Columbia 2016). The court ruled against a conflict of interest, since the relationship in question lasted only for a fraction of the time the arbitrator served as arbitrator and had ended when the final award was issued. See also, *Apperson v. Fleet Carrier Co.*, 879 F.2d 1344 (6th Cir. 1989).

19 N. Andrews/J. Landbrecht, *Schiedsverfahren und Mediation in England*, para. 97.

20 *First Interregional Equity Corp. v. Haughton*, 842 F.Supp. 105 (S.D. New York 1994).

21 BGer, 19 February 2009, 4A_539/2008, para. C 3.2. Cf. BGer, 12 June 2009, 4A_586/2008, para. C 3.1.2; BGer, 20 March 2008, 4A_506/2007, para. C 3.1.1; BGer, 9 February 1998, ASA Bull. 1998, 634-652, 645. In litigation, this higher possibility of being conflicted can be compared to part-time judges.

22 BGer, 4 August 2006, 4P.105/2006/fun, para. C 4.

23 BGer, 12 June 2009, 4A_586/2008, para. C 3.1.2.

4.1.1.1 Arbitrator's Relationship with a Party or Counsel

An arbitrator's relationship with a party is the most frequent ground for challenges in ICC arbitration.[24] An arbitrator should not be linked to the party that appointed him or her in a way that reduces the arbitrator to a mere representative of that party.[25] In accordance with the prerequisites of due process, an arbitrator shall not be a judge in his or her own cause. Hence, identity between the arbitrator and a party amounts to a conflict of interest.[26]

Often, the party itself does not appoint the arbitrator, but, rather, the party's counsel proposes the appointment. Since counsels represent their parties, their relationship with an arbitrator may equally create a conflict of interest, although differences in the argumentation in favour or against a conflict of interest can be observed.[27]

4.1.1.1.1 Professional Ties

Professional Ties with a Party

More often than social ties, professional ties constitute a conflict of interest. In general, an ordinary business relationship does not suffice to constitute a conflict of interest. An ordinary business relationship exists, for example, where the arbitrator and one party belong to the same professional group.[28] The business relationship may be no longer ordinary where the arbitrator and one party are members of a trade association that conducts the arbitral proceedings, and only one party is not a member of this association. Here, a conflict of interests may exist.[29] Similarly, an arbitrator may be conflicted and excluded from deciding a case if he or she is part of the representative organ of a company.[30] Generally, if the professional relationship between an arbitrator and one party is direct,

---

24 S. Greenberg, *Tackling Guerrilla Challenges Against Arbitrators.*

25 BGer, 9 February 1998, ASA Bull. 1998, 634-652, 644. In this regard, see also, Part II, para. 1.1 IBA Guidelines 2014, i.e., the Non-Waivable Red List.

26 In 2017, the German *Bundesgerichtshof* ruled that an arbitration agreement calling for a "tribunal" with two employees of each party and one neutral arbitrator was not in line with German arbitration law. The court denied enforcement of the final award since parties' employees and representatives being arbitrators violated the principle that no one should be judge in his or her own cause. BGH, 11 October 2017, I ZB 12/17, SchiedsVZ 2018, 271-275.

27 The relationship between the arbitrator and the party is generally treated more severely than that of the arbitrator and counsel. E.g., the IBA Guidelines 2014 only name scenarios of the arbitrator and the party or an affiliate on the Non-Waivable Red List. The counsel is not an affiliate in the terminology of the IBA Guidelines 2014.

28 CA Paris, 10 June 2004, YB Com. Arb. XXX (2005), 499-504.

29 According to J.-F. Poudret/S. Besson, *Comparative Law of International Arbitration*, para. 418, it is inadmissible that all members of the tribunal are members of an association and only one party is also a member of that association. More flexible on the constellation of member-tribunals: BGer, 12 February 1958, BGE 84 I 39, 51-52, and BGer, 25 January 1967, BGE 93 I 49.

30 Stein/Jonas/P. Schlosser, § 1036 para. 13.

connected to the dispute, and proximate in time to the arbitration proceedings, the relationship may constitute a ground for finding dependence and partiality.

Often, professional ties include financial relationships. This category is closely linked to employment and a relationship of subordination between the arbitrator and the party.[31] The professional and financial relationship resulting only from the ongoing arbitration is not a conflict of interest.[32] The professional relationship needs to be financially significant for the arbitrator to constitute a conflict of interest. This may be the case where an arbitrator derives a substantial portion of their income from the relationship.[33] Personal financial interests include those of close family members.[34] For example, where the arbitrator's father has ongoing business contacts with one of the parties, the arbitrator can be challenged.[35] However, where the relationship of the close family member is too tenuous there is no conflict of interest.[36]

Also, no conflict of interest exists if the party-appointed arbitrator is a member of the board of directors of the company whose president appointed the arbitrator to the dispute, provided that the arbitrator does not own any stock in the company and the dispute does not concern the company.[37] This decision can be different, however, if the arbitrator

31 See below chapter 4.1.1.1.4, for other employment.

32 The mere payment of arbitration fees does not constitute a conflict of interest: *HSM Const. Services, Inc. v. MDC Systems, Inc.*, 239 Fed.Appx. 748 (3d Cir. 2007), where one party informs the tribunal that the other party intends not to pay arbitration costs. The court denied a conflict of interest since there were other mechanisms for the tribunal to assure payment. However, this might be different where commitment fees are agreed upon bilaterally between one arbitrator and one party, cf. *K/S Norjarl A/S v. Hyundai Heavy Industries Co. Ltd.*, 1991 WL 838002. See below chapter 4.1.1.1.5, on remuneration as a ground for finding dependence and partiality.

33 J.-F. Poudret/S. Besson, *Comparative Law of International Arbitration*, p. 419. In *Commonwealth Coatings Co. v. Continental Casualty Co. et al.*, 89 S.Ct. 337 (1968), the arbitrator had earned 12.000 USD in the last five years in the relationship with one of the parties. According to the U.S. Supreme Court, this was of financial weight. The criterion of deriving a significant financial income from the relationship is also named on the Non-Waivable Red List of the IBA Guidelines 2014: "The arbitrator or his or her firm regularly advises the party, or an affiliate of the party, and the arbitrator or his or her firm derives significant financial income therefrom." Part II, para. 1.4 IBA Guidelines 2014.

34 Part II, para. 2.3.9 IBA Guidelines 2014. A close family relationship between one of the arbitrators and a party "or any person having a controlling influence in one of the parties, or an affiliate of one of the parties" is also placed on the Waivable Red List of the IBA Guidelines 2014, Part II para. 2.3.8.

35 *Sierra Fishing Co. v. Farran*, [2015] EWHC 140 (Comm); affirmative N. Andrews/J. Landbrecht, *Schiedsverfahren und Mediation in England*, paras. 106-108. In this case the court held that the arbitrator's financial interest in his father's law firm was significant. The firm and his father acted for one of the parties and derived significant financial benefit from that continuing commercial relationship.

36 *Stone v. Bear, Stearns & Co., Inc.*, 872 F.Supp.2d 435 (E.D. Pennsylvania 2012). The arbitrator's husband was a well-known finance professor who had worked for one of the respondents until ten years prior to the arbitration proceedings. In addition, a year before the arbitration began the husband gave speeches at a conference sponsored by that respondent.

37 KGer Graubünden, 30 January 1996, ASA Bull. 1996, 264-267.

receives other benefits. With regard to public companies, German case law and literature highlight the role of financial intensity, i.e., the amount of stocks owned: where the arbitrator or judge is a major shareholder, he or she cannot be independent and impartial.[38]

Financial intensity is a criterion also used in the United States to evaluate whether professional ties constitute a conflict of interest. In the words of the U.S. Court of Appeals, Ninth Circuit, the award may not be annulled where the arbitrator's financial relationship to a party is "contingent, attenuated, and merely potential".[39] This was held to be the case where the presiding arbitrator once worked under claimant's principal and main stockholder at another firm;[40] where respondent's party-appointed arbitrator was a non-executive director on the board of directors of a bank that invested together with respondent in Buenos Aires and was also part of the board of a consortium with respondent;[41] and where an arbitrator had previous business relations to claimant's in-house counsels.[42] On the other hand, where the arbitrator was vice-president, chief financial officer, and compliance officer for a third-party investment firm that entered several business relations with respondent, the business relationship between respondent and the arbitrator was "more than trivial".[43] A highly criticised decision was rendered by the U.S. Court of Appeals,

38 German law: MünchKomm ZPO/J. Münch, § 1036 para. 34. See also, BVerwG, 18 April 2001, 8 B 11/0 NJW 2001, 2191 on judges; MünchKomm ZPO/N. Stackmann, § 42 para. 10, with additional references on state court judges. Swiss law: BSK ZPO/M. Weber, Art. 47 para. 20. Case law from the United States differentiates correspondingly: in *Bernstein Seawell & Kove v. Bosarge*, 813 F.2d 726 (5th Cir. 1987), one of the arbitrators owned a "fractional" share of claimant's partnership interest. According to the court, this scenario resulted in "impropriety", but the "appearance of impropriety, standing alone, is insufficient" to constitute evident partiality. Other case law from the United States takes into consideration not the amount of shares the arbitrator owns of one party but the relation of the total amount of shares the arbitrator indirectly owned. In *Standard Tankers (Bahamas) Co., Ltd. v. Motor Tank Vessel, AKTI*, 438 F. Supp. 153 (E.D. North Carolina 1977), two arbitrators owned stocks of the only stockholder of one party. The court ruled that there was no conflict of interest since the stockholder had a vast number of shares (226 million in total) resulting in the relation as rather "trivial".

39 *In re Sussex*, 781 F.3d 1065 (9th Cir. 2015), on domestic arbitration.

40 *Merit Ins. Co. v. Leatherby Ins. Co.*, 714 F.2d 673 (7th Cir. 1983), on domestic arbitration.

41 *Republic of Argentina v. AWG Group Ltd.*, 211 F.Supp.3d 335 (D. Columbia 2016), denying annulment since the relation was too remote and trivial to constitute a conflict of interest. According to the court, the participation of the bank in the consortium was in the context of its overall business "inconsequential", the arbitrator's compensation in bank stocks was, hence, also inconsequential, and the role as non-executive director demonstrated the attenuated nature of the relationship.

42 These business relations were as follows: both were members of the College of Commercial Arbitrators' Corporate Counsel Task Force and members of a small committee of five people at the Civil Justice Reform Group, *Merck & Co., Inc. v. Pericor Therapeutics, Inc.*, 2016 WL 4491441 (S.D. New York), again an example from domestic arbitration.

43 *Olson v. Merrill Lynch, Pierce, Fenner & Smith, Inc.*, 51 F.3d 157 (8th Cir. 1995), 159, on domestic arbitration. These business relations between the firm and the respondent consisted of 225 bond issues managed by the investment firm between 1 January 1992 and 31 August 1993, the arbitrator served as a joint underwriter in seventeen issues, which amounted to nearly 26% of the total face value of the bonds managed or co-managed by the investment firm.

Second Circuit, in *Certain Underwriting Members of Lloyds of London v. Florida*. Respondent's party-appointed arbitrator was president and CEO of another company that had many financially relevant dealings with respondent.[44] The U.S. District Court concluded that there was a conflict of interest, and the U.S. Court of Appeals, Second Circuit, reversed that decision. The criticism focused on the fact that the U.S. Court of Appeals, Second Circuit, applied a different standard of impartiality to party-appointed than presiding arbitrators.[45]

Financial intensity is also a criterion in English case law. According to the England and Wales High Court of Justice, the threshold of intensity of a conflicted professional relationship is met if 25% of an arbitrator's income over the previous three years derived from cases involving the same party.[46] In arbitral proceedings with the LCIA, the threshold of financial intensity is not met where respondent's party-appointed arbitrator rendered service for respondent more than three and a half years ago.[47]

Finally, the French *cour de cassation* rejected a request for annulment of the award where a business relationship existed between the presiding arbitrator and a third party to the arbitration that was guarantor of sums to be paid to either party, depending on the outcome of the arbitration.[48] Since the award had a neutral impact on the guarantor, i.e., payment in any event to one party, there was no conflict of interest.

Professional Ties with Counsel

In general, business relationships between arbitrators and counsels are even more frequent than those with the parties. Arguing that these business relations are frequent and common, most courts are more forgiving with this category. Hence, a business relation between the arbitrator and counsel is even less likely to constitute a ground for dependence and partiality. Courts accept that members of the same bar or the same legal club are more

44 *Certain Underwriting Members of Lloyds of London v. Florida*, 2018 WL 2727492 (2d Cir.), on domestic arbitration. These dealings included joint business projects, the former CFO of respondent provided consulting services to the other company, and one of respondent's directors was CFO of the other company during the summer of 2015.

45 J. Fellas, *Evident Partiality and the Party-Appointed Arbitrator*, N.Y. L.J. 2018, criticising that the default rule on allowing different standards for party-appointed arbitrators had been changed in the AAA/ABA Code of Ethics. On the issue of different standards for party-appointed arbitrators, see below chapter 6.3.

46 *Cofely Ltd. v. Anthony Bingham and Knowles Ltd.*, [2016] EWHC 240 (Comm).

47 LCIA Reference No. UJV3476, LCIA Court, 24 December 2004, Arb. Int'l 27 (2011), 367-370, where the arbitrator had not been the partner in charge of the previous matter, nor had he been in direct contact with the respondent at that time. The LCIA Court held that the professional ties had been severed and possible personal ties to respondent's employees were acceptable and could not be an obstacle to impartiality.

48 Cass civ 1ére, 25 June 2014, 11-16.444, Rev. de l'Arb. 2015, 75-77.

likely to know each other[49] and, hence, appoint each other. In line with this, no conflict of interest was found in the following affiliations between an arbitrator and counsel: were both members of the same association,[50] or a political party,[51] went to the same law school,[52] had presented together at seminars relating to arbitration training, co-authored various articles, were past presidents (at different times) or members of an attorney society, and, in addition, were members of an advisory board developing educational programmes for an arbitral institution.[53] However, where the party-appointed arbitrator worked together with one of the appointing counsels in the same law firm and even the same team, a conflict of interest may exist.[54] In this case before the *Oberlandesgericht* Frankfurt a.M., the judges were not convinced that the business relation ended seventeen years before the arbitration. It was, however, a crucial aspect that the arbitrator and the counsel worked in the same team and both as partners. On the other hand, the mere fact that an arbitrator and counsel had worked together does not justify a challenge.[55]

Especially where the professional relations stem from arbitration-related encounters, excluding reappointments and parallel proceedings, it is less likely that a conflict of interest exists. There is no conflict of interest if the arbitrator knows a party's counsel professionally from having acted together on the same side as counsels representing different parties,[56] the arbitrator and counsel had a previous interaction in an unrelated arbitration,[57] or the counsel to a party regularly recommended a particular arbitrator, also a practicing attorney,

49 J.-F. Poudret/S. Besson, *Comparative Law of International Arbitration*, p. 419. This applies also where they belong to the same discussion group, KG Berlin, 7 June 2010, 20 SchH 2/10, SchiedsVZ 2010, 225-227.

50 BGer, 20 March 2008, 4A_506/2007, para. C 3.3.2; OLG Frankfurt a.M., 4 October 2007, 26 Sch 8/07, SchiedsVZ 2008, 96-102, where one counsel and one arbitrator were board members of the same arbitral institution.

51 Sutter-Somm/Hasenböhler/Leuenberger/S. Wullschleger, Art. 47 para. 41. This might change if there is a concrete connection between the dispute and the political engagement, the purpose of the organisation or the arbitrator and party are both members of a small, non-transparent organisation.

52 Sutter-Somm/Hasenböhler/Leuenberger/S. Wullschleger, Art. 47 para. 31.

53 *Midwest Generation EME, LLC v. Continuum Chemical Corp.*, 768 F.Supp.2d 939 (N.D. Illinois 2010), on domestic arbitration. The court reasoned that the facts do not establish a genuine "system of referrals". It is rather common for lawyers in the branch at question, i.e., construction, to appear as arbitrators. Hence, connections to lawyers are common.

54 OLG Frankfurt a.M., 24 January 2019, 26 SchH 2/18, BeckRS 2019, 848.

55 OLG Frankfurt a.M., 24 January 2019, 26 SchH 2/18, BeckRS 2019, 848. In the same case, the court rejected a second challenge on the presiding arbitrator, who had worked as an employed lawyer in the same law firm as one of the counsels twelve years before the arbitral proceedings. Since both worked in different teams and on different levels, the court rejected the challenge. See also, BGer, 16 October 2019, 4A_292/2019.

56 There were eighteen cases where both acted together, *Ostrom v. Worldventures Marketing, LLC*, 60 F.Supp.3d 942 (M.D. Louisiana 2016). The court denied annulment due to the lack of a "direct financial relationship". This decision on domestic arbitration is to be criticised as applying a threshold that is too low. See below chapters 6.1.2.4 and 6.1.3.1, on the favoured standard for independence and impartiality: justifiable doubts.

57 LCIA Reference No. 81224, LCIA Court, 15 March 2010, Arb. Int'l 27 (2011), 461-470.

to clients in litigation and vice versa.[58] Additionally, visiting the same bar school[59] or publishing in the same paper[60] does not result in a conflict of interest.

4.1.1.1.2 Reappointment

Professional ties may result in numerous appointments of an arbitrator by a party or its counsel. In institutional arbitration, the institution often has discretion to appoint or confirm the arbitrator[61] and may do so notwithstanding previous appointments. Especially where previous or parallel appointments were or are under the auspices of another institution, limiting the risk of reappointments is heavily dependent on a proper disclosure by the arbitrator. If the arbitrator is appointed by the institution, the question arises whether the reappointment can at all be a scenario constituting a ground for dependence and partiality, since neither the party nor counsel directly appointed the arbitrator. This question also arises with regard to the presiding arbitrator.[62]

Some institutions regulate the number of active institutional arbitral proceedings for an arbitrator.[63] The International Cotton Association provides in its ICA Code of Conduct that "[a]n arbitrator should not be able to have more than 8 active first tier cases open at any one time".[64] Although, according to the England and Wales High Court of Justice, the provision's objective is to address concerns about delay in rendering ICA awards, and to promote the expeditious resolutions,[65] it additionally limits reappointments and expands the pool of arbitrators. The ICC Court of Arbitration also takes the number of active ongoing arbitrations into consideration when appointing arbitrators.[66]

58 BGer, 30 June 1994, 4P.292/1993, ASA Bull. 1997, 99-107, arguing that such pattern of recommendation is usual between lawyers practising in a specialised field of law, here intellectual property.

59 On French state court proceedings, C. Chanais/F. Ferrand/S. Guinchard, *Procédure civile*, para. 1061, with additional references to case law.

60 OLG Frankfurt a.M., 4 October 2007, 26 Sch 8/07, SchiedsVZ 2008, 96-102. Additionally, the arbitrator and counsel were even both on the board of editors of the paper.

61 E.g., Art. 13.1 DIS Rules; Art. 13 ICC Rules; Art. 5.6 LCIA Rules; Art. 9.3 SIAC Rules; all usually after nomination by the parties.

62 See BGer, 10 June 2010, 4A_458/2009 ASA Bull. 2010, 520-539, as an example for demonstrating more leeway if the arbitrator appointed repeatedly was previously the presiding arbitrator.

63 But see, S. Wilske/M. Stock, *Rules 3.3.7 IBA Guidelines on Conflicts of Interest in International Arbitration - The Enlargement of the Usual Shortlist?*, ASA Bull. 2005, 45-52, 47, arguing that the income is decisive, not the number of appointments.

64 Cited in *Aldcroft v. International Cotton Association Ltd.*, [2017] EWHC 642 (Comm).

65 *Aldcroft v. International Cotton Association Ltd.*, [2017] EWHC 642 (Comm).

66 Para. 25 ICC Note 30 October 2017, i.e., the previous ICC Note. The current ICC Note merely states in para. 33: "Arbitrators have a duty to devote to the arbitration the time necessary to conduct the proceedings as diligently, efficiently and expeditiously as possible. Accordingly, prospective arbitrators must indicate in the Statement the number of arbitrations in which they are currently acting, specifying whether they are acting as president, sole arbitrator, co-arbitrator or counsel to a party, as well as any other commitments and their availability over the next 24 months."

Generally, when evaluating whether reappointment constitutes a ground for finding dependence and partiality, the interest the party has in the proceedings, the directness of the underlying relationship, and the proximity in time between the relationship and the arbitration proceedings are decisive. Regarding the latter criterion, a cooling-off period may help to ensure that no conflict of interest exists.[67]

Reappointment by a Party

Repeat appointments of the arbitrator by one of the parties, or an affiliated company, is a classic example of a potential conflict of interest.[68] Usually, repeat appointments alone do not create a conflict of interest,[69] especially if there is a substantial period of time between the previous and the current appointment.[70] This might change if the intensity of a resulting financial relationship crosses the threshold of a conflict of interest,[71] or the number of reappointments demonstrates a business stream.[72] The French *cour de cassation* clarified that such a business stream may be established not only by one party but also by a group of companies.[73]

Another example that demonstrates leeway in repeat appointments comes from the United States. The U.S. Court of Appeals, Second Circuit, ruled that nineteen cases in a three year period involving one of the arbitrators and an affiliated company of the claimant merely proved a business relationship but no personal relationship. Since there was no additional financial relationship involved, the affiliated company had no stake in the outcome of the

67 E.g., the Burgh House Principles suggest a cooling-off period of three years after appointment, para. 10. Similarly, some practitioners report on such practice in arbitration, i.e., not accepting reappointments by the same party or counsel within the preceding three years, C. Brower/S. Melikian/M. Daly, *Tall and Small Tales of a Challenged Arbitrator*, p. 336.

68 The IBA Guidelines 2014 demand disclosure of the following scenario: "The arbitrator has, within the past three years, been appointed as arbitrator on two or more occasions by one of the parties, or an affiliate of one of the parties." Part II, para. 3.1.3. Besides the mere fact that an arbitrator had been repeatedly appointed, he or she may lack an open-minded approach to the case and demonstrate respective conduct, see below chapters 4.2.1.2 et seq.

69 BGer, 12 June 2009, 4A_586/2008, para. C 3.1.2; SCAI, *Swiss Rules – Selected Case Law*, reporting on the denial of the challenge of a sole arbitrator who was previously involved in a dispute that did not involve the respondent, but a company of which respondent was a substantial – but not major – shareholder; J. Lew/L. Mistelis/S. Kröll, *Comparative International Commercial Arbitration*, para. 11-27.

70 BGer, 4 January 2015, 4A_598/2014, where the previous appointment was more than fifteen years ago. However, other case law is even more liberal with a short period of time: *Federal Vending, Inc. v. Steak & Ale of Florida, Inc.*, 71 F.Supp.2d 1245 (S.D. Florida 1999).

71 See examples above, in chapter 4.1.1.1.1. Some scholars argue that repeat appointment can be equalised with the underlying economic interest in being appointed again, cf. R. Williams, *The Selection of a Tripartite Panel: You Get What You Contract For*, Rev. Litig. 36 (2018), 767-785, 780.

72 Cass civ 1ère, 20 October 2010, 09-68131.

73 The arbitrator was reappointed by the same group of companies in 34 cases.

case, and the professional relationship did not create a conflict.[74] This case demonstrates the criticised inefficiency of the Orange List of the IBA Guidelines 2014.[75] In both cases, Part II, paras. 3.1.3-3.1.5 IBA Guidelines 2014, i.e., the Orange List, would apply. Unfortunately, the Orange List primarily purports the need for disclosure, but does not clarify its consequences regarding the arbitrator's independence and impartiality.[76] According to the introduction to Part II, para. 3 of the IBA Guidelines 2014, the scenarios listed on the Orange List have to be disclosed and "may, in the eyes of the parties, give rise to doubts as to the arbitrator's impartiality or independence", "depending on the facts of a given case". At the same time, the introduction of the Guidelines clarifies that "the fact of requiring disclosure – or of an arbitrator making a disclosure – does not imply the existence of doubts as to the impartiality or independence of the arbitrator".[77] Therefore, recourse to other applicable rules and laws is necessary for more guidance on the concrete applicable standard.[78]

The English case *Cofely Ltd. v. Anthony Bingham and Knowles Ltd.*, cited previously for the need of financial intensity in case of professional ties, also serves as an example for the threshold of repeat appointments as conflicts of interest.[79] This case involved an arbitrator who acted as arbitrator twenty-five times in cases involving the same respondent. In fact, 18% of the arbitrator's total appointments involved that respondent, and 25% of the arbitrator's total income as arbitrator in the past three years came from appointments involving the respondent. In 72% of these cases the arbitrator found in favour of respondent. This case demonstrates that the scenario of reappointments depends, inter alia, on the number of previous appointments and the impact on the arbitrator's income, both revealing a potential financial interest that can create a conflict of interest.

---

74 *Andros Compania Maritima, SA v. Marc Rich & Co., AG*, 579 F.2d 691 (2d Cir. 1978).

75 See above chapter 2.1.

76 On this criticism, see also, *H v. L and M*, [2017] EWHC 137 (Comm).

77 IBA Guidelines 2014, Introduction, p. iii.

78 Interestingly, according to the QMUL/White & Case, *2015 International Arbitration Survey*, the respondents favoured more regulation of multiple appointments, Chart 34, p. 39.

79 *Cofely Ltd. v. Anthony Bingham and Knowles Ltd.*, [2016] EWHC 240 (Comm). The challenge application under Sect. 24(1)(a) EAA was successful.

Reappointment by Counsel
A similar approach is taken in case law on repeat appointments by counsel.[80] Again, reappointments themselves are unlikely to constitute a conflict of interest.[81] The

> fact that an arbitrator was regularly nominated (by different arbitral parties) on the recommendation of the same counsel or the same firm of solicitors ought not of itself to give rise to justifiable doubts as to his independence and impartiality.[82]

Such reappointments may meet the threshold of a conflict of interest only when they coincide with other factors, such as financial interest or parallel proceedings.[83]

4.1.1.1.3 Parallel Proceedings
Instead, or in addition to previous appointments, one arbitrator may act for the same party or with the same counsel in parallel proceedings. Parallel proceedings and reappointments have similarities but should not be treated alike.[84] In parallel proceedings the reappointment is current, potentially creating closer ties. The decisive criteria for finding dependence and partiality may be the directness of the relationship and the proximity in time between the relationship and the arbitration proceeding. The directness of the relationship may include superior knowledge and information an arbitrator may have where he or she acts in parallel as arbitrator with the same counsel or party and their additional encounters.

---

80 This scenario is also listed on the Orange List of the IBA Guidelines 2014, Part II, para. 3.3.8: "The arbitrator has, within the past three years, been appointed on more than three occasions by the same counsel, or the same law firm." Respondents to the QMUL/White & Case, *2015 International Arbitration Survey*, were slightly less in favour of regulating multiple appointments by counsels (68% compared with 72% favouring the regulation of multiple appointments by the parties), Chart 34, p. 39.

81 In SCC Arbitration 2015/064, SCC Practice Note, p. 9, the respondent successfully challenged the arbitrator appointed by claimant on the grounds that (1) he was co-counsel with the claimant's counsel in another dispute, with the respondent's counsel opposing them, and (2) he had received repeated arbitrator appointments from the claimant's counsel.

82 *Interprods Ltd. v. De La Rue International Ltd.*, [2014] EWHC 68 (Comm). The High Court of Justice, inter alia, relied on the arbitrator's expertise and the size of the law firm to deny the annulment action of the award under Sects. 67, 68 EAA.

83 E.g., the arbitrator being selected for mediation in different proceedings by the same counsel as counsel for respondent and the mediation was parallel to the current arbitration, *Crow Construction v. Jeffrey M. Brown Assoc. Inc.*, 264 F.Supp.2d 217 (E.D. Pennsylvania 2003), on domestic arbitration. The court heavily relied on a breach of the obligation to disclose, see critically on this issue, below chapters 4.2.1.6 and 7.1.4.

84 There are many examples where both scenarios cumulate, e.g., *Crow Construction v. Jeffrey M. Brown Assoc. Inc.*, 264 F.Supp.2d 217 (E.D. Pennsylvania 2003). Parallel proceedings concern only other proceedings as arbitrator. Other involvement of the arbitrator as counsel, expert, witness or any other form will be addressed below, in chapter 4.1.1.1.4. For the opposing view, i.e., that reappointment and parallel proceedings should be treated alike, see O. Froitzheim, *Die Ablehnung von Schiedsrichtern wegen Befangenheit in der internationalen Schiedsgerichtsbarkeit*, p. 220.

Parallel Proceedings with the Same Party

Parallel proceedings with the same party are listed on the Orange List of the IBA Guidelines 2014.[85] Hence, they must be disclosed but are not necessarily grounds for dependence and partiality. In parallel proceedings the arbitrator has an immediate comparison of one party's actions and submissions in two different proceedings. The arbitrator has, to some extent, superior knowledge of that party, thus raising the question of whether and to what extent the arbitrator needs to disclose that knowledge to the opposing party and/or the co-arbitrators.[86]

Superior knowledge on its own usually does not lead to a finding of dependence and partiality.[87] In fact, it may be helpful in the deliberations. Especially in cases where another party may not be joined to the arbitral proceedings, but legal and factual issues are similar, having the same arbitrator on the tribunal, or even the very same tribunal, is often in the interest of the parties. The advantages of superior knowledge also led the England and Wales Court of Appeal in *Halliburton Co v. Chubb Bermuda Insurance Ltd.* to decline the challenge of the arbitrator.[88] The court underlined that having common parties and arbitrators may reduce costs and delay and minimise the risk of inconsistent decisions. The court saw the potential downside of superior knowledge, especially from the other party's perspective, but concluded that

> inside information and knowledge may be a legitimate concern for the parties to have in overlapping arbitrations involving a common arbitrator but only one common party. [H]owever, [...] in itself, it does not justify an inference of apparent bias.[89]

However, superior knowledge may constitute a conflict of interest where the level of familiarity with the subject matter results in a lack of "open mind".[90]

---

85 Part II, para. 3.1.5 IBA Guidelines 2014.

86 In *Beumer Group U.K. Ltd. v. Vinci Construction U.K. Ltd.*, [2016] EWHC 2283 (TCC), the adjudicator failed to communicate that the common party, Beumer, was putting forward mutually inconsistent cases in the two proceedings. The case did not concern arbitration but rather adjudication. Justice Fraser, however, cited many sources on arbitration, e.g., the CIArb Guidelines, and stated that adjudicators and arbitrators are bound by the same principles of disclosure.

87 Stein/Jonas/P. Schlosser, § 1036 para. 46.

88 *Halliburton Co. v. Chubb Bermuda Ins. Ltd.*, [2018] EWCA Civ 817, upheld by *Halliburton Co. v. Chubb Bermuda Ins. Ltd.*, [2020] UKSC 48. The court dealt with a challenge under Sects. 24(1)(a), 33 EAA.

89 *Halliburton Co. v. Chubb Bermuda Ins. Ltd.*, [2018] EWCA Civ 817, upheld by *Halliburton Co. v. Chubb Bermuda Ins. Ltd.*, [2020] UKSC 48. Interestingly, the decision also relied on the expertise of the arbitrator to decide a case merely on the documents before him or her.

90 See below chapter 4.2.1.5.

Parallel Proceedings with the Same Counsel

Again, parallel proceedings with the same counsel are listed on the Orange List of the IBA Guidelines 2014.[91] If one of the arbitrators and a counsel are at the same time involved in another arbitration, e.g., both as arbitrators or one as counsel, the threshold of a conflict of interest is usually not met.[92] Parallel proceedings with the same counsel differ from parallel proceedings with the same party: it is not superior knowledge of facts or the party's activities that are crucial in this scenario, but rather the existence of a potential relationship with the counsel. Such a relationship may result in specific professional[93] or social ties,[94] or even a hierarchy, and the risk of subordination between them.[95] Since there is no hierarchy between the arbitrators, the risk is a minor one where counsel and one arbitrator are co-arbitrators in another arbitration. However, where counsel and one arbitrator are co-counsels (from different firms) in another arbitration, an issue of diametrically opposed hierarchies may result. Where the arbitrator conducts parallel proceedings as counsel with one of the counsels from the arbitration where he or she sits as arbitrator, and if the counsel is instructing the arbitrator as co-counsel, the hierarchies in both parallel scenarios are diametrically opposed.[96] Depending on the arbitrator's financial interest in each arbitration and the arbitrator's conduct, one may conclude that the arbitrator is unconsciously biased.[97]

4.1.1.1.4 Other Employment and Similar Connection

Apart from previous or parallel arbitral proceedings with the same arbitrator, parties and counsels may have professional relations due to other employment forms. The risk of conflicting hierarchy and subordination is also present, for example in the case of a teacher-student-relationship.[98] Generally, other employment may risk a conflict of interest if the professional relationship between an arbitrator and one party or counsel is direct, connected to the dispute,[99] and proximate in time to the arbitration proceedings.

---

91 Part II, para. 3.3.9 IBA Guidelines 2014: "The arbitrator and [...] counsel for one of the parties in the arbitration, currently act or have acted together within the past three years as co- counsel."

92 BGer, 12 June 2009, 4A_586/2008, para. C 3.1.2; BGer, 4 August 2006, 4P.105/2006/fun, para. C 4, rejecting a challenge.

93 See above chapter 4.1.1.1.1.

94 See below chapter 4.1.1.1.7.

95 See below chapter 4.1.1.4, for the treatment of hierarchy and subordination between two arbitrators.

96 In *A v. B*, [2011] EWHC 2345 (Comm), the arbitrator in the disputed arbitration was at the same time solicitor receiving instructions from the barrister counsel of party B.

97 See claimant's argumentation in *A v. B*, [2011] EWHC 2345 (Comm). The court rejected the argumentation and denied the annulment action under Sect. 68 EAA.

98 See Stein/Jonas/P. Schlosser, § 1036 para. 37, arguing that a previous teacher-student-relationship should generally not justify a challenge under § 1036 German ZPO.

99 See Stein/Jonas/P. Schlosser, § 1036 para. 38, highlighting the connection to the dispute for these scenarios.

Other Employment and Similar Connection with the Party

In contrast to reappointments by and parallel proceedings with the same party, the IBA Guidelines 2014 place some scenarios of other employment forms on the Non-Waivable and Waivable Red Lists.[100] An arbitrator can have a previous or ongoing relationship as counsel,[101] expert, witness[102] or mediator, or another employment form, such as being a "manager, director or member of the supervisory board",[103] with one of the parties. Similar to this more strict categorisation in the IBA Guidelines 2014, challenges and annulments are successful before courts in the following scenarios: the arbitrator is the co-CEO of one party;[104] the arbitrator previously acted as expert for one of the parties (on the same matter);[105] the presiding arbitrator was employed by one of the parties directly after the first of numerous awards had been rendered;[106] or the arbitrator is counsel in different proceedings of one of the parties at the same time as the current proceedings.[107] A conflict of interest often depends on whether the employment was previous or is ongoing, whether there is a connection to the subject matter of both proceedings,[108] and to what extent financial interests prevailed. Hence, the U.S. Court of Appeals, Seventh Circuit, denied a conflict of interest where one party-appointed arbitrator was counsel for two months in

100 Part II, para. 1.2 IBA Guidelines 2014, i.e., Non-Waivable Red List: "The arbitrator is a manager, director or member of the supervisory board, or has a controlling influence on one of the parties or an entity that has a direct economic interest in the award to be rendered in the arbitration." Under the same para. 1.2: "There is an identity between a party and the arbitrator, or the arbitrator is a legal representative or employee of an entity that is a party in the arbitration." And Part II, para. 2.1.1 IBA Guidelines 2014, i.e., Waivable Red List, reads: "The arbitrator has given legal advice, or provided an expert opinion, on the dispute to a party or an affiliate of one of the parties." In these scenarios, a conflict of interest exists according to Part II, Introduction, para. 2 IBA Guidelines 2014.

101 OLG Dresden, 27 January 2005, 11 SchH 02/04, SchiedsVZ 2005, 159-163.

102 Stein/Jonas/P. Schlosser, § 1036 para. 38.

103 Part II, para. 1.2 IBA Guidelines 2014.

104 BGH, 11 October 2017, I ZB 12/17, SchiedsVZ 2018, 271-275.

105 E.g., OLG Frankfurt a.M., 13 February 2012, 26 SchH 15/11, BeckRS 2014, 12067, and additional references in D. Effer-Uhe, *Schiedsgerichtliche Unabhängigkeit bei wissenschaftlichen Äußerungen*, SchiedsVZ 2018, 75-80, 80. See also, Part II, para. 2.1.1 IBA Guidelines 2014.

106 CA Paris, 2 July 1992, Rev. de l'Arb. 1996, 411-410. The court reasoned that there must have been a "link of dependency" between the arbitrator and the party even before the date of employment. See also, Stein/Jonas/P. Schlosser, § 1036 para. 44, on an annulment action based on *ordre public*.

107 *Wettstein v. Switzerland*, ECtHR, 21 December 2000, 33958/96; BSK IPRG/W. Peter/C. Brunner, Art. 180 para. 15; J.-F. Poudret/S. Besson, *Comparative Law of International Arbitration*, para. 418. See also, BGer, 9 October 2012, BGE 138 I 406, 408, where the arbitrator regularly was counsel opposing one of the parties and there was additionally an ongoing mandate against that party; and Part II, para. 2.1.1 IBA Guidelines 2014. The Swiss *Bundesgericht* takes a similar approach in disputes regarding independence and impartiality of state court judges: a conflict of interest exists if a judge has an open, ongoing mandate or is in a durable mandate-relation with one of the parties as counsel, Sutter-Somm/Hasenböhler/Leuenberger/S. Wullschleger, Art. 47 paras. 46-47. For the opposing view, see *Sodexo Management, Inc. v. Detroit Public Schools*, 200 F.Supp.3d 679 (E.D. Michigan 2016), on domestic arbitration. Inter alia, the court reasoned that respondent failed to point to specific facts that indicate the arbitrator was improperly motivated.

108 On the latter, see J.-F. Poudret/S. Besson, *Comparative Law of International Arbitration*, para. 418.

an unrelated matter in international insurance arbitration of claimant's subsidiary in another country, four years ago.[109] This case demonstrates that any cooling-off period can be contingent on the total period of the previous employment.[110] In addition, any cooling-off period should be contingent on the concrete employment form and the directness of the relationship during the time of employment. A fixed period, e.g., three years,[111] does not meet the needs of flexibility in arbitration and would not be in line with the high importance of the parties' right to appoint their chosen arbitrator. Following the categories on the Waivable Red List of the IBA Guidelines 2014, there are employment scenarios where the parties should have the chance to waive their right to challenge and annul.

A difficult decision was rendered by the U.S. Court of Appeals, Second Circuit, in *Lucent Technologies Inc. v. Tatung Co.*[112] In a domestic arbitration, claimant's party-appointed arbitrator was an expert witness in a previous unrelated arbitration involving the claimant. The testimony of the expert witness, i.e., the arbitrator, was implicated in a motion for a new trial, which was denied more than six months after the arbitrator's appointment in the arbitration. The U.S. Court of Appeals denied the annulment action, reasoning that the final invoice was paid by the claimant to the expert witness more than a year before the arbitration commenced. It is difficult to assess whether the expert witness (i.e., the arbitrator in question) and the party maintained a relationship during the period awaiting the outcome of the motion for a new trial. There was certainly a risk that the relationship would recur if the motion for new trial was successful. Also, it is possible that the claimant and the expert witness were still in contact at that time. However, neither the mere risk of the ongoing proceedings nor potentially being in contact provides sufficient criteria to result in a definite conflict of interest. Therefore, the restrictive decision rendered is to be welcomed.

109 *Sphere Drake Ins. Ltd. v. All American Life Ins. Co.*, 307 F.3d 617 (7th Cir. 2002), on domestic arbitration.

110 MünchKomm ZPO/J. Münch, § 1036 para. 35, favouring such a contingent cooling-off, and referring to OLG Hamburg, 9 July 2015, 6 SchH 1/14, where the court ruled that in case of forty years employment a cooling-off period of seven years would be too short. On the other hand, the LCIA Court ruled in LCIA Reference No. 971X27, LCIA Court, 23 October 1997, Arb. Int'l 27 (2011), 322-324, that an arbitrator who was an expert witness almost ten years before the ongoing arbitration is not conflicted.

111 This is the cooling-off period suggested by the Burgh House Principles for judges. See critically on the application on arbitrators, Y. Shany, *Squaring the Circle?*, Loyola L.A. Int'l & Comp. L. Rev. 30 (2008), 473-490, 486.

112 *Lucent Technologies Inc. v. Tatung Co.*, 379 F.3d 24 (2d Cir. 2004).

Other Employment and Similar Connection with Counsel

Being employed by counsel also bears the risk of conflicting hierarchies and subordination for the arbitrator and may result in a conflict of interest.[113] Again, meeting the threshold of a conflict of interest will depend on the intensity of the employment, including financial intensity, when the employment began and ended, and the connection to the subject matter.[114] Similar to professional ties in general, the likelihood of being employed by counsel, or counsel's law firm, is higher than the likelihood of being employed by one of the parties. Arbitrators and counsels often work in the same business area. Case law acknowledges this likelihood and tends to recognise a conflict of interest less frequently. Therefore, no conflict of interest existed where the relationship was not ongoing: e.g., a former counsel for the claimant ceased to represent the claimant before the presiding arbitrator had been selected and later joined that arbitrator's law firm.[115]

In 2011, the *Oberlandesgericht* Frankfurt a.M. demonstrated considerable leeway for the employment relationship of an arbitrator and one of the counsels. In an ongoing proceeding, the presiding arbitrator disclosed that he had acted as party-appointed expert in ten cases involving the same counsel.[116] According to the challenging party, the fact that the arbitrator continued to provide expert opinions should have been disclosed at the beginning and constituted a conflict of interest. The court focused on the financial intensity of the relationship between the arbitrator and the counsel. It held that since the arbitrator was a well-known and busy arbitrator, he would not be financially dependent on the employment as expert. Thus, the relationship was not intense, and the court denied the challenge.[117]

4.1.1.1.5 Remuneration

Theoretically, an argument could be constructed that the remuneration of the arbitrator may constitute a conflict of interest. Where, for example, the arbitration agreement provides for individual payment of the party-appointed arbitrators, the question may arise as to

113 Part II, para. 2.3.2 IBA Guidelines 2014: the scenarios that the "arbitrator currently represents or advises the lawyer or law firm acting as counsel for one of the parties" and the "arbitrator is a lawyer in the same law firm as the counsel to one of the parties" are listed on the Waivable Red List.

114 On the lack of connection with the subject matter, see *Taylor v. Lawrence*, [2002] EWCA Civ 90. The challenged judge was a client of respondent's solicitor some years before, and also the night before the judgment was given, in an unrelated and personal matter. The court ruled that "[w]e regard it as unthinkable that an informed observer would regard it as conceivable that a judge would be influenced to favour a party in litigation with whom he has no relationship merely because that party happens to be represented by a firm of solicitors who are acting for the judge in a purely personal matter in connection with a will".

115 *Peoples Sec. Life Ins. Co. v. Monumental Life Ins. Co.*, 991 F.2d 141 (4th Cir. 1993).

116 OLG Frankfurt a.M., 13 February 2012, 26 SchH 15/11, BeckRS 2014, 12067.

117 OLG Frankfurt a.M., 13 February 2012, 26 SchH 15/11, BeckRS 2014, 12067. The challenge was based on §§ 1049(3), 1036(2) German ZPO. See also, KG Berlin, 7 June 2010, 20 SchH 2/10, SchiedsVZ 2010, 225-227, only sustaining the challenge in direct and intense relationships.

whether the individual remuneration casts doubt in regard to the independence and impartiality of the party-appointed arbitrators. This was the case in the Germany-Poland BIT, leading to the Investor-State dispute between TRACO Deutsche Travertin Werke GmbH and The Republic of Poland.[118] The tribunal deviated from the BIT, which provides that each party should "bear the cost of its own member", in accordance with the right to deviate in Article 10(5) Germany-Poland BIT.[119] The tribunal stated that the regulation of individual remuneration is

> based on a misconception of arbitral justice that the Tribunal considers manifestly incompatible with contemporary conceptions of the independence and impartiality of international arbitrators. As the UNCITRAL Arbitration Rules make clear [...], the same standard of impartiality and independence is required for all members of an arbitration tribunal; and an arbitrator cannot be considered, by virtue of his or her appointment by one disputing party, to be that party's "own" arbitrator. In this case, all three arbitrators were and remain required to be arbitrators for both Parties, with the two party-appointed arbitrators under exactly the same duties of independence and impartiality as the chairman.[120]

The theoretical argument that remuneration generally creates a conflict of interest is unconvincing. First, regarding international commercial arbitration, the practice of individual remuneration is abandoned by most institutional rules.[121] Therefore, risks of doubt as to independence and impartiality are diminished. Second, and much more important, remuneration is the parties' primary obligation under their contract with the arbitrators, i.e., a separate contract concluded between the parties and the arbitrators once the tribunal is constituted. Remuneration by the parties is one of the characteristics of the contractual nature of arbitration. It is one of the specificities that the parties may choose their arbitrators and pay for the arbitrators' service in return.[122] If remuneration is the primary obligation for the parties, its fulfilment cannot create any direct relationship or

---

118 The proceedings were conducted applying UNCITRAL Arbitration Rules and an award was rendered on 5 September 2012, but it is not public. The award is partially reported on in L. Peterson, *Citing the Need for Independence and Impartiality for all Arbitrators.*

119 Art. 10(5) of the Germany-Poland BIT stated that "[e]ach Contracting Party shall bear the cost of its own member and of its counsel in the arbitral proceedings; the cost of the chairman and the remaining costs shall be borne in equal parts by the Contracting Parties. The arbitral tribunal may make a different regulation concerning costs".

120 Cited by L. Peterson, *Citing the Need for Independence and Impartiality for all Arbitrators.* On the issue of same standards applying to all members of the tribunal, see below chapter 6.3.

121 The arbitrator's fees are usually part of the costs of the arbitration and determined by the institution in institutional arbitration, e.g., Arts. 32 and 33.1 DIS Rules; Art. 38 ICC Rules.

122 N. Voser/E. Fischer, *The Arbitral Tribunal*, p. 54.

subjective connection that indicates a conflict of interest. This may, however, be different where the arbitrator agrees on any additional remuneration with only one party.[123]

Another argument may be raised regarding remuneration that the arbitrators, when rendering an award on costs, are judges in their own cause, violating independence and impartiality. The German *Bundesgerichtshof* rejected a respondent's annulment action in a case where respondent argued that the arbitrators would act as judges in their own cause when determining their own remuneration, violating German *ordre public.*[124] The court denied the appeal on other grounds but additionally explained that the award on costs requiring respondent to bear claimant's costs did not address the determination of remuneration itself. Also, the court decided that the ruling on costs and the determination that respondent had to bear claimant's costs became binding only between the parties and not between one of the parties and the tribunal. Therefore, there was no judgment on their own cause violating German *ordre public.*[125]

4.1.1.1.6 Legal Disputes with One Party

Legal disputes between an arbitrator and one party may be professional or personal. Irrespective of their nature, their potential impact will usually be on the arbitrator's emotions, bearing a risk of conscious or unconscious bias. Whether a conflict of interest exists must be examined by using the general criteria, i.e., the directness of the relationship, the connection of the relationship to the dispute, and the proximity in time between the relationship and the arbitration proceedings.

No conflict of interest was found where the respondent's manager was sued in his professional capacity in another proceeding by the sole arbitrator in a former proceeding acting as opposing lead counsel – there was no direct contact between the manager and the arbitrator previously, since the manager had no key function either in the old proceedings or in the current ones.[126]

---

123 MünchKomm ZPO/J. Münch, § 1036 para. 35.

124 BGH, 2 March 2017, I ZB 42/16, SchiedsVZ 2017, 200-202.

125 Previously, in BGH, 28 March 2012, III ZB 63/10, NJW 2012, 1811-1812, the German *Bundesgerichtshof* had ruled that the determination of the amount in dispute through the arbitrators according to the decision on costs, based on § 1057 German ZPO, is no improper decision in the arbitral tribunal's own interest even though arbitrator's fees were based on the amount in dispute.

126 *Sodexo Management, Inc. v. Detroit Public Schools*, 200 F.Supp.3d 679 (E.D. Michigan 2016). The case dealt with domestic arbitration. In another domestic arbitration, *Washburn v. McManus*, 895 F.Supp. 392 (D. Connecticut 1994), the court rejected the allegation of evident partiality based on the scenario that the arbitrator previously had a personal lawsuit with one of respondent's former employees.

Although there is not much case law affirming a conflict of interest, legal disputes between the arbitrator and one party may create a conflict of interest.[127] One of the few examples is *Middlesex Mut. Ins. Co. v. Levine*. Here the legal dispute existed with a close family member of the arbitrator. The U.S. Court of Appeals, Eleventh Circuit, ruled that an arbitrator whose family-owned insurance company was entangled in a dispute with the claimant of the arbitral proceedings at the time of the arbitration constitutes a conflict of interest.[128] Such a relation is "direct, definite and capable of demonstration rather than remote, uncertain and speculative".[129] Another example is that an arbitrator who is liable for recourse to one party cannot act as arbitrator.[130]

4.1.1.1.7 Social Ties - Family, Friendship or Enmity

Social ties require a certain degree of closeness to raise a conflict of interest. Again, the directness of the relationship, the connection of the relationship to the dispute, and the proximity in time between the relationship and the arbitration proceedings are decisive criteria. A direct relationship will be present if the personal ties of friendship or family are close. In such a scenario, the arbitrator should be removed.[131] Personal ties include, for example, an engagement to marry, any long-term relationship, close friendship or serious enmity.[132] These ties are usually difficult to prove, especially when it comes to the intensity of a friendship or enmity. Counsels may refer to a certain conduct possibly revealing these emotions. However, except for severe facts, it remains difficult to prove such a conflict of interest.[133]

Social Ties with a Party

According to Part II, para. 1.3 IBA Guidelines 2014, "a significant [...] personal interest in one of the parties, or the outcome of the case" is placed on the Non-Waivable Red List. However, the application and interpretation of a "significant personal interest" is left open. Where an arbitrator's father served as trustee and supervisor of one of the parties, it is not surprising that the court declared it was "bound by [its] strong feeling that sons are more often than not loyal to their fathers, partial to their fathers, and biased on behalf of their

127 OLG Dresden, 12 December 2008, 11 SchH 7/08, OLGR Dresden 2009, 924, sustaining a challenge against the arbitrator under §§ 1036, 1037 German ZPO. But see, BGer, 14 December 2004, 4P.208/2004/lma, para. C 4.1, where one of the parties ordered a private investigator to observe the presiding arbitrator who later pressed charges against that party and ordered it to stop investigating. The court denied the conflict of interest.

128 *Middlesex Mut. Ins. Co. v. Levine*, 675 F.2d 1197 (11th Cir. 1982). The arbitral award in favour of the respondent was annulled.

129 *Middlesex Mut. Ins. Co. v. Levine*, 675 F.2d 1197 (11th Cir. 1982).

130 BGer, 14 March 1985, BGE 111 Ia 72.

131 J.-F. Poudret/S. Besson, *Comparative Law of International Arbitration*, para. 418.

132 MünchKomm ZPO/J. Münch, § 1036 para. 34.

133 See below chapter 4.2, for conduct as a conflict of interest.

fathers".[134] Likewise, a close personal friendship or enmity between an "arbitrator and a manager or director or a member of the supervisory board of" one of the parties, an affiliated entity, or any person having a controlling influence may constitute a conflict of interest, depending on the concrete circumstances.[135] Finally, a close relationship between an arbitrator or one of his or her close family members and "a non-party who may be liable to recourse on the part of the unsuccessful party in the dispute" may also constitute a conflict of interest.[136]

Close personal ties are not present where an arbitrator and a party are both members of the same club.[137] However, such ties may be found, if in addition to the membership both are involved in common activities that lead to friendship. Also, the mere fact that the arbitrator and one of the parties were students at the same school in the same year does not create a conflict of interest.[138]

Social Ties with Counsel

Both social ties with a party and with counsel need a certain degree of intensity to constitute a conflict of interest. However, the IBA Guidelines 2014 demonstrate more leeway for social ties between an arbitrator and a counsel. Whereas the social ties with a party are placed on the Non-Waivable, Waivable and Orange Lists, social ties with counsels are placed only on the Orange List. Similar to professional ties between an arbitrator and one counsel, some scholars argue that social ties between an arbitrator and the counsel are acceptable to a certain degree because both are active in the same field of law.[139] This argument has merit only if the social and professional ties are similar. Where "the shared cup of coffee becomes a deeper relationship" the arbitrator may be challenged successfully.[140] Again, similar to professional ties, the relationship, first, needs to be intense. Whereas a friendly relationship is, in principle, not enough to create a conflict of interest,[141] "profound

134 *Morelite Construction Co. v. New York City District Council Carpenters Benefit Funds*, 748 F.2d 79 (2d Cir. 1984), on domestic arbitration in a Union dispute.

135 This scenario is listed on the Orange List in the IBA Guidelines 2014 and needs to be disclosed but does not necessarily constitute a conflict of interest.

136 Part II, para. 2.2.3 IBA Guidelines 2014, i.e., the Waivable Red List.

137 KGer Graubünden, 30 January 1996, ASA Bull. 1996, 264-267, where the party-appointed arbitrator and the appointing party were members of the same Rotary Club, with approximately sixty members.

138 Cass civ 2ème, 13 July 2005, 04-19962, on a dispute involving the alleged dependence and partiality of a state court judge. See also, *Questar Capital Corp. v. Gorter*, 909 F.Supp.2d 789 (W.D. Kentucky 2012). In this case on domestic arbitration the social interaction of an arbitrator and one of the parties was not sufficient to annul the award.

139 E.g., business associates having lunch, see W. Park, *Arbitrator Integrity: The Transit and the Permanent*, San Diego L. Rev. 46 (2009), 629-704, 641. See also, KG Berlin, 7 June 2010, 20 SchH 2/10, SchiedsVZ 2010, 225-227, 226; Zöller/R. Geimer, § 1036 para. 11.

140 W. Park, *Arbitrator Integrity: The Transit and the Permanent*, San Diego L. Rev. 46 (2009), 629-704, 641.

141 BGer, 12 June 2009, 4A_586/2008, para. C 3.1.2; BGer, 4 August 2006, 4P.105/2006/fun, para. C 4.

hostility" can be a ground for a conflict of interest.[142] The threshold of profound hostility is not met where the challenge of the arbitrator is based on a disagreement between one of the arbitrators and a challenging party's counsel in an earlier arbitration in which they appeared as opposing counsels.[143] Similarly, this threshold of profound hostility was not met where a judge wrote a letter to the head of chambers of counsel for respondent complaining about an article written by another member of the same chambers.[144] According to the England and Wales Court of Appeal, the judge acted deplorably in writing the letter, but it did not follow that the allegation of apparent bias succeeded. This high threshold of intensity is also applied in arbitration.[145]

Applying the additional general criteria of the directness of the relationship, the connection of the relationship to the dispute, and the proximity in time between the relationship and the arbitration proceedings, any cooling-off period must be rather long in case of intense social ties, e.g., serving as best man or godmother.[146] These examples raise the more general question as to whether and to what extent cultural aspects or, more generally, subjective interpretations of a scenario such as being the best man, matter. The answer depends on the applicable standard of independence and impartiality, and especially the perspective to analyse it.[147] Even though the cultural perception of family relations may vary as well, "close family relationships" between the arbitrator and one of the counsels are more likely to create a conflict of interest than personal friendship.[148] Such a relationship was found and the awards annulled in the following three examples: first, where an arbitrator was the stepfather of one of the counsels,[149] second, where the daughter of one of the arbitrators practiced in the same law firm as one of the counsels,[150] and, third, where the arbitrator's wife was working in one of the counsel's law firm.[151]

142 BGer, 20 March 2008, 4A_506/2007.

143 SCAI, *Swiss Rules – Selected Case Law*. The institution dismissed the challenge based on these grounds. On the issue of legal disputes, see above chapter 4.1.1.1.6.

144 *Harb v. Aziz*, [2016] EWCA Civ 556, clarifying that even if a judge showed hostility towards an advocate, it did not follow that there was a real possibility that it would affect his approach to the parties themselves. The case dealt with state court proceedings.

145 OLG München, 10 January 2007, 34 SchH 7/06, BeckRS 2007, 00709, where the arbitrator was challenged according to § 1037(3) German ZPO without success.

146 But see, OLG München, 5 July 2006, 34 SchH 5/06, BeckRS 2006, 8109, dismissing the challenge against an arbitrator who was godfather of another lawyer of counsel's law firm.

147 See below chapter 6.1.1 et seq.

148 They are, hence, placed on the Waivable Red List in Part II, IBA Guidelines 2014.

149 CA Paris, 12 January 1999, Rev. de l'Arb. 1999, 381-384.

150 CA Paris, 18 December 2008, Rev. de l'Arb. 2011, 682-685. The arbitral award was annulled. The IBA Guidelines 2014 place this scenario on the Orange List, Part II, para. 3.3.5.

151 BGer, 26 October 1966, BGE 92 I 271, 276-277, sustaining the challenge.

Intense social ties constituting a conflict of interest cannot be proven by the mere fact that the arbitrator and counsel know each other and are on friendly terms.[152] However, where the arbitrator and a counsel are not merely on friendly terms but also parties to a lease agreement, the German *Oberlandesgericht* Frankfurt a.M. sustained the challenge of the arbitrator.[153] The court underlined that these personal ties do not generally justify a challenge but since the arbitrator failed to disclose the rent agreement earlier, the challenge was granted.[154] In this case, the non-disclosure of the connection, rather than the connection in itself, was the significant factor in granting the challenge. This approach risks being misunderstood as generally accepting non-disclosure as a ground for a challenge or annulment.[155] The court should have analysed the financial intensity of the contract[156] and whether a risk of subordination existed because of the landlord-tenant relationship of an arbitrator and a counsel.

Taking a closer look at the meaning of friendship and enmity, one may question their similar treatment. Personal friendship is a positive emotional connection, while enmity is the opposite, a negative emotion. The IBA Guidelines 2014 place "close personal friendship" and "enmity" on the Orange List and, therefore, mandate disclosure thereof.[157] The wording of the IBA Guidelines 2014 requires the friendship to be close and personal but provide no such qualifiers on enmity. An explanation for the heightened requirements for friendship can be the tendency to be lenient with professional and social ties between arbitrators and counsels due to their common interest in arbitration. However, some case law demonstrates a rather strict approach to enmity as well: an arbitrator who previously insulted one party's counsel in another unrelated matter may be challenged.[158]

4.1.1.1.8 Relationships on Social Networks

Professional and social ties may also be present on social networks.[159] Social networking sites provide for the possibility to befriend (e.g., Facebook), to connect with (e.g., LinkedIn,

152 However, depending on the exact friendly terms an issue of unfair conduct resulting in a conflict of interest might arise, see below chapter 4.2.

153 OLG Frankfurt a.M., 10 January 2008, 26 Sch 21/07, SchiedsVZ 2008, 199-200.

154 The court clarified that the obligation to disclose encompasses not only actual conflicts of interest but also circumstances that are likely to give rise to doubts as to the arbitrator's independence and impartiality.

155 Although some German case law indeed seems to favour that approach, more case law disfavours it. Also, the international approach is not to treat non-disclosure as a ground for challenge or annulment, see below chapter 4.2.1.6.

156 It is reasonable to argue that continuing contractual relations, such as lease agreements, generally constitute a conflict of interest, see MünchKomm ZPO/J. Münch, § 1036 para. 34.

157 Part II, paras. 3.3.6 and 3.3.7 IBA Guidelines 2014.

158 LG Duisburg, 6 October 1981, 15 O 173/81, ZIP 1982, 229.

159 For a detailed analysis of the term social media, see A. Kaplan/M. Haenlein, *Users of the World, Unite!, The Challenges and Opportunities of Social Media*, Bus. Horiz. 53 (2010), 59-68. They differentiate different

Xing) or to follow someone (e.g., Instagram). Additionally, users may form small or large communities and sub-communities in groups, closed or public, focusing on specific topics or events. Potential conflicts of interest may arise where the arbitrator is friends on LinkedIn with the brother of one of the parties; the presiding arbitrator is a friend on Facebook with one of the parties or counsels; or an arbitrator follows one of the parties on Instagram.[160] In all these scenarios the connections and friendships are visible and, thus, may help to prove a conflict of interest. However, it is questionable whether the mere connection or friendship on social networks expresses the intensity or closeness of the underlying professional and social relationship. If the answer is no, the general criteria for analysing the presence of a conflict of interest with regard to relationships help; these are the interest the party has in the proceedings, the directness of the relationship, the connection of the relationship to the dispute, and the proximity in time between the relationship and the arbitration proceeding.

The question whether the mere connection on social networks results in a conflict of interest was recently addressed in state court proceedings in Switzerland and France:

In 2018, the Swiss *Bundesgericht* defined the term "friend" used by Facebook.[161] The court elaborated that

> *[i]l ne suppose pas forcément un sentiment réciproque d'affection et de sympathie ou une connaissance intime qui implique une certaine proximité allant au-delà du simple fait de connaître quelqu'un ou de le tutoye […]. Il atteste uniquement de l'existence de contacts entre des personnes qui partagent les mêmes centres d'intérêt.*[162]

The court held that the term does not differentiate between close and detached connections. The group of people involved with each other on Facebook is thus much larger than one's

---

tools of social media by their degrees of "social presence", "media richness", "self-presentation" and "self-disclosure". Based on these parameters six categories of social media evolve: collaborative projects, blogs, content communities, social networking sites, virtual game worlds and virtual social worlds. For potential conflicts of interest, tools with high degrees in all four parameters are primarily relevant.

160 See for all examples A. Bedoya, *Arbitration, Social Media and Networking Technologies, Latent Existing Conflicts.*

161 BGer, 14 May 2018, 5A_701/2017, para. C 4.5. The dispute was concerned with a child's custody. The father of the child became friends on Facebook with the president of the local authority deciding in first instance on the custody.

162 Translation: "It does not necessarily imply a reciprocal feeling of affection and sympathy or an intimate knowledge that implies a certain proximity going beyond the mere fact of knowing someone or caring for them […]. It only shows the existence of contacts between people who share the same interests."

group of friends as defined by friendship in the traditional sense.[163] The court concluded that the mere fact of being Facebook "friends" cannot constitute a conflict of interest.[164] According to the court, it is the underlying relationship that needs to be analysed for a potential conflict.[165] In view of the great number of connections that most users have on social networks, this decision is to be welcomed.

In 2017, the French *cour de cassation* approached the question in a similar manner.[166] The court dismissed the appeal against a decision of the lower court, which had reasoned that the term "friend" used by social networks does not refer to relations of friendship in a traditional sense and that the mere connection of two people in a social network is insufficient to constitute a conflict of interest.[167] The lower court concluded that social networks are *"simplement un moyen de communication spécifique entre des personnes qui partagent les mêmes centres d'intérêt, et en l'espèce la même profession"*.[168] Therefore, the decisive criterion is the intensity of the relationship itself when analysing a potential conflict of interest through the use of social networking sites. This conclusion is supported by the finding of the anthropologist and evolutionary psychologist Dunbar. He studied social media and people's behaviour and found that only active networks on Facebook were highly identical with face-to-face networks.[169]

At first glance, the IBA Guidelines 2014 leave even more leeway to social networks. They generally place these contacts on the Green List.[170] "[N]o appearance and no actual conflict of interest exists from an objective point of view" in scenarios of the Green List.[171] This general categorisation of any social networking contact as not requiring disclosure generated criticism, and some scholars suggested a qualitative analysis of the contact,[172] in line with the approaches by the French *cour de cassation* and the Swiss *Bundesgericht*. The IBA

163 BGer, 14 May 2018, 5A_701/2017, para. C 4.5.

164 BGer, 14 May 2018, 5A_701/2017, para. C 4.5.

165 As stated earlier, the IBA Guidelines 2014, Part II, paras. 4.3.1 and 4.4.4 could be understood in this sense as well.

166 Cass civ 2ème, 5 January 2017, 16-12394, cited in BGer, 14 May 2018, 5A_701/2017, para. C 4.5.

167 Cass civ 2ème, 5 January 2017, 16-12394.

168 Translation: "simply a means of specific communication between people who share the same interests, and in this case the same profession."

169 R. Dunbar, *The Anatomy of Friendship*, Tr. Cog. Sc. 22 (2018), 32-51, 46.

170 Part II, para. 4.3.1 reads: "The arbitrator has a relationship with another arbitrator, or with the counsel for one of the parties, through membership in the same professional association, or social or charitable organisation, or through a social media network." Para. 4.4.4 reads: "The arbitrator has a relationship with one of the parties or its affiliates through a social media network."

171 Part II, Introduction, para. 7 IBA Guidelines 2014.

172 S. Sanubari, *Arbitrator's Conduct on Social Media*, J. Int'l Disp. Settlement 8 (2017), 483-506, 493-494. The author additionally proposes to differentiate between personal and professional social networks and to place professional networks on the Green List and personal ones on the Orange List.

Guidelines 2014 do not explicitly require differentiating between the contact itself and the underlying relationship. However, interpreting Part II, paras. 4.3.1 and 4.4.4, reveals that a qualitative analysis is implicitly suggested by the IBA Guidelines 2014 or is at least compatible with them. The introductory paragraphs of paras. 4.3.1 and 4.4.4 both refer to "contacts", and paras. 4.3.1 and 4.4.4 speak of whether the "arbitrator has a relationship [...] through social media". Thus, the IBA Guidelines 2014 place only the mere fact that such relationship exists on the Green List. Whether this relationship qualifies as a conflict of interest is not covered by the wording of paras. 4.3.1 or 4.4.4. Considering the system of the IBA Guidelines 2014, Part II, i.e., exemplifying through concrete situations the variety of possible conflicts,[173] one real scenario may fall under several situations listed in the IBA Guidelines 2014, Part II. Hence, considering the foregoing example that the presiding arbitrator is friends on Facebook with one party's counsel and that this friendship is close and personal, the fact that both are friends on Facebook does not need to be disclosed under Part II, para. 4.4.4, but their close personal friendship also falls under Part II, para. 3.3.6. Therefore, the IBA Guidelines 2014 meet the requirements of analysing the quality of a relationship on social networking sites.

Aside from the question of whether the mere connection on social networks results in a conflict of interest, social networking sites may, first, help to prove the existence of a relationship, and, second, to categorise it, i.e., to analyse the nature and intensity of the relationship.

First, the connection on social networks potentially provides more information on the closeness and intensity of the relationship and, hence, simplifies proving a conflict of interest. Social networking sites make relationships more visible.[174] For example, where the arbitrator and counsel are both members of a small group of twenty people named "Gutenberg Friends Fribourg", it is obvious that both have a common interest, a close connection to Fribourg, and it is rather certain that both know each other, since the group consists of only twenty people. The data provided through the social networking activity may help with regard to the general criteria of the directness of the relationship and the proximity in time between the relationship and the arbitration proceeding. It may be visible whether or not the arbitrator and the counsel in the above scenario had contact just before or even during the arbitration proceedings and how they interact with each other. On the other hand, if that group consists of 200.000 people, the mere fact that both are members of the group does not evidence that they know each other.

173 Cf. Part II, Introduction para. 1.

174 J. Kalicki, *Social Media and Arbitration Conflicts of Interest: A Challenge for the 21st Century.*

Second, social networking sites can be categorised according to professional and personal usage. Interaction on professional social networking sites may be less likely to constitute a conflict of interest, similar to professional interaction in face-to-face relationships.[175] Following this approach, the England and Wales High Court of Justice relied on the fact that users have to agree that they will use LinkedIn services in a professional manner when creating an account.[176] However, it is difficult to classify social networking sites as being either categorically professional or personal. Like face-to-face connections, there is often no clear distinction – friends are colleagues and vice versa. Therefore, connections on personal social networking sites should not be treated differently than professional networking sites when determining the existence of a conflict of interest.

In conclusion, relationships on social networks should not be differentiated from other relationships. Social networks provide only tools of interaction. The mere fact that a relation exists in any social network does not constitute a conflict of interest. However, social networks may help to prove a relationship. The decisive criterion for analysing a conflict of interest based on social networking contacts is the nature of the underlying relationship.

4.1.1.1.9 Involvement of a Barrister

If counsel for one of the parties or the arbitrator is a barrister, the analysis of a conflict of interest involves an additional question: whether barristers are to be treated differently in the analysis of conflicts of interest. Barristers are organised in chambers in England and Wales. Their traditional role is to appear before court, whereas solicitors are limited in doing so. Usually, barristers have no direct contact with the parties. They are engaged and instructed by the solicitor of a party. This leads to potential tensions, first, since barristers may join an ongoing arbitration as counsel after the proceedings commenced,[177] second, since the internal structure of chambers differs from law firms and, third, since barristers may not decline the request to act as counsel. The IBA Guidelines 2014 place the scenario on the Orange List.[178]

---

175 See above chapter 4.1.1.1.1. Also, S. Sanubari, *Arbitrator's Conduct on Social Media*, J. Int'l Disp. Settlement 8 (2017), 483-506, 493-494, proposes that professional social networks should be placed on the Green List of the IBA Guidelines and personal social networks on the Orange List.

176 *Hays Specialist Recruitment (Holdings) Ltd., Hays Specialist Recruitment Ltd. v. Mark Ions, Exclusive Human Resources Ltd.*, [2008] EWHC 745 (Ch).

177 See M. Hwang, *Arbitrators and Barristers in the Same Chambers – An Unsuccessful Challenge*, Bus. L. Int'l 6 (2005), 235-257, for an illustrative example.

178 Part II, para. 3.3.2 IBA Guidelines 2014. Listing the scenario on the Orange List is a "good compromise", according to N. Andrews/J. Landbrecht, *Schiedsverfahren und Mediation in England*, paras. 119-120. The authors argue that the "international scepticism" towards the organisation in chambers requires disclosure.

According to the DAC Report, English barristers are to be treated differently in arbitration than international lawyers and solicitors. They are "sole traders" without partnerships.[179] Chambers regularly are office communities of self-employed barristers[180] who may not access confidential information from each other.[181] Also, they usually do not share profits and losses of common businesses within the chambers, although they usually share administrative expenses.[182] In the words of the *cour d'appel de* Paris,

> the function of a barrister is essentially carried out independently and [...] belonging to a set of chambers of barristers [...] is characterised, in essence, by the sharing of premises and support staff, without necessarily creating any professional ties, which would imply [...] common interests or a certain economic or intellectual dependence between various members of a set of chambers who are, between themselves, frequently called, usually because of the specialism of the chambers, to plead against each other or to participate in arbitral tribunals before which other members of the same set of chambers may appear in the capacity as counsel.[183]

179 DAC Report, paras. 287, 288. In fact, para. 211(a) of the English Bar's code of conduct (at that time) stated that "a practising barrister must not enter into a professional partnership with another barrister or enter into a professional partnership or any other form of unincorporated association with any person other than a barrister".

180 The structure of a self-employed bar intends to reinforce the independence of counsels, The General Council of the Bar, Information Note Regarding Barristers in International Arbitration, para. 16.

181 N. Andrews/J. Landbrecht, *Schiedsverfahren und Mediation in England*, para. 95.

182 J. Kendall, *Barristers, Independence and Disclosure*, Arb. Int'l 8 (1992), 287-299, 288. It should be noted that this given structure is currently undergoing important changes and that each chamber needs an individual analysis of the exact organisational structure. New barrister chambers are not necessarily mere office communities of self-employed barristers sharing the same postal address any more. "There is a growing move to a type of branding by the name of the chambers." See Kendall, 347, citing the fact that "chambers' names do not consist, as they used to, simply of the actual geographical address, but of allusions to the previous address of the chambers or of the name of an illustrious former head of chambers". It is difficult to determine whether it is a mere marketing tool or creating an image like a conventional law firm. Kendall argues in favour of creating an image similar to a conventional law firm and concludes that "[the change] goes to confirm the wrong impression the uninformed outsider gets of how barristers' chambers are organized", 348. Also, chambers grew considerably since 1990, potentially creating more conflicts of interest. Finally, a changing role of the solicitors in arbitration proceedings might diminish the difference between barristers and solicitors, 350. Accordingly, the argument of unique specialisation of a barrister for justifying repeat appointments could be weakened. Therefore, a general conclusion that the mere involvement of barristers does not create a conflict of interest could change. Each individual case must be analysed according to the factual organisation of the chamber in question. See also, *Hrvatska Elektroprivreda d.d. v. Republic of Slovenia*, ICSID Tribunal, 17 December 2015, ARB/05/24, on investment arbitration.

183 CA Paris, 29 June 1991, cited in *Laker Airways Inc. v. FLS Aerospace Ltd. & Anor*, [1999] CLC 1124, 1130, where one of respondent's counsel was barrister at the same chambers as the presiding arbitrator. *Laker Airways Inc. v. FLS Aerospace Ltd.*, [1999] CLC 1124, affirms the decision. See also, D. Brown, *Arbitrators, Impartiality and English Law*, J. In'l Arb. 18 (2001), 123-130, for a detailed analysis of these cases.

Therefore, authorities find that, in general, the participation of two barristers from the same chambers in one arbitration, one as counsel and the other as arbitrator, does not create a conflict of interest.[184] In addition, public access to the bar would be severely limited if one were to conclude a conflict of interest on a general basis. Each time a member of a set of chambers accepts instructions, he or she would debar any other member of those chambers.[185] In fact, the specialisation of different barristers within the same chamber often requires that two barristers from the same chamber appear before each other.

However, if the relationship of the barrister-arbitrator and one of the parties' counsel is more intense, through a close friendship, additional financial ties, repeat appointments,[186] or subordination and hierarchy,[187] the conclusion can be different. For example, in *Liverpool Roman Catholic Archdiocesan Trustees Incorporated v. David Goldberg Q.C.*, the England and Wales High Court of Justice refused to admit a barrister belonging to the same chamber as respondent as an expert witness because both barristers were friends.[188] The intensity of instructions received by the barrister-arbitrator in previous or parallel proceedings was explicitly argued in two LCIA Court decisions.[189] In LCIA Reference No. 81132, claimant's party-appointed barrister-arbitrator was instructed by claimant's counsel (and the law firm) on two previous occasions.[190] The barrister-arbitrator was paid less than £1,000 for these instructions. The LCIA Court denied the challenge since it is

184 *Locabail (U.K.) Ltd. v. Bayfield Properties Ltd.*, [2000] QB 451, on state court proceedings; *Laker Airways Inc. v. FLS Aerospace Ltd.*, [1999] CLC 1124; CA Paris, 29 June 1991, cited in *Laker Airways Inc. v. FLS Aerospace Ltd.23 & Anor*, [1999] CLC 1124, 1130; *PPG Industries Inc. v. Pilkington PLC*, EWHC, 1 November 1989, reported in J. Kendall, *Barristers, Independence and Disclosure*, Arb. Int'l 8 (1992), 287-299, 290-291; The General Council of the Bar, Information Note Regarding Barristers in International Arbitration, para. 8.

185 *Laker Airways Inc. v. FLS Aerospace Ltd.*, [1999] CLC 1124; in general affirmative: N. Andrews/J. Landbrecht, *Schiedsverfahren und Mediation in England*, paras. 104-105. To guarantee public access to the bar, another principle applies to barristers, the "cab rank" rule. According to this principle, clients enjoy freedom of choice in selecting their counsel, and barristers may usually not decline appointment, The General Council of the Bar, Information Note Regarding Barristers in International Arbitration, para. 9.

186 For the latter, see J. Kendall, *Barristers, Independence and Disclosure Revisited*, Arb. Int'l 16 (2000), 343-351, 343, in favour of repeat appointments, creating a conflict of interest. See also, *ASM Shipping Ltd. of India v. TTMI Ltd. of England*, [2005] EWHC 2238 (Comm), where one of the grounds creating a conflict of interest was repeat appointments.

187 Senior barristers may have an influence on junior barristers, see W. Park, *Rectitude in International Arbitration*, Arb. Int'l 27 (2011), 473-526, 517.

188 *Liverpool Roman Catholic Archdiocesan Trustees Incorporated v. David Goldberg Q.C.*, [2002] TCLR 4, on state court proceedings.

189 In general, on parallel proceedings, see above chapter 4.1.1.1.3.

190 LCIA Reference No. 81132, LCIA Court, 15 November 2008, Arb. Int'l 27 (2011), 439-441. The previous instructions were two and five years ago and concerned other clients of claimant's counsel.

> commonplace for lawyers, who act both as lawyer and as arbitrator, and particularly for English barristers, to take instructions from firms of solicitors, who, in entirely unrelated matters, appear before them as representatives of parties in an arbitration.[191]

In LCIA Reference No. 81160, respondent's party-appointed arbitrator was a barrister specialising in insurance and reinsurance. He acted previously, inter alia, as a lawyer both for and against various syndicates of respondent. He explained his close professional connection with the respondent with his practice as a "leading insurance Queen's Counsel".[192] In the last 12 months he received less than 5% of all instructions from respondent's counsel and around 11% in the last five years. In addition, the arbitrator received ongoing instructions by respondent's counsel. The LCIA Court accepted the challenge of the arbitrator. The court, inter alia, relied on the "obvious professional importance to the arbitrator of his relationship with Respondents' Counsel, combined with his barrister/client relationship with one of the Respondents".[193] Accordingly, the relationship between two barristers from the same chamber does not constitute a conflict of interest if this relationship does not meet the general criteria, i.e., the directness of the relationship, the connection of the relationship to the dispute, and the proximity in time between the relationship and the arbitration proceeding. Only an intense relationship between the two involved barristers constitutes a conflict of interest.

4.1.1.1.10 Involvement of a Third-Party Funder

The involvement of third-party funders introduces a third actor to the arbitral proceedings. The potential conflicts in disputes involving a third-party funder are diverse and risk the efficiency of the proceedings, since a conflict threatens the valid composition of the arbitral tribunal.[194] The conflicts are similar to those already addressed, e.g., professional ties, repeat appointments, and social ties between the arbitrator and the funder. Identifying the criteria for a conflict of interest with a third-party funder must be the starting point in analysing

191 LCIA Reference No. 81132, LCIA Court, 15 November 2008, Arb. Int'l 27 (2011), 439-441.

192 LCIA Reference No. 81160, LCIA Court, 28 August 2009, Arb. Int'l 27 (2011), 442-454.

193 LCIA Reference No. 81160, LCIA Court, 28 August 2009, Arb. Int'l 27 (2011), 442-454. The court ruled that when examining the instructions received in other cases it is relevant to consider "how recent and frequent the instructions have been, the complexity of the cases involved, and whether further instructions are likely to be forthcoming". In the end, the court relied not primarily on the conflict of interest itself but on the late disclosure. The conflict of interest based on the instructions was not a ground for challenging the arbitrator in this case, since the insurance market requires a special treatment due to a limited pool of arbitrators. For a general analysis of the argument of a limited pool of arbitrators, see below chapter 6.5.1.2. Usually, non-disclosure does not create a ground for challenge or annulment, see below chapter 4.2.1.6.

194 C. Dos Santos, *Third-party Funding in International Commercial Arbitration, A Wolf in Sheep's Clothing?*, ASA Bull. 2017, 918-936, 924. The author primarily names repeat appointments and financial relations as potential conflicts; however, there are more.

potential conflicts of interest in arbitrator-funder relationships. Then, only at a second stage, can potential (hypothetical) scenarios of conflicts of interest be examined using the applicable criteria for evaluating a conflict of interest where third-party funders are involved.

Applicable Criteria for a Conflict of Interest with Third-Party Funders

In recent years many guidelines, policy or practice notes, and even some rules were published that address third-party funding. The practical difficulty involving third-party funders is to become aware of their involvement. Hence, many rules and regulations demand or suggest disclosure of the involvement of a third-party funder.[195] Even though this obligation to disclose and its standard is to be differentiated from the applicable criteria for a conflict of interest,[196] the reference to "economic interest" in many rules and regulations sheds some light on what kind of third-party funding involvement is relevant for examining a potential conflict of interest.[197] Additionally, the general criteria for examining a conflict of interest, i.e., the directness of the relationship, the connection of the relationship to the dispute, and the proximity in time between the relationship and the arbitration proceeding, may help.

The most recent example of the reference to "economic interest" as the decisive criterion when evaluating the role of third-party funders and their need to be disclosed are the new ICC Rules and the ICC Note. Both were introduced in 2021. Article 11(7) ICC Rules requires parties to inform

> of the existence and identity of any non-party which has entered into an arrangement for the funding of claims or defences and under which it has an economic interest in the outcome of the arbitration.

The ICC Note provides an example for economic interest that is present where the "non-party is entitled to receive all or part of the proceeds of the award" and additionally defines the economic interest negatively, as follows:

> Subject to any different determination that may be made by the arbitral tribunal in the circumstances of any given case, Article 11(7) would normally not capture (i) inter-company funding within a group of companies, (ii) fee arrangements between a party and its counsel, or (iii) an indirect interest, such as that of a

195 See for more details on the obligation to disclose below chapter 7.1.
196 See below chapter 7.1.4.1, for a detailed analysis of this differentiation.
197 Third-party funding can take many different forms, e.g., an insurance mechanism or a means of investment.

> bank having granted a loan to the party in the ordinary course of ongoing activities rather than specifically for the funding of the arbitration.[198]

These negative criteria can be used to clarify the directness of the relationship, contained in the general criteria for examining a conflict of interest. They exclude certain forms of funding that will usually not be related to the dispute, e.g., the bank loan in the ordinary course of ongoing activities. The term "any non-party" is broad and may include all sorts of different funders not excluded by the ICC Note. The term does, however, imply that funders are not regarded as parties in ICC arbitral proceedings.

A similar approach was taken by SIAC in 2017, when SIAC published a Practice Note on third-party funding, applicable in SIAC-administered cases under the SIAC Rules.[199] This Note broadly uses the term "External Funder" and defines it as "any person, either legal or natural, who has a Direct Economic Interest in the outcome of the arbitration proceedings". A "Direct Economic Interest" is defined as

> an interest in the arbitration proceedings resulting from the provision by a non-Disputant Party to a Disputant Party of funding for or indemnity against the award to be rendered in the arbitration proceedings.[200]

By generally including all sorts of "funding for or indemnity against the award" the wording is open to different forms of funders, similar to the approach taken by the ICC. This applies, even though the SIAC, Practice Note, PN – 01/17 refers to "Direct Economic Interest". Some authors suggested, with regard to the IBA Guidelines 2014, that loans and corporate finance instruments, such as equity investments, as well as before the event insurances, are probably not covered by the wording of the IBA Guidelines 2014, which refers to a "direct economic interest in [...] the award".[201] However, "the provision by a non-Disputant Party to a Disputant Party of funding" is broad enough to include loans and corporate finance instruments under SIAC, Practice Note, PN – 01/17. In addition, the definition of an External Funder as "any person, either legal or natural, who has a Direct Economic Interest in the outcome of the arbitration proceedings" may include before the event

198 ICC Note para. 21.
199 SIAC, Practice Note, PN – 01/17.
200 SIAC, Practice Note, PN – 01/17, para. 3.a.
201 J. von Goeler, *Third-party Funding*, p. 261. See also, J. Clanchy, *Access to Arbitral Justice: Costs for Arbitration, Third Party Funding in Arbitration: Breaking Down Barriers and Building Bridges*, Croatian Arb. YB 23 (2016), 53-69, 66, on "before the event" insurances.

insurances, since they do have a general interest "in the outcome of the arbitration proceedings".[202]

In the SCC Disclosure Policy of 2019, the SCC introduced an even broader wording than that used by the ICC and SIAC. Para. A encourages each party to disclose "the identity of any third party with a significant interest in the outcome of the dispute, including but not limited to funders, parent companies, and ultimate beneficial owners". Additionally, para. B.3 SCC Disclosure Policy further illustrates parties with a significant interest as

> (a) ultimate beneficial owners; (b) persons obligated to pay an award under an indemnification or other agreement; (c) persons entitled to receive proceeds of an award under a third-party-funding or other agreement; and (d) ultimate parent companies of a party.

Thus, para. B.3 SCC Disclosure Policy clarifies that the significant interest concerns especially economic interests, with regard to funders, but may go beyond.

Economic and financial interests are also at the centre of third-party funding defined by the current Hong Kong AO, although the term is not used. The Hong Kong AO broadly defines third-party funding as "money, or any other financial assistance, in relation to any costs of the arbitration".[203] The Hong Kong AO does not refer to any direct or indirect form of the "financial assistance". Thus, it may cover even more tenuous relationships.

The approach by ICSID in their 2020 Draft Code of Conduct for Adjudicators in Investor-State Dispute Settlement goes in this direction as well. Article 5(2)(a)(iv) ICSID Draft Code of Conduct requires disclosure of

> any professional, business and other significant relationships, within the past [five] years with [...] any third party with a direct or indirect financial interest in the outcome of the proceeding.

202 SIAC, Practice Note, PN – 01/17, para. 3.

203 Part 10A, Div. 2, Sect. 98F Hong Kong AO. A mandatory Code of Practice, published by the Secretary for Justice in December 2018, addresses practices and standards funders are "ordinarily expected to comply" with, see Code of Practice for Third Party Funding of Arbitration, available at gia.info.gov.hk/general/201812/07/P2018120700601_299064_1_1544169372716.pdf. The Code of Practice entered into force on 1 February 2019. According to Hirst and Yeow, the Hong Kong Code of Practice provides a developed level of safety and security to the funded party, P. Hirst/M. Yeow, *Comparing Hong Kong Code of Practice for Third Party Funding Arbitration with the Code of Conduct in England & Wales.*

The Draft underlines its purpose of an extensive disclosure obligation by explicitly referring to "direct or indirect financial interest".[204] Bearing in mind that the standard for disclosure differs from that for a conflict of interest,[205] the guidance on analysing a conflict of interest is limited. However, useful guidance on conflicts of interest may be deduced from the ICSID case *Suez, Sociedad General de Aguas de Barcelona SA, and others v. The Argentine Republic.*[206] The tribunal established four criteria to evaluate whether third-party funding creates a conflict. These criteria concentrate on the arbitrator's relation with the funded party and are:

> **Proximity:** How closely connected is the challenged arbitrator to one of the parties by reason of the alleged connection? The closer the connection between an arbitrator and a party, the more likely that the relationship may influence an arbitrator's independence of judgment and impartiality;
>
> **Intensity:** How intense and frequent are the interactions between challenged arbitrator and one of the parties as a result of the alleged connection? The more frequent and intense the interaction by virtue of the relationship between an arbitrator and a party, the more probable that such relationship will affect the arbitrator's independence of judgment and impartiality;
>
> **Dependence:** To what extent is the challenged arbitrator dependent on one of the parties for benefits as a result of the connection? The more an arbitrator is dependent on a relationship for benefits or advantages, the more likely that the relationship may influence the arbitrator's independence of judgment and impartiality; and
>
> **Materiality:** To what extent are any benefits accruing to the challenged arbitrator as a result of the alleged connection significant and therefore likely to influence in some way the arbitrator's judgment? Obviously, significant

204 Para. 42 of the Draft clarifies: "The mere fact of disclosure does not mean that a conflict exists. The policy reason underlying the disclosure requirement is to permit a full assessment by all parties and to avoid possible problematic situations during the proceedings. For this reason, an adjudicator should err on the side of more extensive disclosure."

205 See in detail below chapter 7.1.1.3, on the scope of disclosure.

206 *Suez, Sociedad General de Aguas de Barcelona SA, and others v. The Argentine Republic*, ICSID Tribunal, 12 May 2008, ICSID Case Nos. ARB/03/19 and ARB/03/17, para. 35. For the idea to apply the principles named in this case, see J. von Goeler, *Third-party Funding*, p. 266.

> benefits derived from a relationship will be more likely to influence an arbitrator's judgment and impartiality than negligible or insignificant benefits.[207]

This concrete elaboration resembles the general criteria, i.e., the directness of the relationship, the connection of the relationship to the dispute, and the proximity in time between the relationship and the arbitration proceeding, but provides a more detailed description.

Finally, the IBA Guidelines 2014 address in General Standard 6(b) a "direct economic interest" and clarify in the Explanation of General Standard 6(b) that this addresses third-party funders. General Standard 6(b) reads as follows:

> If one of the parties is a legal entity, any legal or physical person having a controlling influence on the legal entity, or a direct economic interest in, or a duty to indemnify a party for, the award to be rendered in the arbitration, may be considered to bear the identity of such party.

The wording "may" leaves discretion to the users of the Guidelines. General Standard 6(b) uses a different technique than the approaches taken by the ICC and SIAC, where third-party funders are simply addressed as non-parties. The IBA Guidelines require two steps: first, the funder must be positioned with one of the parties; and, second, where the funder is to be positioned with one of the parties a conflict of interest is to be analysed with the General Standards applicable to parties. Whether or not the funder is to be positioned with one party, depends on the form of funding.[208] Remarkably, the wording merely addresses parties that are a "legal entity". Where a natural person is funded, the Standard would not apply according to its wording. However, third-party funding of a natural person may also lead to a conflict of interest. Here, the general criteria for analysing a conflict of interest may provide guidance. An additional approach may be the application of the IBA Rules 1987 due to the limited scope of General Standard 6(b). According to the IBA Guidelines 2014, the Rules of Ethics "cover more topics than these Guidelines, and they remain in effect as to subjects that are not discussed in the Guidelines".[209] Rule 3.1 IBA Rules 1987 refers to potential dependence in relationships between an arbitrator and "someone closely connected with one of the parties".

207 *Suez, Sociedad General de Aguas de Barcelona SA, and others v. The Argentine Republic*, ICSID Tribunal, 12 May 2008, ICSID Case Nos. ARB/03/19 and ARB/03/17, para. 35, emph. add.

208 Cf. J. von Goeler, *Third-party Funding*, p. 275, who also argues that the form of funding is decisive, but who also prefers to apply the IBA Guidelines 2004 on the issue of third-party funding due to the broad and imprecise wording of General Standard 6(b).

209 Part I, Introduction, para. 8.

The Explanation of General Standard 6(b) IBA Guidelines 2014 additionally clarifies that

> [t]hird-party funders and insurers in relation to the dispute may have a direct economic interest in the award, and as such may be considered to be the equivalent of the party.

The Explanation clarifies the terms third-party funder and insurer to

> refer to any person or entity that is contributing funds, or other material support, to the prosecution or defence of the case and that has a direct economic interest in, or a duty to indemnify a party for, the award to be rendered in the arbitration.

One may argue that the Explanation narrows the scope of application in the General Standard to the second alternative, i.e., direct economic interest,[210] and, thus, certain types of funding or insurance are not addressed by the wording of the Explanation.[211] However, such a reading is unconvincing for two reasons. First, the Explanation uses the term "may", leaving room for different applications, including the other alternatives listed in General Standard 6(b).[212] Second, the introduction to the IBA Guidelines 2014 demands an application "with robust common sense and without unduly formalistic interpretation".[213] The Explanation must, hence, rather be interpreted as an inclusive example of the General Standard and not an exhaustive definition.

Arbitrator's Potential Conflicts of Interest

The arbitrator is at the centre of potential conflicts of interest when third-party funders are involved. Since the third-party funder is an additional actor involving different tasks, e.g., due diligence of claims before accepting to fund, the resulting relationships relevant for conflicts of interests are numerous. Potential typical scenarios are: first, arbitrator A

---

210 Again, J. von Goeler, *Third-party Funding*, p. 261, criticises the Explanation since it complicates the application of the standard – it would be unclear whether the General Standard or the standard in the Explanation prevails.

211 Von Goeler correctly points out that loans and corporate finance instruments, such as equity investments, are probably not covered by the alternative of a "direct economic interest in [...] the award", J. von Goeler, *Third-party Funding*, p. 261. J. Clanchy, *Access to Arbitral Justice: Costs for Arbitration, Third Party Funding in Arbitration: Breaking Down Barriers and Building Bridges*, Croatian Arb. YB 23 (2016), 53-69, 66, points out that "before the event" insurances would also not be covered by this alternative. He argues that these forms of insurances are much more present than third-party funding and pleads for disclosure of all sorts of third parties' funding costs of a dispute, since the potential for conflicts would be the "real concern".

212 The Explanation reads: "[t]hird-party funders and insurers in relation to the dispute may have a direct economic interest in the award".

213 Part I, Introduction, para. 6 IBA Guidelines 2014.

in arbitration 1 is also counsel for the claimant in arbitration 2, and in both proceedings the same funder backs different claimants;[214] second, an arbitrator is repeatedly appointed by different parties, but these parties are backed by the same funder;[215] third, arbitrator B advises a funder in the due diligence process of a potentially funded claim and acts as arbitrator in an arbitration involving the same funder;[216] fourth, an arbitrator holds shares in the funder;[217] or, fifth, there are indirect relationships of the arbitrator's law firm and the funder.[218] Additionally, bundling claims in a portfolio may create conflicts, and personal relationships may exist between an arbitrator and a funder within a portfolio.[219] Each scenario is examined below.

In the first scenario, the arbitrator is, directly or indirectly, paid as counsel by the funder. He or she has an economic interest in having a good relationship with the funder, i.e., potentially in the outcome of the case. This scenario may fall on the Non-Waivable Red List of the IBA Guidelines 2014 if this economic interest in the outcome of the case is present and "significant".[220] In the words of the *Suez* criteria, it is decisive whether the relationship between the arbitrator and the funder is "material", i.e., whether it includes significant benefits. The answer will depend, first, on the funding agreement, especially the mechanism of funding. If the funding is a loan provided by a bank or another private individual, the funder's economic interest is less material than where the funding is contingent on the outcome of the dispute.[221] Whether a contingent fee agreement between the funder and the funded party is a significant economic interest of the arbitrator depends, second, on the materiality of this funding agreement for the arbitrator. One possible criterion is to evaluate the percentage of the arbitrator's income in the second arbitration

214 E.g., L. Barrington, *FS Karrer*, p. 19; V. Frignati, *Ethical Implications of Third-party Funding in International Arbitration*, Arb. Int'l 32 (2016), 505-522, 513; J. von Goeler, *Third-party Funding*, p. 267.

215 V. Frignati, *Ethical Implications of Third-party Funding in International Arbitration*, Arb. Int'l 32 (2016), 505-522, 515; J. von Goeler, *Third-party Funding*, p. 274.

216 N. Darwazeh/A. Leleu, *Disclosure and Security for Costs or How to Address Imbalances Created by Third-Party Funding*, J. Int'l Arb. 33 (2016), 125-150, 132-133; J. von Goeler, *Third-party Funding*, p. 270.

217 V. Frignati, *Ethical Implications of Third-party Funding in International Arbitration*, Arb. Int'l 32 (2016), 505-522, 515. See generally, OLG München, 10 May 2012, 23 U 4635/11, BeckRS 2012, 10669, on lawyers holding shares of third-party funders.

218 N. Darwazeh/A. Leleu, *Disclosure and Security for Costs or How to Address Imbalances Created by Third-Party Funding*, J. Int'l Arb. 33 (2016), 125-150, 132-133; V. Frignati, *Ethical Implications of Third-party Funding in International Arbitration*, Arb. Int'l 32 (2016), 505-522, 515. The more general issues involving law firms will be addressed below, see chapter 4.1.2.

219 For the latter, see J. von Goeler, *Third-party Funding*, p. 264, with additional references.

220 Part II, para. 1.3, depending on the applicability of General Standard 6(b).

221 J. von Goeler, *Third-party Funding*, p. 268.

where he or she acts as counsel, in relation to his or her total income.[222] Alternatively, the relationship of the arbitrator and the funder might be particularly intense due to the dual role of the arbitrator also acting as counsel. If the funder is involved intensely in counselling, the arbitrator may be regarded as being under the control of the funder and not independent.[223]

In the second scenario, i.e., repeat appointments of the arbitrator by different parties backed by the same funder, an intense relationship between the arbitrator and the funder may create a conflict of interest. The *Suez* criteria of intensity and proximity may be particularly at issue in this scenario. The IBA Guidelines 2014 generally list the scenario of repeat appointments through "affiliates" on the Orange List. Whether the third-party funder can be positioned with the party, i.e., as an "affiliate of the party", in appointing the arbitrator depends on the individual case and cannot be generalised.[224] In some cases the funder controls the appointment process, and in others it does not.[225] Even if the funder controls the appointments, there is a general tendency that repeat appointments alone do not create a conflict of interest.[226]

The third scenario is rather a specific third-party funding scenario but resembles the preceding category of other employment.[227] Third-party funders often use other law firms for their due diligence of potentially funded disputes. Within the due diligence process the funder examines whether it will fund the claim by evaluating the prospects of success, the terms of the arbitration agreement, the arbitral institution and composition of the tribunal, the seat of the arbitration, the substantive law of the dispute, any potential jurisdictional issues, the quantum of the claim in comparison with the likely costs and risks of pursuing the claim, possible counterclaims, the likely timing to resolution of the claim, and risks associated with enforcing and obtaining payment under an award.[228] The arbitrator may have another employment relationship with the funder. This creates additional ties between potential arbitrators and third-party funders. The scenario may fall under the Waivable Red List of the IBA Guidelines 2014, stating that "[t]he arbitrator

222 See Example 1 in J. von Goeler, *Third-party Funding*, p. 267. The amount paid to the arbitrator was also a criterion for evaluating a conflict in *Commonwealth Coatings Co. v. Continental Casualty Co. et al.*, 89 S.Ct. 337 (1968), although no third-party funder was involved in that case.

223 For more details on potential influence of the funder on counsel, see below chapter 4.1.4.2.

224 J. von Goeler, *Third-party Funding*, p. 274, with additional references.

225 Where the funder does not approach the arbitrator, only the funder and the funded party are aware of this control, J. von Goeler, *Third-party Funding*, p. 274.

226 See above chapter 4.1.1.1.2, for more details and case law outside third-party funding scenarios.

227 See above chapter 4.1.1.1.4.

228 O. Gayner/A. Croft/K. Hurford, *Third-party Funding for International Arbitration Claims Practical Tips*. The law firm for due diligence is chosen in cooperation with the potentially funded party.

currently represents or advises one of the parties, or an affiliate of one of the parties".[229] Again, the intensity and materiality of the relationship will be decisive for analysing whether a conflict of interest exists. If the funder regularly appoints the same lawyer, i.e., the potential arbitrator, for due diligence, his or her economic interest is at stake. Additionally, the proximity may be an issue, especially where the arbitrator acts in parallel as party-appointed arbitrator for a funded party and as lawyer in due diligence for the same funder.

Fourth, if the arbitrator holds shares in the funding company, the prerequisites of para. 2.2.1 of the IBA Guidelines 2014 Waivable Red List can be met.[230] Similar to the approach in scenarios without a third-party funder, the financial interest must meet a certain threshold to constitute a conflict of interest.[231] Usually, as long as the arbitrator is not a major shareholder, case law is rather liberal. A comparable scenario can be that the arbitrator is directly employed by the third-party funder as investment or case manager. If the employment is parallel to the proceedings, this will most likely constitute a conflict of interest.[232] If the funder employs the arbitrator shortly after the arbitration proceedings ended, it is questionable whether a conflict of interest arises and will depend, inter alia, on the intensity and proximity of a previous relationship.

Fifth, indirect conflicts may arise where the arbitrator's law firm has a significant relationship with a funder.[233] In general, the IBA Guidelines 2014 associate the arbitrator with his or her law firm. They require an examination of the relationship between the party, or affiliate, and the law firm, on the one hand, and the relationship between the law

229 Part II, para. 2.3.1 IBA Guidelines 2014.

230 I.e., "the arbitrator holds shares, either directly or indirectly, in one of the parties, or an affiliate of one of the parties, this party or an affiliate being privately held".

231 See above chapter 4.1.1.1.

232 Depending on the exact scenario and the form of funding, one may apply Part II, para. 1.2 IBA Guidelines 2014: "The arbitrator is a manager, director or member of the supervisory board, or has a controlling influence on one of the parties or an entity that has a direct economic interest in the award to be rendered in the arbitration." Also, para. 1.3 IBA Guidelines 2014 may be relevant: "The arbitrator has a significant financial or personal interest in one of the parties, or the outcome of the case." In these cases, the scenario can meet the standards of the Non-Waivable Red List.
Alternatively, Part II, para. 2.3.4 IBA Guidelines 2014, i.e., the Waivable Red List, may apply where "[t]he arbitrator is a manager, director or member of the supervisory board, or has a controlling influence in an affiliate of one of the parties, if the affiliate is directly involved in the matters in dispute in the arbitration", the arbitrator may be conflicted. However, it will depend on the exact scenario: the wording requests "direct involvement" of the affiliate.
Another alternative is the approach taken by CA Paris, 2 July 1992, Rev. de l'Arb. 1996, 411-410. The court ruled that there must have been a "link of dependency" between the arbitrator and the party even before the date of employment.

233 N. Darwazeh/A. Leleu, *Disclosure and Security for Costs or How to Address Imbalances Created by Third-Party Funding*, J. Int'l Arb. 33 (2016), 125-150, 132-133. On general aspects of law firm conflicts outside third-party funding, see below chapter 4.1.2.

firm and the arbitrator on the other hand. In cases involving third-party funders, a third relationship becomes decisive: that of the third-party funder with the party. Generally, the *Suez* criteria of intensity and proximity in time of these relationships will often be decisive. Regarding potential conflicts arising out of the due diligence activity of the law firm (i.e., the arbitrator's law firm does due diligence for the funder), the scholar and practitioner Bond provides a useful analogy that highlights the caution to be applied due to the additional third relationship:

> If we draw an analogy between the funder and an insurance company that is a client of your firm, does that mean you cannot be an arbitrator if one of the parties in the case has litigation insurance with that company? Or suppose your firm represents a bank; must an arbitrator ask if any of the parties have taken out loans from that bank, either to fund the arbitration or otherwise, given that money is fungible? If so should the arbitrator be disqualified?[234]

Finally, third-party funders often provide either single funding or portfolio funding.[235] Portfolio funding bundles diverse disputes with different risk allocations. Successful disputes within the same portfolio may cover losses of other unsuccessful disputes. At first glance, the argument that grouping together different claims exponentiates the potential for conflicts appears convincing: potential conflicts may arise with all other disputes, arbitrators, counsels or parties involved in the same portfolio. However, under closer examination this argument does not hold water. In most cases, the risk of conflicts will not exponentiate. Where neither the arbitrators nor counsels or parties of different disputes become aware of the fact that they belong to the same bundle of a third-party funder, their relationships do not create a conflict of interest. Since many funding agreements require confidentiality, it is also unlikely that two befriended arbitrators of two different arbitral proceedings in the same portfolio bundle would inform each other of the involved third-party funder. In addition, even if these two arbitrators become aware of such information, their relationship and that with the funder must meet the general threshold of constituting a conflict of interest. Therefore, without concluding on the particular case whether a conflict of interest exists, portfolio cases are not to be treated differently than other third-party funding cases.

234 Cited in J. von Goeler, *Third-party Funding*, p. 270.

235 See examples presented by Woodsford Litigation Funding, available at https://woodsfordlitigationfunding.com/arbitration-funding/portfolio-arbitration-funding/ and https://woodsfordlitigationfunding.com/arbitration-funding/single-case-arbitration-funding/.

4.1.1.2 Arbitrator's Relationship with a Witness

An arbitrator's relationship with one of the witnesses may also create a conflict of interest.[236] Especially the prejudice in favour of or against a witness, "which prevents an impartial assessment of the evidence of that witness", may create a conflict.[237] The right to present witness evidence is covered by the parties' right to be heard and to present their case. Article 18 UNCITRAL Model Law requires that "[t]he parties shall be treated with equality and each party shall be given a full opportunity of presenting his case". The arbitral tribunal must adhere to this mandatory provision.[238] The concrete rights and duties on whether, when, how and for what purpose parties may introduce witness evidence depend on the applicable law, the parties' agreement, and the orders of the tribunals.[239] In any event, a relationship between an arbitrator and one party's witness raises questions of the arbitrator's ability to judge this witness. Witnesses provide evidence of a legal or factual aspect, and the arbitrator needs to assess the credibility and reliability of the witnesses. In order to do so, the arbitrator must be free from a conflict of interest. When examining whether a conflict of interest exists, the general criteria of the directness of the relationship, the connection of the relationship to the dispute, and the proximity in time between the relationship and the arbitration proceeding provide guidance.

The SCC Board ruled that no intense relationship constituting a conflict of interest existed where claimant's party-appointed arbitrator had an ongoing business relationship with the firm at which a witness called by the claimants was working as consultant.[240] He frequently advised that firm on internal matters. In these internal matters the arbitrator had, on a few occasions, been in contact with the witness, but he had never worked with him for a mutual client. Even though the SCC Board's reasoning was not published, an argument justifying professional relationships between arbitrators and witnesses may be their presence in the same legal field. In such cases, professional ties will be common and frequent, usually not constituting a conflict of interest. Thus, an arbitrator's acquaintance with one of the witnesses, e.g., an employee of one of the brokers who testified for the respondent, does not constitute a conflict of interest. The U.S. District Court in this example explained that

236 *Washburn v. McManus*, 895 F.Supp. 392 (D. Connecticut 1994).

237 *Director General of Fair Trading v. Proprietary Association of Great Britain and Proprietary Articles Trade Association*, [2001] EWCA Civ 1217.

238 G. Born, *International Commercial Arbitration*, p. 2327 et seq.

239 On the admissibility of evidence, see G. Born, *International Commercial Arbitration*, p. 2446 et seq.; S. Elsing, *Procedural Efficiency in International Arbitration: Choosing the Best of Both Legal Worlds*, SchiedsVZ 2011, 114-123, 119 et seq.

240 SCC Arbitration V (137/2008), N. Lindström, *Decisions by the SCC Board during 2008 – 2010*, p. 7 et seq.

> the very purpose of arbitration is to have controversies decided by persons knowledgeable in the particular industry, and that it is therefore inevitable that there will be repeated instances of acquaintanceship between arbitrators and parties and witnesses in the proceeding.[241]

The result may be different where the arbitrator knows a witness from previous proceedings and the credibility and reliability of that witness was at issue in those previous proceedings. In *ASM Shipping Ltd. of India v. TTMI Ltd. of England*, the presiding arbitrator knew one of claimant's main witnesses from a previous arbitration where the arbitrator had acted as counsel.[242] The arbitrator did not disclose this fact. The previous proceeding was conducted seven months earlier, and serious allegations were raised against the witness. The England and Wales High Court of Justice concluded that a conflict of interest resulted from these facts.[243] Bearing in mind that the arbitrator's task is to assess the credibility and reliability of a witness, this result is not surprising. However, absent any special circumstance, i.e., allegations against the witness, the mere fact that the arbitrator met the witness in previous proceedings is not likely to give rise to a conflict of interest.[244] Close family relations, e.g., the arbitrator's wife is to be called as a witness in proceedings, constitute a conflict of interest.[245] The IBA Guidelines 2014 place the close personal friendship and enmity between the arbitrator and a witness on the Orange List.[246]

In some jurisdictions and in the IBA Rules 1987, a conflict of interest depends on the role of the witness: only if he or she is of paramount importance and objective grounds for the incredibility exist is there a valid conflict of interest.[247]

241 *Hodges Intern. Inc. v. Rembrandt Fabrics, Ltd.*, 353 N.Y.S.2d 462 (1st Dep't 1974).

242 *ASM Shipping Ltd. of India v. TTMI Ltd. of England*, [2005] EWHC 2238 (Comm). In addition, the arbitrator had received instructions from respondent's solicitor in the previous proceedings.

243 *ASM Shipping Ltd. of India v. TTMI Ltd. of England*, [2005] EWHC 2238 (Comm). However, the court denied the request for annulment of the award since claimant waived its right to rely on the violation.

244 *University Commons-Urbana, Ltd. v. Universal Constructors Inc.*, 304 F.3d 1331 (11th Cir. 2002), on domestic arbitration. Additionally, the arbitrator failed to disclose the previous encounter. The court generally affirmed the U.S. District Court in confirming the award, but remanded the decision for fact-finding on the arbitrator's potential relationship.

245 See A. Denning, *The Independence and Impartiality of the Judges*, S. African L.J. 71 (1954) 345-358, 355, for this example originally referring to a magistrate's wife.

246 Part II, paras. 3.4.3 and 3.4.4.

247 Rule 3.3 IBA Rules 1987: "Any current direct or indirect business relationship between an arbitrator and a party, or with a person who is known to be a potentially important witness, will normally give rise to justifiable doubts as to a prospective arbitrator's impartiality or independence." Sutter-Somm/Hasenböhler/Leuenberger/S. Wullschleger, Art. 47 para. 40, on Swiss state court proceedings. The criterion of the importance of the witness can be applied within the discretion provided by the applicable standard of independence and impartiality. It should not generally lead to directly denying a conflict of interest.

A relationship with a witness is often accompanied or evidenced by certain conduct of the arbitrator, e.g., revealing a friendship or enmity.[248] However, merely cutting off or applying an alleged "extra scrutiny" on a witness does not suffice to create a conflict of interest.[249]

4.1.1.3 Arbitrator's Relationship with an Expert

Similar to witnesses, experts also provide a means of presenting the case for the parties. The right to use an expert witness is covered by the parties' right to be heard and to present their case, protected, inter alia, by Article 18 UNCITRAL Model Law.[250] The expert's role is to provide their genuinely held and sincere professional opinion.[251] Thus, Article 8(4) IBA Rules 2020 requires the expert to affirm in a manner determined appropriate by the arbitral tribunal that it is "his or her genuine belief in the opinions to be expressed at the Evidentiary Hearing". The arbitral tribunal has to "determine the admissibility, relevance, materiality and weight of evidence".[252] An intense relationship between the arbitrator and the expert may impair this determination. Whether or not a conflict of interest exists, again depends on the directness of the relationship, the connection of the relationship to the dispute, and the proximity in time between the relationship and the arbitration proceeding.

Undoubtedly, the arbitrator may not act as an expert in the same case where he or she acts as an arbitrator, and vice versa.[253] A scenario that requires more examination exists where the arbitrator has a professional or personal relationship with an expert. Where this relationship results in a close personal friendship or enmity, a conflict of interest may exist.[254] Where the arbitrator is already familiar with certain expert evidence and decided

---

248 Part II paras. 3.4.3 and 3.4.4 IBA Guidelines 2014 explicitly on "close personal friendship" and "enmity". Other rules require general disclosure of personal relationships: NASD Code of Arbitration Sect. 23(a)(3) "any personal relationships with any party, its counsel, or witness".

249 *Ortiz-Espinosa v. BBVA Securities of Puerto Rico, Inc.*, 852 F.3d 36 (5th Cir. 2017); *Blackwell v. Merrill Lynch, Pierce, Fenner & Smith Inc.*, 22 F.Supp.3d 565 (W.D. North Carolina 2014), on domestic arbitration; *Kolel Beth Yechiel Mechil of Tartikov, Inc. v. YLL Irrevocable Trust*, 878 F.Supp.2d 459 (S.D. New York 2012), also on domestic arbitration. See also, LCIA Reference No. 81007/81008/81024/81025, LCIA Court, 16 June 2008, Arb. Int'l 27 (2011), 425-432; LCIA Reference No. UN7949, LCIA Court, 3 December 2007, Arb. Int'l 27 (2011), 420-424. Additionally, see *Rai v. Barclays Capital Inc.*, 739 F.Supp.2d 364 (S.D. New York 2010), on rejecting evidence, and *Interprods Ltd. v. De La Rue International Ltd.*, [2014] EWHC 68 (Comm), on not questioning a witness. See below chapter 4.2, for a more detailed analysis of the arbitrator's conduct resulting in a conflict of interest.

250 See above chapter 4.1.1.2, for witnesses.

251 G. Born, *International Commercial Arbitration*, p. 2452.

252 Art. 9(1) IBA Rules 2020.

253 Part II, para. 2.1.1 IBA Guidelines 2014. See also, BGer, 7 June 2011, BGE 137 III 289, 292; BSK BV/J. Reich, Art. 30 para. 22, on state court proceedings. Some national laws on state court judges generally forbid judges to act as experts for legal opinions, e.g., § 41(1) German RiG. Also, German judges cannot act in cases where they have been heard as witness or expert, § 41 No. 5 German ZPO.

254 The IBA Guidelines 2014 again require disclosure of these scenarios: Part II, paras. 3.4.3 and 3.4.4.

a legal issue considering that same expert evidence, it is questionable whether a conflict of interest exists. On the one hand, the objective value of an independent and impartial expert opinion should enable the same arbitrator to consider the same expert opinion more than once. On the other hand, arbitrators need to be open-minded and not influenced by prejudgment.[255] Where the arbitrator repeatedly encounters the same expert opinion for the same legal issues, he or she is most likely not open-minded any more. Following this second approach, the U.S. District Court, S.D. Texas, annulled an award where the arbitrator did not disclose that he served as an arbitrator in another case involving the claimant, the same legal issues, and where the arbitrator explicitly relied on an expert presented by the claimant and contested by the respondent.[256] The U.S. District Court did not only rely on this connection of the arbitrator and the expert, but on a cumulation of grounds: repeat appointment, potential lack of an open mind, and non-disclosure. Leaving aside the issues of reappointment and non-disclosure, it is questionable whether the professional relationship and potential lack of an open mind resulting from the previous encounter with the expert witness constitute a conflict of interest in this case. There was no consistent previous relationship between the arbitrator and the expert but a single one. Additionally, the lack of an open mind remained rather suspicious.[257] The U.S. Court of Appeals reversed the U.S. District Court's annulment two years later but with the reasoning that respondent had waived its right.[258]

The threshold of an intense financial relationship resulting in a conflict of interest was not met where a presiding arbitrator and an expert were both passive investors in a limited partnership unrelated to the subject of the dispute.[259]

4.1.1.4 Arbitrator's Relationship with Another Arbitrator

An additional source of conflicts of interest based on relationships are relationships within the arbitral tribunal. In general, arbitrators are obliged to deliberate and render the most important decisions in a plenary session.[260] According to French case law and literature,

---

255 See in detail below chapter 4.2.1.5.

256 *Dealer Computer Services, Inc. v. Michael Motor Co., Inc.*, 761 F.Supp.2d 459 (S.D. Texas 2010), also relying on a failure to disclose these facts. The case dealt with domestic arbitration. See below chapter 7.1, on the obligation to disclose.

257 The court merely stated that "Butner, [the challenged arbitrator,] a party-appointed *neutral* arbitrator, failed to disclose that she was *personally involved* in a prior arbitration that involved the *same issues* of contractual interpretation and damages calculation, as well as related expert witnesses", 466, emph. add. by the court.

258 *Dealer Computer Services, Inc. v. Michael Motor Co., Inc.*, 485 Fed.Appx. 724 (5th Cir. 2012). See below chapter 7.2, on waiver.

259 *Apusento Garden (Guam) Inc. v. Superior Court of Guam*, 94 F.3d 1346 (9th Cir. 1996).

260 C. Seraglini/J. Ortscheidt, *Droit de l'arbitrage interne et international*, paras. 864-867. Deliberations are usually confidential for arbitrators and judges, see, e.g., § 43 German RiG for German judges.

these obligations result in the principles of loyalty and collegiality applicable to arbitral tribunals.[261] Arbitrators should be loyal and collegial with each other. Intense relationships, e.g., enmity or financial dependency, between the arbitrators can impair this goal. Additionally, such intense relationship may create hierarchies and subordination within the arbitral tribunal, risking a balanced approach to the deliberations and potentially resulting in a conflict of interest.[262] In order to prevent any of these conflicts, the IBA Guidelines 2014 call for disclosure of the following scenarios: two arbitrators are lawyers in the same law firm; members of the same barristers' chamber were within the past three years partners or otherwise affiliated; and a lawyer in the arbitrator's law firm is an arbitrator in another dispute involving one of the parties, or an affiliate.[263] Whether or not a conflict of interest exists depends on the impact of the relationship on the arbitrator's obligations and their loyalty and collegiality with each other. Helpful for analysing this relationship are the general criteria of directness of the relationship, the connection of the relationship to the dispute, and the proximity in time between the relationship and the arbitration proceeding.

German case law reveals that, generally, friendship or close relations between the arbitrators do not create a conflict of interest.[264] Similar to the leeway applied to social relationships between arbitrators and counsels,[265] the argument is that arbitrators usually come from the same legal community and, thus, are likely to have connections. Without relying on these arguments, the approach taken by the U.S. Court of Appeals, Second Circuit, in *Lucent Technologies Inc. v. Tatung Co.* is in line with this leniency. One of the alleged grounds for annulment was the fact that claimant's party-appointed arbitrator and the presiding arbitrator owned an airplane together.[266] The U.S. Court of Appeals affirmed the lower court's decision and ruled that the facts did not warrant annulment.[267] Much more rigorous is the approach suggested by French law applicable in court proceedings: it generally forbids spouses, parents, and other family members to sit on the same tribunal

261 E.g., Cass civ 1ère, 29 June 2011, 09-17346. See generally, L. Lévy, *The Chairman's Roles in the Arbitral Tribunal's Dynamics*, p. 68 et seq.

262 See also, below chapter 4.2.1.3, for potential conflicts of interest resulting from the conduct in deliberating and decision-making.

263 Part II, paras. 3.3.1-3.3.4 IBA Guidelines 2014.

264 OLG München, 10 July 2013, 34 SchH 8/12, NJOZ 2014, 1779-1782.

265 See above chapter 4.1.1.1.7.

266 *Lucent Technologies Inc. v. Tatung Co.*, 379 F.3d 24 (2d Cir. 2004), this fact had not been disclosed by either of the arbitrators. In addition, claimant's party-appointed arbitrator failed to disclose a previous relationship with claimant.

267 The U.S. District Court in the first instance held that this would be a "classic example of a losing party seizing upon a pretext for invalidating the award". Additionally, the Court of Appeals relied upon the parties' right to appoint an expert as arbitrator and the existence of a certain trade-off between expertise and impartiality in arbitration.

in court proceedings.[268] It is not necessary to apply such a general prohibition to arbitration. Whether to appoint arbitrators from one family should be up to the parties and covered by the right to appoint their chosen arbitrator. As long as the social ties do not hinder the arbitrators from carrying out their obligations of deliberating and rendering a decision, there is no reason to conclude that a conflict exists.

More often than social ties, there are professional relationships between arbitrators. Here again, the fact that arbitrators have the same profession must be borne in mind. Four groups of cases with regard to professional ties can be differentiated.

First, the mere fact that two co-arbitrators have previously worked together does not by itself create a conflict of interest. No conflict of interest was found where two co-arbitrators were affiliated with the same publisher and met on a study day of that publisher.[269] The *cour d'appel de* Paris reasoned that there was no evidence of any subordination. Also, the mere fact that two arbitrators come from the same law firm should not create a conflict.[270] This is to be welcomed if there is no permanent financial relationship between the two arbitrators and their obligations as arbitrators are separated from their obligations as counsels. However, if the business relationship is more substantial, the relationship may rise to a conflict of interest.[271] For example, a permanent and financial relationship may be created if one arbitrator intends to join one of the co-arbitrator's law firms.

Second, few reappointments by the party-appointed arbitrators in unrelated cases do not create a conflict of interest.[272] This approach is to be welcomed, bearing in mind that few repeat appointments by the counsel and the party are similarly treated. However, a conflict of interest may arise where the party-appointed arbitrator tries to nominate a potentially

268 Art. L. 111-10 French COJ, reading: "*Les conjoints, les parents et alliés jusqu'au troisième degré inclus ne peuvent, sauf dispense, être simultanément membres d'un même tribunal ou d'une même cour en quelque qualité que ce soit.*" In fact, this could also be understood that these groups may not even be judges in the same court. French case law, however, reveals that two spouses may be judges in the same court if they do not sit in the same proceedings, C. Chanais/F. Ferrand/S. Guinchard, *Procédure civile*, para. 1061. Chanais criticises the rigorous solution of Art. L. 111-10.

269 CA Paris, 1 July 2011, Rev. de l'Arb. 2011, 761-765.

270 J.-F. Poudret/S. Besson, *Comparative Law of International Arbitration*, para. 420. Even though this scenario needs to be disclosed according to the IBA Guidelines 2014, Part II, para. 3.3.1.

271 In *LGC Holdings, Inc. v. Julius Klein Diamonds, LLC*, 238 F.Supp.3d 452 (S.D. New York 2017), the U.S. District Court concluded that the request for annulment was procedurally too late. Claimant's party-appointed arbitrator and the presiding arbitrator were partners in two businesses. Since respondent failed to object when the presiding arbitrator disclosed this fact during the proceedings, the court concluded that respondent had waived its right to rely on the conflict.

272 E.g., *Ario v. Cologne Reinsurance (Barbados), Ltd.*, 2009 WL 3818626 (M.D. Pennsylvania), where the presiding arbitrator had been selected twice by the same party-appointed arbitrator.

biased presiding arbitrator.[273] In one case, the challenged arbitrator first rejected another candidate and then proposed a lawyer who was consistently chosen by the party that nominated the arbitrator. The *Oberlandesgericht* Karlsruhe did not decide whether this scenario met the threshold of a conflict of interest since it based its decision to sustain the challenge on another ground.

Third, some parties have argued that the fact that another arbitrator was successfully challenged constituted a new ground for challenge regarding the remaining arbitrators. Usually, this does not create a ground for challenge of the remaining arbitrators or later annulment.[274] Without demonstrating that these remaining arbitrators are themselves conflicted, it is not possible to successfully challenge the whole tribunal.[275] This may be different where there is a risk that the removed arbitrator "infected" the remaining arbitrators during the deliberations[276] or where the co-arbitrator's reaction to the third arbitrator's challenge demonstrates conduct meeting the threshold of a conflict of interest.[277]

Finally, it is questionable whether a professional relationship that creates an imbalance or hierarchy between the arbitrators, e.g., a relationship of subordination, constitutes a conflict. Mere collegiality between arbitrators cannot create a conflict.[278] In general, such a relationship is difficult to prove. The LCIA Court rendered two decisions in this regard. In LCIA Reference No. 3488, it denied respondent's challenge based on the allegation of divergence in the tribunal.[279] According to the respondent, its party-appointed arbitrator was forced into the minority.[280] However, the respondent failed to prove its allegations. The LCIA Court held that the respondent would be required to prove that the majority of arbitrators were "rascals". The minority arbitrator would need to "express himself with

273 OLG Karlsruhe, 14 July 2006, 10 Sch 1/06, BeckRS 2006, 19851.

274 *ASM Shipping Ltd. v. Harris & Ors.*, [2007] EWHC 1513 (Comm); affirmative G. Born, *International Commercial Arbitration*, p. 2028.

275 With regard to state court proceedings, BGH, 19 September 2016, IX ZA 37/15, BeckRS 2016, 18053.

276 CA Paris, 21 February 2012, Rev. de l'Arb. 2012, 587-595. However, this "infection" was only an additional argument for granting the annulment.

277 See below chapter 4.2, on conduct in general.

278 In state court proceedings neither collegiality between members of the same tribunal, nor that between judges of different instances creates a conflict of interest, BGer, 7 December 2006, BGE 133 I 1; *Steck-Risch and others v. Liechtenstein*, ECtHR, 19 May 2005, 63151/00; BSK BV/J. Reich, Art. 30 para. 33. For a different view on judges in different instances, see R. Kiener, *Richterliche Unabhängigkeit*, p. 133. According to Kiener, collegiality may lead to unconscious or subjective bias. However, a ground for finding dependence and partiality requires more.

279 LCIA Reference No. 3488, LCIA Court, 11 July 2007, Arb. Int'l 27 (2011), 413-419.

280 Regarding the substance, respondent alleged that the two other arbitrators were prejudging the case. Regarding the procedure, the presiding arbitrator offended respondent in one of the procedural orders. Respondent alleged that its party-appointed arbitrator did not support the offences.

force and clarity if he considered his co-arbitrators to be guilty of bias".[281] In its second decision on this matter, the LCIA Court refrained from considering whether the relationship disqualified the two arbitrators but asked the presiding arbitrator to stand down.[282] The relationship in question was an alleged hierarchy between claimant's party-appointed arbitrator and the presiding arbitrator. The former had been instructed in several matters in the past by the presiding arbitrator. In addition, there existed a long-standing continuing relationship between the two. The presiding arbitrator stood down to avoid needless controversy at an early stage of the arbitration.

4.1.1.5 Arbitrator's Relationship with an Appointing Authority or Institution

Finally, it is possible that an arbitrator has a relationship with the appointing authority or institution, e.g., he or she is a member of a committee or board, or social or professional ties exist with a member or employee of the institution. According to the IBA Guidelines 2014, any such relationship needs to be disclosed.[283] However, whether a conflict of interest exists will depend on the directness of the relationship, the connection of the relationship to the dispute, and the proximity in time between the relationship and the arbitration proceeding.

Where the institution is involved in the arbitrator's appointment,[284] the question arises as to whether institutional personnel may be appointed. A full-time employee should not be able to serve as an arbitrator.[285] The appointment of members of institutional courts, however, is often allowed.[286] Bearing in mind that the members of the institutional courts are often not (fully) employed by the institution, but are practitioners themselves, this approach is to be welcomed. Moreover, a close connection between the institution and the tribunal can be advantageous in keeping the arbitral proceedings efficient.

---

281 LCIA Reference No. 3488, LCIA Court, 11 July 2007, Arb. Int'l 27 (2011), 413-419, 418. The court added that, in any event, it would be the division of the court judging whether the challenged arbitrators had done anything wrong. Otherwise, the efficiency and fairness of the arbitral process would be easily derailed if a minority arbitrator could stop proceedings based on ill-founded negative feelings towards his colleagues and baseless accusations of impropriety against them.

282 LCIA Reference No. 81132, LCIA Court, 15 November 2008, Arb. Int'l 27 (2011), 439-441.

283 Part II, para. 3.5.3 IBA Guidelines 2014.

284 In fact, this is one of the essential advantages of institutional arbitration, to have a helping hand in constituting the arbitral tribunal, F. Schäfer, *Institutionelle Schiedsgerichtsbarkeit*, para. 110 et seq. Often, the institution appoints in default for the parties, e.g., Sect. R-13(c) AAA Rules; Art. 12.3 DIS Rules; Arts. 7.2 and 8 HKIAC Rules. Interestingly, Art. 7.5 JAMS Rules even includes the parties in the default situation through a list mechanism.

285 In this regard, institutions forbid their own personnel and members of the board to act as arbitrator under their own rules, e.g., paras. 4 and 5 DIS-Integrity Principles; Art. 2(1) ICC Internal Rules.

286 E.g., Art. 5.10 LCIA Rules, allowing the appointment if the parties agree in writing; Art. 2(2) ICC Internal Rules limits the allowance to the vice-presidents and the ordinary members of the ICC Court of Arbitration.

4.1.2 Law Firm Conflicts

In past years, the number of arbitrators quitting large law firms to pursue careers as independent arbitrators has increased. The number of conflicts created by their employment or partnership with a large law firm is one of the main reasons for this decision. Whether or not the arbitrator bears the identity of his or her law firm when analysing a potential conflict of interest is, however, questionable. On the one hand, the paramount importance of independence and impartiality for the arbitral process may favour the identity between the arbitrators and their law firms.[287] A practical argument in favour of identity is the difficulty of establishing a real "Chinese Wall" within a law firm. On the other hand, the fact that law firm conflicts are more indirect relations, and that indirect relations are less likely to create a conflict of interest,[288] speaks against such a general identity.[289] In globally organised law firms, lawyers simply do not know each other or the work of unknown colleagues. It is questionable whether the mere possibility to know each other and each other's work is sufficient to constitute a conflict of interest.

The IBA Guidelines 2014 General Standard 6(a) applies a differentiated approach.

> [I]n principle, [the arbitrator] bear[s] the identity of his or her law firm, but when considering the relevance of facts or circumstances to determine whether a potential conflict of interest exists [...] the activities of an arbitrator's law firm, if any, and the relationship of the arbitrator with the law firm, should be considered in each individual case. The fact that the activities of the arbitrator's firm involve one of the parties shall not necessarily constitute a source of such conflict.[290]

In the Explanation to this General Standard, the IBA Guidelines 2014 refer to the growing size of law firms and the need to balance the parties' right to appoint their arbitrator of choice and the "importance of maintaining confidence in the impartiality and independence

287 See O. Froitzheim, *Die Kanzleimitgliedschaft und die Ablehnung von Schiedsrichtern in der internationalen Schiedsgerichtsbarkeit*, SchiedsVZ 2017, 172-176, 174, generally favouring this approach and with additional references.

288 Sutter-Somm/Hasenböhler/Leuenberger/S. Wullschleger, Art. 47 para. 38, primarily on state court judges.

289 See also, G. Nicholas/C. Partasides, *LCIA Court Decisions on Challenges to Arbitrators: A Proposal to Publish*, Arb. Int'l 23 (2007), 1-41, 25, referring to the "significance of the relationship".

290 General Standard 6(a) IBA Guidelines 2014. The prerequisite to analyse "each individual case" was already present in General Standard 6(a) IBA Guidelines 2004. However, the predecessor of the current version did not state that, in principle, the arbitrator is to be regarded as bearing the identity of the law firm. Instead, the 2004 version emphasised that "the fact that the activities of the arbitrator's firm involve one of the parties shall not automatically constitute a source of such conflict or a reason for disclosure".

of international arbitrators".[291] The Lists of Part II IBA Guidelines 2014 follow the principle that the arbitrator bears the identity of his or her law firm.[292]

4.1.2.1 Relationship between the Arbitrator's Law Firm and a Party

4.1.2.1.1 Relationships with the Party

The arbitrator's law firm may have a relationship with one of the parties or an affiliated company of one of the parties. Whether these relationships constitute a conflict of interest depends on the interest the party has in the proceedings, the directness of the relationship between the party and the law firm, the connection of this relationship to the dispute, and the proximity in time between the relationship and the arbitration proceeding.

Direct relations with the party in connection to the same subject matter of the dispute may prevent an institution or appointing authority from confirming the nomination of an arbitrator. The LCIA Court refrained from confirming respondent's nominated arbitrator since he was a partner in a law firm that had previously represented the respondent with respect to the contractual arrangements with which the present arbitration agreement was concerned, though he himself had not been party to the advice given to the respondent.[293] The court emphasised that declining the appointment was necessary to avoid any risk of embarrassment to the arbitrator or parties at an early stage of the proceedings. However, where the previous representation of one of the parties was on matters unrelated to the dispute, the U.S. Court of Appeals, District of Columbia Circuit, declined to annul the award.[294]

Besides the connection to the subject matter of the dispute, the size of the law firm and the internal organisation are factors for evaluating the risk of creating a conflict of interest. Where the arbitrator was personally involved in representing the party, the differentiation in examining the conflict of interest between the arbitrator (direct) and the law firm (indirect) is void. Here, the intensity of the direct relationship, i.e., that of the arbitrator with the party, is decisive.[295] In order to distinguish direct from indirect relations, a criterion

291 Explanation to General Standard 6(a) IBA Guidelines 2014.

292 E.g., Part II, para. 1.4 for regular advice and deriving significant income; para. 2.3.3, on current representation and advice; or para. 2.3.6, on a current significant commercial relationship of the arbitrator's law firm with a party.

293 In LCIA Reference No. 9147, LCIA Court, 27 January 2000, Arb. Int'l 27 (2011), 334-335.

294 *Al-Harbi v. Citibank*, 85 F.3d 680 (D.C. Cir. 1996). More precisely, claimant relied on the arbitrator's failure to disclose the relevant fact. The court ruled that claimant's argumentation did not meet the "onerous standard for" annulment.

295 It is particularly the financial intensity that is decisive in professional relations. Cf. the IBA Guidelines 2014 in its Explanation to General Standard 6(a): "The relevance of the activities of the arbitrator's firm, such as

can be whether the arbitrator was involved in strategic or legal decisions while representing the party.[296] In line with this criterion, the U.S. District Court, E.D. North Carolina, dismissed respondent's action to annul the arbitral award. Respondent argued that the arbitrator's law firm was engaged in three actions against the respondent and that the arbitrator participated in at least one of them. However, the arbitrator had not been involved directly in the legal strategies regarding those previous actions.

In state court proceedings, relationships between law firms and judges, including deputy or part-time judges, tend to be less restrictively handled. In *Locabail (U.K.) Ltd. v. Bayfield Properties Ltd.*, no conflict of interest existed where one of the deputy judges was a partner of a law firm that had represented a third company in its dispute against the owner of the respondent.[297]

4.1.2.1.2 Relationships with an Affiliate

The IBA Guidelines 2014 differentiate between relationships with the party and those with an affiliate of one of the parties.[298] The IBA Guidelines 2014 refrain from providing a "catch-all rule" on this matter since relationships between the arbitrator's law firm and an affiliate are often complex and individual.[299] Thus, case law may give helpful guidance. Additionally, the analysis of whether a conflict of interest exists may be guided by the general criteria, namely the interest the affiliate has in the proceedings, the directness of the relationship between the affiliate and the law firm, the connection of this relationship to the dispute, and the proximity in time between the relationship and the arbitration proceeding.

Where the relationship between the law firm and the affiliate itself is not close or material, the threshold of a conflict of interest is not crossed. Per contra, where the relationship is intense and even important for the law firm, the threshold may be crossed. For example, the importance of a relationship was demonstrated by extreme publicity of the relationship, even though the arbitrator's law firm represented the mother company of the main shareholder of claimant in an unrelated matter.[300] Furthermore, naming the respondent's group of companies among the high-profile clients of the firm on the law firm's web page

---

the nature, timing and scope of the work by the law firm, and the relationship of the arbitrator with the law firm, should be considered in each case."

296 *Standard Tankers (Bahamas) Co., Ltd. v. Motor Tank Vessel, AKTI*, 438 F. Supp. 153 (E.D. North Carolina 1977).

297 *Locabail (U.K.) Ltd. v. Bayfield Properties Ltd.*, [2000] QB 451. The law firm had 145 partners.

298 E.g., in Part II, paras. 1.4 and 2.3.6 IBA Guidelines 2014.

299 Explanation to General Standard 6(a).

300 CA Paris, 14 October 2014, Rev. de l'Arb. 2015, 151-155, 152-153. The arguments of publicity also touched on the issue of a potential obligation to investigate, see below chapter 7.1.5.

can demonstrate the importance of the relationship.[301] In addition, the LCIA Court accepted a challenge where the arbitrator disclosed that his law firm previously represented affiliated companies of the respondent in several matters not related to the dispute and without his involvement.[302] The court relied on the general identity of the arbitrator and his or her law firm, at least insofar as their professional activities were concerned.[303] Where the arbitrator's law firm advised a party's affiliate in a matter related to the dispute, the relationship is even closer and likely to result in challenge or annulment.[304] The three latter scenarios are in line with the IBA Guidelines 2014, favouring a conflict where the arbitrator's "firm regularly advises the party, or an affiliate of the party, and the arbitrator or his or her firm derives significant financial income therefrom".[305]

Even in case of a financially intense relationship between the arbitrator's law firm and the affiliate, no conflict of interest arises if the arbitrator's relationship with the law firm is loose.[306] Any law firm conflict requires the analysis of the relationship between the arbitrator and the law firm. To that end, the England and Wales High Court of Justice denied an action for annulment even though there was an intense financial relationship between the arbitrator's law firm and the affiliated company. The High Court reasoned that the arbitrator himself was not involved personally in the relationship but that, in fact, he used the law firm as an independent arbitrator merely for administrative assistance, and the affiliated company was not a parent company.[307] The court explicitly declined to apply the IBA Guidelines 2014 in this matter since they were "not [...] correct".[308] The court's reluctance to apply the IBA Guidelines 2014 is understandable. In pointing at General Standard 6(a), and especially the requested individual approach to law firm contacts, the IBA Guidelines 2014 should not require a definite conflict of interest in the scenario of Part II, para. 1.4, i.e., the Non-Waivable Red List.

Finally, if the relationship between the arbitrator's law firm and the affiliate is not linked to the dispute, and no additional criteria of a conflict of interest are met, the relationship

301 Challenge decision reported in SCAI, *Swiss Rules – Selected Case Law*.
302 LCIA Reference No. UN96/X15, LCIA Court, 29 May 1996, Arb. Int'l 27 (2011), 317-319.
303 The division of the court added that it was in the interest of all parties that the arbitration resulted in a valid award that would not be subject to challenge later for alleged lack of independence and impartiality. Such general argument applies, however, to every arbitral proceeding.
304 Such a challenge was granted by the tribunal in DIS – SV – 217/00, SchiedsVZ 2003, 94-96.
305 Part II, para. 1.4 and Introduction, para. 2 IBA Guidelines 2014.
306 See generally, above chapter 4.1.2.
307 *W Ltd. v. M Sdn Bhd.*, [2016] 1 CLC 437. In addition, the court decided that the facts that the arbitrator did a conflict check and disclosed these and "[t]hat he would have made a disclosure if he had been alerted to the situation involving the affiliate showed a commitment to transparency". His experience as an arbitrator added that his involvement could not lead to a conflict of interest.
308 *W Ltd. v. M Sdn Bhd.*, [2016] 1 CLC 437, 446.

is less likely to give rise to a conflict.[309] However, if there is a link to the dispute in question and the affiliate has an interest in the outcome of the proceedings, a conflict may be affirmed.[310]

4.1.2.2 Relationship between the Arbitrator's Law Firm and Counsel's Law Firm

As with relationships between arbitrators and counsels, relationships between their law firms are rather common. Arbitration involves a group of actively networking arbitrators. Case law on this category deals predominantly with professional ties. In line with the general approach to professional ties of allowing leeway,[311] there is not much case law positively finding a conflict of interest. Generally, the analysis is guided by the directness of the relationship between the two law firms, the connection of this relationship to the dispute, and the proximity in time between the relationship and the arbitration proceeding. Additionally, the analysis in this category of law firms involves the question of whether the arbitrator and counsel each bear the identity of their law firms.

Annulment was not granted where the presiding arbitrator's law firm merged with the law firm of counsel for respondent ten years before the arbitration commenced but separated again after one year.[312] The U.S. Court of Appeals, Fourth Circuit, rejected claimant's allegation that a conflict of interest resulted from respondent's legal representation by its counsel's law firm during that merger. The Court of Appeals, inter alia, relied on the fact that the presiding arbitrator was ill during that year of the merger and was thus not involved. Annulment was also denied where the arbitrator's former law firm represented the same party as counsel for respondent, in litigation proceedings, and one of the attorneys working for the law firm of counsel for respondent was involved in both cases.[313] The U.S. District

309 *NGC Network Asia, LLC v. PAC Pacific Group Intern., Inc.*, 511 Fed.Appx. 86 (2d Cir. 2013), on domestic arbitration, where the arbitrator's law firm had a business relation with a third company and that third company had an indirect, non-controlling ownership interest in claimant. The court denied a conflict of interest since the third company had no management rights or control over claimant. *Gianelli Money Purchase Plan and Trust v. ADM Investor Services Inc.*, 146 F.3d 1309 (11th Cir. 1998), where the arbitrator's law firm had represented an affiliated company to respondent in several disputes in the last 20 years and the last one approximately three years before the current dispute. Depending on the financial intensity in this second decision, it is questionable whether this scenario should not create a conflict of interest.

310 BGer, 27 August 2013, BGE 139 III 433, on Swiss state court proceedings. The judge disclosed that his law firm represented Migros France, a sister company of respondent. Since the dispute dealt with patent issues which were regulated by the mother company, Migros-Genossenschafts-Bund, the close connection and interest of Migros-Genossenschafts-Bund on the outcome of the proceedings precluded a judge from the same law firm as one of Migros-Genossenschafts-Bund's counsels from acting as judge.

311 See above chapter 4.1.1.1.1.

312 *ANR Coal Co., Inc. v. Cogentrix of North Carolina, Inc.*, 173 F.3d 493 (4th Cir. 1999), on domestic arbitration.

313 *Positive Software Solutions, Inc. v. New Century Mortg. Corp.*, 476 F.3d 278 (5th Cir. 2007), 285-286, on domestic arbitration. The litigation proceedings were six different lawsuits, and all took place ten years prior to the arbitration in question.

Court, N.D. Texas, first granted annulment, but the U.S. Court of Appeals, Fifth Circuit, reversed the decision, reasoning that these were "attenuated facts".[314]

Professional ties include business contacts outside the traditional attorney-business. The U.S. Court of Appeals, Second Circuit, denied annulment where the presiding arbitrator was involved in another dispute where his firm was represented by claimant's law firm and an additional dispute where his firm was not directly involved but managed the ship that was the object of the additional dispute.[315] On that latter dispute, the ship's owners were opposed by respondent's law firm and the presiding arbitrator was called as witness and cross-examined. The U.S. Court of Appeals established that, first, the arbitrator fully disclosed the relations; second, the latter case did not involve any of the parties; third, the arbitrator's role was merely being a witness; and, fourth, the maritime business knows only a limited number of people potentially acting as arbitrator. The U.S. District Court previously found that this multitude of connections was an unusual conjunction of contacts and granted annulment.[316]

4.1.2.3 Relationship between the Arbitrator's Law Firm and a Witness

The indirect relationship between the arbitrator's law firm and a witness rarely creates conflicts of interest. It is possible that a law firm operating in a specialised business area faces conflicts with witnesses where that same law firm has other ongoing business relationships or legal disputes with the same witnesses. However, a conflict of interest arises only where these relationships are intense, i.e., close and material enough to justify a challenge.

4.1.2.4 Relationship between the Arbitrator's Law Firm and Another Arbitrator's Law Firm

The relationship between two arbitrators' law firms is even more unlikely to create a conflict of interest. One case granting an annulment of the award was criticised as a "mess of an arbitration".[317] It was a dispute that faced allegations of partiality on grounds of relationships

314 *Positive Software Solutions, Inc. v. New Century Mortg. Corp.*, 476 F.3d 278 (5th Cir. 2007), 285-286.

315 *International Produce, Inc. v. A/S Rosshavet*, 638 F.2d 548 (2d Cir. 1981), on domestic arbitration.

316 *International Produce, Inc. v. A/S Rosshavet*, 504 F.Supp. 736 (S.D. New York 1980). In fact, there was even a third connection: the arbitrator was also vice-president of a firm rendering management services in the same field as the arbitration was dealing with. The U.S. District Court based its decision especially on the arbitrator's function as a witness in the third case. According to the court, "[t]he relationship between a witness and the lawyer cross-examining him may be an intensely adversarial one".

317 M. Zaremski, *The 'Back Story'*, Alternatives To High Cost Litig. 31 (2013), 107-108, 107.

and conduct of the arbitrators.[318] Regarding the conflicts of interest based on relationships, the presiding arbitrator disclosed five years after the commencement of the arbitration that a partner in his law firm was retained as an expert in a malpractice action against the law firm of one of the party-appointed arbitrators. The U.S. District Court, E.D. Michigan, held that although the disclosed facts alone would not require a reasonable person to conclude that the presiding arbitrator was partial, the timing of the disclosures made the relationship particularly troublesome. Stressing the importance of the parties' right to appoint their arbitrator, the court reasoned that "mid-arbitration business relationships undermine the ability of the parties to make informed decisions regarding the members of their arbitration panel".[319] The claimant was deprived of its right to make an informed decision, and the award was ultimately annulled. This decision was rightly criticised.[320] The decision mischaracterises non-disclosure as a ground for dependence and partiality. This approach diminishes the correct differences between disclosure and the standard of independence and impartiality.[321]

4.1.3 Tribunal Secretary's Relationships

4.1.3.1 Status of Tribunal Secretaries

The general use of tribunal secretaries in international arbitration has been a highly debated issue.[322] The pros and cons have been weighed up against each other: strengthening the efficiency of the proceedings versus the risk of a conflicted person judging the dispute.[323] By now, most authorities seem to agree that some involvement of tribunal secretaries assisting the tribunal can be useful and appropriate.[324] Some authors even suggest that tribunal secretaries have an important role as they are "the glue that keeps the whole show on the road".[325]

318 *Thomas Kinkade Co. v. Lighthouse Galleries, LLC*, 2010 WL 436604 (E.D. Michigan), affirmed by *Thomas Kinkade Co. v. White*, 711 F.3d 719 (6th Cir. 2013), on domestic arbitration. For more details on the conduct as a ground for dependence and partiality, see below chapter 4.2.

319 *Thomas Kinkade Co. v. Lighthouse Galleries, LLC*, 2010 WL 436604 (E.D. Michigan), affirmed by *Thomas Kinkade Co. v. White*, 711 F.3d 719 (6th Cir. 2013), on domestic arbitration.

320 E.g., in M. Zaremski, *The 'Back Story'*, Alternatives To High Cost Litig. 31 (2013), 107-108.

321 See below chapter 7.1.4.1.

322 See O. Jensen, *Tribunal Secretaries in International Arbitration*, for an overview.

323 See, e.g., P. Tercier, *The Role of the Secretary to the Arbitral Tribunal*, p. 531 et seq., for a detailed overview, and C. Spalton, *Are Tribunal Secretaries Writing Awards?*, for different voices from practice on pros and cons.

324 In the words of Menz, the market already decided in favour of the use of secretaries, J. Menz, *The Fourth Arbitrator?, Die Rolle des Administrativen Secretary im Scheidsverfahren*, SchiedsVZ 2015, 210-218, 213.

325 M. Hwang, *Introduction, Musings on International Arbitration*, p. 16.

Besides the general debate about whether to use secretaries or not, an additional debate evolved on the appropriate degree of their involvement. The debate focuses on the extent of secretaries' involvement in the arbitrator's core function of decision-making and deliberating. In theory, the secretary may perform any task between administrating and drafting parts of the award, e.g., the procedural history. In practice, secretaries appear to exceed the role of an administrator, sometimes even without the permission of the institution.[326] Multiple surveys on the use of tribunal secretaries reveal that many users approve of tasks including those moving away from pure administration, but, at the same time, would exclude secretaries from deliberations.[327] Where the tribunal secretary is not only involved in administration, he or she may influence the arbitral proceedings. Thus, his or her independence and impartiality are decisive for the process.

4.1.3.1.1 Case Law

Different courts have addressed the role of secretaries. These courts analysed the general role of the arbitrators, what kind of tasks the arbitrator is obliged to perform personally, i.e., the principle of *intuitu personae*, and, ultimately, how the parties' right to appoint an arbitrator influences this analysis.

In 2017, the England and Wales High Court of Justice reflected in depth on the role of the arbitrator and the secretary and concluded

> that the use of a tribunal secretary must not involve any member of the tribunal abrogating or impairing his non-delegable and personal decision-making function. That function requires each member of the tribunal to bring his own personal and independent judgment to bear on the decision in question, taking account of the rival submissions of the parties; and to exercise reasonable diligence in going about discharging that function.[328]

---

326 E.g., C. Spalton, *Are Tribunal Secretaries Writing Awards?*, reporting on a conference where practitioners addressed the use of secretaries and that some colleagues "allow their secretaries to do 'much more' than what is allowed by the ICC". In this regard also J. Menz, *The Fourth Arbitrator?, Die Rolle des Administrativen Secretary im Scheidsverfahren*, SchiedsVZ 2015, 210-218.

327 Young ICCA, *Young ICCA Guide on Arbitral Secretaries*, pp. 2-3, citing the 2013 and 2012 Young ICCA surveys. The 2013 survey revealed that 83.5% of respondents voted against secretaries participating in the deliberations. According to the 2012 survey, 68.8% of users favour secretaries to perform legal research, 60.2% to draft procedural orders, 57% to communicate with the parties and 54.8% to communicate with the institution, and 45.2% favour secretaries drafting parts of the award. Another survey, the 2012 QMUL – White & Case survey, revealed slightly different numbers: 77% of the respondents declared that secretaries communicate with the parties, 70% that secretaries prepare drafts for procedural orders, 47% that secretaries conduct legal research, and 10% that secretaries prepare drafts for substantive parts of the award, QMUL/White & Case, *2012 International Arbitration Survey*, p. 12.

328 *P v. Q, R, S, U*, [2017] EWHC 194 (Comm), para. 65.

The High Court also advised that

> [b]est practice is [...] to avoid involving a tribunal secretary in anything which could be characterised as expressing a view on the substance of that which the tribunal is called upon to decide.[329]

The High Court ruled on a challenge against both co-arbitrators, based on the argument that the arbitrators' workload in hours was below that of the secretary, proving that the co-arbitrators personally failed "to exercise their decision-making functions and responsibilities, and [... improperly delegated] those responsibilities [...] to the Secretary. The functions and responsibilities said to be improperly delegated were adjudicative". However, this presumptive evidence did not convince the High Court, and it rejected the challenge. It also acknowledged that

> performing the adjudicatory function is often an iterative process. There is nothing offensive per se to performance of that function in receiving the views of others, provided the adjudicator makes his own mind up by the exercise of independent judgment.[330]

In 2015, the Swiss *Bundesgericht* recognised the fundamental principle of the arbitrator's mission being personal in nature, i.e., *intuitu personae*, and acknowledged that the core duties and obligations of an arbitrator cannot be delegated. The court ruled that the principle of *intuitu personae* is not violated where the arbitrator uses a secretary to assist him or her if the decision-making authority is not delegated.[331] This is the case where a legal secretary drafts an arbitral award if the draft follows the parameters set out by the arbitrator. Applying these rules to the dispute, the court rejected respondent's annulment action.[332] The dispute involved a sole arbitrator who was not a lawyer but rather the architect of the project in dispute. The sole arbitrator received assistance from a secretary and a consultant, especially on legal procedural matters. The court outlined some of the appropriate tasks undertaken by a secretary: preparing for hearings, organising documents,

329 *P v. Q, R, S, U*, [2017] EWHC 194 (Comm), paras. 67-69.

330 *P v. Q, R, S, U*, [2017] EWHC 194 (Comm), paras. 67-69.

331 BGer, 21 May 2015, 4A_709/2014.

332 The Swiss *Bundesgericht*, inter alia, relied on the arbitrator's statement that he rendered the award and did not delegate his decision-making authority to either the secretary or the consultant. The decision was interpreted as being "more permissive" and liberal regarding appointment and duties of the secretary, J. Menz/A. George, *How Much Assistance Is Permissible?, A Note on the Swiss Supreme Court's Decision on Arbitral Secretaries and Consultants*, J. Int'l Arb. 33 (2016), 311-324, 321. Others criticised the decision for being too vague on the exact line of decision-making authority, T. Timlin, *The Swiss Supreme Court on the Use of Secretaries and Consultants in the Arbitral Process*, YB Arb. Med. 8 (2016), 268-296, 286 et seq.

maintaining the record, and other tasks that might typically be thought of as purely administrative.

Another often cited case when analysing the role of secretaries is the *Yukos* case before the *Rechtbank* Den Haag, although the court was ultimately not required to rule on their role.[333] The court was asked to set aside an award against Russia, inter alia, because of the absence of a valid arbitration agreement and irregularities in the tribunal's composition. The Russian Federation based its action on alleged excess of arbitral authority, failure of substantiation and violation of Dutch *ordre public* and, therefore, alleged deficiencies of the award according to Articles 1065(1)(a)-(e) Dutch BRv. The court granted the action on the very first ground, the absence of a valid arbitration agreement.[334] Therefore, it was not required to address the issue of secretaries and refrained from doing so. Nevertheless, the parties' submissions on the involved secretary's role prompted many authors to address the issue. The Russian Federation's submission challenging the regularity of the secretary's role was based on three pieces of presumptive evidence: first, the fact that the PCA provides administration reveals that the tribunal's secretary was meant to serve on substantive matters; second, the workload of the secretary, in terms of hours spent, was much higher than that of the tribunal; and, third, the fact that the secretary was at the beginning of the proceedings an associate, but at the end, when the award was rendered, a partner at a law firm leads to the assumption that an interaction on substantive matters was likely.[335] The arguments were echoed by different authors. In his criticism, Menz argued that, first, it is not forbidden to charge tribunal secretaries with any substantive tasks, as many surveys support the view that some substantive tasks can be undertaken by secretaries.[336] He added, second, that the hourly workload was not surprising considering the overall document load in the case, and, third, the fact that the secretary was partner at a law firm in the end cannot support the argument since the proceedings lasted ten years. Others interpreted the facts differently, i.e., suggesting that the secretary overstepped the line of appropriate tasks, especially relying on the vast number of hours spent.[337] In addition, it would have been questionable whether the presumptive character of the evidence was strong enough

333 *Russian Federation v. Veteran Petroleum, Ltd., Yukos Universal Ltd. and Hulley Enterprises, Ltd.*, RB Den Haag, 20 April 2016, C/09/477160 / HA ZA 15-1, C/09/477162 / HA ZA 15-2, and C/09/481619 / HA ZA 15-112.

334 The court had to decide whether the Russian Federation was bound by Art. 45(1) ECT, i.e., the provisional application of the ECT, and Art. 26 ECT, i.e., the arbitration agreement. The Russian Federation had signed the ECT but never ratified it. The Dutch court concluded that a provisional application of the ECT was not in accordance with Russian Law and, hence, that no arbitration agreement existed between the parties.

335 The Russian Federation, Writ of Summons Regarding Veteran Petroleum Ltd., paras. 492 et seq.

336 J. Menz, *The Fourth Arbitrator?*, *Die Rolle des Administrativen Secretary im Scheidsverfahren*, SchiedsVZ 2015, 210-218, 212.

337 G. Bermann, *The Yukos Annulment, Answered and Unanswered Questions*, Am. Rev. Int'l Arb. 27 (2016), 1-20, 19 et seq. Bermann clarified, however, that parties can agree on a more substantive role of the secretary.

to meet the burden of proof for setting aside the award under the notion of an irregularly constituted tribunal.[338]

This case law demonstrates that the exact determination of appropriate tasks of the secretary is of paramount importance. All three cases underscore the global importance of the principle of *intuitu personae* and party autonomy in the form of the parties' right to choose their arbitrator, i.e., the "cardinal feature of international arbitration proceedings".[339]

4.1.3.1.2 Rules and Regulations

The principles of *intuitu personae* and party autonomy in the form of the parties' right to choose their arbitrator are also upheld by regulations and guidelines addressing the role of secretaries. However, they grant the arbitrator differing degrees of discretion in delegating tasks to a secretary. At the liberal end of the tableau are the guidelines delivered by Young ICCA in the 2014 report[340] and the HKIAC Rules.[341] Both grant the delegation of more than administrative tasks, especially regarding the attendance of the tribunal's deliberations and the drafting of relevant parts of the award. Both sets of rules also require independence and impartiality of the tribunal secretary.[342] The Young ICCA Task Force highlights in its

---

338 G. Bermann, *The Yukos Annulment, Answered and Unanswered Questions*, Am. Rev. Int'l Arb. 27 (2016), 1-20, 19 et seq.

339 G. Bermann, *The Yukos Annulment, Answered and Unanswered Questions*, Am. Rev. Int'l Arb. 27 (2016), 1-20, 15.

340 Particularly Art. 3(1), and Art. 3(2)(i) and (j), Young ICCA, *Young ICCA Guide on Arbitral Secretaries*, p. 5 and p. 11. They comment that, first, the importance of the principle of the arbitrator's mandate being *intuitu personae* is paramount and 80% of those respondents who opposed the use of arbitral secretaries chose the "[d]erogation from an arbitrator's responsibilities" as the reason for opposition, p. 5. Second, and regarding Art. 3, the report relies on the fact that in practice the use of secretaries is often beyond the mere administrative use, p. 11. It differentiates between attending the deliberations and participating in them, and allows merely the first, since 72.3% of respondents in the 2013 survey supported this, p. 15. The report comments on Art. 3(2)(j) that the efficiency of the proceedings may demand the assistance of the secretary in drafting the award, backed up by 63.5% of the respondents to the 2013 survey allowing some assistance of the secretary, p. 15.

341 According to Art. 13.4 HKIAC Rules, an arbitral tribunal may appoint a secretary "after consulting with the parties", and additional detailed Guidelines on the Use of a Secretary to the Arbitral Tribunal provide that the secretary may attend deliberations, conduct research and draft "non-substantive parts of the tribunal's orders, decisions and awards", provided that the tribunal "ensures that the secretary does not perform any decision-making function or otherwise influence the arbitral tribunal's decisions in any manner", HKIAC Secretary Guidelines, para. 3.4. However, it appears that the tribunal has a veto in appointing the secretary, cf. para. 2.9.

342 Art. 2(3) Young ICCA Guide and Art. 13.4 HKIAC Rules 2018. The Young ICCA Guide additionally states that the "arbitral tribunal shall confirm to the parties that the proposed candidate for arbitral secretary is independent, impartial and free of any conflicts of interest" and, additionally, "shall notify the parties if the circumstances of the arbitral secretary's independence and impartiality change", Young ICCA, *Young ICCA Guide on Arbitral Secretaries*, p. 7. The Guide proceeds: "Although it has not been the historical practice to require an arbitral tribunal to confirm that an arbitral secretary is independent, impartial and free of any conflicts of interest, given the duties and responsibilities of an arbitral secretary in modern international

comment that they "[believe] that the arbitral secretary's independence and impartiality should be the responsibility of the arbitral tribunal" and hence, the tribunal has to confirm to the parties the secretary's independence and impartiality.[343] Moreover, the comment suggests the application of the IBA Guidelines 2014.[344]

A less detailed approach to the regulation of the use of secretaries is found in the rules, codes and guidelines of JAMS,[345] the AAA,[346] ICSID,[347] and UNCITRAL.[348] All briefly state that it is generally possible to use a secretary and highlight the principle of *intuitu personae*. All these rules clarify that the decision-making cannot be delegated to the secretary. The Swiss Rules take the position in Article 15(5) that the provisions on independence and challenge of arbitrators, i.e., Articles 9-11 Swiss Rules, apply to tribunal secretaries. Article 15(5) Swiss Rules grants the tribunal the power to appoint a secretary after

---

arbitration, it is important to ensure their independence and impartiality throughout the course of an arbitration", p. 9. This approach is backed up by results of the 2013 survey, which showed that 83.5% supported a requirement for the arbitral secretary to file a statement of independence and impartiality. The HKIAC Secretary Guidelines provide for a challenge proceeding of the secretary in case of lack of independence and impartiality, similar to that for an arbitrator, HKIAC Secretary Guidelines, para. 2.

343 Young ICCA, *Young ICCA Guide on Arbitral Secretaries*, p. 9. Other approaches are that the secretary submits his or her statement of independence and impartiality to the parties, see, e.g., Sect. 8.2, p. 73.

344 Young ICCA, *Young ICCA Guide on Arbitral Secretaries*, p. 9. The Task Force argues that the Guidelines are "most widely utilized and accepted". 54.2% of respondents in the 2012 Survey support this view.

345 Secretaries acting for JAMS International arbitrators may be assigned with tasks such as "research and/or drafting". The limitation to the assignment is that the secretary may not "engage in deliberations or decision-making on behalf of an arbitrator or tribunal". JAMS, Guidelines for Use of Clerks and Tribunal Secretaries, point 3.

346 Canon VI(B) AAA/ABA Code of Ethics states: "An arbitrator may obtain help from an associate, a research assistant or other persons in connection with reaching his or her decision if the arbitrator informs the parties of the use of such assistance and such persons agree to be bound by the provisions of this Canon." When addressing the arbitrator's role, the Code provides for the need "not [to] delegate the duty to decide to any other person", Canon V(C) AAA/ABA Code of Ethics.

347 Art. 25(d) ICSID Administrative and Financial Regulations provides that the secretary "shall [...] perform other functions with respect to the proceeding at the request of the President of the Commission, Tribunal or Committee, or at the direction of the Secretary-General".

348 UNCITRAL, Notes on Organizing Arbitral Proceedings provide a very broad frame of regulation, para. 35 et seq. They describe that "[s]ome arbitral tribunals wish to have secretaries carry out more substantive functions", para. 36. The listed substantive functions include "legal research and other professional assistance, such as preparing a summary of the facts or the procedural history of the arbitral proceedings, collecting or summarizing case law or published commentaries on legal issues defined by the arbitral tribunal, and preparing draft procedural decisions". The Notes additionally state that "it is recognized that secretaries are not involved and do not participate in the decision-making of the arbitral tribunal, except in certain rare, specialized types of arbitration [...]". Regarding the appointment mechanism, the Notes are similarly broad: "If the arbitral tribunal wishes to appoint a secretary, it would normally disclose this fact to the parties, along with the identity of the proposed secretary, the nature of the tasks to be performed by the secretary, and the amount and source of any proposed remuneration. The parties may wish to agree on the role and practices to be adopted in respect of the secretaries, as well as on the financial conditions applicable to their services", para. 38. The requirement of independence and impartiality, on the other hand, is concretely listed, para. 37.

consultation with the parties. The Swiss Rules do not explicitly address the exact role and the tasks of the secretary.[349] However, the explicit reference to Articles 9-11 Swiss Rules provides legal security to the users with regard to the challenge procedure of secretaries and clarifies the importance of independence and impartiality for secretaries.[350]

Less liberal regarding both or either the role of secretaries and the appointment are guidelines and notes proposed by the ICC, LCIA, SCC, and SIAC. The ICC Note regulates the use of administrative secretaries in detail, devoting chapter XX to them.[351] Similar to the Swiss Rules, the ICC Note clarifies that "administrative secretaries must satisfy the same independence and impartiality requirements as those which apply to arbitrators under the Rules".[352] Where the parties object to the proposed secretary, he or she cannot act as secretary.[353] The scope of tasks allocated to the secretary is limited to "organisational and administrative tasks".[354] The ICC Note explicitly clarifies that

> under no circumstances may the arbitral tribunal delegate its decision-making functions to an administrative secretary or rely on an administrative secretary to perform on its behalf any of the essential duties of an arbitrator.

The approach taken by the LCIA in its rules is rather similar. Article 14A LCIA Rules provides a detailed regulation on tribunal secretaries. Secretaries may be removed by the arbitral tribunal or challenged by the parties.[355] As with the ICC Note, the LCIA Rules forbid delegating the decision-making function to the tribunal secretary.[356] The LCIA further provides a strict appointing mechanism of secretaries, where the parties may veto the appointment.[357] Likewise, in SCC proceedings, the parties may veto the appointment of the secretary, and the tribunal should consult with the parties when defining the role

349 According to Swiss Rules Commentary/C. Jermini/A. Gamba, Art. 15 para. 21, the secretary may not be allowed to exercise any influence on the decisions of the arbitral tribunal and the authors refer to the ICC Note. It remains unclear where the reference to the ICC Note and their importance for interpreting the Swiss Rules come from.

350 Swiss Rules Commentary/C. Jermini/A. Gamba, Art. 15 paras. 21, 21a.

351 Paras. 216-230 ICC Note.

352 Para. 219 ICC Note.

353 Para. 221 ICC Note.

354 Para. 224 ICC Note.

355 Art. 14.15 LCIA Rules.

356 Art. 14.8 sentence 2 LCIA Rules.

357 Art. 14.10 LCIA Rules. See also, LCIA Notes for Arbitrators, para. 74 et seq. Especially, the parties need to confirm the tasks the tribunal wishes to assign to the secretary, para. 71 and Art. 14.10(i) LCIA Rules. The tribunal may propose to the parties that the secretary carries out substantive tasks, but it may not "delegate its fundamental decision-making function", paras. 71 lit. c and 68.

of the secretary.[358] Under SIAC arbitrations, the appointment of secretaries is limited to "appropriate cases", with the "consent of all parties".[359] Although these institutional approaches differ, e.g., on the appointment and the exact role of the secretaries, there is a general standard, namely that the decision-making function cannot be discharged.[360] It is the "core element" of the arbitral process that the decision is the "fruit of the arbitrator's personal commitment".[361] Some of the rules and guidelines allowing the use of tribunal secretaries oblige the arbitrator to monitor or supervise the work of the secretary. For example, the ICC Note reads in para. 222:

> Administrative secretaries act upon the arbitral tribunal's instructions and under its strict and continuous supervision. At all times, the arbitral tribunal is responsible for the administrative secretary's conduct during the arbitration.

Thus, it is the arbitrator who remains responsible for the secretary's performance.[362] Since it is usually the arbitral tribunal that choses the secretary, this approach is reasonable.

Finally, several institutions do not (yet) address the scope of the role of secretaries.[363] If no applicable rules and regulations address the use and degree of involvement of tribunal secretaries, one may draw a comparison with state court assistants.[364] However, regulating the appointment and especially providing for the requirement of independence and

---

358 SCC Arbitrator's Guidelines, Sect. 2, p. 8. The SCC Guidelines take a default approach that "[u]nless the parties agree otherwise, the administrative secretary's duties shall be limited to organizational, clerical and administrative functions". In addition, the Guidelines provide that "[t]he arbitral tribunal may not delegate to the administrative secretary any decision-making or drafting of substantive parts of decisions or awards", and "it is the tribunal's responsibility to ensure that the secretary remains impartial and independent throughout the proceedings. Parties may challenge an administrative secretary on the same basis and according to the procedure that apply to arbitrators".

359 SIAC, Practice Note, PN – 01/17, para. 3 et seq. As C. Spalton, *Tribunal Secretaries*, points out it is not clear whether the final decision on appointment lies with the parties or the tribunal. However, the author interprets the wording in favour of the decision lying with the tribunal.

360 See also, J. Menz/A. George, *How Much Assistance Is Permissible?, A Note on the Swiss Supreme Court's Decision on Arbitral Secretaries and Consultants*, J. Int'l Arb. 33 (2016), 311-324, 320, and G. Bermann, *The Yukos Annulment, Answered and Unanswered Questions*, Am. Rev. Int'l Arb. 27 (2016), 1-20, 16.

361 P. Tercier, *The Role of the Secretary to the Arbitral Tribunal*, p. 539 et seq. The author differentiates "between what an arbitrator must personally *do* and what he or she must personally *oversee*" and concludes that this differentiation is "a legitimate one", emph. add. by the author. However, according to Tercier, even assistance in decision-making is feasible if it is conducted under the responsibility of the arbitrator and in accordance with the specific instructions, p. 541. Concretely, Tercier provides the example that the arbitrator should prepare the first document as basis for future work, and the secretary may assist in making chronology, organising exhibits, writing brief reports and organising witness statements, p. 546.

362 See also, Art. 14.8 sentence 3 LCIA Rules for a similar approach.

363 E.g., the DIS Rules.

364 E.g., C. Partasides, *Secretaries to Arbitral Tribunals*, p. 84; M. Hwang, *Introduction, Musings on International Arbitration*, p. 18 et seq.

impartiality of secretaries tackles potential risks of "undisclosed secretaries"[365] and safeguards the integrity and legitimacy of the arbitral proceedings.[366] The particular advantage of using secretaries, the efficiency of the proceedings regarding costs, time and even enabling the arbitrator to focus on more substantive aspects, are apparent.[367] In addition, allowing the appointment of secretaries provides a valuable training system of young arbitration professionals.[368] The potential risks of arbitrators abusing the use of secretaries, and potentially even violating their personal obligations to render a decision,[369] are handled by a profound regulation of the use of secretaries and a concrete, detailed description of their tasks in assisting in decision-making, but not replacing the decision maker,[370] and supervised by the arbitrator.[371] In light of these advantages, several authors additionally suggested guidelines and best practice statement in the past.[372]

4.1.3.2 Potential Conflicts of Interest in Form of Relationships

A tribunal secretary is an assistant to the arbitrator, operating under the framework set out by the arbitrator. The arbitrator remains responsible for all work provided by the

---

365 J. Menz, *The Fourth Arbitrator?, Die Rolle des Administrativen Secretary im Scheidsverfahren*, SchiedsVZ 2015, 210-218, 214.

366 Cf. Young ICCA, *Young ICCA Guide on Arbitral Secretaries*, p. 1.

367 M. Hwang, *Introduction, Musings on International Arbitration*, p. 16; C. Partasides, *Secretaries to Arbitral Tribunals*, p. 85. In this regard also, T. Timlin, *The Swiss Supreme Court on the Use of Secretaries and Consultants in the Arbitral Process*, YB Arb. Med. 8 (2016), 268-296, 270-271.

368 T. Clay, *Le secretaire arbitral*, Rev. de l'Arb. 2005, 931-957, 931.

369 T. Timlin, *The Swiss Supreme Court on the Use of Secretaries and Consultants in the Arbitral Process*, YB Arb. Med. 8 (2016), 268-296, 272-273. The author stresses that this, in addition, violates the parties' right to appoint their arbitrator.

370 C. Partasides, *Secretaries to Arbitral Tribunals*, p. 85. Tercier points out that such general criticism reveals a general "suspicion" towards arbitration, since the criticism targets the arbitrator chosen by the parties as their trusted expert, P. Tercier, *The Role of the Secretary to the Arbitral Tribunal*, p. 542. Cf. M. Polkinghorne/C. Rosenberg, *The Role of the Tribunal Secretary in International Arbitration*, Disp. Res. Int'l 8 (2014), 107-128.

371 J. Menz, *The Fourth Arbitrator?, Die Rolle des Administrativen Secretary im Scheidsverfahren*, SchiedsVZ 2015, 210-218, 217, who highlights that a trustworthy personality of the arbitrator is more decisive than regulation.

372 Hwang proposes the following precise guidelines: "(a) By defining the points or law and/or issues in dispute as well as specifying the areas of factual inquiry, the Tribunal will be retaining control of the decision-making process. The Tribunal will thus restrict the Legal Assistant to highly structured and closely supervised tasks. (b) The Tribunal will also retain control of the decision-making process by subjecting the Legal Assistant's output to critical review. (c) The Tribunal's reliance on the Legal Assistant's work product is acceptable so long as the Tribunal does not forgo its review of the parties' written submissions and the evidence. (d) The Tribunal will retain the ultimate responsibility for the Award since the Legal Assistant will only be asked to prepare an early draft of the formal and uncontroversial parts of any decision or award made by the Tribunal, which draft will be subject to the final approval of the Tribunal", M. Hwang, *Introduction, Musings on International Arbitration*, p. 17.
C. Partasides/N. Bassiri/U. Gantenberg/L. Bruton/A. Riccio, *Arbitral Secretaries*, p. 338 et seq., suggest guidelines for a statement of best practice, including regulations on the appointment, the role, setting out a list of what an arbitral secretary can legitimately do and a list of what a secretary should not do, and costs.

secretary.[373] Therefore, the secretary must generally be placed in a position similar to that of the arbitrator for evaluating conflicts of interest.[374] Irrespective of the nature of the task of the secretary and the concrete role, his or her work may influence the arbitral proceeding.[375] His or her partiality or dependence may put the integrity of the whole proceedings at risk. This understanding is highlighted by the parties' right to challenge the tribunal secretary, explicitly named in the LCIA and Swiss Rules.[376]

In line with the Young ICCA Guidelines, the IBA Guidelines 2014 should be applied to supplement other applicable rules and guidelines to analyse and judge potential conflicts of interest of secretaries.[377] The IBA Guidelines 2014

> seek to balance the various interests of parties, representatives, arbitrators and arbitration institutions, all of whom have a responsibility for ensuring the integrity, reputation and efficiency of international arbitration.[378]

They aim to "assist parties, practitioners, arbitrators, institutions and courts in dealing with the [...] important questions of impartiality and independence".[379] To efficiently adhere to this purpose of the IBA Guidelines 2014, they should be applied in addition to other rules and guidelines in scenarios dealing with tribunal secretaries. Secretaries are included in the scope of the IBA Guidelines 2014.[380] Additionally, and with regard to conflicts of interest based on relationships, an analysis of the general criteria may be helpful – namely the directness of the relationship between the tribunal secretary and one of the parties, counsels, arbitrators, witnesses or experts, the connection of the relationship

---

373 Cf. Art. 1(5) and the comment, Young ICCA, *Young ICCA Guide on Arbitral Secretaries*, pp. 6-7; *P v. Q, R, S, U*, [2017] EWHC 194 (Comm), para. 31, stating, "it is normal for a Secretary to work under the direct supervision of the Chairman, who will give multiple written and oral instructions to the Secretary in relation to the work which he/she wants the Secretary to do. The Secretary's job (among other things) is to assist the Chairman to prepare the work product for the review of the co-arbitrators. It is unnecessary and impractical for the co-arbitrators to be apprised of all communications between the Chairman and the Secretary".

374 But see, T. Clay, *Le secretaire arbitral*, Rev. de l'Arb. 2005, 931-957, 947 et seq., differentiating between the tribunal secretary and the arbitral tribunal in some scenarios, e.g., with regard to ex parte communication.

375 One may argue that this positioning with the arbitrator is applicable only where the tasks fulfilled by the secretary are substantive or nearly substantive. However, such a differentiation is not convincing, since, first, the arbitrator is also responsible for the secretaries' purely administrative tasks and, second, a conflict of interest may also arise in conduct scenarios.

376 Art. 14.15 LCIA Rules; Arts. 15(5) and 10 Swiss Rules.

377 Young ICCA, *Young ICCA Guide on Arbitral Secretaries*, p. 9. See also, O. Jensen, *Tribunal Secretaries in International Arbitration*, para. 4.50.

378 IBA Guidelines 2014, Introduction para. 4.

379 IBA Guidelines 2014, Introduction para. 6.

380 General Standard 5(b) IBA Guidelines 2014.

to the dispute, and the proximity in time between the relationship and the arbitration proceeding.

The tribunal secretary may have social or professional ties that create a conflict of interest. Generally, when positioning a secretary with a tribunal, similar potential conflicts of interest may arise for the secretary as for the arbitrators. Thus, intense personal or professional relationships to either of the parties or affiliates of the parties may create a conflict of interest.[381] Since tribunal secretaries are most often junior lawyers,[382] the proximity of their relationship with one counsel, his or her law firm, or one of the parties can be an issue. Secretaries may have worked as an intern previously for one of the parties, their counsels or their law firms. An ICSID Tribunal accepted the challenge of a tribunal secretary who interned with the claimant's counsel long before he joined the ICSID staff.[383] In these internship scenarios whether an issue of independence and impartiality exists or not will depend on the financial interest, and the hierarchy or subordination.[384] Where close social ties have evolved from the internship, there can be a reason to argue in favour of a conflict of interest. Social or professional ties between the secretary and an expert or witness should be addressed in parallel to arbitrators.[385]

Regarding the relationships of secretaries with arbitrators, it is questionable whether they should be treated like relationships between two arbitrators. The relationship between two arbitrators has led at least to allegations of conflicts of interest where an unusual hierarchy and subordination existed.[386] The very nature of secretaries is, however, to work under the supervision of the arbitrators, usually in subordination and hierarchy. The secretary has to fulfil tasks allocated by the arbitrator(s). Hierarchy and subordination are inherent to the secretaries' role. Concluding that a conflict of interest exists in case of hierarchy and subordination between the secretary and the arbitrator would contradict this role. Even

381 See generally for these categories, above chapters 4.1.1.1.1 and 4.1.1.1.7.

382 C. Partasides/N. Bassiri/U. Gantenberg/L. Bruton/A. Riccio, *Arbitral Secretaries*, p. 333.

383 In ICSID arbitrations the ICSID staff acts as secretary. See *Víctor Pey Casado and Foundation President Allende v. Republic of Chile*, ICSID Tribunal, 18 May 2014, ICSID Case No. ARB/98/2, Annex 2, para. 12 for the facts of the challenge and *Víctor Pey Casado and Foundation President Allende v. Republic of Chile*, ICSID Tribunal, 21 February 2017, ICSID Case No. ARB/98/2, on the challenge itself. However, it remains unclear whether the tribunal was convinced that the scenario met the threshold of dependence and partiality or whether the arbitrators regarded the secretary's role not as important to not challenge him, O. Jensen, *Tribunal Secretaries in International Arbitration*, para. 7.16.

384 Potentially denying a conflict of interest for most instances: O. Jensen, *Tribunal Secretaries in International Arbitration*, para. 7.17, with the argument that there will be no financial interest or loyalty with a law firm the secretary has already left.

385 See above chapters 4.1.1.1.1 and 4.1.1.1.7.

386 Although the aforementioned scenarios did not lead to positive challenges, the courts and tribunals faced with the argument did not decide that this allegation would generally be impossible to create a conflict of interest. See in general above chapter 4.1.1.4.

the rather theoretical risk that the presiding arbitrator might use the secretary to pursue a hierarchy upon the co-arbitrators could be tackled by a system where secretaries provide assistance and are supervised by the whole arbitral tribunal.[387]

4.1.4 Counsel's Relationships

Counsel's relationships are not directly at issue when analysing conflicts of interest creating risks for the independence and impartiality of the arbitral proceedings. Counsels are not decision makers, do not have the judicial function of arbitrators, and, hence, the standard of independence and impartiality applied to arbitrators does not apply to them.[388] According to the England and Wales High Court of Justice,

> it is the duty of counsel to advance the case of his client within the limits of his professional responsibilities, while it is the duty of the arbitrator to adjudicate impartially between the parties.[389]

Counsels are, however, involved in the arbitrator's independence and impartiality.

4.1.4.1 Potential Conflicts of Interest

Relationships between counsels and arbitrators may lead to a conflict of interest.[390] Where a counsel joins the arbitral proceeding after the constitution of the arbitral tribunal, and this counsel creates a conflict of interest with one of the arbitrators, the question arises as to whether the counsel should refrain from joining the arbitral proceedings.[391] The parties' right to choose their counsel and the parties' right to appoint their arbitrator may collide here.[392] The IBA Guidelines 2013 require counsels to act accordingly. Guideline 5 IBA Guidelines 2013 provides that

> [o]nce the Arbitral Tribunal has been constituted, a person should not accept representation of a Party in the arbitration when a relationship exists between

387 The latter is proposed by Young ICCA, *Young ICCA Guide on Arbitral Secretaries*, pp. 6-7, in order to tackle the risk of the presiding arbitrator diluting his or her mandate.

388 See below chapter 6.1, for the evaluation of the standard for arbitrators.

389 *Laker Airways Inc. v. FLS Aerospace Ltd.*, [1999] CLC 1124; affirmative N. Andrews/J. Landbrecht, *Schiedsverfahren und Mediation in England*, paras. 104-105.

390 See above chapter 4.1.1.1.

391 See below chapter 7.3.3, on the arbitral tribunal's possibility to order the exclusion of a counsel.

392 See generally on this collusion, J. Waincymer, *Reconciling Conflicting Rights in International Arbitration*, Arb. Int'l 26 (2010), 597-624.

> the person and an Arbitrator that would create a conflict of interest, unless none of the Parties objects after proper disclosure.

And according to Guideline 6,

> [t]he Arbitral Tribunal may, in case of breach of Guideline 5, take measures appropriate to safeguard the integrity of the proceedings, including the exclusion of the new Party Representative from participating in all or part of the arbitral proceedings.

This position is criticised in scholarly writing as "unusual" and doubtfully reflecting "either customary practice or the professional obligations of counsel under most national codes of conduct".[393] The IBA Guidelines 2013 do not, however, address the issue of conflicts of interest.

In addition, counsels may try to communicate ex parte with one of the arbitrators, potentially creating a conflict of interest.[394] Depending on the counsel's intention, such behaviour can be categorised as guerrilla tactics.[395] The lack of sufficient regulation of counsel's ethics in international arbitration may facilitate such guerrilla tactics.

> Differences in ethical obligations that give a party an advantage are problematic and the size of the amount at stake can drive counsel over the line from zealous representation to guerrilla tactics.[396]

These references demonstrate that counsel's work may contribute to safeguarding the integrity of the arbitral process, i.e., a judicial process. The Swiss *Bundesgericht* reasoned that the principle of counsel's independence is a prerequisite for the client's trust in the judiciary.[397] Counsels are integral participants in arbitration. Thus, it is not surprising that scholars understand today's concept of independence and impartiality in a way that the

393 G. Born, *International Commercial Arbitration*, p. 3100.

394 See below chapter 4.2.2, for counsel's conduct relevant for conflicts of interest. See also, J. Waincymer, *Regulatory Developments in the Control of Counsel in International Arbitration*, Arb. Int'l 30 (2014), 513-552, 516, for additional scenarios.

395 See below chapter 4.2.1.7, for tactical challenges.

396 E. Sussman, *Can Counsel Ethics Beat Guerrilla Tactics?*, Rev. Brasileira Arb. 10 (2013), 98-105, 102. See also, A. Mourre, *FS Karrer*, p. 239 et seq., on the use of the IBA Guidelines 2013 as a flexible tool of soft law.

397 The Swiss *Bundesgericht* highlighted the counsel's role in BGer, 10 December 2004, BGE 131 I 223, 232, on state court litigation.

> actual and the perceived neutrality of the arbitrators [...] extends not only towards the parties in the case, but also towards the parties' legal representatives and others involved in or affected by the proceeding, e.g., a real party in interest, the principal witnesses, or the experts.[398]

Depending on the country of admission to the bar, counsels are respectively bound by ethical rules and guidelines. Accordingly, conflicts of interest may arise under national laws precluding counsels from representing parties in certain matters because of their responsibilities to other parties or their personal responsibilities.[399] In the following, only the involvement of third-party funders will be addressed as a practical example.

4.1.4.2 Involvement of a Third-Party Funder

Involvement of a third-party funder may not only raise issues of conflicts of interest for arbitrators[400] but may, additionally, include potential conflicts of interest between the counsel, the third-party funder and the funded party, as it may affect the relationship between the counsel and the funded party. Legal systems that regard acting as counsel as an independent profession restrict the use of third-party funding. The degree of control of the funder in the dispute may collide with the counsel's function. Here, issues of conflict may arise. Where the funder strategically advises the funded party or its counsel, e.g., in selecting the counsel and controlling the case strategy and management, it influences the relationship between counsel and the funded party.[401] Similarly, a conflict of interest may arise where arbitrator A in arbitration 1 is also counsel for the claimant in arbitration 2, and in both proceedings the same funder backs different claimants.[402] Also, settlement negotiations may create a potential conflict between the interests of the funder and the funded party and may interfere with counsel's rights.[403]

Some of the national rules and guidelines addressing counsel's role explicitly address third-party funding, though primarily in the context of state court proceedings.

398 D. Lawson, *Impartiality and Independence of International Arbitrators, Commentary on the 2004 IBA Guidelines on Conflicts of Interest in International Arbitration*, ASA Bull. 2005, 22-45, 25.

399 G. Born, *International Commercial Arbitration*, p. 3099.

400 See above chapter 4.1.1.1.10.

401 G. Born, *International Commercial Arbitration*, p. 3100.

402 See above chapter 4.1.1.1.10, for the solution of this example from the arbitrator's perspective.

403 L. Barrington, *FS Karrer*, p. 19.

In the United Kingdom, the ALF Code of Conduct[404] includes rules on the party-counsel relationship. Particularly, paras. 9.2 and 9.3 demand the funder to refrain from controlling the dispute and, generally, from taking steps "that cause or are likely to cause the Funded Party's solicitor or barrister to act in breach of their professional duties".[405] In the civil law systems of France, Germany, and Switzerland, lawyers are obliged to act in a "liberal and independent" manner.[406] As a consequence, counsels may not be controlled by the funder when advising their clients. Similarly, the New York Rules of Professional Conduct[407] forbid compensation from a person other than the client[408] and highlight the "independent professional judgment" of counsel.[409] Thus, these approaches coincide to the extent that a funder should not control the case to the detriment of the funded party.

It is questionable at what point the funder's control and dominance creates a conflict of interest impairing the integrity of the arbitral process. Where the counsel acts for the funder, i.e., the counsel primarily regards the funder's interest, the threshold for a conflict of interest will be crossed.[410] Moreover, final decisions on the legal strategy of the case and the management should be taken by the counsel.[411] These issues may be addressed and, ideally, prevented by regulation in the funding agreement. This agreement may help to clarify the rights and obligations of the funder, the counsel, and the funded party. To the extent possible, the parties should address these rights and obligations precisely in the funding agreement.[412]

---

404 The Code of Conduct applies to all third-party funders that are members in the Association of Litigation Funders. Although the Code expressly only addresses litigation funders, many of these also fund arbitration cases. There is no reason why the same funders funding an arbitration should act different in arbitration.

405 Additionally, in England and Wales, the SRA Code of Conduct regulates in chapter 3 conflicts of interest and provides additional guidelines. The SRA Code of Conduct accompanies ten mandatory SRA Principles, regulating the conduct of solicitors and their employees, registered European lawyers, recognised bodies and their managers and employees, and licensed bodies and their managers and employees. The SRA Code of Conduct is available at https://sra.org.uk/solicitors/handbook/code/content.page.

406 Art. 1.1 French RIN: "*La profession d'avocat est une profession libérale et indépendante quel que soit son mode d'exercice.*" Translation: "The legal profession is a liberal and independent profession, regardless of how it is practised." § 1 German BRAO: "*Der Rechtsanwalt ist ein unabhängiges Organ der Rechtspflege.*" Translation: "A Rechtsanwalt is an independent organ in the administration of justice." And Art. 12(b) Swiss BGFA: "*[Anwältinnen und Anwälte] üben ihren Beruf unabhängig, in eigenem Namen und auf eigene Verantwortung aus.*" Translation: "[Anwältinnen und Anwälte] exercise their profession independently, in their own name and on their own responsibility."

407 In the United States, the applicable law or code of conduct depends on the States.

408 Rule 1.8(f) New York Rules of Professional Conduct, naming a few exceptions. One exception is that there is no interference with the counsel's "independent professional judgment or with the client-lawyer relationship".

409 Rule 2 New York Rules of Professional Conduct. See also, Rule 5.4 New York Rules of Professional Conduct.

410 BGer, 22 January 2015, 2C_814/2014. Additionally, counsel's employment by the third-party funder is forbidden in Switzerland: Art. 8(1)(d) Swiss BGFA.

411 L. Bench Nieuwveld/V. Shannon Sahani, *Third-party Funding in International Arbitration*, pp. 108-109.

412 O. Gayner/A. Croft/K. Hurford, *Third-party Funding for International Arbitration Claims Practical Tips.*

Another possible conflict may arise where the counsel has a financial interest in the third-party funder, e.g., through a partnership or shares.[413] Depending on the applicable rules and guidelines, and the intensity of the financial interest, such a scenario may constitute a conflict of interest.[414] Also, conflicts of interest may arise with regard to due diligence and portfolio claims. It is advisable that the due diligence law firm does not act as counsel for the funded party, and, at least in jurisdictions with strict ethical regulations for counsels, that the same counsel acts for all disputes in portfolios, in order to prevent conflicts of interest.

The mere existence of third-party funding does not create a conflict of interest for the counsel. Arguing that counsels generally prefer a good relationship with any funder for future business, and thus would primarily regard the funder's interest, cannot convince on such a general basis. To the contrary, the Swiss *Bundesgericht* held that a general advantage of third-party funding is that the funded party could benefit from the additional legal expertise.[415]

4.1.5 *Expert's Relationship*

Like counsels, experts are not decision makers. Experts appear before an arbitral tribunal to provide an expert analysis or opinion on specific issues determined by a party or the arbitral tribunal, e.g., calculation of damages or the applicable law.

> Unlike fact witnesses, expert witnesses do not testify about events in which they were personally involved. The role of the expert witness is to provide opinion evidence to assist the tribunal in understanding and deciding specialised issues that go beyond the ordinary experience and knowledge of the layperson.[416]

Usually, both the tribunal and the parties have the right to appoint experts.[417] Even though the application of independence and impartiality deviates between party-appointed and tribunal-appointed experts, it is, first, questionable within both groups whether experts

413 See, e.g., OLG München, 31 March 2015, 15 U 2227/14, NJW-RR 2015, 1333-1338.

414 In OLG München, 31 March 2015, 15 U 2227/14, NJW-RR 2015, 1333-1338, the court stated that such an indirect payment may constitute a violation of the German principle to forbid *quota litis*. In the concrete case, however, the court was only asked to declare the funding agreement void in general. This request was denied.

415 BGer, 10 December 2004, BGE 131 I 223, 238. See also, J. von Goeler, *Third-party Funding*, p. 271.

416 M. Burianski/A. Lang, *"Challenges" to Party-Appointed Experts*, SchiedsVZ 2017, 269-277, 270.

417 According to the CIArb Guideline on Experts, Preamble, p. 1, the individual appointment by each party is the most frequent method used in international arbitration. This CIArb Guideline on Experts highlights that the appointment is an integral part of the parties' right to submit evidence and to be heard.

must be independent and impartial and what the applicable standards are.[418] Second, where requirements of independence and impartiality apply (to some extent), the expert's relationships may create a conflict of interest. This will depend on the directness of the relationship between the expert and one party or an affiliate, its counsel or the arbitrator, the connection of the relationship to the dispute, and the proximity in time between the relationship and the arbitration proceeding.

4.1.5.1 Tribunal-Appointed Experts

Tribunal-appointed experts are not decision makers but assist the tribunal in arriving at a decision.[419] They "report [...] on specific issues designated by the Arbitral Tribunal".[420] An ICSID Tribunal even stated that the tribunal-appointed expert's "role forms part of the adjudicative process".[421] Where experts participate in the adjudicative process, these experts must be independent and impartial.[422] Similarly, courts reviewing arbitral proceedings in France,[423] Germany,[424] and Switzerland[425] generally apply the obligation of arbitrators and judges to act independently and impartially to tribunal-appointed experts.[426] Additionally, the CIArb Guideline on Experts suggests that tribunal-appointed experts shall be independent and impartial.[427]

The expert's relationships with a party are similarly treated as relationships of arbitrators and parties. The expert may not have close social ties or intense financial interests in the

418 For an analysis of the applicable standard for experts, see below chapter 6.6. A majority of 69% of the respondents in QMUL/White & Case, *2018 International Arbitration Survey*, Chart 38, p. 34, favours the regulation of standards for independence and impartiality for experts in arbitration rules. The survey explains this result with an increasing role of experts in arbitration proceedings, pp. 33-34.

419 C. Brunner, *Note – Federal Supreme Court, 28 April 2000*, ASA Bull. 2000, 566-581, 577, referring to BGer, 28 April 2000, BGE 126 III 249. Brunner defines experts as "auxiliary persons of the tribunal". See also, BSK BV/J. Reich, Art. 30 para. 8.

420 Art. 6(1) sentence 1 IBA Rules 2020.

421 *Bridgestone Licensing Services, Inc. and Bridgestone Americas, Inc. v. Republic of Panama*, ICSID Tribunal, 13 December 2018, ARB/16/34, paras. 14-39.

422 See, e.g., Art. 6(1) sentence 1 IBA Rules 2020; LCIA Note to Arbitrators, Sect. 9, para. 84; *Bridgestone Licensing Services, Inc. and Bridgestone Americas, Inc. v. Republic of Panama*, ICSID Tribunal, 13 December 2018, ARB/16/34, paras. 14-39. See also, BSK BV/J. Reich, Art. 30, para. 8, applying the requirement of independence and impartiality for decision makers to experts by analogy.

423 E.g., Cass civ 2ème, 21 January 2010, 09-10144.

424 E.g., BGH, 2 May 2017, I ZB 1/16, SchiedsVZ 2017, 317-323.

425 E.g., BGer, 28 April 2000, BGE 126 III 249, 253-256.

426 Some of these countries foresee in their national arbitration laws that the obligation to disclose, and to be independent and impartial, applies to experts: § 1049(3) German ZPO; Switzerland: no statute but an analogy to Art. 30(1) Swiss BV and Art. 6 ECHR. For more details on the applicable standard of independence and impartiality, see below chapter 6.1.

427 Commentary on Art. 3 CIArb Guideline on Experts.

outcome of the proceedings.[428] Hence, the appointment of a close friend and colleague as expert witness can be rejected.[429] Difficulties may arise with regard to reappointments. Generally, where the expert is repeatedly appointed and intense financial relationships and professional ties are present, a conflict of interest may exist.[430] However, experts may be even more specialised and limited in number than arbitrators. Thus, repeat appointments may occur more often for specialised experts. Case law on repeat appointments is divergent. On the one hand, the French *cour de cassation* denied the challenge of an expert in state court proceedings between a tenant and a landlord, although the expert previously provided opinions in favour of other landlords in the same neighbourhood.[431] On the other hand, also in French case law, the French *cour de cassation* reversed a decision that denied a challenge of an expert chosen by the court who was appointed previously by a competitor of one of the parties in the same field of expertise.[432] The court of first instance decided that a rather small number of previous interactions between a competitor and the expert cannot establish a "relationship of subordination or economic dependence".[433] The French *cour de cassation* reversed this decision without providing detailed arguments.[434] Further, a lawsuit between the expert and one party was found to raise a conflict of interest.[435]

A relationship between the expert and a third-party funder may also arise to a conflict of interest. For example, it is possible that it is not the party or counsel that (repeatedly) suggests the appointment of one expert, but the third-party funder. Depending on the intensity of the relationship, a conflict of interest may exist. The expert's potential lack of an open mind, and therefore a lack of objectivity together with a financial interest in the relationship with the third-party funder, can be significant. Similar to conflicts involving counsels and third-party funders,[436] one may argue that, theoretically, the expert has a high interest in preserving a relationship with the funder in order to guarantee reappointments. One may conclude, therefore, that the expert will provide an opinion within the interest

428 BGer, 28 April 2000, BGE 126 III 249, 253-256. See also, BSK IPRG/S. Pfisterer, Art. 190 para. 103.
429 *Liverpool Roman Catholic Archdiocesan Trustees Incorporated v. David Goldberg Q.C.*, [2002] TCLR 4, on state court proceedings.
430 See above chapter 4.1.1.1.2, for repeat appointments of arbitrators.
431 Cass civ 2ème, 21 January 2010, 09-10144, on state court proceedings.
432 Cass civ 2ème, 5 December 2002, 01-00224, on state court proceedings.
433 See Cass civ 2ème, 5 December 2002, 01-00224, on state court proceedings.
434 The French *cour de cassation* only reasoned that Art. 341 French CPC is not exhaustive on the grounds for challenging an expert and that the expert had to be impartial.
435 Cf. Cass civ 2ème, 13 October 2005, 04-10834, regarding state court proceedings. According to the court, the existence of a lawsuit constitutes a peremptory cause for a challenge, without distinguishing whether the trial was instituted before or after the commencement of the expert's investigation or whether it derives its reasoning from facts not related to the course of operations.
436 See above chapter 4.1.4.2.

of the funder that is no longer objective. However, the mere existence of third-party funding cannot lead to such a conclusion.

Besides these scenarios where the expert had a potential relationship with a party, the expert may also have relationships with one of the arbitrators or counsels. An expert repeatedly appearing before the same arbitrator usually does not provide a ground for dependence or partiality, since the expert assists the arbitrator. If, however, an arbitrator consistently appoints the same expert, knowing or predicting the outcome of the expert's opinion, the open-mindedness of the arbitrator may be called into question. The arbitrator may face the criticism of prejudging the case.[437] Finally, scenarios of potential relationships with one of the counsels are to be treated like relationships between arbitrators and counsels.

4.1.5.2 Party-Appointed Experts

In contrast to tribunal-appointed experts, party-appointed experts are individually appointed and paid for by the parties. They provide evidence in support of that party's case.[438] The right to use an expert witness is covered by the parties' right to be heard and to present their case, protected, inter alia, by Article 18 UNCITRAL Model Law.[439] Party-appointed experts are comparable to witnesses. Their relationships with the party appointing them are less significant and will usually not create a conflict of interest. However, since the expert's role is to provide their genuinely held and sincere professional opinion,[440] while the arbitral tribunal has to "determine the admissibility, relevance, materiality and weight of evidence",[441] an intense relationship between the arbitrator and the expert may impair this determination. Comparing party-appointed and tribunal-appointed experts, one may conclude that for tribunal-appointed experts the relationship with the parties or counsels may be rather crucial and that for party-appointed experts the crucial relationship is that with the arbitrator. In line with this approach, the Iran-U.S. Claims Tribunal rejected the challenge of claimant's party-appointed expert in *Sedco Inc. v. Iranian National Oil Co. and the Islamic Republic of Iran*, holding that the existence of a master-servant relationship between the expert and the claimant alone did not render the expert unreliable, but could have caused subjectivity.[442]

437 Primarily, this is an issue of the arbitrator's conduct. See in more detail below chapter 4.2.

438 *Bridgestone Licensing Services, Inc. and Bridgestone Americas, Inc. v. Republic of Panama*, ICSID Tribunal, 13 December 2018, ARB/16/34, where the parties' right to be heard and present their case is upheld by the possibility to appoint an expert. See also, M. Altenkirch/R. Raheja, *Quo Vadis Party-appointed Experts?*, on the criticism raised on party-appointed experts and possible solutions.

439 See above chapter 4.1.1.2, for witnesses.

440 Art. 8(4) IBA Rules 2020; G. Born, *International Commercial Arbitration*, p. 2452.

441 Art. 9(1) IBA Rules 2020.

442 *Sedco Inc. v. Iranian National Oil Co. and the Islamic Republic of Iran*, Iran-U.S. Claims Tribunal, Award, 7 July 1987 – No. 309-129-3, para. 75.

This does not leave the party-appointed expert without duties. The CIArb Guideline on Experts generally requires the expert's opinion to be impartial and objective.[443] Finding a balance between the remaining need for objectivity and neutrality of party-appointed experts and a potential consequence of a conflict of interest with party-appointed experts, an ICSID Tribunal established that

> [a] party-appointed expert witness will normally be, and be expected to be, independent of the party calling him. The best expert witnesses will also be impartial. They will give their evidence honestly and objectively in accordance with their sincere beliefs and experience. Judges and arbitrators are familiar, however, with the expert witness whose evidence manifestly lacks objectivity and favours the party paying his fees. An appearance of partiality does not result in the disqualification of an expert witness. It detracts from the weight that the Tribunal will accord to his evidence.[444]

Therefore, where a party-appointed expert appears dependent and partial towards its nominating party, the tribunal may include its observance in its determination of the admissibility, relevance, materiality, and weight of the evidence.[445] To avoid this consequence as well as increased costs and conflicting views from different party-appointed experts, the CIArb Guideline on Experts recommends having either one jointly party-appointed or, where appropriate, a tribunal-appointed expert.[446]

4.2 Conduct

Besides relationships, the conduct of actors involved in an arbitral proceeding may demonstrate a conflict of interest and provide a ground for finding dependence and

443 Art. 4.1 CIArb Protocol for the Use of Party-Appointed Expert Witnesses in International Arbitration.

444 *Bridgestone Licensing Services, Inc. and Bridgestone Americas, Inc. v. Republic of Panama*, ICSID Tribunal, 13 December 2018, ARB/16/34, where the tribunal was additionally faced with the question of whether the expert can be challenged due to breach of privilege. It ruled that the communication between a party seeking an expert and the potential expert is not privileged.

445 See below chapter 7.3.1, on the exclusion of experts.

446 Preamble, p. 2, CIArb Guideline on Experts. Additionally, this approach circumvents issues that arose in *Flughafen Zürich AG and Gestión e Ingeniería IDC SA v. Republic of Venezuela*, ICSID Tribunal, 29 August 2012, ICSID Case No. ARB/10/19, where an expert was appointed by respondent after having already received information related to the case from the claimants, who considered retaining the expert as well, but eventually decided against it. The claimants challenged the expert on the grounds that he was in possession of allegedly confidential documents, which included the contract, the claimants' business plan and damages calculations, as well as the request for arbitration. See below chapter 7.3.1, on the exclusion of experts.

partiality.[447] The parties' right to have a fair proceeding, including equal treatment, demands unbiased conduct. Even though conduct is less persuasive or more difficult to prove compared with relationships,[448] it is often argued by parties, and much case law has evolved. Conduct usually needs to show a certain degree of intensity to constitute a conflict of interest that grants a challenge or annulment. A dominant style in handling the proceedings is not enough, at least if no violation of the right to be heard is apparent.[449]

In the following section, the main focus is on the arbitrator's conduct as the most common scenario for finding a conflict of interest.[450] Additionally, the conduct of tribunal secretaries and consultants will be addressed. The conduct of experts, institutions, counsels, and parties is less frequently an issue since their role in the proceedings differs fundamentally from that of the arbitrators as decision makers.[451]

4.2.1 *Arbitrator's Conduct*

The conduct of the arbitrator is a frequent ground for challenges and annulments.[452] The arbitrator's conduct in granting or denying procedural orders; when providing guidance or even settlement options for the parties; when communicating with one of the parties or their counsels ex parte, are just a few examples. However, the conduct of arbitrators may generally only rise to a conflict of interest if, under objective consideration, its content or the way of communication reveals special sympathy or antipathy or unequal treatment of parties.[453]

447 Conduct may also give rise to other grounds for annulment, e.g., misconduct under Sect. 10(a)(3) FAA; excess of power under Art. 1520(3) French CPC, Art. 190(2)(a) Swiss IPRG, Sect. 10(a)(4) FAA; or violation of public policy under Art. 1520(5) French CPC, or § 1059(2)(b) German ZPO.

448 Cf. *Ostrom v. Worldventures Marketing, LLC*, 60 F.Supp.3d 942 (M.D. Louisiana 2016). The decision on domestic arbitration stated that conduct is seldom used to demonstrate evident partiality.

449 C. Armbrüster/V. Wächter, *Ablehnung von Schiedsrichtern wegen Befangenheit im Verfahren*, SchiedsVZ 2017, 213-223, 216. See also, KG Berlin, 7 June 2010, 20 SchH 2/10, SchiedsVZ, 225-227.

450 Cf. C. Armbrüster/V. Wächter, *Ablehnung von Schiedsrichtern wegen Befangenheit im Verfahren*, SchiedsVZ 2017, 213-223, 216.

451 Experts' support of arbitrators in decision-making is limited to providing their expert opinions. There is, hence, not much room for showing bias in conduct. On the issue of expert's relationships, see above chapters 4.1.1.3 and 4.1.5. Institutions, on the other hand, interfere in the proceedings and control them, depending on the applicable institutional rules. E.g., in *Ray v. Chafetz*, 236 F.Supp.3d 66 (D. Columbia 2017), the court was faced with the action for annulment based on bias demonstrated by the institution, i.e., the AAA, when deciding on the reopening of the proceedings, accepting illegal money, and generally favouring respondent. The case dealt with domestic arbitration.

452 S. Greenberg, *Tackling Guerrilla Challenges Against Arbitrators*.

453 Cf. Sutter-Somm/Hasenböhler/Leuenberger/S. Wullschleger, Art. 47 para. 33 et seq. Wullschleger focuses on state court judges and requests a "restrictive analysis" for conduct rising to the level of a conflict of interest.

Issues of the arbitrator's conduct touch upon the right to be heard,[454] e.g., where the arbitrator refuses to admit some evidence. Any examination of a potential violation of either the right to be heard or the principles of independence and impartiality needs to balance additional rights and principles of international arbitration: on the conduct of the arbitrator, these are especially the arbitrator's right to determine the procedure and the general principle of efficiency of the proceedings.[455]

Grounds for challenging an arbitrator are multifaceted: specific closeness, personal interest, factual pre-treatment, concrete conduct of the proceedings, and many more. In the following, a broad understanding of conduct of the arbitrator will be applied. This section will not only deal with the concrete conduct of the proceedings, but also conduct outside the proceeding.

Challenges based on the conduct of the arbitrator often bear a risk of being described as "tactical challenges".[456] Tactical challenges are challenges raised by a party not primarily to safeguard the due process of arbitration, but to misuse challenges to gain a procedural advantage. Apart from challenges based on a conflict of interest due to lack of independence and impartiality, tactical challenges may be based on the excess of power, misconduct, or even disregard of the law.[457] The conduct of an arbitrator often opens different doors of grounds for challenge and annulment, and the line differentiating the various grounds is not clear cut.[458] Misconduct and partiality may be differentiated by finding that "misconduct

454 J.-F. Poudret/S. Besson, *Comparative Law of International Arbitration*, para. 421. The authors argue in favour of a general high threshold to confirm a violation of the right to be heard in these scenarios.

455 *Ballantine Books, Inc. v. Capital Distributing Co.*, 302 F.2d 17 (2d Cir. 1962), reasoning that "[a] judge is not wholly at the mercy of counsel, and would be remiss if he did not participate in questioning to speed proceedings and eliminate irrelevancies. [...] A fortiori an arbitrator should act affirmatively to simplify and expedite the proceedings before him, since among the virtues of arbitration which presumably have moved the parties to agree upon it are speed and informality. [...] It is to be expected that after a judge or an arbitrator has heard considerable testimony, he will have some view of the case. As long as that view is one which arises from the evidence and the conduct of the parties it cannot be fairly claimed that some expression of that view amounts to bias".

456 C. Armbrüster/V. Wächter, *Ablehnung von Schiedsrichtern wegen Befangenheit im Verfahren*, SchiedsVZ 2017, 213-223, 214, clearly stating that the line for a successful challenge should be that a party cannot "simply ditch" an unpleasant arbitrator. Depending on the available procedural mechanism of the applicable law and rules, tactical challenges may be challenges of an arbitrator or expert, the jurisdiction of the tribunal, or other delaying mechanisms.

457 The exact term deviates in different laws and rules. Additionally, the procedural mechanism used deviates according to the point in time of the proceedings.

458 E.g., in *Rai v. Barclays Capital Inc.*, 739 F.Supp.2d 364 (S.D. New York 2010), the court found that claimant "confuses the bases for relief under the FAA". According to the court, claimant's allegations did not support the claims of partiality. There was no reason to believe the lack of a transcript or brief deliberations prejudiced the determination of the case. In *Thian Lok Tio v. Washington Hosp. Center*, 753 F.Supp.2d 9 (D. Columbia 2010), the parties argued the same scenario under partiality, misconduct and excess of power or disregard of the law. *Ostrom v. Worldventures Marketing, LLC*, 60 F.Supp.3d 942 (M.D. Louisiana 2016) is an additional

requires prejudice of the parties' rights, and such prejudice is separate from the bias or impartiality required to vacate an arbitration award on the grounds of bias".[459] On excess of power, the claimant "needs to show that the agreement contained 'express contractual provisions' that created a 'plain limitation on the authority of the arbitrator' which the arbitrator exceeded".[460] Often, courts examine or parties try to establish that the arbitrator or judge potentially prejudged the case, and that this prejudgment is demonstrated by excess of power, misconduct, or disregard of the law. Prejudgment is the underlying issue of independence and impartiality.[461] However, the terminology used in case law deviates.[462] In the following, there will be no explicit distinction between excess of power, misconduct, or disregard of law and independence and impartiality, except for a short note in the footnotes where the court explicitly based the case on one of the grounds.

4.2.1.1 Ex Parte Communication with the Parties

Examining the issue of ex parte communication between the parties and an arbitrator, both parties' rights to be treated equally must be balanced. Equality of the parties means that the parties have the same access to the arbitrator.[463] If an arbitrator communicates individually with only one party, that party may exercise some additional control, and the principle of equal treatment of both parties can be violated. The individual communication may create a special bond between the arbitrator and the party, potentially leading to a conflict of interest impairing the independence and impartiality of the arbitral tribunal.

Different legal systems approach the scenario of ex parte communication differently. At first sight, one may draw a general line between common and civil law systems. There are indeed many examples of ex parte communication where United States law was the *lex*

---

example, and in LCIA Reference No. 81007/81008/81024/81025, LCIA Court, 16 June 2008, Arb. Int'l 27 (2011), 425-432, claimant based its challenge for a lack of independence and impartiality on the arbitrator's disregard of the law.

459 C. Palo, *Bias of Arbitrator as Ground for Vacatur of Arbitration Award*, Sect. 7.

460 C. Palo, *Bias of Arbitrator as Ground for Vacatur of Arbitration Award*, Sect. 8.

461 *Dera Commercial Estate v. Derya Inc.*, [2018] EWHC 1673 (Comm), where a lack of independence and impartiality "may be established if the fair-minded observer concludes that the arbitrators had, by their conduct of and during proceedings, apparently already closed their minds".

462 Alternatively to prejudgement or independence and impartiality, some authorities require the evidence of injustice, see LCIA Reference No. 5665, LCIA Court, 30 August 2006, Arb. Int'l 27 (2011), 395-412. The court required "at least some degree of injustice or harm [...] demonstrated by an applicant before an arbitrator may be considered unfit in the opinion of the LCIA Court and removed".

463 C. Seraglini/J. Ortscheidt, *Droit de l'arbitrage interne et international*, paras. 257-258. The principle of equality is, hence, a limitation to the parties' general right to agree on the mechanism for appointment, N. Voser/E. Fischer, *The Arbitral Tribunal*, p. 59. The application of the principle of equality is, however, not limited to the commencement of the arbitral proceeding, C. Seraglini/J. Ortscheidt, *Droit de l'arbitrage interne et international*, paras. 257-258. They base the application of the principle of equality of the parties on the jurisdictional nature of arbitration and the jurisdictional power of arbitrators.

loci arbitri[464] and just a few from Germany and Switzerland.[465] However, examining cases from civil and common law jurisdictions, the differentiating criterion is not so much the jurisdiction as the facts: the permissibility of ex parte communication depends on the point in time when the communication takes place and the materiality of the communication. Both common and civil law authorities stress the need to respect the parties' right of equal treatment, but allow limited ex parte communication.[466] In addition, even the AAA Rules, applicable to domestic arbitration in the United States, were changed in 2004. According to Rule R-19(a) AAA Rules,

> [n]o party [...] shall communicate ex parte with an arbitrator or a candidate for arbitrator concerning the arbitration, except that a party, [...] may communicate ex parte with a candidate for direct appointment.

This rule is excluded only where the parties explicitly agreed on non-neutral arbitrators under Rule R-18(b) AAA Rules.[467] This shift in the AAA Rules towards a default rule prohibiting ex parte communication demonstrates a more general dedication to rewriting the standard for arbitrators in the United States that is more similar to that embraced by the international community.[468]

This new dedication in Rule R-19(a) AAA Rules is in line with para. 4.4.1 IBA Guidelines 2014, allowing ex parte communication only before the appointment and on limited

---

464 E.g., *Savers Property and Cas. Ins. Co. v. National Union Fire Ins. Comp.*, 748 F.3d 708 (6th Cir. 2014); *National Indemnity Co. v. IRB Brasil Resseguros SA*, 164 F.Supp.3d 457 (S.D. New York 2016), *Continental Cas. Co. v. Staffing Concepts, Inc.*, 2011 WL 7459781 (M.D. Florida).

465 BGer, 16 October 2019, 4A_292/2019; BGer, 14 December 2004, 4P.208/2004/lma, para. C 4.1-5. For a general overview on German case law on this issue, see C. Armbrüster/V. Wächter, *Ablehnung von Schiedsrichtern wegen Befangenheit im Verfahren*, SchiedsVZ 2017, 213-223, 216.

466 On common law jurisdictions: N. Andrews/J. Landbrecht, *Schiedsverfahren und Mediation in England*, paras. 99-100; D. McLaren, *Party-Appointed vs List-Appointed Arbitrators: A Comparison*, J. Int'l Arb. 20 (2003), 233-245, 238-239. On civil law jurisdictions: KG Berlin, 7 June 2010, 20 SchH 2/10, SchiedsVZ, 225-227, denying a challenge. The arbitrator only communicated some information on the outcome of the deliberations ex parte, and all other arbitrators were informed about this conduct. BGer, 14 December 2004, 4P.208/2004/lma, para. C 4.1-5, where the ex parte communication was not material for decision-making.

467 But even in that case, the "AAA shall as an administrative practice suggest to the parties that they agree further that Sect. R-19(a) should nonetheless apply prospectively", Sect. R-19(b) AAA Rules. In general on these changes to the AAA Rules, B. Meyerson/J. Townsend, *Revised Code of Ethics for Commercial Arbitrators Explained*, Disp. Res. J. 59 (2004), 10-17, 15-16.

468 O. Byrne, *A New Code of Ethics for Commercial Arbitrators: The Neutrality of Party-Appointed Arbitrators on a Tripartite Panel*, Fordham Urban L. J. 30 (2003), 1815-1847, 1829. The issue of ex parte communication is also linked to that of different standards applicable to party-appointed arbitrators, see in general, D. Branson, *American Party-Appointed Arbitrators – Not the Three Monkeys*, U. Dayton L. Rev. 30 (2004), 1-62, 13 et seq. Branson clarifies that the allowed conduct depends on the parties' agreement. If parties approve ex parte communication, it should not be an issue.

information.[469] Other international soft laws, e.g., the IBA Rules 1987, also address ex parte communication. Rules 5.3 and 5.4 IBA Rules 1987 stress the need for disclosure once any improper communication occurred, and Guideline 7 IBA Guidelines 2013 generally prohibits ex parte communication,[470] while Guideline 8 provides some exceptions.[471]

Differentiating for the permissibility of ex parte communication on the point in time, it is relevant whether the communication took place before or after the arbitral proceedings commenced.

4.2.1.1.1 Before the Proceedings Commenced

Ex parte communication between a potential arbitrator and one of the parties is generally allowed before the proceedings commence, as long as the points discussed are appropriate, i.e., they concern the prospective arbitrator's expertise, experience, ability, availability, willingness, and the existence of potential conflicts of interest.[472] The parties' right to appoint their chosen expert needs to be adhered to at this point in time. They need a reasonable opportunity to find out whether a potential arbitrator has the required expertise,

---

469 Part II, IBA Guidelines 2014, i.e., the Green List. The limited information is on the arbitrator's availability and qualifications to serve or the names of possible candidates for a chairperson. It is forbidden to address the merits or procedural aspects of the dispute, other than to provide the arbitrator with a basic understanding of the case.

470 It reads: "Unless agreed otherwise by the Parties, and subject to the exceptions below, a Party Representative should not engage in any Ex Parte Communications with an Arbitrator concerning the arbitration."

471 Guideline 8 IBA Guidelines 2013 reads: "(a) A Party Representative may communicate with a prospective Party-Nominated Arbitrator to determine his or her expertise, experience, ability, availability, willingness and the existence of potential conflicts of interest. (b) A Party Representative may communicate with a prospective or appointed Party-Nominated Arbitrator for the purpose of the selection of the Presiding Arbitrator. (c) A Party Representative may, if the Parties are in agreement that such a communication is permissible, communicate with a prospective Presiding Arbitrator to determine his or her expertise, experience, ability, availability, willingness and the existence of potential conflicts of interest. (d) While communications with a prospective Party-Nominated Arbitrator or Presiding Arbitrator may include a general description of the dispute, a Party Representative should not seek the views of the prospective Party-Nominated Arbitrator or Presiding Arbitrator on the substance of the dispute." In addition, many institutional rules address ex parte communication and allow similar exceptions, e.g., Art. 13(6) ICDR Rules; Art. 13.6 SIAC Rules.

472 Comments on Guideline 8, IBA Guidelines 2013. See also, Art. 11.5 HKIAC Rules; Art. 13(6) ICDR Rules; Art. 13.6 SIAC Rules; ICC Note, para. 68 lit. a. Generally allowing ex parte communication at that point in time: *Stef Shipping Corp. v. Norris Grain Co.*, 209 F.Supp. 249 (S.D. New York 1962), stressing the parties' right to appoint and possibly applying a different standard of independence and impartiality on the party-appointed arbitrator; LCIA Reference No. UN96/X15, LCIA Court, 29 May 1996, Arb. Int'l 27 (2011), 317-319. See also, Sutter-Somm/Hasenböhler/Leuenberger/S. Wullschleger, Art. 47 para. 36; C. Armbrüster/V. Wächter, *Ablehnung von Schiedsrichtern wegen Befangenheit im Verfahren*, SchiedsVZ 2017, 213-223, 216; N. Andrews/J. Landbrecht, *Schiedsverfahren und Mediation in England*, paras. 99-100.

experience, and time.[473] There is an old, and probably exaggerated, explanation of how arbitrators are appointed:

> A number of businessmen seem to make it their practice to present the facts of the case to a colleague, then ask him how he would decide it, and if his view coincides with their own, request him to sit as their appointee.[474]

Another description, more recent, but similar in approach is the following:

> The way I approach an arbitration is, the party tells me what the case is and what their side of it is. If I disagree with them, I tell them you better not appoint me. If their case seems right, I tell them I think they're right but I haven't heard the other side so I cannot guarantee that I will vote your way. I have to hear all the evidence before I make up my mind.[475]

Even if exaggerated, both examples illustrate how the right to appoint may be used to select an arbitrator that is thought to be likely to vote in the appointing party's favour.[476]

Where the communication exceeds the limits of the necessary information on selecting an arbitrator, ex parte communication can be a ground for challenging an arbitrator or annulling the award.[477] Many authorities deal with ex parte communication with the party-appointed arbitrator on his or her appointment, a scenario where the parties' right

---

473 D. Branson, *American Party-Appointed Arbitrators – Not the Three Monkeys*, U. Dayton L. Rev. 30 (2004), 1-62, 51.

474 B. Gold/H. Furth, *The Use of Tripartite Boards in Labor, Commercial, and International Arbitration*, Harvard L. Rev. 68 (1954), 293-339, 319.

475 *Nationwide Mut. Ins. Co. v. First St. Ins. Co.*, 213 F. Supp. 2d 10 (D. Massachusetts 2002), 18.

476 Following the line of argumentation on trust in the arbitrator, one may question whether the mere interview creates a specific bond between the arbitrator candidate and the interviewing party, potentially excluding the candidate as arbitrator for the opposing party. In *Flughafen Zürich AG and Gestión e Ingeniería IDC SA v. Republic of Venezuela*, ICSID Tribunal, 29 August 2012, ICSID Case No. ARB/10/19, the ICSID Tribunal was faced with such an allegation towards an expert who had been interviewed by the opposing party in advance. The tribunal denied a conflict of interest. The same should be the answer for the arbitrator: appropriate ex parte communication with the party not appointing the arbitrator is no ground for dependence and partiality of that arbitrator.

477 E.g., in *Metropolitan Property and Cas. Ins. Co. v. J.C. Penney Casualty Ins. Co.*, 780 F.Supp. 885 (D. Connecticut 1991), where the party-appointed arbitrator discussed with respondent the merits of the case. The case concerned domestic arbitration and the court applied different standards for the presiding and the party-appointed arbitrators. In United States case law, these scenarios often do not deal with a lack of independence and impartiality but rather misconduct, D. Branson, *American Party-Appointed Arbitrators – Not the Three Monkeys*, U. Dayton L. Rev. 30 (2004), 1-62, 33 et seq. In favour of applying the lack of independence and impartiality as a potential ground for challenge or annulment in these cases, N. Sievi, *Pre-Appointment Communications with Prospective Arbitrators*, SchiedsVZ 2021, 1-6, 3 et seq.

to appoint is directly applicable. Another scenario is the parties' interview of their already chosen party-appointed arbitrator on the appointment of the presiding arbitrator. Some rules address this scenario as well and admit the interview. For example, Article 13.5 LCIA Rules explicitly allows such conduct but demands transparency with other arbitrators and the institution.[478] To assure that the presiding arbitrator is acceptable to all concerned, it may be seen as "common and generally accepted" for party-appointed arbitrators to confer with the parties.[479] Additionally, Article 4 CIArb Guideline on Interviews permits parties to interview the presiding arbitrator and sets some standards for such interviews.[480] However, some institutional rules prohibit such conduct.[481]

In conclusion,

> some degree of ex parte communication between an arbitrator and one party's representatives may occur as part of the selection process. Party-appointed arbitrators typically are consulted ex parte about their own ability to serve and related matters, and such arbitrators may consult with the appointing parties or their counsel about the choice of a third arbitrator if they are to have a role in that selection. However, the arbitrators may not have ex parte communications after the tribunal is fully constituted.[482]

---

478 It reads: "Prior to the Arbitral Tribunal's formation, unless the parties agree otherwise in writing, any arbitrator, candidate or nominee who is required to participate in the selection of a presiding arbitrator may consult any party in order to obtain the views of that party as to the suitability of any candidate or nominee as presiding arbitrator, provided that such arbitrator, candidate or nominee promptly informs any other arbitrator, candidate or nominee involved in the selection process and the Registrar of such consultation." Cf. Art. 12.2 sentence 2 DIS Rules; Art. 11.5 HKIAC Rules; Art. 13(6) ICDR Rules; Art. 13.6 SIAC Rules.

479 S. Elsing/A. Shchavelev, *FS Karrer*, p. 72 et seq. See also, BGer, 16 October 2019, 4A_292/2019, explicitly allowing ex parte communication with the appointed arbitrator on the selection of the presiding arbitrator and dismissing the annulment. The court examined in detail Guidelines 7 and 8 IBA Guidelines 2013, i.e., counsel's communication with the arbitrator. See on counsel's conduct, below chapter 4.2.2. But see, G. Aksen, *The Tribunal's Appointment*, p. 340, disfavouring consultations as party-appointed arbitrator with parties or counsel on the selection of the chair.

480 It reads: "If a prospective sole or presiding arbitrator is invited to an interview by one party, they should only agree to be interviewed by all parties jointly. If, however, a candidate is satisfied that a party who chooses not to attend such an interview was invited to attend and given reasonable notice of the interview, and does not object to the interview and/or the agenda, the interview may proceed in the absence of that party. In these circumstances, the prospective arbitrator should make a contemporaneous note of matters discussed in the interview and send it to all of the parties, any co-arbitrators and any institution, promptly after their appointment."

481 E.g., Art. 11.5 HKIAC Rules; Art. 13.6 SIAC Rules.

482 J. Carter, *Improving Life with the Party-Appointed Arbitrator: Clearer Conduct Guidelines for "Nonneutrals"*, Am. Rev. Int'l Arb. 11 (2000), 295-305, 296.

4.2.1.1.2 After the Proceedings Commenced

If the arbitral tribunal is already appointed, there is no longer any need to interview the potential arbitrator. The parties' right to appoint is less effective at this stage, whereas the principle of equality demands the arbitrators to treat both parties equally and, generally, refrain from communicating with one party ex parte.

Some scenarios, however, do not meet the threshold of violating the principle of equal treatment and do not constitute a conflict of interest. For example, ex parte communication is allowed as long as it is limited in substance, e.g., to the outcome of deliberations, all other arbitrators are informed about this conduct, and everyone is aware that the deliberations may be taken up anew.[483] Also, minor procedural or administrative communications may be communicated ex parte.[484] It should be noted that in the cited case law, it was not only one arbitrator communicating ex parte but rather the whole tribunal.

The permissibility of ex parte communication primarily depends on the materiality of the communication.[485] If the communication is not material, e.g., minor organisational matters are communicated, there is little to no risk that the arbitrator will be influenced in his or her decision-making. Decision-making is the elementary aspect of the arbitrator's role, and independence and impartiality safeguard this role. In addition, where the parties are

483 KG Berlin, 7 June 2010, 20 SchH 2/10, SchiedsVZ, 225-227, denying a challenge. Cf. *Sunoco Overseas, Inc. v. Texaco Intern. Trader, Inc.*, 69 F.Supp.2d 502 (S.D. New York 1999). The mere allegation that one of the parties had some knowledge of the final award before all parties were notified did not demonstrate a conflict of interest. However, where the deliberations have already officially ended, the arbitrators should refrain from communicating ex parte the outcome of the final award before it is officially rendered, LCIA Reference No. 0252, LCIA Court, 1 July 2002, Arb. Int'l 27 (2011), 351-354.

484 E.g., when the tribunal finds it easier to agree on dates with both parties individually. However, no legal issues can be discussed, C. Armbrüster/V. Wächter, *Ablehnung von Schiedsrichtern wegen Befangenheit im Verfahren*, SchiedsVZ 2017, 213-223, 216. In *WellPoint Health Networks, Inc. v. John Hancock Life Ins. Co.*, 547 F.Supp.2d 899 (N.D. Illinois 2008), the parties were additionally informed in advance on ex parte communication. See also, *Continental Cas. Co. v. Staffing Concepts, Inc.*, 2011 WL 7459781 (M.D. Florida); *Dow Corning Corp. v. Safety National Cas. Corp.*, 335 F.3d 742 (8th Cir. 2003); *Kolel Beth Yechiel Mechil of Tartikov, Inc. v. YLL Irrevocable Trust*, 878 F.Supp.2d 459 (S.D. New York 2012), later affirmed by *Kolel Beth Yechiel Mechil of Tartikov, Inc. v. YLL Irrevocable Trust*, 729 F.3d 99 (2d Cir. 2013). All cases concern domestic arbitration. In line with these cases, the IBA Guidelines 2013, in their Comments to Guidelines 7-8, provide that ex parte communication is allowed in some procedural actions, e.g., where interim measures are requested.

485 *AMEC Capital Projects Ltd. v. Whitefriars City Estates Ltd.*, [2004] EWCA Civ 1418, stating that communication of the adjudicator and a counsel would be "unwise in principle" but that there was nothing in the conversation capable of giving rise to a real possibility of bias. Additional examples: *Nationwide Mutual Ins. Co. v. Home Ins. Co.*, 90 F.Supp.2d 893 (S.D. Ohio 2000), affirmed by *Nationwide Mutual Ins. Co. v. Home Ins. Co.*, 429 F.3d 640 (6th Cir. 2005); *WellPoint Health Networks, Inc. v. John Hancock Life Ins. Co.*, 547 F.Supp.2d 899 (N.D. Illinois 2008); *Brown v. Brown-Thill*, 762 F.3d 814 (8th Cir. 2014). All cases concern domestic arbitration.

informed in advance about the communication, courts have ruled that ex parte communication did not amount to a conflict of interest.[486] Sometimes, informing the parties after the conversation took place even has a curing effect.[487] However, where ex parte communication concerns the merits of the case or procedural strategies, it may result in a conflict of interest.[488]

Some examples from United States case law concern scenarios that would most likely constitute a conflict in other jurisdictions.[489] Courts in these examples suggested that there is a conflict of interest. But due to different applicable standards of independence and impartiality for party-appointed arbitrators, the courts did not conclude that the conflict requires the arbitrator to be challenged or the award to be annulled. For example, in *Sunkist Soft Drinks, Inc. v. Sunkist Growers, Inc.*, the court pointed out that under the applicable AAA Rules and the 1977 ABA/AAA Code of Ethics, the obligation to act impartial applies only to the neutral arbitrator, whereas party-appointed arbitrators "may be predisposed toward the party who appointed them but in all other respects are obligated to act in good faith and with integrity and fairness".[490] Claimant's party-appointed arbitrator, first, attended meetings with claimant's employees who were to be witnesses; second, assisted claimant's counsel in selecting consultants; third, gave advice to "his" party's expert witness; and, fourth, suggested lines of testimony to counsel. In *Delta Mine Holding Co. v. AFC Coal Properties, Inc.*, claimant's party-appointed arbitrator helped to prepare witnesses, participated in a mock arbitration a few days before the hearings, and communicated the neutral arbitrator's draft award to "his" party to obtain comments before again consulting with the neutral arbitrator.[491] The arbitrator acknowledged he was trying "to sway the [neutral] arbitrators to rule in Delta Mine's favor". These are rather extreme examples, to

486 LCIA Reference No. 0256, LCIA Court, 13 February 2002, Arb. Int'l 27 (2011), 345-350, where the LCIA additionally informed claimant about the facts and substance of the ex parte meeting the following day. According to the court, the arbitrator acted unfairly and deliberately breached rules, but his conduct did not amount to justifiable doubts as to his independence and impartiality.

487 Cf. *Bubbles & Wine Limited v. Reshat Lusha*, [2018] EWCA Civ 468, on state court proceedings.

488 LCIA Reference No. UN3490, LCIA Court, 21 October 2005, 27 December 2005, Arb. Int'l 27 (2011), 377-394, generally holding that it is not unacceptable in all circumstances for an arbitrator to hold meetings with representatives of only one party. But accepting a meeting behind closed doors and addressing issues of the arbitration was a step too far and would, indeed, raise suspicions of unequal treatment between the parties. The court concluded that two private meetings of claimant's party-appointed arbitrator and counsel for claimant in the retiring rooms of the arbitrator, speaking about the merits of the case, lead to justifiable doubts on the arbitrator's independence and impartiality. See also, *Metropolitan Property and Cas. Ins. Co. v. J.C. Penney Casualty Ins. Co.*, 780 F.Supp. 885 (D. Connecticut 1991), on domestic arbitration.

489 E.g., *Delta Mine Holding Co. v. AFC Coal Properties, Inc.*, 280 F.3d 815 (8th Cir. 2001); *Sunkist Soft Drinks, Inc. v. Sunkist Growers, Inc.*, 10 F.3d 753 (11th Cir. 1993).

490 *Sunkist Soft Drinks, Inc. v. Sunkist Growers, Inc.*, 10 F.3d 753 (11th Cir. 1993).

491 *Delta Mine Holding Co. v. AFC Coal Properties, Inc.*, 280 F.3d 815 (8th Cir. 2001).

be explained with the former AAA Rules and the differences in standards for the party-appointed arbitrator.[492]

In some specific procedures and scenarios ex parte communication may be particularly useful after the proceedings commenced. For example, settlement attempts may be more effective when they are addressed ex parte. Likewise, in deadlock situations between the parties and the tribunal, some ex parte communication can help to find a solution. It offers an additional tool for the tribunal to proceed efficiently. This positive use of ex parte communication may weigh against prohibiting it here. Even another example of permitted ex parte communication are default proceedings where only one party participates.[493] Here, there is usually no violation of the defaulting party's rights if the tribunal proceeds with the case. Most arbitration laws and rules encourage that the defaulting party is informed throughout the proceedings and provided with sufficient possibility to be heard. Although ex parte communication may have some positive impact on the efficiency, it is questionable whether it may be used without the parties' consent. Where both parties explicitly agree on ex parte communication in settlement or deadlock situations, there will usually not be an issue.[494] More delicate is whether the tribunal may opt for ex parte communication without the parties' consent or even against express disagreement. In that situation, communicating ex parte against the will of the parties will not be in line with the parties' right to determine the procedure.[495] Where the parties do not guide the tribunal on the procedure of ex parte communication, it will depend on the applicable laws and rules, and the particular scenario: whether efficiency trumps the limitation of ex parte communication to pre-arbitral scenarios. In any event, ex parte communication needs to be conducted in a way that respects the parties' general right of equal treatment, e.g., by granting the same amount of time for communications or informing the opposing party of the communication.

In conclusion, the dominant view remains to be that ex parte communication is generally prohibited after the proceedings have commenced. Only non-material communication or specific scenarios may be in line with a fair proceeding.

---

492 Based on the assumption of applying different standards for party-appointed arbitrators, it may appear feasible to allow each party to communicate ex parte with "its" party-appointed arbitrator. However, the assumption cannot be followed, as will be shown below, chapter 6.3.

493 IBA Guidelines 2013 in their Comments to Guidelines 7-8 provide that ex parte communication is allowed if one party defaults. See also, A. Mourre/E. Zuleta, *The IBA Guidelines on Party Representation in International Arbitration*, Disp. Resol. Int'l 7 (2013), 135-158, 138.

494 This is covered by party autonomy. E.g., Sect. 38(1) EAA.

495 E.g., Sect. 38(2) EAA.

4.2.1.2 Comments and Actions during the Proceedings

An arbitrator may be faced with the allegation of dependent and partial conduct due to his or her conduct in hearings, calls, or written communication with the parties and counsels. Only serious procedural mistakes may be an indication for a ground of finding dependence and partiality.[496] In most cases, these comments or actions do not meet the threshold of constituting a conflict of interest. The context of the scenario is highly important for the analysis of whether the comment reveals dependent and partial conduct.[497] Dependent and partial conduct eliminates the violated party's trust in the arbitrator's ability to provide fair and equal proceedings. Apart from the context, the object of the comments and actions may be decisive for evaluating conflicts of interest. The *Oberlandesgericht* München ruled that comments addressed to counsel are to be treated less critically than comments towards a party.[498] The court, inter alia, reasoned that the counsel has no right to challenge – the counsel is not the one who appoints the arbitrator. Therefore, comments towards counsel do not offend the party directly. The decision is correct where the arbitrator's comments concern the counsel and not the party. In the case before the *Oberlandesgericht* München, the comments raised by the arbitrator concerned the behaviour of the counsel. However, if the comments concern the party, and are just addressed towards the counsel, the approach may be different.

In the following, offending comments or tone, comments or questions strengthening one party's position, settlement actions and other procedural actions will be addressed.

4.2.1.2.1 Offending Comments or Tone

Comments made in jest generally do not suffice to demonstrate partiality.[499] But offending comments or comments without connection to the legal issues may result in an impression of bias and constitute a conflict of interest.[500] Personal insults, in particular, may evidence

---

496 OLG München, 10 July 2013, 34 SchH 8/12, NJOZ 2014, 1779-1782; Musielak/Voit/W. Voit, § 1036 para. 8.

497 LCIA Reference No. UN7949, LCIA Court, 3 December 2007, Arb. Int'l 27 (2011), 420-424. See also, *Magill v. Porter*, [2001] UKHL 67, 105.

498 OLG München, 10 January 2007, 34 SchH 7/06, BeckRS 2007, 00709.

499 BGer, 15 February 1990, BGE 116 Ia 14, para. E 4-7c, on state court proceedings.

500 C. Armbrüster/V. Wächter, *Ablehnung von Schiedsrichtern wegen Befangenheit im Verfahren*, SchiedsVZ 2017, 213-223, 216. See also, KuKo ZPO/R. Kiener, Art. 47 para. 19, primarily on state court judges. E.g., where the arbitrator used expressions such as "fictitious, false and malevolent" in his characterisation of the claimant's submissions and "viciously attributed by [claimant's counsel]", the LCIA Court accepted a challenge considering that the self-evident tension and ill-feeling that had arisen as a result of the challenge created circumstances that may, of themselves, gave rise to justifiable doubts as to the arbitrator's impartiality, LCIA Reference No. 1303, LCIA Court, 22 November 2001, Arb. Int'l 27 (2011), 342-344.

bias.[501] Personal insults are, however, not often present. Where the presiding arbitrator in a conference call said to counsel that they

> tried not to be prejudiced toward [claimant] because he was a pro se claimant, but it has been very difficult [and] [w]e are so glad to have you on board,

no conflict of interest was present.[502] Also, slightly critical comments or general comments that one of the parties lacked seriousness usually do not create conflicts of interest.[503] Decisions made on comments and tone may often be borderline cases, since words and tone are open to interpretation.[504]

In addition, the tone, rather than the content, of some comments may give rise to an argument of a lack of independence and impartiality. The mere general allegation of a hostile tone is no basis for a conflict of interest. In an unpublished ICC case, one of the parties challenged the presiding arbitrator on the basis of having addressed its counsel in a "scolding tone". The challenge was dismissed.[505]

501 This should apply to insults of a party or their counsel. Where the presiding arbitrator publicly questioned the ethics of one party's counsel, that arbitrator may be challenged, see example in J. Hamilton/F. Jijon/E. Corzo, *Arbitrator Challenges in Latin America*, p. 420 lit. d.

502 *Blackwell v. Merrill Lynch, Pierce, Fenner & Smith Inc.*, 22 F.Supp.3d 565 (W.D. North Carolina 2014), explicitly relying on the "heavy burden" of evident partiality.

503 *Ortiz-Espinosa v. BBVA Securities of Puerto Rico, Inc.*, 852 F.3d 36 (5th Cir. 2017), where the arbitrator said: "If I were [defendants' counsel], I would have a sore throat from objection for irrelevancies." The court interpreted the comment as indicating that the arbitrator was concerned with the number and length of the hearings, as well as the potential for scheduling issues if the hearings needed to be prolonged. Without additional facts, the threshold of lack of independence and impartiality would not be met. Another example is LCIA Reference No. 5665, LCIA Court, 30 August 2006, Arb. Int'l 27 (2011), 395-412, where the presiding arbitrator sent an email to all parties instead of merely his or her co-arbitrators and that email read, inter alia, that "it reads to me as if [sic] [claimants' counsel] gets his pleasure in abusing us and when it comes to a crunch he does not want any particular orders now. I do not like his floating threats. All we may do is give him lashings of fair procedure". The LCIA Court did not grant the following challenge.

504 E.g., in BGer, 7 January 2004, 4P.196/2003/ech, the court rejected the challenge with resentment. The arbitrator said to counsel that counsel would be "more occupied by mounting a case than by advancing the construction project". Generally, comments and tone may demonstrate the underlying relationship. Positive comments may also demonstrate friendship or another similar connection. A presiding arbitrator who had publicly praised one party's counsel was challenged due to justifiable doubts as to his or her relationship with that counsel, see example in J. Hamilton/F. Jijon/E. Corzo, *Arbitrator Challenges in Latin America*, p. 420 lit. e.

505 S. Greenberg, *Tackling Guerrilla Challenges Against Arbitrators*, considering this case a possible example of a tactical challenge. An additional reason why the threshold of a conflict of interest was not met could be that the comment concerned the counsel and not the party. Since the former is less critical, it is more difficult to base a challenge on comments concerning the counsel.

Finally, offensive conduct may, theoretically, create an impression of bias. However, picking up the phone during the hearing (in another matter) should not be a ground for challenge.[506]

4.2.1.2.2 Comments or Questions Strengthening One Party's Position

Parties and counsels may have the impression that an arbitrator's questions reveal that he or she is prejudging the case or even strengthening the opposing party's position. From the arbitrator's point of view, he or she may not partially prejudge the case but question efficiently by pointing at the legally weak aspects. Arbitrators enjoy some discretion in conducting the proceedings.[507] Hence, there are not many cases challenging an arbitrator or annulling an award successfully on this ground.

Pointing one party to specific evidence when questioning and creating the impression of providing legal advice to that party was not enough to successfully challenge an arbitrator under the Swiss Rules.[508] Also, raising "leading" and "suggestive" questions, and by that prompting a party with arguments in support of its case, may look somewhat closed-minded, or even rude. But such questioning usually does not evidence that the arbitrator had a closed mind towards the case and, hence, does not give rise to a conflict of interest.[509] Similarly, the *Oberlandesgericht* Frankfurt a.M. rejected a challenge which was based on claimant's allegation that respondent's party-appointed arbitrator took the lead in significant stages of the proceedings, the evidentiary hearing, and cross-examined respondent's witnesses in a manner that was useful for respondent, i.e., avoiding attacking contradictions of claimant's case.[510] Additionally, that arbitrator used respondent's submissions during the evidentiary hearing. The court argued that this conduct did not meet the threshold of challenging the arbitrator.

---

506 According to Art. 10(2) CIETAC Rules for Evaluating the Behavior of Arbitrators, this behaviour may damage the parties' confidence in the arbitrator and can lead to a "warning" by the commission. Cf. C. Armbrüster/V. Wächter, *Ablehnung von Schiedsrichtern wegen Befangenheit im Verfahren*, SchiedsVZ 2017, 213-223, 216.

507 E.g., Art. 22(2) ICC Rules on effective case management; Art. 14.5 LCIA Rules on "fair, efficient and expeditious conduct"; Arts. 19.1, 19.4 SIAC Rules on ensuring "the fair, expeditious, economical and final resolution of the dispute".

508 SCAI, *Swiss Rules – Selected Case Law.*

509 LCIA Reference No. 81224, LCIA Court, 15 March 2010, Arb. Int'l 27 (2011), 461-470, explicitly relying on *El Farargy v. El Farargy and others*, [2007] EWCA Civ 1149, for the fact that an arbitrator formed and expressed preliminary views was part and parcel of the normal process of considering a case. The LCIA Court accepted that this view was not shared by all jurisdictions such that respondent's reaction might be understandable, but this was clearly not a reason for considering that the arbitrator was biased. In this direction, see also, LCIA Reference No. UN7949, LCIA Court, 3 December 2007, Arb. Int'l 27 (2011), 420-424.

510 OLG Frankfurt a.M., 24 January 2019, 26 SchH 2/18, BeckRS 2019, 848.

However, where the comments and questions are objectively primarily useful as a legal argument and not within the interest of efficiency, the impression of bias may arise.[511] This may be the case, for example, where the tribunal comments on the statute of limitations without any party having argued it.[512] It will always be difficult to draw a line between comments and questions covered by the tribunal's discretion to act efficiently and those questions guiding one party. The applicable procedural rules and laws and the issue of whether the tribunal must address certain aspects ex officio are highly important here.[513]

4.2.1.2.3 Settlement and Mediation

Like comments and questions raised by the tribunal to conduct the proceedings efficiently, some arbitrators may initiate settlement proceedings or even a mediation phase within the arbitral proceedings to resolve the dispute more rapidly.[514] Again, from the parties'

---

511 BGer, 28 April 2008, BGE 134 I 238, on state court proceedings. The judge explicitly recommended to one party to withdraw its claim. The Swiss *Bundesgericht* ruled that even though there is a need to act efficiently, and judges may have preliminary views on a case, they are not supposed to communicate this view to the parties and provide legal recommendation. In line with this thought, one might interpret such questioning as an advice to the party. Some rules expressly forbid the arbitrator to advise the parties, e.g., Art. 5.3 LCIA Rules.

512 C. Armbrüster/V. Wächter, *Ablehnung von Schiedsrichtern wegen Befangenheit im Verfahren*, SchiedsVZ 2017, 213-223, 216. They propose to use § 139 German ZPO in order to differentiate between useful and forbidden comments. § 139 German ZPO provides: "(1) To the extent required, the court is to discuss with the parties the circumstances and facts as well as the relationship of the parties to the dispute, both in terms of the factual aspects of the matter and of its legal ramifications, and it is to ask questions. The court is to work towards ensuring that the parties to the dispute make declarations in due time and completely, regarding all significant facts, and in particular is to ensure that the parties amend by further information those facts that they have asserted only incompletely, that they designate the evidence, and that they file the relevant petitions.
(2) The court may base its decision on an aspect that a party has recognisably overlooked or has deemed to be insignificant, provided that this does not merely concern an ancillary claim, but only if it has given corresponding notice of this fact and has allowed the opportunity to address the matter. The same shall apply for any aspect that the court assesses differently than both parties do.
(3) The court is to draw the parties' attention to its concerns regarding any items it is to take into account ex officio.
(4) Notice by the court as provided for by this rule is to be given at the earliest possible time, and a written record is to be prepared. The fact of such notice having been given may be proven only by the content of the files. The content of the files may be challenged exclusively by submitting proof that they have been forged.
(5) If it is not possible for a party to immediately make a declaration regarding a notice from the court, then the court is to determine a period, upon the party having filed a corresponding application, within which this party may supplement its declaration in a written pleading."

513 E.g., the newly adopted Prague Rules require arbitrators to express their preliminary views on the case in the case management conference, Art. 2.4.e. Prague Rules. The article also states that "[e]xpressing such preliminary views shall not by itself be considered as evidence of the arbitral tribunal's lack of independence or impartiality, and cannot constitute grounds for disqualification".

514 Settlement may be conducted according to, e.g., Art. 47 CIETAC Rules; Art. 26 DIS Rules (with an extensive power of the tribunal); General Standard 4(d) IBA Guidelines 2014; Art. 9 Prague Rules; Art. 15(8) Swiss Rules; Sect. 12 UNCITRAL, Notes on Organizing Arbitral Proceedings; Art. 9 Prague Rules. Mediation

point of view, such behaviour may appear biased, whereas the arbitrator may find it useful to discuss and point out the issues relevant for the outcome of the case to enable a settlement or mediation.[515] On this issue, there is a rather clear divide between civil and common law.[516] Under a civil law approach, settlement entails an arbitrator actively suggesting proposals to settle and mediate between the parties.[517] Thus, case law demonstrates more leeway on the arbitrator's conduct in trying to settle the case or mediate between the parties.[518] Under a common law approach, the arbitrator must decide the case and not settle it.[519] Hence, it is important to consult the applicable rules and laws in regard to whether they include the power to conduct settlement proceedings.[520] In the words of UNCITRAL:

> In appropriate circumstances, the arbitral tribunal may raise the possibility of a settlement between the parties. In some jurisdictions, the arbitration law permits facilitation of a settlement by the arbitral tribunal with the agreement of the parties. In other jurisdictions, it is not permissible for the arbitral tribunal to do more than raise the prospect of a settlement that would not involve the arbitral tribunal. Where the applicable arbitration law permits the arbitral tribunal to facilitate a settlement, it may, if so requested by the parties, guide or assist the parties in their negotiations. Certain sets of arbitration rules provide for facilitation of a settlement by the arbitral tribunal.[521]

Following this divergence of different laws and rules, it is questionable whether an arbitrator may also act as mediator in the same case. He or she may lack an open mind. Some authorities regard participants in settlement or mediation proceedings unfit to serve as an

---

may be proposed according to, e.g., Art. 27.4(iii) DIS Rules; General Standard 4(d) IBA Guidelines 2014. Some institutions also provide for multi-tiered clauses mixing mediation and arbitration, or a "Mediator in Reserve" (Mediator-in-Reserve Policy for International Arbitrations under JAMS).

515 See generally, H. Raeschke-Kessler, *The Arbitrator as Settlement Facilitator*, Arb. Int'l 21 (2005), 523-536.

516 Cf. Explanation to General Standard 4(d) IBA Guidelines 2014, referring to divergence in different jurisdictions.

517 S. Elsing, *Procedural Efficiency in International Arbitration: Choosing the Best of Both Legal Worlds*, SchiedsVZ 2011, 114-123, 118. Cf. the extensive approach under Arts. 26 DIS Rules and 9 Prague Rules.

518 E.g., OLG München, 3 January 2008, 34 SchH 3/07, SchiedsVZ 2008, 102-104; OLG Frankfurt a.M., 27 April 2006, 26 SchH 1/06, SchiedsVZ 329-331. But see, Stein/Jonas/P. Schlosser, § 1036 paras. 38 and 45.

519 C. Armbrüster/V. Wächter, *Ablehnung von Schiedsrichtern wegen Befangenheit im Verfahren*, SchiedsVZ 2017, 213-223, 216. Cf. *Ballantine Books, Inc. v. Capital Distributing Co.*, 302 F.2d 17 (2d Cir. 1962). In general, settlement proceedings initiated by the arbitrators are seen critical in English arbitration and may constitute a ground for challenge, N. Andrews/J. Landbrecht, *Schiedsverfahren und Mediation in England*, para. 101.

520 E.g., Art. 26 DIS Rules: "Unless any party objects thereto, the arbitral tribunal shall, at every stage of the arbitration, seek to encourage an amicable settlement of the dispute or of individual disputed issues."

521 UNCITRAL, Notes on Organizing Arbitral Proceedings, para. 72.

arbitrator.[522] The settlement initiative must, however, meet a certain threshold to qualify as evidence for a conflict of interest or misconduct.[523] In the end, whether an arbitrator may act after participating in settlement or mediation proceedings with the parties will, again, depend on the applicable laws and rules.[524]

4.2.1.2.4 Procedural Actions

Finally, there may be additional procedural actions giving one party the impression of a lack of independence and impartiality. These are often procedural actions regarding evidence, additional submissions, protocols, or other procedural requests. Whether these actions violate the arbitrator's obligation to act independently and impartially depends on the arbitrator's discretion under the applicable laws and rules.

In general, minor procedural flaws do not provide a ground for conflicts of interest or misconduct.[525] Only if they are intense and repeated will they violate the arbitrator's obligation to act independently and impartially.[526] Denials of procedural requests often do not rise to the level of a conflict.[527] These might be denying the admission of evidence;[528]

522 *Glencot Development and Design Co. Ltd. v. Ben Barrett & Son (Contractors) Ltd.*, [2001] EWHC 15. Interestingly, in this direction also on civil law C. Müller, *Swiss Case Law in International Arbitration*, Art. 180 para. 1.3.9. Swiss state court judges may, however, act as judges after having participated in a mediation, Art. 47(2)(b) Swiss ZPO; BSK BV/J. Reich, Art. 30 para. 27.

523 E.g., in *Ballantine Books, Inc. v. Capital Distributing Co.*, 302 F.2d 17 (2d Cir. 1962), this threshold was not met. The arbitrator communicated off the record with the parties on settlement – including a hint that he had a "tentative view" that there should be an award in favour of claimant. The dispute concerned domestic arbitration.

524 E.g., Art. 9.3 Prague Rules explicitly allows the arbitrator to act if the parties agree in writing. Due to party autonomy, the same approach should apply in cases not applying the Prague Rules.

525 BGer, 7 January 2004, 4P.196/2003/ech, para. C 3.1; BGer, 11 May 1992, ASA Bull. 1992, 381-401, 392; OLG München, 17 November 2016, 34 SchH 13/16, NJOZ 2018, 437-439. See also, Sutter-Somm/Hasenböhler/Leuenberger/S. Wullschleger, Art. 4 para. 35, on judges in Switzerland.

526 BGer, 27 April 2015, BGE 141 IV 178; BGer, 19 February 2009, 4A_539/2008, para. C 3.2; *Standard Tankers (Bahamas) Co., Ltd. v. Motor Tank Vessel, AKTI*, 438 F. Supp. 153 (E.D. North Carolina 1977), on the general principle of fair treatment. Additionally, on Swiss state court judges, where procedural mistakes revealing the judge's lack of independence and impartiality may constitute a ground for challenge, BGG PK/D. Vock Art. 34 para. 3.

527 *British Ins. Co. of Cayman v. Water Street Ins. Co., Ltd.*, 93 F.Supp.2d 506 (S.D. New York 2000); C. Armbrüster/V. Wächter, *Ablehnung von Schiedsrichtern wegen Befangenheit im Verfahren*, SchiedsVZ 2017, 213-223, 216.

528 *Fairchild Corp. v. Alcoa, Inc.*, 510 F.Supp.2d 280 (S.D. New York 2007), examining bias under misconduct in this scenario. See generally, E. Sussman, *Arbitrator Decision Making – Unconscious Psychological Influences and What You Can Do About Them*, YB Int'l Arb. IV (2015), 70-96; *Amerisure Mut. Ins. Co. v. Everest Reinsurance Co.*, 109 F.Supp.3d 969 (E.D. Michigan 2015).

refusing to hear a witness;[529] not granting an oral hearing on preliminary matters;[530] denying the request for protocols to a hearing;[531] denying to change dates;[532] denying time extensions, or denying a request to stay.[533] In addition, other examples from case law not granting a challenge of an arbitrator or annulment of the award are as follows: fixing dates for a hearing and not questioning a witness in detail when the opposing party is absent;[534] allowing the opposing party to hear a witness that was not mentioned on the list;[535] granting a protective order;[536] or rejecting submissions on new factual evidence handed in during the first hearing.[537] Especially, procedural actions that are required by the institution administering the case may not evidence biased conduct of the arbitrators.[538] Furthermore, the style of questioning a witness usually does not amount to a conflict of interest.[539]

Generally, the parties' right to be heard is often touched upon in these scenarios – either the parties address it in their arguments or the courts address it in examining the arguments.[540] Placing the risk and costs for a videoconference on the party requesting this

529 *Kolel Beth Yechiel Mechil of Tartikov, Inc. v. YLL Irrevocable Trust*, 878 F.Supp.2d 459 (S.D. New York 2012), affirmed by *Kolel Beth Yechiel Mechil of Tartikov, Inc. v. YLL Irrevocable Trust*, 729 F.3d 99 (2d Cir. 2013). The U.S. District Court reasoned that, first, arbitrators are accorded great deference in their evidentiary determinations, and, second, the legal arguments were considered in detail in seven or eight sessions. Additionally, interfering when a witness is heard is by itself no conduct evidencing bias, *Amerisure Mut. Ins. Co. v. Everest Reinsurance Co.*, 109 F.Supp.3d 969 (E.D. Michigan 2015).

530 LCIA Reference No. 1291, LCIA Court, 1 October 2002, Arb. Int'l 27 (2011), 355-357. See also, *British Ins. Co. of Cayman v. Water Street Ins. Co., Ltd.*, 93 F.Supp.2d 506 (S.D. New York 2000).

531 C. Armbrüster/V. Wächter, *Ablehnung von Schiedsrichtern wegen Befangenheit im Verfahren*, SchiedsVZ 2017, 213-223, 216, arguing that, under German *lex loci arbitri*, no obligation to take a protocol exists.

532 OLG München, 1 July 2009, 34 SchH 4/09, BeckRS 2011, 7079. See also, BGH, 6 April 2006, V ZB 194/05, NJW 2006, 2492-2495, on state court proceedings.

533 SCAI, *Swiss Rules – Selected Case Law*.

534 *Interprods Ltd. v. De La Rue International Ltd.*, [2014] EWHC 68 (Comm), relying in detail on an analysis of the arbitrator's obligation to act fairly: "It cannot be said that an arbitrator must always put points to a party's witnesses in the absence of the other party. Whether fairness requires him to do so depends upon all the circumstances of the case, including the nature of the point, its importance and whether the witness has sufficiently dealt with the point."

535 *Ostrom v. Worldventures Marketing, LLC*, 60 F.Supp.3d 942 (M.D. Louisiana 2016), examining misconduct rather than evident partiality.

536 *Fowler v. Ritz-Carlton Hotel Co., LLC*, 579 Fed.Appx. 693 (11th Cir. 2014), arguing that courts generally refrain from reviewing the substance of arbitrator's judgments and that an adverse ruling alone rarely evidences partiality. The dispute concerned domestic arbitration.

537 OLG Frankfurt a.M., 24 January 2019, 26 SchH 2/18, BeckRS 2019, 848.

538 *Ray v. Chafetz*, 236 F.Supp.3d 66 (D. Columbia 2017), on domestic arbitration; LCIA Reference No. 7990, LCIA Court, 21 May 2010, Arb. Int'l 27 (2011), 471-473.

539 See *Interprods Ltd. v. De La Rue International Ltd.*, [2014] EWHC 68 (Comm).

540 E.g., in LCIA Reference No. 1291, LCIA Court, 1 October 2002, Arb. Int'l 27 (2011), 355-357; *Oracle Corp. v. Wilson*, 276 F.Supp.3d 22 (S.D. New York 2017); *Ostrom v. Worldventures Marketing, LLC*, 60 F.Supp.3d 942 (M.D. Louisiana 2016), both on domestic arbitration.

tool does not violate this party's right to be heard.[541] Also, conducting a telephone conference merely to set dates for potential hearings does not give rise to a conflict of interest.[542]

Some procedural actions may interfere with the arbitrator's obligations to remain confidential. For example, he or she may inform a third party potentially acting as mediator or expert about the proceedings. It is questionable whether an arbitrator's breach of confidentiality may create the impression of bias in such a scenario.[543] A breach of confidentiality can be of such nature that it violates the obligation to act independently and impartially, e.g., where additional facts support the ground for a conflict of interest. However, where no party is unilaterally favoured, the breach of confidentiality should not constitute a conflict.[544]

4.2.1.3 Deliberating and Decision-Making

The arbitrator's core function is to render a decision.[545] He or she may not delegate the obligation to decide and must participate personally in the deliberations.[546] During deliberations and decision-making, both counsels and parties are usually not present. It will, therefore, be difficult to notice unequal treatment or other violation of independence and impartiality that constitutes a conflict of interest.[547] Besides difficulties in proving a conflict of interest, the threshold of conflicts is generally high in these scenarios. A premature conclusion on a conflict of interest would risk affecting the arbitrator's role as a decision maker and his or her discretion on acting in this role. Hence, the mere allegation that a decision was rendered prematurely, and that the arbitrators failed to consider the evidence in detail is not enough to cross the threshold.[548] Additionally, an arbitrator does

541 LCIA Reference Nos. 81209 and 81210, LCIA Court, 16 November 2009, Arb. Int'l 27 (2011), 455-460, where the court concluded that "it was more likely that a fair-minded and informed observer would conclude that the challenge had been motivated by a desire to delay the proceedings".

542 *Interprods Ltd. v. De La Rue International Ltd.*, [2014] EWHC 68 (Comm).

543 OLG Frankfurt a.M., 26 June 2008, 26 SchH 2/08, BeckRS 2008, 13980, denying the challenge under § 1036(2) German ZPO.

544 C. Armbrüster/V. Wächter, *Ablehnung von Schiedsrichtern wegen Befangenheit im Verfahren*, SchiedsVZ 2017, 213-223, 220.

545 This is the case in common and civil law systems. Cf. C. Seraglini/J. Ortscheidt, *Droit de l'arbitrage interne et international*, paras. 789-790, explicitly pointing at the arbitrator's duties stemming from both the contractual and jurisdictional nature of arbitration. Adding that deliberation and decision-making need to be seen as fulfilling due process principles: N. Andrews/J. Landbrecht, *Schiedsverfahren und Mediation in England*, para. 68. See also, *Mantle v. Upper Deck Co.*, 956 F.Supp. 719 (N.D. Texas 1997).

546 C. Seraglini/J. Ortscheidt, *Droit de l'arbitrage interne et international*, paras. 789-790.

547 *ASM Shipping Ltd. of India v. TTMI Ltd. of England*, [2005] EWHC 2238 (Comm).

548 *Kolel Beth Yechiel Mechil of Tartikov, Inc. v. YLL Irrevocable Trust*, 878 F.Supp.2d 459 (S.D. New York 2012), affirmed by *Kolel Beth Yechiel Mechil of Tartikov, Inc. v. YLL Irrevocable Trust*, 729 F.3d 99 (2d Cir. 2013), on domestic arbitration. Also, the fact that the tribunal deliberated for five minutes is no proof of a

not impair the decision-making by reading potentially privileged documents, since he or she must render a decision on the question of whether or not documents are privileged.[549]

In some scenarios, the question arises of whether the arbitrators' interaction within the tribunal creates a conflict of interest. First, the mere fact that one of the arbitrators has already been challenged successfully or withdrew does not constitute a ground for challenge or annulment with the possible argument that he or she influenced the remaining arbitrators in their decision-making or deliberations.[550] Second, certain hierarchies and unconscious bias between the arbitrators may arguably create conflicts of interest. For example, if the most senior arbitrator commences in the deliberations, would a younger, less experienced arbitrator feel free to disagree and openly speak his or her mind?[551] The underlying issue is whether hierarchies within the tribunal may create a conflict at all. There may be a conflict where one follows the approach of applying different standards of independence and impartiality to party-appointed and presiding arbitrators. In that case, one may argue that the party-appointed arbitrator has a specific role in safeguarding the parties' interests. If the arbitrator is hindered in safeguarding these interests, e.g., by not being heard in the deliberations, there may be an issue. However, arguing that the tribunal in total is obliged under its contractual and judicial duties to render a fair and just award, hierarchies between the arbitrators are less likely to amount to a conflict of interest. Besides, they are difficult to prove.[552]

Additionally, some jurisdictions have upheld the principle of collegiality in arbitration. Where the conduct crosses the limits of this principle, a conflict of interest may exist.

---

premature decision, *Rai v. Barclays Capital Inc.*, 739 F.Supp.2d 364 (S.D. New York 2010). The arbitrator may prejudge the case during the hearings and, hence, only deliberate shortly, cf. Sutter-Somm/Hasenböhler/Leuenberger/S. Wullschleger, Art. 47 para. 49.

549 *Mantle v. Upper Deck Co.*, 956 F.Supp. 719 (N.D. Texas 1997), on domestic arbitration.

550 BGer, 4 May 2011, BGE 137 I 227, 230; *Tamari v. Bache Halsey Stuart Inc.*, 619 F.2d 1196 (7th Cir. 1980). See also, *ASM Shipping Ltd. v. Harris & Ors.*, [2007] EWHC 1513 (Comm), reasoning that this allegation would be "fanciful" but that "[n]o fair minded and informed observer would conclude that there was any real possibility that there had been [...] that might improperly [...] detract from [the arbitrators'] impartiality". However, on using the potential risk of affecting other arbitrators in the deliberations and decision-making, see CA Paris, 21 February 2012, Rev. de l'Arb. 2012, 587-595. The successful annulment was based on another argument. See generally, above chapter 4.1.1.4, on relationships between arbitrators.

551 In order to safeguard impartiality, in French state court proceedings the youngest judge is usually asked to commence with presenting his or her opinion so that he or she is not influenced by the more senior ones, C. Chanais/F. Ferrand/S. Guinchard, *Procédure civile*, para. 1071.

552 It should be noted that the co-arbitrators may delegate preparation of drafts and similar tasks to the presiding arbitrator, *P v. Q, R, S, U*, [2017] EWHC 194 (Comm).

Where two out of three arbitrators actively exclude the third arbitrator from deliberations, the principle of collegiality is violated, and the rendered award may be annulled.[553]

4.2.1.4 Tribunal Orders and the Arbitral Award

The arbitrator may also show bias within procedural orders or arbitral awards.[554] Even though this may be easier to prove than bias in deliberations and decision-making – there is written evidence – the threshold is again high to constitute a conflict of interest. Like the previous scenarios, the allegation of dependence and partiality in orders or the arbitral award may not only be based on a conflict of interest, but may also include allegations of disregard of law and misconduct.

There is substantial case law concerning orders not being grounds for challenging an arbitrator or annulling the award.[555] Only where orders severely violate the parties' procedural rights have courts accepted challenges or annulment actions. Even if an arbitrator made a "regrettable mistake" in issuing an order without having first considered the application made by one party a few days earlier, and even granted that "that order should not have been made", this does not cross the threshold.[556] Often, the presiding arbitrator is able to issue procedural orders alone. Therefore, he or she does not need to consult with the co-arbitrators.[557]

---

553 J. De La Jara/J. Olórtegui, *Puma v. Estudio 2000*. The authors report on a dispute that led to the annulment of the award and to the arbitrator's liability. Puma was awarded partial payback of the legal fees paid to the two arbitrators who excluded Puma's party-appointed arbitrator. Both cases are also reported on in S. Wilske/L. Markert/L. Bräuninger, *Entwicklungen in der internationalen Schiedsgerichtsbarkeit im Jahr 2017 und Ausblick auf 2018*, SchiedsVZ 2018, 134-158, 149.

554 According to C. Armbrüster/V. Wächter, *Ablehnung von Schiedsrichtern wegen Befangenheit im Verfahren*, SchiedsVZ 2017, 213-223, 216, informative orders are particularly used to establish bias. The authors regret this since the challenging party oversees the use for efficiency of these orders.

555 OLG Frankfurt a.M., 24 January 2019, 26 SchH 2/18, BeckRS 2019, 848; OLG München, 10 July 2013, 34 SchH 8/12, NJOZ 2014, 1779-1782; LCIA Reference No. 3488, LCIA Court, 11 July 2007, Arb. Int'l 27 (2011), 413-419; LCIA Reference No. UN0239, LCIA Court, 22 June 2001, 3 July 2001, 3 October 2001, Arb. Int'l 27 (2011), 336-341; SCAI, *Swiss Rules – Selected Case Law*. See also, S. Greenberg, *Tackling Guerrilla Challenges Against Arbitrators*, stating that the ICC Court has rarely upheld challenges based on procedural decisions; BSK IPRG/W. Peter/C. Brunner, Art. 180 para. 16, with further references.

556 LCIA Reference No. 7932, LCIA Court, 17 June 2008, Arb. Int'l 27 (2011), 433-438. See also, OLG München, 10 July 2013, 34 SchH 8/12, NJOZ 2014, 1779-1782.

557 OLG Frankfurt a.M., 4 October 2007, 26 Sch 8/07, SchiedsVZ 2008, 96-102. The presiding arbitrator ordered closure of the arguments although he had not consulted the co-arbitrators on the objections raised against his impartiality and independence. The court reasoned that the presiding arbitrator had dealt with the objections at length before.

A similar high threshold applies to awards. Notably, the mere adverse ruling does not create the impression of bias.[558] Likewise, it is no ground for the challenge that two arbitrators only signed a partial award after the third arbitrator resigned due to disagreement and left the meeting of the arbitral tribunal.[559] It is no ground for annulment that the award merely cited one reference and did not cite the evidence.[560] Especially when examining the orders and the award, courts and institutions tend to judge any potential of bias by considering the "full circumstances surrounding the Tribunal's [...] orders and directions, and of the conduct of the arbitration as a whole".[561]

4.2.1.5 Familiarity with the Subject Matter

In any given arbitration, the arbitrator may not be dealing with a particular subject matter for the first time. He or she may have expressed an opinion on the subject matter or served as an arbitrator or in another capacity in different proceedings concerning the same, or a similar, subject matter. Issues of conflict of interest occur where the arbitrator was previously involved in the same dispute as a lawyer drafting the contract and the arbitration agreement in question,[562] or when arbitrators sit on several tribunals in connected disputes.[563] The decisive criterion is whether the arbitrator remained open-minded for the dispute in question. This group of familiarity with the subject matter as a potential conflict of interest has intersections with relationships based on reappointments.[564] However, they are not identical. Reappointments may include financial interests and other social ties, whereas the familiarity with the subject matter may lead to a lack of an open mind.

Again, several fundamental procedural principles may be touched upon when evaluating whether a conflict of interest exists, including the right to be heard. In line with the

558 *Blackwell v. Merrill Lynch, Pierce, Fenner & Smith Inc.*, 22 F.Supp.3d 565 (W.D. North Carolina 2014), examining partiality under excess of power; LCIA Reference No. 96/X22, LCIA Court, 22 July 1998, Arb. Int'l 27 (2011), 325-327; *Scandinavian Reinsurance Co. Ltd. v. Saint Paul Fire and Marine Ins. Co.*, 668 F.3d 60 (2d Cir. 2012); S. Feldman, *Contract Law and Practice*, Sect. 14:35. Particularly, this must be the case where the rules provide for the possibility to draft a dissenting opinion, *RSM Production Corp. v. Saint Lucia*, ICSID Tribunal, 23 October 2014, ARB/12/10, 79. See also, Art. 47(3) ICSID Rules.

559 BGer, 20 December 1989, BGE 115 Ia 400, 404-405.

560 *Thian Lok Tio v. Washington Hosp. Center*, 753 F.Supp.2d 9 (D. Columbia, 2010), relying on the fact that there was no motive for acting biased. See also, *Ostrom v. Worldventures Marketing, LLC*, 60 F.Supp.3d 942 (M.D. Louisiana 2016).

561 *Dera Commercial Estate v. Derya Inc.*, [2018] EWHC 1673 (Comm).

562 BezGer Affoltern am Albis, 26 May 1994, ASA Bull. 1997, 262-273, arguing that such an arbitrator may not be impartial when interpreting the said contract. The request for enforcement was not granted due to violation of the Swiss *ordre public*, according to Art. V(2)(b) New York Convention.

563 J.-F. Poudret/S. Besson, *Comparative Law of International Arbitration*, para. 421. But see, *Halliburton Co. v. Chubb Bermuda Ins. Ltd.*, [2018] EWCA Civ 817, upheld by *Halliburton Co. v. Chubb Bermuda Ins. Ltd.*, [2020] UKSC 48.

564 See above chapter 4.1.1.1.2.

tendencies of a high threshold for the arbitrator's conduct constituting a conflict of interest, authors and courts favour a high threshold on the issue of familiarity with the subject matter.[565] A high threshold in these scenarios ensures the parties' right to appoint their arbitrator.

An arbitrator's familiarity with the subject matter as a potential conflict of interest will often be demonstrated by expressing a legal opinion or previous and parallel proceedings.

4.2.1.5.1 Expressing a Legal Opinion

Most cases reveal that usually expressing an opinion on legal issues to be decided in an arbitral proceeding does not create a conflict of interest or violate another procedural principle. Notably, where the arbitrator publishes before the proceedings commenced, the publication cannot create a conflict of interest. It is the parties' right to choose an arbitrator who has a favourable legal opinion. Additionally, an academic and scientific exchange of thoughts is indispensable for decision makers.[566] Generally prohibiting such exchange could have a detrimental effect on arbitration as a dispute settlement mechanism. In these scenarios of expressing an opinion on legal issues before the proceedings commenced, there is no genuine connection to the ongoing dispute,[567] and the arbitrator or judge remained open-minded towards deciding the concrete legal issues.[568] Where one of the arbitrators published his opinion on the first out of three awards in an ongoing arbitration, these prerequisites were not fulfilled, and a conflict of interest may exist.[569] Thus, one criterion is the point in time of the conduct in question. If the comments are published during the proceedings before the award is rendered, it is more likely to constitute a conflict since the arbitrator no longer appears open-minded.[570]

565 J.-F. Poudret/S. Besson, *Comparative Law of International Arbitration*, para. 421. E.g., the mere membership in an organisation is no proof for prejudging a case. Cf. *Helow v. Advocate General for Scotland*, [2008] UKHL 62, allowing state court judges to be members in organisations. In this regard, see also, Code of Conduct for the Justices of the Federal Constitutional Court (Germany), para. 3.

566 Cf. BGH, 13 January 2016, VII ZR 36/14, NJW 2016, 1022-1025 and BGH, 14 May 2002, XI ZR 388/01, NJW 2002, 2396-2397, on state court judges. The first decision dealt with conduct during ongoing but suspended proceedings.

567 On state court judges: BGer, 17 February 1982, BGE 108 Ia 48; Sutter-Somm/Hasenböhler/Leuenberger/S. Wullschleger, Art. 47 para. 45; BSK BV/J. Reich, Art. 30 para. 29; BGG PK/D. Vock Art. 34 para. 10.

568 OLG Frankfurt a.M., 4 October 2007, 26 Sch 8/07, SchiedsVZ 2008, 96-102, on both criteria; P. Mankowski, *Die Ablehnung von Schiedsrichtern*, SchiedsVZ 2004, 304-313, 311; BGG PK/D. Vock Art. 34 para. 10.

569 BGer, 7 November 2006, BGE 133 I 89, affirming the successful challenge of the arbitrator.

570 C. Armbrüster/V. Wächter, *Ablehnung von Schiedsrichtern wegen Befangenheit im Verfahren*, SchiedsVZ 2017, 213-223, 216. In this direction also, BSK IPRG/W. Peter/C. Brunner, Art. 180 para. 15, citing BGer, 7 November 2006, BGE 133 I 89, ruling that a conflict of interest exists where an arbitrator states that the outcome of another very similar arbitration was "obviously wrong".

Another criterion is the material connection to the case. This is also the criterion applied by the IBA Guidelines 2014. Where the expression is "a position on the case", the arbitrator needs to disclose this previous expression, but the expression is in itself no ground for challenge or annulment.[571] Where the arbitrator previously expressed a legal opinion that is not focused on in the current dispute, he or she does not have to disclose it nor does it create a conflict of interest.[572] This approach may be described as requiring central similarities. Only expressing an opinion on the core issues of the dispute in question falls under the Orange List. It leaves some leeway for finding a conflict of interest since central similarities are limited by their nature. The differentiation under the IBA Guidelines 2014 between central similarities on the Orange List and peripheral similarities on the Green List may create difficulties. The arbitrator needs to determine how close his or her expression is connected to the dispute. With regard to expressions of legal opinions before the proceedings commenced, or before the arbitrator is appointed, this may cause insecurities in handling disclosure obligations. Opposing the approach under the IBA Guidelines 2014, one could argue that expressing a legal opinion, and especially publishing it, generally reveals a prejudgment of this legal issue. Following this approach, any legal similarity of the expressed opinion with the case in dispute proves prejudgment cumulating in a conflict of interest.[573] It would be unrealistic to assume that the arbitrator would deviate in the proceedings from his or her previous postulations, thus providing the absence of being open-minded. Some authors differentiate in this regard between party-appointed and the presiding arbitrator: expressing a legal opinion previously should not be a ground for finding dependence and partiality for the party-appointed arbitrator, but only for the presiding arbitrator, due to the parties' right to appoint their arbitrator.[574] Such general approaches on finding dependence and partiality should be rejected. It limits the appointing party's right to appoint and rejects the general interest in arbitrators who actively exchange their thoughts.

Finally, the arbitrator may also express a political opinion. Whether this creates a conflict of interest again depends on the connection to the dispute in question[575] and the point in time of expressing the opinion.

---

571 Part II, para. 3.5.2 IBA Guidelines 2014, i.e., the Orange List.

572 Part II, para. 4.1.1 IBA Guidelines 2014, i.e., the Green List.

573 This approach is also in line with the requirement for German judges of the *Bundesverfassungsgericht*, Code of Conduct for the Justices of the Federal Constitutional Court (Germany), para. 11, which demands judges not to "give expert opinions concerning constitutional matters" or to "offer predictions as to the outcome of pending proceedings or matters that will likely be brought before the Court".

574 D. Effer-Uhe, *Schiedsgerichtliche Unabhängigkeit bei wissenschaftlichen Äußerungen*, SchiedsVZ 2018, 75-80, 78-80. But see, O. Froitzheim, *Schiedsrichterliche Befangenheit durch Äußerungen zu Rechtsfragen – Eine Antwort auf Effer-Uhe*, SchiedsVZ 2019, 10-16, critically replying to Effer-Uhe.

575 KuKo ZPO/R. Kiener, Art. 47 para. 21.

4.2.1.5.2 Previous and Parallel Proceedings

The arbitrator may be involved previously or in parallel in similar legal and factual issues as those of the current dispute. His or her involvement may create a conflict of interest. The issue of previous and parallel conduct likely overlaps with the issue of repeat appointments and expressing an opinion. However, the focus will be, first, on conflicts of interest in the subject matter of the dispute, legally and factually, and not the relationship between the arbitrator and one of the parties or counsels. Second, previous and parallel proceedings include different scenarios than expressing an opinion, e.g., not the mere publication in a journal.

As an Arbitrator

Previous or parallel conduct in other proceedings as an adjudicator can pose a risk to the open-mindedness in the current proceedings. This lack of open-mindedness may be present where both factual and legal issues are similar.[576] Some business industries encounter this issue more frequently than others.[577] In case law, the scenario of previous proceedings is more prevalent than parallel proceedings. If there are no factual similarities, i.e., same parties or counsels involved, both scenarios should be handled alike. If there are no factual similarities, a series of similar previous rulings may not create a conflict.[578] As long as the arbitrator remains open-minded, he or she may act as an arbitrator.[579] Where another party in the same branch and with the same size as the current party previously appointed the same arbitrator, there are no factual similarities leading to a conflict of interest.[580] The similar parties had the same market position in the same market, but the disputes were not connected. However, if factual similarities are present, the involvement in a similar dispute may create a conflict of interest.[581] Courts may base the conflict, inter alia, on the

576 *Dealer Computer Services, Inc. v. Michael Motor Co., Inc.*, 761 F.Supp.2d 459 (S.D. Texas 2010). The U.S. Court of Appeals reversed the decision due to a waiver in *Dealer Computer Services, Inc. v. Michael Motor Co., Inc.*, 485 Fed.Appx. 724 (5th Cir. 2012). See also, TGI Paris, 13 January 1986, Rev. de l'Arb. 1987, 63-66, sustaining the challenge of the arbitrator.

577 E.g., insurance or maritime disputes. But see, BGer, 10 June 2010, 4A_458/2009 ASA Bull. 2010, 520-539, rejecting the challenge.

578 *Prince Jefri Bolkiah v. State of Brunei Darussalam*, [2007] UKPC 62, regarding state court proceedings; *Thian Lok Tio v. Washington Hosp. Center*, 753 F.Supp.2d 9 (D. Columbia 2010), on domestic arbitration; *Anderson, Inc. v. Horton Farms, Inc.*, 166 F.3d 308 (6th Cir. 1998), also on domestic arbitration.

579 The requirement of being "open-minded" applies also to state court judges. In France, the French COJ stipulates in Art. L. 111-9 that the "freedom of judgment" must be altered by prior participation in order to disqualify a judge.

580 CA Paris, 1 July 2011, Rev. de l'Arb. 2011, 761-765.

581 C. Chanais/F. Ferrand/S. Guinchard, *Procédure civile*, para. 1061, on French state court proceedings involving the same parties. The authors provide case law on, e.g., prior involvement in preliminary judgments and different instances of the same judges. See also, BSK BV/J. Reich, Art. 30 para. 26, providing the example that a judge is involved in the same dispute as a civil judge and later in criminal court as a criminal judge.

fact that the arbitrator previously favoured a specific position advocated by the same or an affiliated party in previous proceedings.[582]

Generally, the mere legal similarity with previous or parallel proceedings does not create a conflict of interest. Like the treatment of expressing a legal opinion, the fact that an arbitrator has a specific legal opinion, and experience in judging with it, is usually the reason for appointing him or her. The parties' right to appoint a trusted and experienced arbitrator is of major importance in arbitration and an effect of the contractual nature of arbitration.[583] Alternatively, one could base a similar argument on the purely judicial nature of arbitration and function of the arbitrators: in line with the judicial role, the arbitrator has to apply his or her legal position in decision-making, irrespective of who appointed the arbitrator.[584] Therefore, previous dissenting or majority opinions are far from demonstrating a conflict of interest. This judicial role was highlighted by the Court of Appeal in England and Wales for adjudicators elaborating that

> [j]udges are assumed to be trustworthy and to understand that they should approach every case with an open mind. The same applies to adjudicators, who are almost always professional persons. That is not to say that, if it is asked to re-determine an issue and the evidence and arguments are merely a repeat of what went before, the tribunal will not be likely to reach the same conclusion as before. It would be unrealistic, indeed absurd, to expect the tribunal in such circumstances to ignore its earlier decision and not to be inclined to come to the same conclusion as before, particularly if the previous decision was carefully reasoned.[585]

In Another Capacity

Arbitrators may have been involved with the same subject matter in another capacity, e.g., as counsel, expert, or mediator. Generally, the same prerequisites as for arbitral proceedings apply: if the arbitrator remains open-minded and there are no strong factual similarities,

582 *Cofely Ltd. v. Anthony Bingham and Knowles Ltd.*, [2016] EWHC 240 (Comm). However, the main criterion was that the same party repeatedly appointed the same arbitrator.

583 See above chapter 1.3.2.

584 Cf. *Andros Compania Maritima, SA v. Marc Rich & Co., AG*, 579 F.2d 691 (2d Cir. 1978).

585 *AMEC Capital Projects Ltd. v. Whitefriars City Estates Ltd.*, [2004] EWCA Civ 1418, para. 20. The professionalism and procedural expertise of arbitrators were also arguments in *Halliburton Co. v. Chubb Bermuda Ins. Ltd.*, [2018] EWCA Civ 817, not to disqualify an arbitrator, upheld by *Halliburton Co. v. Chubb Bermuda Ins. Ltd.*, [2020] UKSC 48. See also, *Prince Jefri Bolkiah v. State of Brunei Darussalam*, [2007] UKPC 62, reasoning that "judicial experience, by its nature, conditions the mind to independence of thought and impartiality of decision", regarding state court judges.

no conflict of interest is apparent.[586] However, where the arbitrator was previously an expert for third parties not directly involved in the current dispute but closely connected to one of the parties, a conflict of interest may arise.[587] Where the expert opinion or prior legal advice concerned the same dispute, the legal and factual similarities create a conflict of interest.[588]

4.2.1.6 Non-Disclosure as a Ground for Finding Dependence and Partiality

According to the prevailing current case law, non-disclosure is, in itself, not a ground for finding dependence and partiality.[589] This majority marks a difference from older case law. The most famous and divergently discussed decision in this regard is *Commonwealth Coatings Corp. v. Continental Casualty Co. et al.* Justice Black's majority opinion stressed the role of independence and impartiality in arbitral proceedings, writing that

> [he] cannot believe that it was the purpose of Congress to authorize litigants to submit their cases and controversies to arbitration boards that might reasonably be thought biased against one litigant and favourable to another

and based this conclusion on a violation of the obligation to disclose.[590] Slightly deviating from this reasoning, Justice White wrote the opinion that is most often cited. He agreed on the result to annul the award but focused on the materiality of the undisclosed facts. He clarified that not every violation of the obligation to disclose creates a ground for annulling an arbitral award.[591]

---

586 S. Greenberg, *Tackling Guerrilla Challenges Against Arbitrators*. The challenge was based on the presiding arbitrator's conduct as a lawyer in an unrelated dispute twenty years ago, where he had allegedly acted racist. The ICC Court dismissed the challenge. Greenberg considers this case as a possible example of a tactical challenge. The challenge was additionally based on the fact that the presiding arbitrator had been challenged in an unrelated LCIA proceeding previously.

587 *Sphere Drake Ins. v. American Reliable Ins. Co.*, [2004] EWHC 796 (Comm).

588 The IBA Guidelines 2014 place this scenario in the Waivable Red List, Part II, para. 2.1.1. Likewise, these scenarios create conflicts of interest for state court judges, e.g., Art. 47(1)(b) Swiss ZPO.

589 There are, however, some rules providing for this effect, e.g., Rule 2 HKIAC Code of Conduct. See below chapter 6.2.2, on the possible approach to differentiate the standard of independence and impartiality in non-disclosure scenarios, and chapter 7.1.4, on the consequences of non-disclosure.

590 *Commonwealth Coatings Co. v. Continental Casualty Co. et al.*, 89 S.Ct. 337 (1968), comparing arbitration with state court litigation, the court ruled that the independence and impartiality of arbitrators is even more important since there is no appellate review in arbitration.

591 He generally stressed the role of the obligation to disclose "the judiciary should minimize its role in arbitration as judge of the arbitrator's impartiality. That role is best consigned to the parties, who are the architects of their own arbitration process, and are far better informed of the prevailing ethical standards and reputations within their business". *Commonwealth Coatings Co. v. Continental Casualty Co. et al.*, 89 S.Ct. 337 (1968), Dissenting Op. White. The dissenting opinion written by Justice Fortas stressed that a general rule of non-disclosure being a ground for vacating an award cannot be upheld with the FAA, *Commonwealth Coatings Co. v. Continental Casualty Co. et al.*, 89 S.Ct. 337 (1968), Dissenting Op. Fortas.

Following only a slim majority of Justice Black's opinion, and a wider approval of Justice White's concurring opinion, the latter is applied more often. The criticism of Justice Black's opinion is summed up in the following decision:

> Requiring vacatur on these attenuated facts would rob arbitration of one of its most attractive features apart from speed and finality-expertise. Arbitration would lose the benefit of specialized knowledge, because the best lawyers and professionals, who normally have the longest lists of potential connections to disclose, have no need to risk blemishes on their reputations from post-arbitration lawsuits attacking them as biased.[592]

Many other courts and authors follow Justice White. They conclude that non-disclosure is in itself not grounds for annulling the award,[593] but that the additional evaluation of the undisclosed fact may lead to a challenge of the arbitrator or annulling the award.[594] For example,

> where an arbitrator has accepted an appointment in such multiple references in circumstances which might reasonably give rise to justifiable doubts as to his or her impartiality, or is aware of other matters which might reasonably give rise to those doubts, a failure in his or her duty to disclose those matters to the party who is not the common party to the references deprives that party of the opportunity to address and perhaps resolve the matters which should have been disclosed. The failure to disclose may demonstrate a lack of regard

---

592 *Positive Software Solutions, Inc. v. New Century Mortg. Corp.*, 476 F.3d 278 (5th Cir. 2007), 285-286, on domestic arbitration.

593 *Johnson v. Directory Assistants Inc.*, 797 F.3d 1294 (11th Cir. 2015); *Scandinavian Reinsurance Co. Ltd. v. Saint Paul Fire and Marine Ins. Co.*, 668 F.3d 60 (2d Cir. 2012); *Sphere Drake Ins. Ltd. v. All American Life Ins. Co.*, 307 F.3d 617 (7th Cir. 2002); *Federal Vending, Inc. v. Steak & Ale of Florida, Inc.*, 71 F.Supp.2d 1245 (S.D. Florida 1999). See also, BGer, 15 October 2001, 4P.188/2001; N. Voser/E. Fischer, *The Arbitral Tribunal*, p. 67. This is especially the case where there is an explanation for non-disclosure, *H v. L and M*, [2017] EWHC 137 (Comm). See generally, S. Feldman, *Contract Law and Practice*, Sect. 14:35; C. Jarrosson, *A propos de l'obligation de révélation, Une leçon de méthode de la Cour de cassation, Note sous Cass. civ. 1re, 10 octobre 2012*, Rev. de l'Arb. 2013, 130-137, 132; C. Palo, *Bias of Arbitrator as Ground for Vacatur of Arbitration Award*, Sect. 13.

594 English case law: *Halliburton Co. v. Chubb Bermuda Ins. Ltd.*, [2018] EWCA Civ 817, upheld by *Halliburton Co. v. Chubb Bermuda Ins. Ltd.*, [2020] UKSC 48; *Sierra Fishing Co. v. Farran*, [2015] EWHC 140 (Comm). French case law: Cass civ 1ére, 25 June 2014, 11-16.444, Rev. de l'Arb. 2015, 75-77; Cass civ 1ère, 20 October 2010, 09-68131. German case law: BGH, 2 May 2017, I ZB 1/16, SchiedsVZ 2017, 317-323; BGH, 4 March 1999, III ZR 72/98, NJW 1999, 2370-2372; OLG Frankfurt a.M., 10 January 2008, 26 Sch 21/07, SchiedsVZ 2008, 199-200; OLG Naumburg, 19 December 2001, 10 SchH 3/01, SchiedsVZ 2003, 134-142. United States case law: *Dow Corning Corp. v. Safety National Cas. Corp.*, 335 F.3d 742 (8th Cir. 2003); *Olson v. Merrill Lynch, Pierce, Fenner & Smith, Inc.*, 51 F.3d 157 (8th Cir. 1995). However, non-disclosure may be important for upholding the challenge, CA Paris, 14 October 2014, Rev. de l'Arb. 2015, 151-155, 154.

to the interests of the non-common party and may in certain circumstances amount to apparent bias.[595]

Initially, some French decisions were also interpreted to sanction primarily the violation of the obligation to disclose.[596] However, this approach has changed.[597]

Some courts and scholars differentiate in regard to whether non-disclosure was intentional. An intentional non-disclosure would undermine the parties' agreement.[598] Thus, it should constitute an exception to the general rule that non-disclosure in itself does not constitute a ground for challenge or annulment.[599] The German *Bundesgerichtshof* clarified that non-disclosure in itself does not constitute a ground for finding dependence and partiality. However, in case of suspicion of intentional non-disclosure, the standard of a lack of independence and impartiality, i.e., justifiable doubts, is met.[600] In fact, by analysing whether the facts met the applicable standard of independence and impartiality, the court had recourse to the initial examination of grounds for finding dependence and partiality. It, thus, underlined that non-disclosure in itself does not constitute such a ground.[601]

The obligation to disclose has the purpose of strengthening the parties' confidence in the tribunal, to enable their right to appoint, and continues throughout the proceedings until the end of the mission of the arbitrators.[602] Hence, where an arbitrator failed to disclose a fact that may give rise to justifiable doubts as to his or her independence and impartiality,

595 *Halliburton Co. v. Chubb Bermuda Ins. Ltd.*, [2020] UKSC 48, Lord Hodge, para. 118.

596 E.g., CA Paris, 12 February 2009, Rev. de l'Arb. 2009, 186-190.

597 T. Heintz/G. da Costa Cerquiera, *Vers une rationalisation de l'obligation de révélation de l'arbitre en droit français*, ASA Bull. 2013, 448-461, 451-457.

598 L. Gross, *Should Parties' Disclosure Requirements For Arbitrators Be Honored by Courts: Positive Software Solutions, Inc. v. New Century Mortgage Corporation*, S. Illinois U.L.J. 33 (2008), 71-93, 72.

599 BGH, 2 May 2017, I ZB 1/16, SchiedsVZ 2017, 317-323 and BGH, 31 January 2019, I ZB 46/18, NZM 2020, 334-336, both on an expert's non-disclosure in the same dispute. See generally, N. Schmidt-Ahrendts/ V. Schneider, *„Gut Ding will Weile haben"*, SchiedsVZ 2020, 35-41, outlining both decisions and their consequences. Cf. in this direction also, C. Palo, *Bias of Arbitrator as Ground for Vacatur of Arbitration Award*, Sect. 14.

600 BGH, 31 January 2019, I ZB 46/18, NZM 2020, 334-336, 336.

601 The decision rendered by the German *Bundesgerichtshof* dealt with an expert's non-disclosure. The approach to examining whether the non-disclosure meets the threshold of ruling on dependence and partiality is also applied to arbitrators in the same manner, see, e.g., OLG Frankfurt a.M., 24 January 2019, 26 SchH 2/18, BeckRS 2019, 848; OLG München, 10 July 2013, 34 SchH 8/12, NJOZ 2014, 1779-1782. But see, OLG Karlsruhe, 14 July 2006, 10 Sch 1/06, BeckRS 2006, 19851; OLG Naumburg, 19 December 2001, 10 SchH 3/01, SchiedsVZ 2003, 134-142.

602 CA Reims, 2 November 2011, Rev. de l'Arb. 2012, 112-119. See in more detail below chapter 7.1, on the purpose.

the violation of the obligation to disclose may result in the annulment of the award.[603] Where the omitted fact does not create reasonable doubts, the arbitrator likely will not be challenged nor the award annulled.[604] "Materiality of the undisclosed conflict drives a finding of evident partiality, not the failure to disclose or investigate per se."[605] This approach fosters the importance of the obligation to be independent and not the obligation to disclose. There is "no ipso facto violation of the principle of independence when the duty to disclose is violated".[606]

4.2.1.7 Conduct Provoking (Tactical) Challenges

Some challenges are difficult to categorise. It may be the case that the party requesting the challenge provoked the grounds for that challenge, that the arbitrator reacted too emotionally to the request to step down, or that there are other facts suggesting a tactical challenge.[607] In any case, it is difficult to spot and classify these groups of challenges.[608]

There are cases where it appears that one party provokes the arbitrator's reaction and that this reaction leads to the challenge or request for annulment by that same party. For example, the Swiss *Bundesgericht* denied the annulment of an award where one of the parties ordered a private investigator to observe the presiding arbitrator and that arbitrator pressed criminal charges against the party ordering investigation.[609] The Swiss *Bundesgericht* reasoned that the arbitrator's reaction to press criminal charges was objectively reasonable.[610]

603 Cass civ 1ère, 10 October 2012, 11-20.299, Rev. de l'Arb. 2013, 129-130; *Scandinavian Reinsurance Co. Ltd. v. Saint Paul Fire and Marine Ins. Co.*, 668 F.3d 60 (2d Cir. 2012); *LGC Holdings, Inc. v. Julius Klein Diamonds, LLC*, 238 F.Supp.3d 452 (S.D. New York 2017); *Midwest Generation EME, LLC v. Continuum Chemical Corp.*, 768 F.Supp.2d 939 (N.D. Illinois 2010); C. Palo, *Bias of Arbitrator as Ground for Vacatur of Arbitration Award*, Sect. 14.

604 CA Paris, 1 July 2011, Rev. de l'Arb. 2011, 761-765.

605 *National Indemnity Co. v. IRB Brasil Resseguros SA*, 164 F.Supp.3d 457 (S.D. New York 2016).

606 T. Heintz/G. da Costa Cerquiera, *Vers une rationalisation de l'obligation de révélation de l'arbitre en droit français*, ASA Bull. 2013, 448-461, 455-456.

607 A. Hosang, *Obstructionist Behavior in International Commercial Arbitration*, p. 105 et seq., on "undue challenges". The author warns arbitrators "not to hastily assume bad intentions of the party submitting a challenge", p. 106.

608 Although several statistics show a general increase in numbers of challenges, it cannot be concluded that likewise the number of challenges in an attempt to "bully the arbitrator" rose as well, S. Greenberg, *Tackling Guerrilla Challenges Against Arbitrators*. According to Greenberg, the percentage of cases with challenges varies from year to year, but there is no "discernible trend up or down". Others explain the increase with the general fact of an increasing market of international commercial arbitration, S. Luttrell, *Bias Challenges in International Commercial Arbitration*, p. 250.

609 BGer, 14 December 2004, 4P.208/2004/lma, para. C 4.1. However, in that case the arbitrator did not know whether it was claimant or respondent who ordered the investigator.

610 The criteria of "objective and reasonable" for the arbitrator's reactions to a provocation are also used by OLG München, 10 January 2007, 34 SchH 7/06, BeckRS 2007, 00709. On state court judges, see also, MünchKomm ZPO/N. Stackmann, § 42 para. 24.

This decision is to be welcomed, since otherwise, a party may tactically arrange the grounds of a conflict of interest. This reasoning also applies to scenarios where one party raised claims against the arbitrator, e.g., civil claims due to alleged misconduct.[611] An additional example of provocation may be initiating a press campaign.[612] A typical example is where the situation heats up by several challenges raised by both parties.[613]

Additionally, an arbitrator may be provoked by the challenge itself. There are several examples where the arbitrator's reaction to a previous challenge gave reason for a new challenge. In general, when the tribunal must render a decision on a challenge it has to act objectively. Evident unobjective behaviour or dismissive conduct may reveal a negative attitude towards the challenging party.[614] Even if the arbitrator does not decide the challenge, he or she may "respond so immoderately that the arbitrator's response (rather than the original challenge) produces doubts about the arbitrator's impartiality".[615] Merely expressing discomfort does not meet the threshold of creating a conflict of interest in these scenarios.[616] However, where the presiding arbitrator has been successfully challenged, and the co-arbitrators react so emotionally and defensively that it may be perceived as offending the parties, and it appears that the co-arbitrators took the challenge personally, a conflict of interest may arise. Thus, one may advise an arbitrator not to react to such a challenge.[617] Also, where the tone of subsequent disclosures and the reaction to a challenge are so high tensioned that, from an objective point of view, the arbitrator's ability to assess future submissions impassively and objectively is not given, the arbitrator's reaction may constitute a conflict of interest. The reaction to a challenge as a ground for challenge or annulment needs to be assessed for each arbitrator individually. Arbitrators are not liable for each other's conduct where the ground for a conflict of interest is personal.[618]

---

611 C. Armbrüster/V. Wächter, *Ablehnung von Schiedsrichtern wegen Befangenheit im Verfahren*, SchiedsVZ 2017, 213-223, 216. According to the authors, raising claims against the arbitrator cannot constitute a conflict of interest.

612 BGer, 15 February 1990, BGE 116 Ia 14, para. E 4-7c, regarding state court judges. According to the Swiss *Bundesgericht*, only virulent press campaigns may infringe the independence and impartiality of judges.

613 *Stef Shipping Corp. v. Norris Grain Co.*, 209 F.Supp. 249 (S.D. New York 1962), the annulment was not successful.

614 OLG Frankfurt a.M., 13 February 2012, 26 SchH 15/11, BeckRS 2014, 12067. The challenge was not successful. Affirmative, C. Armbrüster/V. Wächter, *Ablehnung von Schiedsrichtern wegen Befangenheit im Verfahren*, SchiedsVZ 2017, 213-223, 216. See also, Sutter-Somm/Hasenböhler/Leuenberger/S. Wullschleger, Art. 47 para. 33 et seq.

615 D. Hacking, *Challenges: Theirs Is to Reason Why*, GAR 5 (2006), 26-30, 28.

616 *H v. L and M*, [2017] EWHC 137 (Comm), denying the challenge, inter alia, based on the arbitrator's response to his challenge and stressing the high threshold for a conflict of interest violating independence and impartiality.

617 N. Blackaby/C. Partasides/A. Redfern, *Redfern and Hunter*, para. 4.90.

618 C. Armbrüster/V. Wächter, *Ablehnung von Schiedsrichtern wegen Befangenheit im Verfahren*, SchiedsVZ 2017, 213-223, 215, adding that knowledge of the conduct is itself no ground for a conflict of interest.

Besides these two groups of challenges referring to provocation, other scenarios can also be grouped as tactical challenges. This category refers to scenarios where it appears the challenge is made to gain a procedural advantage.[619] In other words, in these scenarios, challenges are used as a "cost-effective way to ensure an expensive delay".[620] The group of tactical challenges can be categorised into challenges relating to the frequency of a challenge, the timing, and its content.[621]

First, regarding the frequency of challenges, Greenberg argues that frequent challenges in a remarkably short period "may give rise to doubts about the motives". He provides the example of an unpublished ICC case where the claimant placed 23 challenges that were all denied.[622] In an example of another unpublished ICC case, one party filed six challenges and six objections, causing one arbitrator to resign and delaying the proceedings. In the end, all challenges were denied.[623]

Second, the challenge may be placed at a particular point in time of the proceedings. A classic example of such a tactical challenge is where the challenge is placed right before the hearing, causing the hearing to be adjourned.[624] Also, where institutional rules provide for circulation of statements of independence and impartiality before the appointment, challenges on facts disclosed in the statement and placed right after the appointment can appear suspicious as delaying tactics.[625] Suspicion may also arise where the challenge is placed after the tribunal deliberated but before the final award is communicated to the

619 D. Hacking, *Challenges: Theirs Is to Reason Why*, GAR 5 (2006), 26-30, 26. Tactical challenges belong to the broader group of "guerrilla tactics" in arbitration, including other procedural vehicles, e.g., the refusal to pay the share of the advance on costs; the deliberate nomination of a "biased, recalcitrant or unresponsive arbitrator"; and forcing the appointed arbitrator to resign, see S. Greenberg, *Tackling Guerrilla Challenges Against Arbitrators.*

620 M. Baker/L. Greenwood, *Are Challenges Overused in International Arbitration?*, J. Int'l Arb. 30 (2013), 101-112, 102.

621 S. Greenberg, *Tackling Guerrilla Challenges Against Arbitrators.*

622 S. Greenberg, *Tackling Guerrilla Challenges Against Arbitrators.*

623 S. Greenberg, *Tackling Guerrilla Challenges Against Arbitrators.*

624 S. Greenberg, *Tackling Guerrilla Challenges Against Arbitrators.* Greenberg provides an example of an unpublished ICC case where the challenge was placed one week before the hearing. In the end, the hearing was cancelled and the challenge dismissed.

625 S. Greenberg, *Tackling Guerrilla Challenges Against Arbitrators.* See also, N. Blackaby/C. Partasides/A. Redfern, *Redfern and Hunter*, para. 4.90.

parties.[626] Such a challenge may reveal that the challenging party suspects that the tribunal is not persuaded of the merits of the challenging party's arguments.[627]

Finally, the content of the challenge may give rise to the suspicion of being a tactical challenge. The examples Greenberg provides in his article *Tackling Guerrilla Challenges Against Arbitrators: Institutional Perspective* all belong to scenarios where one of the parties alleged that the conduct of an arbitrator constituted a conflict of interest, often additionally alleging excess of power and a violation of the right to be heard. This group is, hence, diverse and especially difficult to detect. A combination of different scenarios may give a stronger appearance of guerrilla tactics.[628]

4.2.1.8 Involvement of Social Networks

Besides the relationship on social networking sites,[629] the conduct on these sites, e.g., liking and sharing posts, raises the question of whether a conflict of interest may result. In general, there is no reason to differentiate the conduct on social networking sites from that of face-to-face scenarios or other conduct, e.g., in publishing an article or giving a speech. Therefore, the general principles apply.[630] In line with these principles, a mere "like" on Facebook does not constitute a conflict of interest.[631] A "like" demonstrates the person's approval of a post. In particular, where the post is not related to the dispute, a "like" cannot constitute a conflict of interest. Even if the post would be related to the dispute, the intentions of the person liking the post must be evaluated. In parallel to expressing a legal opinion elsewhere, arbitrators should refrain from commenting on ongoing arbitral proceedings on social networks.

---

626 S. Greenberg, *Tackling Guerrilla Challenges Against Arbitrators*, providing examples of different unpublished ICC cases: respondent challenging the presiding arbitrator between approval of the draft final award and notification; challenging the presiding arbitrator after the proceedings had been closed and just one month before the final award was rendered; placing the challenge after notification of the award and at the same time applying for correction of the award; challenge after the notification arguing that the award had never been received because the counsel had been sacked a few weeks prior to the final award. All these challenges were dismissed by the ICC Court.

627 N. Blackaby/C. Partasides/A. Redfern, *Redfern and Hunter*, para. 4.90.

628 S. Greenberg, *Tackling Guerrilla Challenges Against Arbitrators.*

629 See above chapter 4.1.1.1.8.

630 See above chapter 4.2.1.

631 CA Lyon, 11 March 2014, 13/00447, where the presiding arbitrator had been friends on Facebook with respondent's counsel. In fact, the counsel liked the arbitrator's fan page for the latter's campaign in the election of the Paris Bar Council after the arbitral proceedings ended. The *cour d'appel de* Paris previously annulled the award, however, based on other arguments, CA Paris, 10 March 2011, 09/28537, ASA Bull. 2013, 443-447, and the French *cour de cassation* reversed the decision, Cass civ 1ére, 10 October 2012, 11-20.299, Rev. de l'Arb. 2013, 129-130.

As already discussed previously (above chapter 4.1.1.1.8), conduct on social networks differs in regard to issues of proof from face-to-face conduct.[632] Social networking sites preserve conduct and, therefore, facilitate proof.[633] However, this, again, does not change the fact that the underlying conduct that is provable must meet the threshold of a conflict of interest.

Looking at regulations for state court judges, different notes and guidelines in the United States are noteworthy and "could be instructive for arbitrators".[634] Although the guidelines differ on the degree of use of social networks,[635] they do not forbid or suggest abstinence from using social media at all.[636]

4.2.1.9 Involvement of Third-Party Funding

Finally, the arbitrator's conduct in cases involving a third-party funder may demonstrate a conflict of interest.

First, a conflict of interest may occur due to the mere fact that the funder is engaged. The conclusion of the funding agreement may trigger the argument that the funded party has a stronger case. The underlying reasoning is that funders are investors and "only agree to fund the strongest claims, after having conducted a rigorous assessment of the case".[637] They invest where the chances of success are around or above 50%.[638] However, the mere

---

632 A. Rojahn/C. Jerger, *Richterliche Unparteilichkeit und Anabhängigkeit im Zeitalter sozialer Netzwerke*, NJW 2014, 1147-1150, 1150.

633 In German state court proceedings on criminal matters, a judge was found to create justifiable doubts as to his independence and impartiality by wearing a T-shirt stating, "We give your future a home: jail". A picture of him wearing the T-shirt was on his Facebook profile. The challenge was successful. BGH, 12 January 2016, 3 StR 482/15, NStZ 2016, 218-219.

634 R. Glick/L. Stipanowich, *Arbitrator Disclosure in the Internet Age*, Disp. Res. J. 67 (2012), 1-7, 3-4, referring to guidelines in California (Calif. Judges Ass'n Judicial Ethics Comm. Op. 66 (23 November 2010)), Florida (Fla. S. Ct. Jud. Ethics Advisory Comm. Ops. 2009-20, 2010-04, 2010-05, 2010-06), New York (N.Y. Jud. Ethics Advisory Op. 08-176 (29 January 2009)), Ohio (Ohio Sup. Ct. Bd. of Comm'rs on Grievances and Discipline, Op. 2010-7), Oklahoma (Okla. Jud. Ethics Advisory Bd., Jud. Op. 2011-3 (6 July 2011)), and South Carolina (S.C. Advisory Comm. on Standards of Judicial Conduct, Op. 17-2009 (October 2009)).

635 E.g., California forbids mere contact between judges and counsels on pending cases; Florida prohibits posting information on pending cases and is concerned in general about friending between judges and counsels; New York takes a similar approach to California, adding that judges should use their good judgment for reflecting on any activities in social media; and Oklahoma takes a similar position to Florida's.

636 R. Glick/L. Stipanowich, *Arbitrator Disclosure in the Internet Age*, Disp. Res. J. 67 (2012), 1-7, 3-4. The authors, however, conclude that judges should be cautioned to "(1) exercise an appropriate discretion in how they use such a network, (2) be familiar with the site's privacy settings and how to modify them, and (3) continue to monitor the features of the network's services as new developments may have an impact on their duties" and that these advices should be applied to arbitrators with the addition to refrain from ex parte communication via social media.

637 J. von Goeler, *Third-party Funding*, p. 271.

638 L. Barrington, *FS Karrer*, p. 19.

presence of a third-party funder cannot create a conflict of interest. This scenario is a classic example of a potential risk of bias. Something more than the mere risk of bias is usually needed to constitute a conflict of interest.[639] Without any showing of being biased through actual conduct, there is no conflict of interest. Additionally, the fact that the chances of success need to be around 50% to convince the funder does not indicate a clear-cut case.[640] Also, the line of argumentation is not without an alternative. Where claims are funded in a portfolio, not all of them need to have a 50% chance of success. Without knowing whether the funded case is a portfolio case, the arbitrator cannot derive any conclusion. Therefore, there is no definite conflict of interest based on third-party funding as an investment.[641]

Second, where additional conduct of the arbitrator demonstrates bias, this conduct may meet the threshold of a conflict of interest. The conduct may be as diverse as in the preceding examples. For example, it is questionable whether a party may challenge an arbitrator who expressed a concrete opinion on third-party funding.[642] Generally, the threshold for constituting a conflict of interest due to conduct is rather high. Conduct may always be interpreted divergently and, hence, must be clear enough to justify the consequences of a conflict of interest. One approach to this scenario of the arbitrator expressing his or her opinion on third-party funding is to differentiate between the funded party and its funder generally. Thus, the arbitrator would not address the party with the expression, and a conflict of interest would, arguably, be less likely. However, such a general differentiation is not in line with the possibility to position third-party funders with the funded party.[643] Another approach is to contextualise the comment and analyse its connection to the dispute, similar to other comments and actions during the proceedings.[644] An example of this approach is found in the decision on the arbitrator's reaction to a request for security for costs in *RSM Production Corp. v. Saint Lucia*.[645] The arbitrator appointed by the respondent drafted assenting reasons to the tribunal's rejection of respondent's request for security for costs and generally criticised third-party funding: "a business plan for a related or professional funder is to embrace the gambler's Nirvana:

---

639 See below chapter 6, for the applicable standards for dependence and partiality.

640 L. Barrington, *FS Karrer*, p. 19. See also, J. von Goeler, *Third-party Funding*, p. 271, who compares this scenario with adding a famous party-appointed expert, which does not serve as an argument for a conflict of bias.

641 J. von Goeler, *Third-party Funding*, p. 269.

642 Von Goeler provides the possible statement: "Litigation funders are highly sophisticated and responsible investors. Litigation funding sends a clear message to the other party as to the limited merits of its case", J. von Goeler, *Third-party Funding*, p. 272. According to the author, this statement is rather "problematic" and may demonstrate a conflict of interest.

643 See above chapter 4.1.1.1.10.

644 See above chapter 4.2.1.2.

645 *RSM Production Corp. v. Saint Lucia*, ICSID Tribunal, 23 October 2014, ARB/12/10.

Heads I win, and Tails I do not lose".[646] The ICSID Tribunal denied the challenge and relied on the fact that the comments were raised in a procedural decision, i.e., the decision on security for costs. The "decision did not deal in any respect with the merits of [the] arbitration, i.e., the contractual relationship between the Parties".[647] The Tribunal concluded that the language used by the arbitrator might have been "radical and perhaps extreme in tone, but not to a degree as to justify a disqualification".[648] The high threshold applied by the tribunal in scenarios of comments is in line with other case law.[649] Likewise, publications, speeches, and previous decisions in other proceedings regarding third-party funding are to be treated no differently from the existing case law not involving third-party funding.

4.2.2 *Counsel's Conduct*

4.2.2.1 General Remarks

Although counsels' conflicts of interest are not directly at issue when analysing independence and impartiality, their conduct may affect the arbitrator's independence and impartiality and the overall integrity of the proceedings. Depending on the country of admission to the bar, counsels are bound by ethical rules and guidelines, even in international arbitration.[650] These rules may provide for some codes of conduct. Besides, the IBA Guidelines 2013 provide in Guideline 5 that the counsel should refrain from accepting representation of a party to the arbitration if a relationship exists that creates a conflict of interest between one of the arbitrators and counsel.[651] Guideline 6 enables the tribunal to implement measures to enact Guideline 5.[652] Both Guidelines aim to tackle threats to the integrity of the arbitral proceedings.[653] Guideline 6 is a powerful tool for the tribunal to safeguard its independence and impartiality.

646 *RSM Production Corp. v. Saint Lucia*, ICSID Tribunal, 23 October 2014, ARB/12/10, para. 41.
647 *RSM Production Corp. v. Saint Lucia*, ICSID Tribunal, 23 October 2014, ARB/12/10, para. 77.
648 *RSM Production Corp. v. Saint Lucia*, ICSID Tribunal, 23 October 2014, ARB/12/10, para. 86.
649 See generally, case law cited above in chapter 4.2.1.2.
650 C. Rogers, *Ethics in International Arbitration*, p. 104.
651 Guideline 5 reads: "Once the Arbitral Tribunal has been constituted, a person should not accept representation of a Party in the arbitration when a relationship exists between the person and an Arbitrator that would create a conflict of interest, unless none of the Parties objects after proper disclosure."
652 Guideline 6 reads: "The Arbitral Tribunal may, in case of breach of Guideline 5, take measures appropriate to safeguard the integrity of the proceedings, including the exclusion of the new Party Representative from participating in all or part of the arbitral proceedings."
653 See Comments to Guidelines 4-6, IBA Guidelines 2013.

The IBA Guidelines 2013 also address counsels' conduct in ex parte communication. They provide a detailed list of permitted ex parte communication.[654] Additionally, some institutional rules define the range for party-appointed arbitrator's ex parte communication with a candidate for the tribunal's chair.[655]

4.2.2.2 Interviewing and Briefing an Expert or Witness

The counsel's role can be notably decisive when interviewing and potentially briefing an expert or witness before his or her involvement in the proceedings. In this situation, the counsel may influence the conduct of the proceedings. Again, the IBA Guidelines 2013 address this issue. They provide for a liberal approach and allow assistance in preparation of both expert and witness statements and preparation of the testimony by a briefing.[656] Guidelines 21 and 22 set some limitations. The party representative should seek to ensure that the witness statement and the expert report reflect the thoughts of the witness and expert. Although the approach by the IBA Guidelines 2013 is liberal, the Comments clarify that they require upholding the integrity of the arbitral proceedings by proposing transparent and predictable standards.[657]

The liberal approach is also reflected by other authorities. For example, Article 25(2) sentence 2 Swiss Rules and Article 20.6 LCIA Rules allow interviewing a witness. Highlighting the potential of limited interviewing and briefing for an efficient conduct of the proceedings and for safeguarding the witness' rights,[658] interviewing and briefing of witnesses and experts may be useful in the permissible limits.

654 Comments to Guidelines 7-8, IBA Guidelines 2013: "(a) the prospective Arbitrator's publications, including books, articles and conference papers or engagements; (b) any activities of the prospective Arbitrator and his or her law firm or organisation within which he or she operates, that may raise justifiable doubts as to the prospective Arbitrator's independence or impartiality; (c) a description of the general nature of the dispute; (d) the terms of the arbitration agreement, and in particular any agreement as to the seat, language, applicable law and rules of the arbitration; (e) the identities of the Parties, Party Representatives, Witnesses, Experts and interested parties; and (f) the anticipated timetable and general conduct of the proceedings."

655 See in more detail above chapter 4.2.1.1.

656 Guidelines 20 and 24 IBA Guidelines 2013 read: "A Party Representative may assist Witnesses in the preparation of Witness Statements and Experts in the preparation of Expert Reports." "A Party Representative may, consistent with the principle that the evidence given should reflect the Witness's own account of relevant facts, events or circumstances, or the Expert's own analysis or opinion, meet or interact with Witnesses and Experts in order to discuss and prepare their prospective testimony." Also, Art. 26.5 JAMS Rules permits the interviewing and briefing of a witness.

657 Comments to Guidelines 18-25, IBA Guidelines 2013.

658 A.-K. Bertke/H.-P. Schroeder, *Grenzen der Zeugenvorbereitung im staatlichen Zivilprozess und im Schiedsverfahren*, SchiedsVZ 2014, 80-86, 82 et seq.

4.2.3 *Conduct of the Tribunal Secretary*

Regarding conflicts of interest based on the conduct of the secretary, there is a general parallelism to the approach to conflicts of interest of arbitrators. The secretary is the arbitrator's helping hand and should be positioned with the latter.[659] The risk of the secretary's conduct violating the parties' right to be heard is apparent. Where the secretary is additionally used to support the tribunal in more substantive matters, his or her conduct may have an indirect influence on the decision-making process.[660] Hence, the secretary's conduct must remain independent and impartial. It should be noted that difficulties of proving a conflict of interest based on conduct are even more pronounced for the secretary: his or her work may remain non-transparent for the parties and their counsels.

Some English and Swiss case law on state court assistants may help to outline potential conflicts of interest and to guide the evaluation of the tribunal secretaries' conduct.

First, the England and Wales High Court of Justice rendered a decision on clerks and their potential conflicts of interest in a criminal procedure.[661] In *R v. Camborne Justices, Ex p. Pearce*, the High Court of Justice held that in order to challenge the clerk in his judicial or quasi-judicial role due to a conflict of interest, a real likelihood of bias must be shown.[662] The facts revealed that the clerk previously acted for another court where the claimant argued the same case. The clerk's open mind was, thus, at issue. However, the High Court of Justice ruled that there was no real likelihood of bias in this scenario, since the clerk was not a member of the committee that decided the case.[663] Where an arbitrator previously dealt with the case, it is important that he or she remain open-minded in order not to prejudge the dispute and constitute a conflict of interest.[664] The same should generally

659 Cf. above chapter 4.1.3. Administration of the secretary may include: "(a) Undertaking administrative matters as necessary in the absence of an institution; (b) Communicating with the arbitral institution and parties; (c) Organizing meetings and hearings with the parties; (d) Handling and organizing correspondence, submissions and evidence on behalf of the arbitral tribunal", Art. 3(2), Young ICCA, *Young ICCA Guide on Arbitral Secretaries*, p. 11.

660 E.g., "(e) Researching questions of law; (f) Researching discrete questions relating to factual evidence and witness testimony; (g) Drafting procedural orders and similar documents; (h) Reviewing the parties' submissions and evidence, and drafting factual chronologies and memoranda summarizing the parties' submissions and evidence; (i) Attending the arbitral tribunal's deliberations; and (j) Drafting appropriate parts of the award", Art. 3(2), Young ICCA, *Young ICCA Guide on Arbitral Secretaries*, p. 11.

661 *R v. Camborne Justices, Ex p. Pearce*, [1955] 1 QB 41, regarding state court proceedings.

662 See below chapter 6.7, for the analysis of the standard of independence and impartiality applicable to secretaries.

663 *R v. Camborne Justices, Ex p. Pearce*, [1955] 1 QB 41, regarding state court proceedings.

664 See above chapter 4.2.1.5.

apply to secretaries.[665] Holding that a tribunal secretary is not a member of the committee and, thus, may not influence the decision would be too short-sighted. It appears more useful to, first, determine the secretaries' role and, second, examine whether the previous encounter with the subject matter led to a lack of open mind. If the tribunal secretary has to research questions of law and outline the facts, lacking an open mind may influence his or her work and consequently the result presented to the arbitrator.

Second, and similar to the decision rendered by the England and Wales High Court of Justice, the Swiss *Bundesgericht* was faced with a scenario where the state court assistant, i.e., the *Gerichtsschreiber*, previously acted as counsel in proceedings against the same claimant.[666] In addition, the *Gerichtsschreiber* was involved as *Gerichstschreiber* previously in three decisions against the same claimant. All these decisions rendered against the claimant were based on the same argumentation. The court ruled that these facts did not meet the threshold of a conflict of interest.[667] The court held that, first, the *Gerichtsschreiber* acted only for a short period of time as counsel, i.e., sixteen months, and, second, that the argumentation in all previous decisions was based on logic and, hence, not particular. It is to be welcomed that the court analysed whether the secretary's previous interaction with the subject matter and parties constituted a conflict of interest. However, when comparing Swiss *Gerichtsschreiber* and tribunal secretaries, it should be noted that the *Gerichtsschreiber* may perform rather substantial tasks, e.g., drafting judgments, and assisting in deliberating and decision-making.

Third, the Swiss *Bundesgericht* ruled that where the *Gerichtsschreiber* participates substantively in assisting in rendering a decision, and he is not only acting as a *Gerichtsschreiber*, but additionally works for another administration office to which the respondent also belongs, a conflict of interest existed.[668] The court highlighted the different duties the *Gerichtsschreiber* must comply with towards the court and the administration office and noted that these different duties may collide.[669]

Finally, an arbitrator may arguably be challenged based on an inappropriate delegation of his or her tasks to the tribunal secretary. The England and Wales High Court of Justice

665 But see, O. Jensen, *Tribunal Secretaries in International Arbitration*, para. 7.21. Jensen suggests that issue conflicts should not create a ground for dependence and partiality for secretaries.

666 BGer, 30 October 2008, 9C_836/2008, on state court proceedings.

667 BGer, 30 October 2008, 9C_836/2008, para. E 4.4.3. Cf. O. Jensen, *Tribunal Secretaries in International Arbitration*, para. 7.22. Jensen stresses, again, that it will depend on the arbitrator's impartiality and independence, not that of the tribunal secretary.

668 BGer, 22 August 2014, BGE 140 I 271, citing BGer, 10 January 2002, 4P.272/2001. Both decisions deal with cases in administrative fiscal matters.

669 The Swiss *Bundesgericht* used the wording "conflict of loyalty".

had to decide such a challenge of the co-arbitrators.[670] The challenge under Section 24(1)(d)(i) EAA was placed after the presiding arbitrator was already challenged successfully. The challenging party argued that there was a discrepancy of time spent by the co-arbitrators and the secretary and that the co-arbitrators failed to participate properly in the deliberations.

> The complaint was of a personal failure by the Co-Arbitrators properly to exercise their decision-making functions and responsibilities, and of an improper delegation of those responsibilities by them to the Secretary. The functions and responsibilities said to be improperly delegated were adjudicative.[671]

The court rejected the challenge and ruled that

> the Tribunal Secretary has assisted the Tribunal "with the internal management of the case" and has engaged in such matters as organising papers for the Tribunal, highlighting relevant legal authorities, maintaining factual chronologies, preparing drafts of orders and correspondence for consideration by the Tribunal, and sending correspondence on behalf of the Tribunal. Therefore there has been no occasion for any of the members of the Tribunal to have "passed [communications] between [them] in connection with the role of and the tasks delegated to [the Secretary] in this arbitration," and in fact none exist.[672]

All these cases demonstrate that a conflict of interest creating a ground for finding dependence and partiality may arise only if the tribunal secretary performs substantive tasks and may indirectly influence the arbitrator's decision-making. In such a case, the evaluation of whether the tribunal secretary's conduct meets the threshold of a conflict of interest may be similar to that applied to the arbitrator.

A different treatment of secretaries and arbitrators may be applied regarding ex parte communication. The arbitration practitioner Hwang seems to allow secretaries' conduct potentially falling under unauthorised ex parte communication of arbitrators. He states that

670 *P v. Q, R, S, U*, [2017] EWHC 194 (Comm), paras. 31 and 47.
671 *P v. Q, R, S, U*, [2017] EWHC 194 (Comm), para. 24.
672 *P v. Q, R, S, U*, [2017] EWHC 194 (Comm), para. 47.

> [i]n nearly all cases where I have had the opportunity to explain to the parties why I propose engaging a legal assistant and his scope of work, parties have responded positively and in fact appreciate having a point of contact which enables a party to communicate directly with the tribunal for clarification on administrative or logistical matters without the spectre of an unauthorised ex parte communication with the tribunal members themselves.[673]

Indeed, it would appear useful to have the secretary solve administrative issues also by using ex parte communication where this is more efficient. However, some rules explicitly prohibit any ex parte communication of the secretary.[674] Additionally, since the secretary is to be positioned with the tribunal, allowing ex parte communication in scenarios unauthorised for the arbitrator would lead to friction with the fact that the secretary is supervised and limited by the discretion of the tribunal. It appears improbable that the secretary will not inform the arbitrator of the exact ex parte communication, and it will be the arbitrator who decides what to do with the information. Therefore, the secretary is merely an agent of the arbitrator. This agency, however, does not materially change any of the issues of ex parte communication.[675] In the end, such differentiation may also bear the risk of non-transparency and potentially offending the legitimacy of the arbitral process.

4.2.4 *Conduct of the Arbitral Institution*

In rare cases, the conduct of the arbitral institution may raise issues of independence and impartiality. The contractual relationship between the arbitral institution and the parties, as well as the applicable law, determine the parties' expectations on the institutional conduct.[676]

Two German decisions, both rendered in 2014, dealt with alleged biased conduct of the DIS in connection with the contract between the institution and the parties. On 14 July 2014, the *Landgericht* Berlin found that the arbitral institution violated its obligation to act neutrally by sending a witness statement to the *Oberlandesgericht* München referring to an ongoing arbitration proceeding.[677] Claimant requested termination of the contract with the arbitral institution. Although the institution failed to comply with its obligation,

673 M. Hwang, *Introduction, Musings on International Arbitration*, p. 17.
674 HKIAC Secretary Guidelines, para. 3.5; Art. 13.4 LCIA Rules.
675 See above chapter 4.2.1.1.
676 See MünchKomm ZPO/J. Münch, Vor § 1034 para. 80, for a general classification of the contract between the institution and the parties.
677 LG Berlin, 14 July 2014, 33 O 494/13, BeckRS 2015, 2546.

the court ruled that the threshold for an extraordinary termination was not met.[678] One of the parties had asked the institution to provide the witness statement. According to the *Landgericht* Berlin, the institutions should have either refrained from providing the statement or informed the other party before submitting it and asked for that party's comments. However, six months later, the *Oberlandesgericht* München declared that the same action did not violate the obligation to act neutrally.[679] The *Oberlandesgericht* München reasoned that any such obligation for the institution must be extenuated compared with that of the arbitrator, provided for in § 1036 German ZPO.[680]

Additionally, the (contractual) relationship between the institution and the arbitrators[681] may raise issues of independence and impartiality. However, these issues often concern the relationship between the arbitrator and the institution and not the conduct.[682] One specific example of potential conduct of the arbitral institution towards an arbitrator is the scrutiny process under Article 34 ICC Rules. It reads as follows:

> [...] The ICC Court may lay down modifications as to the form of the award and, without affecting the arbitral tribunal's liberty of decision, may also draw its attention to points of substance. No award shall be rendered by the arbitral tribunal until it has been approved by the Court as to its form.

As long as such scrutiny process only addresses formal aspects and does not interfere with the tribunal's power and obligation to decide, the arbitral tribunal remains independent of the institution.[683]

678 § 626(1) German BGB.

679 OLG München, 18 December 2014, 34 SchH 3/14, NJOZ, 893-896, where claimants requested a declaration of inadmissibility and lacking jurisdiction, since they terminated the contract with the arbitral institution. The court denied any right to terminate and, hence, did not declare the arbitration proceeding inadmissible and lacking jurisdiction.

680 OLG München, 18 December 2014, 34 SchH 3/14, NJOZ, 893-896. § 1036 German ZPO reads: "(1) A person asked to serve as an arbitral judge is to disclose any and all circumstances that might give rise to doubts as to his impartiality. An arbitral judge is under obligation to disclose such circumstances to the parties without undue delay, also after his appointment and until the close of the arbitration proceedings, if he has failed to so inform them previously. (2) The appointment of an arbitral judge may be refused only if any circumstances give rise to justified doubts as to his impartiality or independence, or if he does not meet the prerequisites established by the parties. A party may recuse an arbitral judge whom it has itself appointed, or in the appointment of whom it has assisted, only for reasons of which it became aware only after he was appointed."

681 It is disputed how to classify this relationship. See F. Schäfer, *Institutionelle Schiedsgerichtsbarkeit*, para. 116 et seq., for an overview.

682 See above chapter 4.1.1.5, on the relationship of the arbitrator and the institution.

683 Cf. Stein/Jonas/P. Schlosser, § 1036 para. 60 et seq.

4.2.5 *Arbitrator's Nationality, Language, or Cultural Affiliations*

If the arbitrator is of a particular nationality, speaks a specific language, or has other cultural affiliations, the parties may arguably question his or her independence and impartiality on these grounds.[684] However, much case law indicates that there is usually no conflict of interest. For example, the common nationality of respondent's company and the chambers the presiding arbitrator belonged to, was not grounds for a conflict of interest.[685] Also, the mere fact that the arbitrator had the same nationality and resided in the same country as one of the parties was no ground for constituting a conflict of interest.[686] The LCIA Court even decided that it is against international commercial arbitration practice to disqualify an arbitrator from the appointment because he was of the same nationality as counsel for a party to the dispute.[687]

Likewise, a tribunal under Swiss Rules dismissed the challenge of a Swiss arbitrator whose mother tongue was Italian, in a dispute between a Cypriot company with a branch in Lugano, represented by counsel from Lugano, and an Italian individual.[688] The mere fact that one party had a branch in the Italian-speaking part of Switzerland and was represented by a counsel from that region did not create a conflict of interest. To be distinguished is a scenario where the parties choose to have a specific language for the proceedings and one of the arbitrators does not speak that language. One may argue that it is necessary to speak the language of the proceedings to safeguard a fair process. However, if parties make use of their right to appoint and choose to appoint an arbitrator who is not firm in the language of the proceedings, they make use of their party autonomy.[689] In such a scenario, additional measures, including appointment of a translator, may be suitable. The mere appointment of an arbitrator who is not fluent in the language of the proceedings cannot, however, violate the parties' right to have an independent and impartial arbitrator.

---

684 Accordingly, many institutional rules provide some (default) provisions on the nationality of the arbitrators. E.g., Rule R-15 AAA Rules, Art. 30 CIETAC Rules, Arts. 11 and 12.3 DIS Rules, Arts. 11.2 and 11.3 HKIAC Rules, Arts. 13(1), (5) and (6) ICC Rules, Art. 6 LCIA Rules; Art. 17(6) SCC Rules, Art. 6(7) UNCITRAL Arbitration Rules.

685 LCIA Reference No. 5665, LCIA Court, 30 August 2006, Arb. Int'l 27 (2011), 395-412.

686 BGer, 12 February 1958, BGE 84 I 39, 51-52.

687 LCIA Reference No. UN9155, LCIA Court, 10 November 1999, Arb. Int'l 27 (2011), 332-333, where the UNCITRAL Arbitration Rules applied. Respondent based its challenge on Art. 6(4) UNCITRAL Arbitration Rules, nowadays Art. 6(7), which provides that "[t]he appointing authority shall have regard to such considerations as are likely to secure the appointment of an independent and impartial arbitrator and shall take into account the advisability of appointing an arbitrator of a nationality other than the nationalities of the parties". Besides basing the denial of the challenge on international commercial arbitration practice, the division pointed at the non-mandatory character of Art. 6(4).

688 SCAI, *Swiss Rules – Selected Case Law.*

689 In line with this, the Swiss IPRG provides in Art. 180(1)(a) that an arbitrator may be challenged "if he does not meet the qualifications agreed upon by the parties".

Also concerning other cultural affiliations, case law points in the same direction. In 2005, the LCIA Court denied a challenge that was based on the sole arbitrator's long-standing commitment to Arab studies and Arab culture.[690] The claimant argued that this might prevent the arbitrator from being as objective and impartial as the role of a sole arbitrator in this matter required.

Since these scenarios are all unlikely to meet the threshold of a conflict of interest, they may raise concerns as being tactical challenges. At least one ICC case where the respondent challenged the presiding arbitrator at a late stage on the fact that he objected from the outset to a Swiss presiding arbitrator, but the presiding arbitrator was a U.S. national, who permanently resided in Switzerland, was classified as a tactical challenge.[691] To prevent these potential conflicts of interest, many institutions prefer to appoint arbitrators with other nationalities than the parties.

4.3 Concluding Remarks

Grounds for finding dependence and partiality are diverse in presentation and success. Depending on the actor's role in question, the scenario is more or less likely to constitute a ground for dependence and partiality. In general, relationships more often provide a successful ground for a challenge or an annulment than conduct. The evaluation of a relationship meeting the threshold of a conflict of interest usually involves the interest the party has in the proceedings, the directness of the relationship, the connection of the relationship to the dispute, and the proximity in time between the relationship and the arbitration proceedings. Applying this general formula, case law demonstrates some leeway for the professional relationship between arbitrators and counsel, arguing that their common background includes frequent ties. Thus, relationships between the arbitrator and a party more often meet the threshold of a ground for finding dependence and partiality. However, even in this category, the specificities of arbitration are acknowledged, e.g., by allowing repeat appointments to some extent. The threshold of a conflict of interest is usually met if repeat appointments create a financially intense relationship. Besides the criterion of financial intensity, conflicting hierarchies and subordination between the arbitrator and

690 LCIA Reference No. 5660, LCIA Court, 5 August 2005, Arb. Int'l 27 (2011), 371-373, arguing that the challenge lacked legitimacy since there was not "a scintilla of evidence" that, beyond his technical expertise in Arab and Islamic law, the arbitrator should have been so exposed to Arab and Islamic culture as to have become biased or more receptive to the case of the respondent.

691 S. Greenberg, *Tackling Guerrilla Challenges Against Arbitrators*. This also applies to a case where one party tried to establish a "de facto" nationality of one of the arbitrators, who was rather a cosmopolite, allegedly establishing bias, LCIA Reference No. 8086, LCIA Court, 30 September 1998, Arb. Int'l 27 (2011), 328-331. The division of the LCIA Court, however, did not classify this challenge as a tactical one but denied it.

the party or counsel may guide the analysis, e.g., in cases involving other employment connections. These criteria may also apply to the analysis of arbitrators' relationships with each other. An additional criterion for analysing whether relationships constitute a ground for finding dependence and partiality is superior knowledge, e.g., in parallel proceedings. Likewise, the arbitrator's ability to judge the case independently and impartially is questioned where he or she has a material relationship with a witness or an expert. Although the threshold is high to find a conflict of interest, due to the parties' right to present their case, some scenarios constitute a ground for finding dependence and partiality.

Regarding current issues of social networks, third-party funding, and tribunal secretaries, case law first clarifies that relationships on social networking sites should not be differentiated from face-to-face relationships. They may, however, be useful when proving the existence of relationships or conduct. Second, on third-party funding, the evaluation of current laws, rules, guidelines, and case law demonstrates that it is necessary to identify the role of the third-party funder. Where the third-party funder is actively involved and is to be positioned with the funded party, the analysis of a conflict of interest may apply the general formula, i.e., evaluating the interest the party has in the proceedings, the directness of the relationship, the connection of the relationship to the dispute, and the proximity in time between the relationship and the arbitration proceedings. Third, on tribunal secretaries, the decisive question is their degree of involvement in the proceedings. The more material their involvement, the more involved they are in evaluating conflicts of interest. Similar to the method applied to third-party funders, relationships of law firms include, in a first step, the determination of whether the arbitrator, or counsel respectively, can be positioned with their law firm when evaluating conflicts of interest.

Compared to relationships, conduct is less often effective as a ground for finding dependence and partiality. Some of the challenges based on conduct may even be categorised as tactical challenges. No general formula guides the analysis of a conflict of interest based on conduct. Instead, it includes examining and balancing different rights and principles of international arbitration: the parties' right to be heard and treated equally, the arbitrator's right to determine the procedure, and the general principle of efficiency of the proceedings. For example, the arbitrator's right to determine the procedure generally prevails with regard to comments and actions during the proceedings, conduct in connection to the deliberations and decision-making, and tribunal orders and their awards. These categories often do not constitute a ground for finding dependence and partiality. However, where the conduct reveals that the arbitrator is not open-minded, the parties' interest in an independent and impartial tribunal may prevail.

Furthermore, the analysis of different sources reveals that ex parte communication may be permissible, depending on the point in time when the communication takes place and the materiality of the communication. After the proceedings commence, only non-material communication or specific scenarios may be in line with a fair proceeding.

Finally, the above case law outlined on the grounds for challenges or annulments of arbitrators, including some case law on state court judges, demonstrates a detailed casuistic. Even though such a detailed casuistic helps courts and adjudicators facing a dispute on independence and impartiality, the individual analysis will hinge on the individual facts. The principles outlined in this detailed casuistic, i.e., the parties' right to appoint their arbitrator and the procedural need of an independent and impartial tribunal, can be generalised and used accordingly. When balancing these principles and the involved interests, the dual nature of arbitration should be borne in mind.

5 Other Potential Grounds for Challenge or Annulment Based on Dependence and Partiality

Some scenarios raise issues of independence and impartiality and may be a ground for challenge or annulment but are not to be classified as a conflict of interest. They do not directly concern issues of relationships or conduct in connection with the proceedings. Due to this lack of connection to the dispute, the scenarios in this category often do not constitute a ground for challenge or annulment.

The following chapter, first, outlines the potential argument that certain scenarios demonstrate a general improper character of an arbitrator: previous challenges of the arbitrator in unrelated proceedings (5.1) and the arbitrator's conviction (5.2). Second, certain institutional appointment mechanisms, e.g., arbitrator's lists, may raise allegations of fostering dependence and partiality (5.3). Finally, the question will be addressed whether cumulating different grounds may sustain a challenge or annulment, even though the individual grounds are not sufficient (5.4). Finally, concluding remarks summarise the key findings (5.5).

5.1 Previous Challenge of the Arbitrator in Unrelated Proceedings

Theoretically, parties could argue that the mere fact that an arbitrator was challenged previously in non-related proceedings demonstrates that this arbitrator is generally unfit to serve as an independent and impartial arbitrator. One party in an unpublished ICC case argued, inter alia, in this direction.[1] In this case, the presiding arbitrator was challenged as an arbitrator in an unrelated LCIA proceeding. This first challenge was unsuccessful. The ICC dismissed the challenge, and it may serve as an example of a tactical challenge.[2] Indeed, where the previous challenge was unsuccessful, the initial argument is void. But even where the challenge was successful, or issues of independence and impartiality of a specific arbitrator led to an annulment of a previous award, this cannot sustain a ground of challenge or annulment in completely unrelated proceedings. An argument that the

1 S. Greenberg, *Tackling Guerrilla Challenges Against Arbitrators*. The challenge was additionally based on previous conduct of the presiding arbitrator twenty years ago as a lawyer.

2 S. Greenberg, *Tackling Guerrilla Challenges Against Arbitrators*.

character of an arbitrator generally demonstrates bias cannot convince. Such an argument thwarts the parties' right to choose their arbitrator as the threshold for a challenge or annulment would be set rather low.

5.2 Arbitrator Being Convicted

A similar line of argumentation, i.e., a generally biased character, can be raised against an arbitrator who is convicted of a crime. Case law from the United States reveals that there needs to be a connection between the ground for being convicted and the arbitration, or "that the legal trouble affected the outcome of the arbitration in some demonstrable way".[3] In *LGC Holdings, Inc. v. Julius Klein Diamond, LLC*, the U.S. District Court, S.D. New York, was faced with the argument raised by the respondent that the arbitrator's indictment and conviction were "directly related" to the arbitration because they pertained to his "'substantial experience in the diamond industry', which was the basis of his qualification as an arbitrator under the parties' agreements".[4] However, the U.S. District Court rejected this argument, as it did not meet the threshold of annulment. The court cited Judge Posner in *United Transp. Union v. Gateway Western Ry. Co.*, who faced a similar argument.[5] Posner stated that the arbitrator's failure to

> disclose his criminal conviction was, we may assume, material in the sense that one or both parties might well have decided that they did not want to have a criminal resolve their dispute. But it does not follow that it should be a basis for setting aside his award.[6]

Posner concluded that "there can be no case in which a fraud that does not induce bias on the part of the arbitrator warrants the setting aside of the award".[7]

Thus, the mere fact that the arbitrator was convicted in the past does not in itself constitute a ground for challenge or annulment. Without any connection between the events leading to the verdict and the arbitral proceedings, and, especially, no suggestions that the events influenced or otherwise prejudiced the arbitrator's independence and impartiality,

3 *LGC Holdings, Inc. v. Julius Klein Diamonds, LLC*, 238 F.Supp.3d 452 (S.D. New York 2017), concerning a domestic arbitration.

4 *LGC Holdings, Inc. v. Julius Klein Diamonds, LLC*, 238 F.Supp.3d 452 (S.D. New York 2017), 471.

5 *United Transp. Union v. Gateway Western Ry. Co.*, 284 F.3d 710 (7th Cir. 2002), where respondent requested annulment of a domestic award rendered by an arbitrator who was charged with and pleaded guilty to feloniously assisting in the preparation of a fraudulent federal income tax return.

6 *United Transp. Union v. Gateway Western Ry. Co.*, 284 F.3d 710 (7th Cir. 2002), 712.

7 *United Transp. Union v. Gateway Western Ry. Co.*, 284 F.3d 710 (7th Cir. 2002), 713.

challenges based on previous imprisonment are unlikely to succeed. Therefore, a ground for challenge or annulment based on a conviction requires a link between the ground for conviction and the arbitration in question. A general argument that the conviction demonstrates a generally biased character cannot be deduced.

In 2015, the U.S. Court of Appeals, Third Circuit, reversed a decision annulling an award rendered by an arbitrator who received numerous regulatory complaints.[8] The U.S. District Court previously held that respondent's rights were compromised by an arbitrator who misrepresented his ability to serve on the arbitration tribunal.[9] However, it should be noted that the Court of Appeals based its decision on the parties' obligation to investigate, requiring them to do "a cursory background check" before appointing or refraining from objecting to an arbitrator.[10]

5.3 Institutional Dependence and Partiality

The preceding analyses on independence and impartiality focused on the arbitrator as being the centre of decision-making, with few exceptions of short references to counsels and experts. Broadening this scope may bring additional issues of independence and impartiality to light.

> Based on the attitudinal assumption that judicial behaviour is almost exclusively influenced by the personal traits and policy preferences of the individuals acting as arbitrators, the main question of all empirical studies on arbitral decision-making to date has been whether arbitrators decide politically or not. However, to unravel arbitral decision-making we need to shift the focus of our analysis from the individual decisionmakers to the institution surrounding them.[11]

The term institutional dependence and partiality not only refers to arbitral institutions, but also encompasses all sorts of institutionalised forms of dependence and partiality or

---

8 *Goldman, Sachs & Co. v. Athena Venture Partners, L.P.*, 803 F.3d 144 (3d Cir. 2015), concerning domestic FINRA arbitration.

9 *Goldman, Sachs & Co. v. Athena Venture Partners, L.P.*, 803 F.3d 144 (3d Cir. 2015), 145.

10 *Goldman, Sachs & Co. v. Athena Venture Partners, L.P.*, 803 F.3d 144 (3d Cir. 2015), 149. See below chapter 7.1.5, for the obligation to investigate.

11 S. Brekoulakis, *Systematic Bias and the Institution of International Arbitration*, J. Int'l Disp. Settlement 4 (2013), 553-585, 580.

mechanisms that abet conflicts of interest.[12] These may include institutions providing lists of arbitrators, specified arbitral institutions having a member scheme but allowing non-members to arbitrate as well, or arbitration agreements providing for a partial mechanism in the appointment procedure.[13] Apart from these selection mechanisms, the term may also encompass the judicial motivation of arbitrators. It covers an analysis of the "main institutional structures, processes and actors of international arbitration, and how they all influence the judicial behaviour of arbitrators".[14] The following overview focuses on selection mechanisms, which have been raised as grounds for challenge or annulment actions. This overview allows only a limited picture of the general issue.[15]

Already in 1958, the Swiss *Bundesgericht* ruled that no issue of independence and impartiality existed where one party was a member of the chamber of commerce, i.e., the arbitral institution, and arbitrators needed to be selected from a list only naming members. The court held that the member-party had merely an "indirect influence" on the procedure.[16] A similar scenario arose in arbitration proceedings under the French association for chocolate trade.[17] Since the tribunal was appointed by the president of the association, who was a representative of the respondent, claimant argued that this mechanism led to an irregularly constituted tribunal. Claimant requested annulment under Article 1520(2) French CPC.[18] The president had appointed a second tribunal, and this second appointment was an instance of appeal foreseen by the rules of the association. Although the *cour d'appel de* Paris sustained the annulment, it based its decision on other grounds and did not address the selection mechanism.

These issues of independence and impartiality in regard to list procedures also arose under a NGFA arbitration.[19] Claimant was a paying member of the NGFA, and one of its

12 The issue of institutional dependence and partiality may overlap with other relationships and conduct, e.g., the familiarity with the subject matter.

13 According to Froitzheim, the main issue is that of partial institutions putting pressure on the arbitrator who is dependent on the institution, O. Froitzheim, *Die Ablehnung von Schiedsrichtern wegen Befangenheit in der internationalen Schiedsgerichtsbarkeit*, pp. 39-40. For the issue of arbitrator's relationship with an institution, see above chapter 4.1.1.5.

14 S. Brekoulakis, *Systematic Bias and the Institution of International Arbitration*, J. Int'l Disp. Settlement 4 (2013), 553-585, 580-581.

15 For a detailed analysis of institutional dependence and partiality, see, e.g., R. Kiener, *Richterliche Unabhängigkeit*, primarily on state court judges; S. Brekoulakis, *Systematic Bias and the Institution of International Arbitration*, J. Int'l Disp. Settlement 4 (2013), 553-585, 339-374, and F. Gélinas, *The Independence of International Arbitrators and Judges: Tampered With or Well Tempered?*, N.Y. Int'l Rev. 24 (2011), 1-48.

16 BGer, 12 February 1958, BGE 84 I 39, 51-52. Regarding the ECHR, see ECtHR, Guide on Art. 6 ECHR, for an overview.

17 CA Paris, 2 July 1992, Rev. de l'Arb. 1996, 411-410.

18 Art. 1502 French CPC is now Art. 1520(2).

19 *Anderson, Inc. v. Horton Farms, Inc.*, 166 F.3d 308 (6th Cir. 1998).

employees was on the NGFA board of directors. The NGFA Rules required every arbitrator to be a dues-paying member. This requirement itself led to inherent dependence and partiality, according to the respondent. The court examined whether the NGFA Rules and their selection mechanism were partial and concluded that this was not the case.

Finally, the issue of independence and impartiality of the arbitral institution also arose in regard to the CAS and its list procedure, in cases where the IOC was a party. Arbitrators acting in the CAS need to be listed members. In 2003, the Swiss *Bundesgericht* ruled that the CAS is sufficiently independent from the IOC, the founding institution of the CAS.[20] The court reasoned that, first, the appointment procedure of the members of the CAS was sufficiently independent, and second, the list procedure generally has the positive effect of guaranteeing efficiency due to the expertise in sports arbitration of the CAS members.[21] Therefore, a prior selection of arbitrators through lists may serve efficiency and is to be tolerated.[22]

Moreover, arbitration agreements may provide for a partial selection mechanism. United States case law provides some insights. In *Johnson v. Directory Assistants Inc.*, the parties agreed on the following arbitration agreement:

> [W]e both agree to resolve any dispute arising out of or relating to this contract through confidential binding arbitration and agree to try to mutually choose the arbitration service, the location and which state's law will govern. If we are unable to come to a mutual agreement, or if one of us refuses to participate in choosing, the party filing the demand will have the right to make the choices unilaterally, as long as the filing party has made a good faith attempt to come to a mutual agreement. The non-filing party expressly consents to and waives any and all objections to the choices made.[23]

---

20 BGer, 27 May 2003, BGE 129 III 445, dealing with the annulment of a CAS award disqualifying two Russian skiers from the Olympic Games due to alleged doping. The court briefly outlined the history of the CAS in connection with the IOC, in para. 3.3.1: in the beginning, the IOC handled all costs of the CAS and directly or indirectly appointed thirty of its sixty members. In 1993, the Swiss *Bundesgericht* declared that the CAS is merely to be regarded independent in disputes excluding the IOC, cf. BGer, 27 May 2003, BGE 129 III 445; BGer, 15 March 1993, BGE 119 II 271. This judgment triggered reforms in the CAS and, especially, formed the CIAS, which obtained the task to appoint the members of the CAS. Notwithstanding the reform, the Russian skiers argued that, in addition, the CIAS is not sufficiently independent of the IOC.

21 BGer, 27 May 2003, BGE 129 III 445, 461, comparing the degree of potential dependency of the CAS to the IOC with state courts where the state might be party before as well.

22 See also, O. Froitzheim, *Die Ablehnung von Schiedsrichtern wegen Befangenheit in der internationalen Schiedsgerichtsbarkeit*, pp. 39-40.

23 *Johnson v. Directory Assistants Inc.*, 797 F.3d 1294 (11th Cir. 2015), 1297, on domestic arbitration.

The respondent/appellant chose an arbitral institution it previously used, and the claimant/appellee argued that this, inter alia, constituted an impression of bias.[24] The U.S. Court of Appeals, Eleventh Circuit, refused claimant's argument.[25] First, the Court of Appeals pointed out that claimant did not provide evidence concerning when or how they requested additional information from the institution, i.e., investigated the issue.[26] Second, even if the claimant could show that they asked the institution to disclose how many times respondent used the arbitration service, the Court of Appeals was unconvinced that the failure to disclose that information would justify annulment. Finally, assuming that the respondent used the institution to conduct several arbitrations, the court did not think this fact alone would lead a reasonable person to suspect partiality, especially because the institution used a variety of arbitrators.

Considering, first, that the wording of the arbitration agreement provided enough room not to lead to an irregular composition and, second, that the mere fact of conducting several arbitration proceedings with one institution does not provide grounds for annulment, the court's decision is to be welcomed. However, where the arbitration agreement does not leave room for appointing an unbiased tribunal, courts have ruled differently. Notably, where the arbitration agreement names precisely the persons to act as arbitrator, or the appointing authority, and this person lacks independence and impartiality, the award rendered risks annulment. For example, naming a future arbitrator whom one works with at a law firm that represented respondent's mother entity in other negotiations may lack independence and impartiality.[27] Likewise, difficulty may arise in naming a former counsel of one of the parties as arbitrator[28] or naming another partner of counsel's law firm to either act as arbitrator or appoint the arbitrator.[29]

---

24 Precisely, claimant alleged that "[t]he arbitrator and ADRC [i.e., the institution,] both refused to provide information to [plaintiffs] regarding how many arbitrations the service had conducted with DAI in the past", which "created a reasonable impression of bias". *Johnson v. Directory Assistants Inc.*, 797 F.3d 1294 (11th Cir. 2015), 1300.

25 *Johnson v. Directory Assistants Inc.*, 797 F.3d 1294 (11th Cir. 2015), 1300-1301.

26 See below chapter 7.1.5.1, on parties' obligation to investigate.

27 *HSMV Corp. v. ADI Ltd.*, 72 F.Supp.2d 1122 (C.D. California 1999).

28 *Cristina Blouse Corp. v. International Ladies Garment Workers Union, Local 162*, 492 F.Supp. 508 (S.D. New York 1980), on domestic union arbitration. The court was requested not to annul the award but to order the parties to agree on a different arbitrator.

29 *Erving v. Virginia Squires Basketball Club*, 349 F.Supp. 716 (E.D. New York 1972), on domestic sports arbitration. The court ordered another arbitrator to act.

5.4 Cumulation of Grounds

The cumulation of grounds is itself no ground for challenge or annulment. However, courts often analyse whether scenarios that on their own do not meet the threshold of a ground for finding dependence and partiality may cumulatively cross the threshold and sustain a challenge or annulment. Case law from Germany, the United Kingdom, and the United States indicates an affirmative approach to the method of cumulating grounds. Additionally, Swiss law arguably provides for a legal basis for cumulating grounds.

In 2008, the *Oberlandesgericht* Frankfurt a.M. concluded that the following grounds cumulatively constituted a ground for challenge: a rent agreement between counsel for the claimant and the presiding arbitrator, a familiar way of addressing each other, and non-disclosure of the rent agreement.[30] In 2012, the same court deviated slightly from this approach: it did not deny the general possibility to examine grounds cumulatively but did not cumulate the non-disclosure of a ground that in itself was no ground for challenge or annulment.[31] The issue of whether non-disclosure can be regarded as ground for crossing the threshold for finding dependence and partiality touches a different question: whether non-disclosure is a ground in itself.[32]

In *Thomas Kinkade Co. v. White*, the U.S. Court of Appeals, Sixth Circuit, held that reappointments and the arbitrator's conduct considered together established a ground for annulment.[33] In *Crow Construction v. Jeffrey M. Brown Assoc. Inc.*, the U.S. District Court, E.D. Pennsylvania, first, reached the conclusion that grounds for annulment were present, and, additionally, pointed out that the cumulation clarified that the threshold was undoubtedly met.[34]

Much case law from the United Kingdom follows similar approaches. Even case law denying challenges or annulments clarify that the general possibility to analyse the grounds

30 OLG Frankfurt a.M., 10 January 2008, 26 Sch 21/07, SchiedsVZ 2008, 199-200. The challenge was successful.

31 OLG Frankfurt a.M., 13 February 2012, 26 SchH 15/11, BeckRS 2014, 12067. The challenge was based on the fact that the presiding arbitrator continuously provided expert opinions including for counsels opposing the counsel for respondent in the present proceeding. In addition, claimant argued that this fact had not been disclosed. The court rejected the challenge, arguing that the presiding arbitrator's work as an expert in completely unrelated proceedings was not a fact that required disclosure.

32 See above chapter 4.2.1.6, for more details on non-disclosure as a ground for dependence and partiality.

33 *Thomas Kinkade Co. v. White*, 711 F.3d 719 (6th Cir. 2013).

34 *Crow Construction v. Jeffrey M. Brown Assoc. Inc.*, 264 F.Supp.2d 217 (E.D. Pennsylvania 2003), "[w]hen considered individually, any one of the above-described failed disclosures constitutes an appearance of bias. Viewed together as a whole, they constitute not only the appearance of bias but, perhaps, a suggestion of bias". The U.S. District Court, therefore, used the cumulation of grounds to avoid deciding which standard applied.

cumulatively exists. This was explicitly acknowledged in *H v. L and M*[35] and *Dera Commercial Estate v. Derya Inc.*, where the England and Wales High Court of Justice concluded that

> it is clear from a review of the full circumstances surrounding the Tribunal's interlocutory orders and directions, and of the conduct of the arbitration as a whole, that none of the matters relied on by Dera demonstrate the existence of apparent bias on a cumulative basis as asserted.[36]

In addition, in *Cofely Ltd. v. Anthony Bingham and Knowles Ltd.*, the High Court of Justice sustained a challenge reviewing the grounds for the challenge cumulatively.[37]

LCIA case law follows this lead. The LCIA Court denied a challenge, but explicitly stated that the Division considered the facts cumulatively,[38] and upheld a challenge, inter alia, based on a cumulation of the grounds.[39]

In Switzerland, Article 47(1)(f) Swiss ZPO, dealing with recusal for judges, is interpreted to enable a cumulative analysis of grounds for challenge.[40] It reads:

> Judges and judicial officers shall recuse themselves if: [...] they may not be impartial for other reasons, notably due to friendship or enmity with a party or his or her representative.

It is generally accepted that this provision applies to arbitrators.[41] The wording of the provision is indeed framed as broadly as to possibly include cumulation.

This precedence from Germany, the United Kingdom, the United States, and Switzerland demonstrates a general acceptance of cumulation of grounds. One may stress that cumulation of grounds safeguards the parties' confidence in the proceedings and values their interest in not accepting an arbitral tribunal that repeatedly provided slight impressions of partiality and dependence.

35 *H v. L and M*, [2017] EWHC 137 (Comm), on a challenge.
36 *Dera Commercial Estate v. Derya Inc.*, [2018] EWHC 1673 (Comm).
37 *Cofely Ltd. v. Anthony Bingham and Knowles Ltd.*, [2016] EWHC 240 (Comm).
38 LCIA Reference No. 5665, LCIA Court, 30 August 2006, Arb. Int'l 27 (2011), 395-412.
39 LCIA Reference No. UN3490, LCIA Court, 21 October 2005, 27 December 2005, Arb. Int'l 27 (2011), 377-394, where the challenge was based on ex parte communication and following biased conduct in the hearing.
40 KuKo ZPO/R. Kiener, Art. 47 para. 18.
41 KuKo ZPO/R. Kiener, Art. 47 para. 7.

5.5 Concluding Remarks

Compared with conflicts of interests, this category of other grounds for challenge or annulment does not provide much space for arguing dependence and partiality. Previous challenges of the arbitrator in unrelated proceedings cannot serve as a ground for finding dependence and partiality. Otherwise, the interests of the party appointing the arbitrator in question would be disproportionately frustrated. Likewise, the mere fact that the arbitrator was convicted of an offense in the past does not constitute a ground for challenge or annulment. Absent any connection between the events leading to the conviction and the arbitral proceedings, there is not sufficient reason to doubt the arbitrator's independence and impartiality. Furthermore, institutional dependence and partiality do usually not entail arguments that succeed in international commercial arbitration for finding dependence and partiality.

Finally, the only helpful resource for parties' pursuing a challenge or annulment action in the above category is the cumulation of grounds. Most case law demonstrates that scenarios that on their own do not meet the threshold of a ground for finding dependence and partiality may cumulatively cross the threshold.

6 The Applicable Standard of Independence and Impartiality

The applicable standard of independence and impartiality will determine whether or not a conflict of interest providing sufficient ground for a challenge or an annulment action exists. The international casuistic in chapters 4 and 5 demonstrates deviations and similarities in the application of independence and impartiality. Different factual circumstances and the use of different standards of independence and impartiality cause these deviations.

In general, any standard of independence and impartiality has the purpose of balancing party autonomy in the form of the parties' right to appoint their chosen arbitrator and the judicial need of a due process to equate the arbitral award with any other legal judgment.

> It is axiomatic that a neutral decision-maker may not decide disputes in which he or she has a personal stake. However, the unique role of arbitrators, whose special expertise arises from wide experience in their fields, sometimes leads to a gain of their professional knowledge and skill at the cost of the appearance of less than complete impartiality.[1]

Often, the professional knowledge and skill are precisely the characteristics that induce the appointing party to choose the arbitrator in question. Demanding the appointing party to choose an arbitrator who is independent and impartial limits this party's full discretion when choosing its arbitrator. The standard of independence and impartiality defines the degree of adjustment. Where the party challenging the arbitrator is required to demonstrate definite dependence and partiality, the other party's right to appoint is less limited. The requirement of demonstrating absolute dependence and partiality reveals a low standard of independence and impartiality. Where the party challenging the arbitrator is required to demonstrate only potential dependence and partiality, the opposite is the case. The other party's right to appoint is more limited since the standard of independence and impartiality is higher. By touching upon the party's right to appoint its arbitrator, the standard of independence and impartiality affects the contractual nature of arbitration.[2] The standard also affects the judicial nature of arbitration. On the judicial side, arbitration,

1 *Pitta v. Hotel Ass'n of New York City, Inc.*, 806 F.2d 419 (2d Cir. 1986), on domestic arbitration.
2 See above chapter 1.3, on the dualistic nature of arbitration.

inter alia, needs to safeguard the users' trust in the judicial function of an arbitral award. Since, in the end, the "users of the legal system matter", their interest in an enforceable award matters.[3] Varieties in the applicable standard of independence and impartiality address this need to safeguard the users' trust differently.

Different standards of independence and impartiality vary between definite dependence and partiality and potential dependence and partiality (6.1). It is striking that different standards may be used for different scenarios. It will be analysed when and why different scenarios may lead to different applicable standards of independence and impartiality (6.2), and whether the standard varies between the arbitrators within the arbitral tribunal (6.3). Additionally, the particular issue of unconscious bias of arbitrators (6.4), and the parties' possibility to modify the standard will be analysed (6.5). Finally, the standards applicable to experts (6.6) and tribunal secretaries (6.7) are outlined, before concluding with final remarks (6.8).

6.1 Definite Dependence and Partiality versus Potential Dependence and Partiality

In theory, the standard of independence and impartiality may vary between proof of absolute dependence and partiality and mere potential dependence and partiality. Most case law and applicable laws as well as rules centre in the middle of these extremes, i.e., they apply a standard between an actual possibility of bias and the impression or appearance of bias. However, case law even within one jurisdiction deviates between these approaches.

Dependence and partiality, and also bias, include internal and external elements, i.e., subjective and objective aspects. Both are highly important: Since justice does not need to be only done, but also requires parties to recognise and see it,[4] independence and impartiality in practice are determined by subjective and objective elements. However, by varying the weight of both elements, different case law comes to divergent applicable standards of independence and impartiality. In addition to different material degrees of independence and impartiality required in case law and statutes, the perspective of the observer may vary.

---

3 D. Lawson, *Impartiality and Independence of International Arbitrators, Commentary on the 2004 IBA Guidelines on Conflicts of Interest in International Arbitration*, ASA Bull. 2005, 22-45, 25.

4 Lord Hewart, in *R v. Sussex Justices, Ex p. McCarthy*, [1924] 1 KB 256. See also, C. Rogers, *Ethics in International Arbitration*, p. 91.

6.1.1 *Perspective*

Case law and statutes apply different perspectives to scenarios that potentially constitute grounds for challenge or annulment.[5] The perspective determines from whose point of view the material standard is to be applied. Possibilities for defining the perspective are a reasonable third or fair-minded person, a reasonable person in the shoes of the applicant, and the eyes of the applicant. The first perspective is a purely objective one, the second is both objective and subjective, and the last a strictly subjective perspective. Most rules do not explicitly refer to the perspective to be applied in the analysis of a conflict of interest.[6]

Primarily, case law from the United States favours a purely objective perspective, and refers to a "reasonable person".[7] Also, some French case law[8] and most of the Swiss case law[9] refer to an objective perspective. The challenging party has to prove facts that objectively demonstrate the distrust in the arbitrator. Such distrust cannot be based on a subjective feeling of one of the parties but must be based on concrete circumstances which are themselves capable of objectively and reasonably arousing distrust of the arbitrator's independence in a "normally sensing" person.[10] Thus, in order to challenge an arbitrator, it is sufficient if the circumstances, when assessed objectively, give rise to the appearance

5 Some authors argue that the issue of perspective is the decisive issue that leads to different results, not the question of defining the terms dependence and partiality, e.g., D. Lawson, *Impartiality and Independence of International Arbitrators, Commentary on the 2004 IBA Guidelines on Conflicts of Interest in International Arbitration*, ASA Bull. 2005, 22-45, 25 et seq. On the standard of proof for challenging an arbitrator, see M. Hwang/L. Lee, *FS Karrer*, p. 169 et seq.

6 Where challenge decisions are made public, the institutional approach can be analysed through these decisions. The LCIA Court repeatedly confirmed the objective perspective, e.g., LCIA Reference No. 81160, LCIA Court, 28 August 2009, Arb. Int'l 27 (2011), 442-454, 452. Sometimes, the material standard of "justifiable doubts" is categorised as demanding an objective perspective, see D. Lawson, *Impartiality and Independence of International Arbitrators, Commentary on the 2004 IBA Guidelines on Conflicts of Interest in International Arbitration*, ASA Bull. 2005, 22-45, 25 et seq.; LCIA Reference No. UN7949, LCIA Court, 3 December 2007, Arb. Int'l 27 (2011), 420-424, both concerning the UNCITRAL Model Law wording. See on this issue also, G. Born, *International Commercial Arbitration*, p. 1913.

7 *Ploetz for Laudine L. Ploetz, 1985 Trust v. Morgan Stanley Smith Barney LLC*, 2018 WL 3213877 (8th Cir.); *National Indemnity Co. v. IRB Brasil Resseguros SA*, 164 F.Supp.3d 457 (S.D. New York 2016). See also, *Morelite Construction Co. v. New York City District Council Carpenters Benefit Funds*, 748 F.2d 79 (2d Cir. 1984), affirmed by, inter alia, *Scandinavian Reinsurance Co. Ltd. v. Saint Paul Fire and Marine Ins. Co.*, 668 F.3d 60 (2d Cir. 2012); *Rai v. Barclays Capital Inc.*, 739 F.Supp.2d 364 (S.D. New York 2010); *Apperson v. Fleet Carrier Co.*, 879 F.2d 1344 (6th Cir. 1989).

8 E.g., Cass com, 16 March 1993, 91-10314; Cass com, 3 November 1992, 90-16751.

9 E.g., BGer, 7 January 2004, 4P.196/2003/ech; BGer, 9 February 1998, ASA Bull. 1998, 634-652; BGer, 18 August 1992, BGE 118 II 359, 362; BGer, 20 December 1989, BGE 115 Ia 400, 405.

10 BSK IPRG/W. Peter/C. Brunner, Art. 180 para. 17.

of bias on the part of the judge, even if this bias does not actually exist.[11] The subjective point of view of the parties is irrelevant for the assessment.[12]

Case law from the United Kingdom refers to a "fair-minded and informed observer" and explains, often in great detail, what this exactly includes.[13] The fair-minded and informed observer is fully informed and not "unduly sensitive or suspicious".[14] The perspective is based "on the correct facts"[15] or the observer being "in possession of all the facts which bear on the question and expected to be aware of the way in which the legal profession operates in practice".[16] Some cases even specify that the informed observer "takes a balanced approached [sic] and appreciates that context forms an important part of the material to be considered".[17] Also, the fair-minded and informed observer is not dependent on the characteristics of the parties, e.g., their nationalities.[18] In sum, the observer

> is gender neutral, is not unduly sensitive or suspicious, reserves judgment on every point until he or she has fully understood both sides of the argument, is not complacent and is aware that judges and other tribunals have their weaknesses. The "informed" observer is informed on all matters which are relevant to put the matter into its overall social, political or geographical context. These include the local legal framework, including the law and practice governing the arbitral process and the practices of those involved as parties, lawyers and arbitrators.[19]

11 BGer, 20 December 1989, BGE 115 Ia 400, 403.

12 BGer, 20 December 1989, BGE 115 Ia 400, 405. See also, BGer, 18 August 1992, BGE 118 II 359, 362.

13 *Magill v. Porter*, [2001] UKHL 67; affirmed, inter alia, by *Beumer Group U.K. Ltd. v. Vinci Construction U.K. Ltd.*, [2016] EWHC 2283 (TCC); LCIA Reference Nos. 81209 and 81210, LCIA Court, 16 November 2009, Arb. Int'l 27 (2011), 455-460. See also, LCIA Reference No. UN7949, LCIA Court, 3 December 2007, Arb. Int'l 27 (2011), 420-424.

14 *Dera Commercial Estate v. Derya Inc.*, [2018] EWHC 1673 (Comm), citing *Helow v. Advocate General for Scotland*, [2008] UKHL 62.

15 *Dera Commercial Estate v. Derya Inc.*, [2018] EWHC 1673 (Comm), citing *Locabail (U.K.) Ltd. v. Bayfield Properties Ltd.*, [2000] QB 451.

16 *Taylor v. Lawrence*, [2002] EWCA Civ 90.

17 *Cofely Ltd. v. Anthony Bingham and Knowles Ltd.*, [2016] EWHC 240 (Comm), para. 72.

18 *H v. L and M*, [2017] EWHC 137 (Comm), para. 118. See already *ASM Shipping Ltd. of India v. TTMI Ltd. of England*, [2005] EWHC 2238 (Comm); and similarly, LCIA Reference No. 81160, LCIA Court, 28 August 2009, Arb. Int'l 27 (2011), 442-454.

19 *H v. L and M*, [2017] EWHC 137 (Comm), para. 118, citing *Helow v. Advocate General for Scotland*, [2008] UKHL 62, paras. 1-3.

The fair-minded and informed observer, a "legal fiction designed to assist the court in assessing something objectively",[20] usefully brings objectivity and provability to the proceedings. Although this perspective is not dependent on the characteristics of the parties, the informed observer includes the social, political or geographical context, as well as the practices of those involved as parties, lawyers and, arbitrators in his or her assessment. He or she takes into account the circumstances of the individual case and applies a realistic point of view. Thus, this perspective is not purely objective but includes subjective elements.[21] Such a mixed perspective is also favoured by the IBA Guidelines 2014.[22] The perspective is informed, i.e., has "knowledge of the relevant facts and circumstances". The use of some subjective elements may secure acceptance of users as they see their interests and individual circumstances considered. Therefore, such a mixed objective-subjective perspective ensures that "justice is seen to be done".[23]

Some German case law also applies an objective perspective,[24] other case law references a reasonable third person in the shoes of the challenging party.[25] An apprehension of partiality exists if, from the party's point of view, there are sufficient objective reasons which, in the eyes of a reasonable person, are likely to create mistrust in the impartiality of the arbitrator.[26] This approach resembles a mixed objective-subjective perspective.

A critique may arise regarding uncertainty as to the exact balance between the objective and subjective elements, and, therefore, a particular risk that the perspective is not

20 N. Beale/J. Lancaster/S. Geesink, *Removing an Arbitrator: Recent Decisions of the English Court on Apparent Bias in International Arbitration*, 2 ASA Bull. 34 (2016), 322-341, 326.

21 But the U.K. Supreme Court refers to this perspective as the "objective observer" when approaching the appearance of bias, *Halliburton Co. v. Chubb Bermuda Ins. Ltd.*, [2020] UKSC 48, Lord Hodge, para. 52.

22 Part I, General Standard 2(c): "Doubts are justifiable if a reasonable third person, having knowledge of the relevant facts and circumstances, would reach the conclusion that there is a likelihood that the arbitrator may be influenced by factors other than the merits of the case as presented by the parties in reaching his or her decision." Applied by LCIA Reference No. UN7949, LCIA Court, 3 December 2007, Arb. Int'l 27 (2011), 420-424.

23 "[J]ustice should not only be done, but should manifestly and undoubtedly be seen to be done", Lord Hewart in *R v. Sussex Justices, Ex p. McCarthy*, [1924] 1 KB 256. Also, the ECtHR can be understood in line with this argument: "What is at stake is the confidence which the courts in a democratic society must inspire in the public. […] This implies that in deciding whether in a given case there is a legitimate reason to fear that a particular judge lacks impartiality, the standpoint of the person concerned is important but not decisive. What is decisive is whether this fear can be held to be objectively justified." *Wettstein v. Switzerland*, ECtHR, 21 December 2000, 33958/96, para. 44.

24 OLG München, 17 November 2016, 34 SchH 13/16, NJOZ 2018, 437-439; OLG Frankfurt a.M., 13 February 2012, 26 SchH 15/11, BeckRS 2014, 12067.

25 OLG Köln, 28 June 2011, 19 Sch 11/10, SchiedsVZ 2012, 161-168; OLG Frankfurt a.M., 28 March 2011, 26 SchH 2/11, SchiedsVZ 2011, 342-344; BGH, 10 December 2019, II ZB 14/19, NJW 2020, 1680-1681, on state court judges and § 42(2) German ZPO; BGH, 31 January 2019, I ZB 46/18, NZM 2020, 334-336, on experts.

26 K. Schwab/G. Walter, *Schiedsgerichtsbarkeit*, Chap. 14 para. 6.

sufficiently usable. However, the detailed description of the fair-minded and informed observer clarifies that the objective elements prevail. The approach must not be unduly sensitive or suspicious. Reserving the judgment under this perspective until the observer has fully understood both sides of the argument enables a fair balance.

Finally, a purely subjective perspective is not often used.[27] This approach lacks provability, and thus bears the risk of misuse. It is rather unpractical and should not be applied.

6.1.2 *Different Standards*

The following categorisation of standards serves to outline possible interpretations of standards for independence and impartiality, and their application in practice in France, Germany, Switzerland, the United Kingdom, and the United States. Case law within one jurisdiction may use different labelling for similar or diverging standards so that different cases from one jurisdiction appear in different categories.

6.1.2.1 Definite Dependence and Partiality or Actual Bias

If the standard requires definite dependence and partiality, the party alleging it must prove circumstances revealing actual bias on the arbitrator's side. Courts from the United States[28] interpret the wording of the FAA to demand definite dependence and partiality of the arbitrators.[29] The FAA demands a general "pro-arbitration bias", only allowing annulment in limited circumstances.[30] Besides the wording of the FAA, the very nature of arbitration and its fundamental difference to state court litigation weigh in favour of this high threshold

27 Explicitly rejecting such approach, OLG Köln, 28 June 2011, 19 Sch 11/10, SchiedsVZ 2012, 161-168.

28 *Cooper v. WestEnd Capital Management, LLC*, 832 F.3d 534, (5th Cir. 2016); *Gianelli Money Purchase Plan and Trust v. ADM Investor Services Inc.*, 146 F.3d 1309 (11th Cir. 1998). Cf. *Certain Underwriting Members of Lloyds of London v. Florida*, 2018 WL 2727492 (2d Cir.).

29 Art. 10(a)(2) FAA requires "evident partiality". Cf. *National Indemnity Co. v. IRB Brasil Resseguros SA*, 164 F.Supp.3d 457 (S.D. New York 2016); *Stone v. Bear, Stearns & Co., Inc.*, 872 F.Supp.2d 435 (E.D. Pennsylvania 2012).

30 Art. 10(a) FAA: "(a) In any of the following cases the United States court in and for the district wherein the award was made may make an order vacating the award upon the application of any party to the arbitration – (1) where the award was procured by corruption, fraud, or undue means; (2) where there was evident partiality or corruption in the arbitrators, or either of them; (3) where the arbitrators were guilty of misconduct in refusing to postpone the hearing, upon sufficient cause shown, or in refusing to hear evidence pertinent and material to the controversy; or of any other misbehavior by which the rights of any party have been prejudiced; or (4) where the arbitrators exceeded their powers, or so imperfectly executed them that a mutual, final, and definite award upon the subject matter submitted was not made." The FAA only refers to annulment, not a challenge action. See above chapter 3.5, for general information on the FAA, and below chapter 6.2, for the differentiation of the applicable standard at different stages of the proceeding.

for dependence and partiality in an annulment action.[31] The contractual nature of arbitration implies a "trade-off between expertise and impartiality".[32] The purpose of the FAA as the arbitration law cannot be to "make it too easy for arbitration losers to overturn unfavourable decisions [...]. The 'actual bias' standard protects an arbitration award against [...] easily manufactured and largely frivolous challenges".[33] Additionally, the contractual aspect leads to a differentiation from state court judges:

> [u]nlike a judge, who can be disqualified in any proceeding in which his impartiality might reasonably be questioned, an arbitrator is disqualified only when a reasonable person, considering all of the circumstances, would have to conclude that an arbitrator was partial to one side.[34]

Indeed, the wording "evident partiality" in the FAA may support this approach. It deviates from other provisions in arbitration laws and rules, usually using the terms of "independence and impartiality", and "justifiable doubts". The FAA refers to the positive term "partiality" instead of the negative term "impartiality". Thereby it can be interpreted to require proof of partiality. According to the U.S. Court of Appeals, Second Circuit, "evident partiality" most naturally means "actual bias".[35] Citing this case, the U.S. District Court, E.D. Pennsylvania, in *Stone v. Bear, Stearns & Co., Inc.*, added that "[t]his has particular importance given the current court's views on the primacy of statutory text and 'ordinary meaning' when it comes to statutory interpretation".[36]

At the same time, case law from the United States also questions whether the wording of the FAA and the nature of arbitration demand proof of definite dependence and partiality. The main criticism derives from the fact that it is difficult to prove actual bias.

31 *National Indemnity Co. v. IRB Brasil Resseguros SA*, 164 F.Supp.3d 457 (S.D. New York 2016). Cf. also, BGer, 6 August 2019, 4A_62/2019; BGer, 27 May 2003, BGE 129 III 445.

32 *National Indemnity Co. v. IRB Brasil Resseguros SA*, 164 F.Supp.3d 457 (S.D. New York 2016). The trade-off is especially apparent in disputes of industries where only a small number of experts is present, *Sphere Drake Ins. Ltd. v. All American Life Ins. Co.*, 307 F.3d 617 (7th Cir. 2002), citing *Merit Ins. Co. v. Leatherby Ins. Co.*, 714 F.2d 673 (7th Cir. 1983).

33 *Stone v. Bear, Stearns & Co., Inc.*, 872 F.Supp.2d 435 (E.D. Pennsylvania 2012). The allegation of dependence and partiality was, inter alia, based on the arbitrator's non-disclosure. For non-disclosure as a ground for dependence and partiality, see above chapter 4.2.1.6. See also, below chapters 6.2.2 and 7.1.4.1.

34 *National Indemnity Co. v. IRB Brasil Resseguros SA*, 164 F.Supp.3d 457 (S.D. New York 2016), citing *Applied Industrial Materials Co. v. Ovalar Makine Ticaret Ve Sanayi, A.S. and Ural Ataman*, Docket No. 06-3297-cv (2d Cir. 9 July 2007), on this sequence. Similar also *Merck & Co., Inc. v. Pericor Therapeutics, Inc.*, 2016 WL 4491441 (S.D. New York); *Scandinavian Reinsurance Co. Ltd. v. Saint Paul Fire and Marine Ins. Co.*, 668 F.3d 60 (2d Cir. 2012).

35 *Morelite Construction Co. v. New York City District Council Carpenters Benefit Funds*, 748 F.2d 79 (2d Cir. 1984).

36 *Stone v. Bear, Stearns & Co., Inc.*, 872 F.Supp.2d 435 (E.D. Pennsylvania 2012).

> Bias is always difficult, and indeed often impossible, to "prove". Unless an arbitrator publicly announces his partiality, or is overheard on a moment of private admission, it is difficult to imagine how "proof" would be obtained.[37]

Such a high hurdle may result in an arbitrator who is in fact partial, being treated by the law as impartial. This is contrary to the desires and intentions of the parties who want a fair proceeding,[38] and "clearly repugnant" to the "sense of fairness" of judges enforcing an award rendered by such an arbitrator.[39]

The difficulties in proving actual bias also led English courts to criticise this approach.

> The proof of actual bias is very difficult, because the law does not countenance the questioning of a judge about extraneous influences affecting his mind; and the policy of the common law is to protect litigants who can discharge the lesser burden of showing a real danger of bias without requiring them to show that such bias actually exists.[40]

Conflicts of interest based on conduct, and probably indirect relationships, may be practically excluded by this standard. The applicant will face difficulties in establishing sufficient proof that particular conduct demonstrates partiality as an inner state of mind. Likewise, an indirect relationship, e.g., between the arbitrator's law firm and counsel's law firm of an affiliate of the party, may be unable to meet the threshold of "definite", even if this relationship is rather intense. Thereby, this standard does not respect this party's interest in independence and impartiality, i.e., the integrity of the proceedings. The party applying for an annulment (or even a challenge) would not be able to effectively protect this interest as the procedural hurdle is too high. On the other hand, such a high threshold effectively guarantees the opposing party's interest in having its chosen arbitrator decide the dispute. Thus, this party's right to appoint is ultimately respected. In sum, this standard appears to create an imbalance between both parties' interests.[41]

---

37 *Morelite Construction Co. v. New York City District Council Carpenters Benefit Funds*, 748 F.2d 79 (2d Cir. 1984).

38 J. Bailey, *The Search to Clarify an Elusive Standard: What Relationships Between Arbitrator and Party Demonstrate Evident Partiality?, ANR Coal Co. v. Cogentrix of North Carolina, Inc.*, J. Disp. Resol. (2000), 153-163, 161-162.

39 *Morelite Construction Co. v. New York City District Council Carpenters Benefit Funds*, 748 F.2d 79 (2d Cir. 1984).

40 *Locabail (U.K.) Ltd. v. Bayfield Properties Ltd.*, [2000] QB 451.

41 See chapter 6.1.3.1, for a detailed evaluation of all standards.

6.1.2.2 Real Possibility of Dependence and Partiality

The real possibility of dependence and partiality, also referred to as a "real possibility of bias" or a "real danger of bias", requires less of a demonstration of dependence and partiality. Case law from the United Kingdom[42] and the LCIA Court[43] often refer to this standard.

English courts regularly cite two cases in arbitration matters: *R v. Gough* and *Porter v. Magill.*[44] Both cases dealt with independence and impartiality in state court proceedings. According to these cases, the decisive questions in regard to independence and impartiality are whether there was a real danger that the appellant had not had a fair trial[45] and "whether the fair-minded and informed observer, having considered the facts, would conclude that there was a real possibility that the tribunal was biased".[46] *Porter v. Magill* changed the wording from "a real danger" to a "real possibility". Today this change in wording has been adopted by much of the case law from the United Kingdom and by the LCIA Court when applying the EAA.[47]

Contrary to the approach of United States case law cited in chapter 6.1.2.1, relying on the contractual nature of arbitration and, therefore, the difference to state court litigation, the English courts held that the standard may be the same for arbitrators and judges.[48] This

---

42 E.g., *AT & T Corp. & Anor v. Saudi Cable Co.*, [2000] CLC 220. Case law from the United Kingdom on the standard of independence and impartiality varies from reasonable suspicion of bias to real danger or real possibility of bias. Other common law jurisdictions, such as Australia, Scotland, and South Africa use the wording of "reasonable suspicion" or "reasonable apprehension of bias", which is arguably the standard of "real possibility of bias". For more details, see G. Born, *International Commercial Arbitration*, p. 1902 et seq. Interestingly, the wording of the EAA uses the terms "circumstances exist that give rise to justifiable doubts", in Sect. 24(1)(a) EAA for challenging an arbitrator.

43 Although the wording of the LCIA Rules refers to "justifiable doubts", challenges in cases where the EAA applies use the standard of real possibility of bias.

44 *R v. Gough (Robert)*, [1993] A.C. 646 (HL); *Magill v. Porter*, [2001] UKHL 67.

45 *R v. Gough (Robert)*, [1993] A.C. 646 (HL). In this case the independence and impartiality of a jury member was at issue. The potential ground for a conflict of interest was a relationship of that jury member with the brother of the accused, being the neighbour of the jury member. The House of Lords ruled that there was no conflict of interest.

46 *Magill v. Porter*, [2001] UKHL 67, 103. The case dealt with the alleged bias of a council auditor. The House of Lords examined *R v. Gough*, and applied the standard in light of the ECHR. The House of Lords explicitly denied the wording of "real danger", since that would not be used by the ECtHR. Affirmed, inter alia, by LCIA Reference Nos. 81209 and 81210, LCIA Court, 16 November 2009, Arb. Int'l 27 (2011), 455-460.

47 *Bubbles & Wine Limited v. Reshat Lusha*, [2018] EWCA Civ 468; *Harb v. Aziz*, [2016] EWCA Civ 556; *A v. B*, [2011] EWHC 2345 (Comm); *ASM Shipping Ltd. v. Harris & Ors.*, [2007] EWHC 1513 (Comm); *W Ltd. v. M Sdn Bhd.*, [2016] 1 CLC 437; LCIA Reference No. 7932, LCIA Court, 17 June 2008, Arb. Int'l 27 (2011), 433-438.

48 *Dera Commercial Estate v. Derya Inc.*, [2018] EWHC 1673 (Comm); *AT & T Corp. & Anor v. Saudi Cable Co.*, [2000] CLC 220. See also, H.-L. Yu/L. Shore, *Independence, Impartiality, and Immunity of Arbitrators: US and English Perspectives*, Int'l & Comp. L.Q. 52 (2003), 935-967, 939.

English case law relies on the judicial nature of arbitration. It is difficult and burdensome for the party alleging dependence and partiality of an arbitrator to demonstrate definite dependence and partiality. The approach of a real possibility of bias more realistically and efficiently enables the party applying for challenge or annulment to enforce its interest in the independence and impartiality of the arbitral tribunal. Due to lower prerequisites for demonstrating bias, this standard is more likely to include conduct, indirect relationships or even unconscious bias as a ground for a conflict of interest.[49] Thus, this standard respects the judicial nature of arbitration to a greater extent, and recognises the fact that arbitral awards may be enforced and implemented into national judicial systems like judgments.

Some case law from the United States arguably fits this standard of real possibility of dependence and partiality as well. Deviating from other case law demanding actual bias,[50] this case law elaborates that the "standard requires a showing greater than an 'appearance of bias' but less than 'actual bias'".[51] This statement is rather broad and could refer to a variety of different standards between actual bias and the appearance of bias. However, some cases additionally indicate that the "alleged partiality must be direct, definite, and capable of demonstration rather than remote, uncertain or speculative".[52] This specification demands intensity, with the terms "direct, definite", and the possibility of proof, with the terms "capable of demonstration". It positions the applicable standard for a conflict of interest closer to a high standard of dependence and partiality. Taking a closer look at the application of the standard in this case law, the reliance on the contractual nature of arbitration becomes again apparent. Underlying that the standard must meet the "twin goals of arbitration, namely settling disputes efficiently and avoiding long and expensive litigation",[53] it is uncertain whether the case law aims to lower the threshold compared with that of actual bias.

---

49 See on unconscious bias, e.g., *A v. B*, [2011] EWHC 2345 (Comm); *Lawal v. Northern Spirit*, [2003] UKHL 35; *AT & T Corp. & Anor v. Saudi Cable Co.*, [2000] CLC 220. On conduct, cf. *Dera Commercial Estate v. Derya Inc.*, [2018] EWHC 1673 (Comm).

50 See case law above in chapter 6.1.2.1.

51 *Nationwide Mutual Ins. Co. v. Home Ins. Co.*, 90 F.Supp.2d 893 (S.D. Ohio 2000). See also, *Sodexo Management, Inc. v. Detroit Public Schools*, 200 F.Supp.3d 679 (E.D. Michigan 2016); *Questar Capital Corp. v. Gorter*, 909 F.Supp.2d 789 (W.D. Kentucky 2012).

52 *Republic of Argentina v. AWG Group Ltd.*, 211 F.Supp.3d 335 (D. Columbia, 2016), regarding Investor-State arbitration. See also, *Fowler v. Ritz-Carlton Hotel Co., LLC*, 579 Fed.Appx. 693 (11th Cir. 2014); *Thian Lok Tio v. Washington Hosp. Center*, 753 F.Supp.2d 9 (D. Columbia, 2010); *Gianelli Money Purchase Plan and Trust v. ADM Investor Services Inc.*, 146 F.3d 1309 (11th Cir. 1998); *Tamari v. Bache Halsey Stuart Inc.*, 619 F.2d 1196 (7th Cir. 1980).

53 *Kolel Beth Yechiel Mechil of Tartikov, Inc. v. YLL Irrevocable Trust*, 729 F.3d 99 (2d Cir. 2013); *Gianelli Money Purchase Plan and Trust v. ADM Investor Services Inc.*, 146 F.3d 1309 (11th Cir. 1998).

The approach of a real possibility of dependence and partiality is not without criticism. Categorising arbitration as "private justice", Yu and Shore demand a lower standard for finding dependence and partiality. Since "private justice affords fewer appellate protections, and public policy promotes and recognises private justice as justice, private 'judges' should be removable on the basis of a lesser showing".[54] However, even if "[s]tate courts frame the boundaries within which matters of disclosure, independence and impartiality are finally decided",[55] arbitration remains an alternative dispute resolution, i.e., where the parties agreed on arbitration state courts are not competent to decide the parties' dispute.[56] The parties to an arbitration agreement deliberately chose arbitrators to decide their case. This choice may be rooted in the trust in the efficiency of arbitration, the expertise of the arbitrators, or any other reason. The fact that arbitration affords fewer appellate protections is an advantage of arbitration for some parties. These differences and advantages are, however, accepted by national legal systems implementing arbitration in their judicial system. Arbitration awards are enforced, subject only to a limited review.[57] Arbitration and state court litigation fulfil the same function in rendering final and binding decisions, and both have similar effects.[58] This requires a similar application of independence and impartiality.

6.1.2.3 Definite Risk of Dependence and Partiality

Close to the standard of a real possibility is the French terminology of a definite risk of dependence and partiality, applied in some French cases. Both standards require less certainty in proof than definite dependence and partiality. French courts require the definite risk of bias to be caused by a "material" or "intellectual" connection with one of the parties to the dispute, affecting the arbitrator's judgment.[59]

Some German cases also use the term "risk of bias" and refer to the standard applicable to judges.[60] § 42(2) German ZPO states that "[a] judge will be recused for fear of bias if sound

54 H.-L. Yu/L. Shore, *Independence, Impartiality, and Immunity of Arbitrators: US and English Perspectives*, Int'l & Comp. L.Q. 52 (2003), 935-967, 940. The authors explicitly criticise the High Court of Justice in *AT & T Corp & Anor v. Saudi Cable Co.* According to them, Lord Woolf failed to explain why arbitration and state court litigation should bear the same standard of dependence and partiality.

55 H.-L. Yu/L. Shore, *Independence, Impartiality, and Immunity of Arbitrators: US and English Perspectives*, Int'l & Comp. L.Q. 52 (2003), 935-967, 942.

56 Cf. Art. II New York Convention.

57 Art. V New York Convention and Art. 34(2) UNCITRAL Model Law.

58 But see, BGH, 11 October 2017, I ZB 12/17, SchiedsVZ 2018, 271-275, relying on different purposes: arbitration is not in the public interest, 273.

59 CA Paris, 29 June 1991, cited in *Laker Airways Inc v. FLS Aerospace Ltd & Anor*, [1999] CLC 1124, 1130.

60 E.g., OLG Frankfurt a.M., 29 October 2009, 26 Sch 12/09, SchiedsVZ 2010, 52-56; OLG Köln, 2 April 2004, 9 SchH 22/03, Beck RS 2012, 10537.

reasons justify a lack of confidence in his impartiality".[61] The German wording uses the noun *Misstrauen*, which can also be translated as "mistrust", instead of "fear". Some scholars interpret § 42(2) German ZPO to refer to a serious appearance of bias in the context of arbitration.[62] The German arbitration law deviates from this wording and refers to "circumstances [that] give rise to justified doubts".[63] The previous version of the German arbitration law, i.e., the old § 1032(1) German ZPO, explicitly referred to the grounds for the challenge of judges in § 42 German ZPO. Although the new version omits this reference, the prevailing view still refers to § 42 German ZPO.[64] However, recent case law from Germany applies § 42 German ZPO as referring to justifiable doubts.[65]

Similar to this recent German case law, Born understands the definite risk of dependence and partiality to be very close to the standard applied by the UNCITRAL Model Law, i.e., justifiable doubts.[66] Indeed, many French cases use the wording of "reasonable doubt", which is close to justifiable doubts.[67] In general, it will be difficult to draw the line between a real possibility of dependence and partiality, a definite risk, and justifiable doubts.[68]

6.1.2.4 Justifiable Doubts on Independence and Impartiality

The standard of justifiable doubts in independence and impartiality is probably the common standard. Many institutional rules and much case law refer to the standard of justifiable doubts or similar wordings.[69] Courts in the United States, for example, also use the terms

---

61 In German it reads: "*Wegen Besorgnis der Befangenheit findet die Ablehnung statt, wenn ein Grund vorliegt, der geeignet ist, Misstrauen gegen die Unparteilichkeit eines Richters zu rechtfertigen.*"

62 Stein/Jonas/P. Schlosser, § 1036 para. 22.

63 Art. 1036(2) German ZPO.

64 OLG Frankfurt a.M., 13 February 2012, 26 SchH 15/11, BeckRS 2014, 12067, para. II. The court reasoned that § 1036(2) German ZPO was purposely based on the old § 1032(1) German ZPO. See also, P. Mankowski, *Die Ablehnung von Schiedsrichtern*, SchiedsVZ 2004, 304-313.

65 BGH, 10 December 2019, II ZB 14/19, NJW 2020, 1680-1681.

66 G. Born, *International Commercial Arbitration*, p. 1905.

67 See generally, on the standard of proof for justifiable doubts and General Standard 2(c) IBA Guidelines 2014, M. Hwang/L. Lee, *FS Karrer*, p. 178 et seq.

68 See chapter 6.1.3, for a detailed evaluation and comparison of the different standards.

69 E.g., Art. 11.6 HKIAC Rules: "Any arbitrator may be challenged if circumstances exist that give rise to justifiable doubts as to the arbitrator's impartiality or independence." Art. 14(1) ICDR Rules: "A party may challenge an arbitrator whenever circumstances exist that give rise to justifiable doubts as to the arbitrator's impartiality or independence." Art. 19(1) SCC Rules: "A party may challenge any arbitrator if circumstances exist that give rise to justifiable doubts as to the arbitrator's impartiality or independence or if the arbitrator does not possess the qualifications agreed by the parties." Art. 14.1 SIAC Rules: "Any arbitrator may be challenged if circumstances exist that give rise to justifiable doubts as to the arbitrator's impartiality or independence." Art. 12(2) UNCITRAL Model Law: "An arbitrator may be challenged only if circumstances exist that give rise to justifiable doubts as to his impartiality or independence, or if he does not possess qualifications agreed to by the parties."

of "serious doubts"[70] or "reasonably construed bias".[71] Moreover, the IBA Guidelines 2014 General Standard 2(c) speak of "justifiable doubts", and case law from Germany[72] and Switzerland[73] fits this category. Both the German and the Swiss arbitration laws are in line with the standard of justifiable doubts.[74]

The *Oberlandesgericht* Frankfurt a.M. explained that it is not decisive whether the challenged arbitrator was biased or held himself or herself to be biased. Rather it is decisive whether sufficient objective reasons exist which can give rise to the concern that the arbitrator in question was not unbiased and, therefore, impartial.[75] Also, a challenge is justified if there are objective reasons which could, upon reasonable and prudent consideration, give rise to the fear that the arbitrator is not impartial to the arbitral proceedings, and thus not impartial.[76] The German *Bundesverfassungsgericht* even clarified that any standard where justifiable doubts are irrelevant for constituting a ground to challenge a judge violates the German Constitution and the general principle ensuring that the person seeking justice does not stand before a judge who – for example, because of close relationship, friendship or even enmity with a party – lacks the required neutrality and distance.[77]

Case law in the United States applying the standard of justifiable doubts consistently uses the broad expression of "more than the mere appearance of bias but less than proof of actual bias", with an emphasis that appearance of impropriety, standing alone, is insufficient.[78] It also refers to "serious doubts"[79] or "reasonably construed bias".[80] Some courts concretised that the party alleging a lack of independence and impartiality "must

---

70 *Washburn v. McManus*, 895 F.Supp. 392 (D. Connecticut 1994), citing *Merit Ins. Co. v. Leatherby Ins. Co.*, 714 F.2d 673 (7th Cir. 1983).

71 *HSM Const. Services, Inc. v. MDC Systems, Inc.*, 239 Fed.Appx. 748 (3d Cir. 2007).

72 OLG Frankfurt a.M., 13 February 2012, 26 SchH 15/11, BeckRS 2014, 12067. The court found that the standard of "justifiable doubts" was the same in § 1036(2) German ZPO and Art. 18.1 DIS Rules 1998, the old version.

73 BGer, 18 August 1992, BGE 118 II 359. The court referred to a "serious doubt with regard to the independence of the arbitrator must be based on concrete facts which are objectively and reasonably capable of giving rise to distrust with regard to the arbitral independence", and in German *"ein ernsthafter Zweifel an der Unabhängigkeit des Schiedsrichters [muss sich] auf konkrete Tatsachen stützen, die objektiv und vernünftigerweise geeignet sind, Misstrauen gegen die schiedsrichterliche Unabhängigkeit zu erwecken"*.

74 § 1036(2) German ZPO and Art. 180(1)(c) Swiss IPRG. The latter explicitly provides for a challenge "if circumstances exist that give rise to justifiable doubts as to that arbitrator's independence or impartiality".

75 OLG Frankfurt a.M., 28 March 2011, 26 SchH 2/11, SchiedsVZ 2011, 342-344.

76 OLG Frankfurt a.M., 24 January 2019, 26 SchH 2/18, BeckRS 2019, 848, para. 74.

77 BVerfG, 8 February 1967, 2 BvR 235/64, NJW 1967, 1123-1124, referring to judges.

78 *Bernstein Seawell & Kove v. Bosarge*, 813 F.2d 726 (5th Cir. 1987).

79 *Washburn v. McManus*, 895 F.Supp. 392 (D. Connecticut 1994), citing *Merit Ins. Co. v. Leatherby Ins. Co.*, 714 F.2d 673 (7th Cir. 1983).

80 *HSM Const. Services, Inc. v. MDC Systems, Inc.*, 239 Fed.Appx. 748 (3d Cir. 2007).

establish facts that create a reasonable impression of bias or misconduct".[81] This reasonably construed bias standard requires proof of circumstances "powerfully suggestive of bias".[82] "This standard is neither too low nor too high, which allows competing interests to receive fair and equal treatment."[83] The standard of serious doubts in United States case law is not without criticism. Some authors argue that it lowers the threshold of independence and impartiality; thus, "impartiality diminishes in importance".[84] It fashions "a new and vague standard" that is not in line with the U.S. Supreme Court's approach or the parties' expectations.[85] However, the ALI Restatement of the FAA also prefers the standard of "serious doubts".[86] Determining whether there is a difference between "justifiable" and "serious" and where it lies will be difficult and depend on the concrete application. For example, in *Washburn v. McManus*, the U.S. District Court, D. Connecticut, used the term "serious doubts" while concretising that the facts must "create a reasonable impression of bias or misconduct".[87]

Courts from the United Kingdom illuminated the standard of justifiable doubts similarly.

> [T]he court must find that circumstances exist, and are not merely believed to exist [...]; and secondly, those circumstances must justify doubts as to impartiality. An unjustifiable or perhaps unreasonable doubt is not sufficient: it is not enough honestly to say that one has lost confidence in the arbitrator's impartiality. On the other hand, doubts, if justifiable, are sufficient: it is not necessary to prove actual bias.[88]

81 *Washburn v. McManus*, 895 F.Supp. 392 (D. Connecticut 1994), citing *Metropolitan Property and Cas. Ins. Co. v. J.C. Penney Casualty Ins. Co.*, 780 F.Supp. 885 (D. Connecticut 1991). See also, *Positive Software Solutions, Inc. v. New Century Mortg. Corp.*, 476 F.3d 278 (5th Cir. 2007).

82 *HSM Const. Services, Inc. v. MDC Systems, Inc.*, 239 Fed.Appx. 748 (3d Cir. 2007); *Merit Ins. Co. v. Leatherby Ins. Co.*, 714 F.2d 673 (7th Cir. 1983).

83 J. Bailey, *The Search to Clarify an Elusive Standard: What Relationships Between Arbitrator and Party Demonstrate Evident Partiality?, ANR Coal Co. v. Cogentrix of North Carolina, Inc.*, J. Disp. Resol. (2000), 153-163, 158.

84 H.-L. Yu/L. Shore, *Independence, Impartiality, and Immunity of Arbitrators: US and English Perspectives*, Int'l & Comp. L.Q. 52 (2003), 935-967, 948.

85 H.-L. Yu/L. Shore, *Independence, Impartiality, and Immunity of Arbitrators: US and English Perspectives*, Int'l & Comp. L.Q. 52 (2003), 935-967, 947.

86 The ALI Restatement provides: "Evident partiality requires proof that would cause an objective, disinterested observer who is fully informed of the relevant facts relating to the arbitrators' conduct or alleged conflicts of interest to have a serious doubt regarding the fundamental fairness of the arbitral proceedings." Printed in G. Born, *International Commercial Arbitration*, p. 1902, n. 826.

87 *Washburn v. McManus*, 895 F.Supp. 392 (D. Connecticut 1994), citing *Metropolitan Property and Cas. Ins. Co. v. J.C. Penney Casualty Ins. Co.*, 780 F.Supp. 885 (D. Connecticut 1991). See also, *Positive Software Solutions, Inc. v. New Century Mortg. Corp.*, 476 F.3d 278 (5th Cir. 2007).

88 *Laker Airways Inc. v. FLS Aerospace Ltd.*, [1999] CLC 1124, 1127. Additionally, cf. *Sierra Fishing Co. v. Farran*, [2015] EWHC 140 (Comm), for a good example of the application.

When applying the EAA and UNCITRAL Arbitration Rules, the LCIA Court stated that neither required proof of "actual bias", but a real possibility that the arbitrator is biased (as to which the justifiable doubts are those of the court deciding on the challenge), or that the arbitrator has displayed an appearance of bias (as to which the justifiable doubts are those of an informed and fair-minded observer).[89] Additionally, the wording of "justifiable doubts" used by the LCIA Rules "mirrors" the language under Section 24 EAA, according to the LCIA.[90] Also, the U.K. Supreme Court clarified that "appearance of bias" is similar to the test of "justifiable doubts" used by Article 12(2) UNCITRAL Model Law, the IBA Guidelines 2014, and the LCIA Rules.[91] This approach of merging the "justifiable doubts" standard with the "real possibility of bias" or "appearance of bias" may not clarify as much the substance of the standard but demonstrates, at least, that justifiable doubts serve as the unified standard. In another decision, the LCIA Court underlined the need of any standard to be in line with the more general principle of the arbitrator acting "fairly and impartially".[92]

The approach of English courts, i.e., to apply the justifiable doubts standard as the unified or merged standard of different variations between real possibility and impression of bias, is echoed by some authors. Born, for example, states, first, that the "formula has several important corollaries, which apply generally, despite the divergent legislative approaches to standards of arbitrator independence and impartiality". Second, he concludes that this demands the existence of risks or possibilities of partiality, rather than requiring a certainty or probability of partiality.[93] Having found that it is one general standard that applies, Born favours the wording of "risk and possibility" over "doubt and suspicion" since the latter connotes subjective elements that are misleading.[94] In practice, the standard should disqualify an arbitrator where there is a fifty-fifty risk of partiality.

> Where the integrity of an ongoing adjudicative process is at issue, and possible defects in that process can be corrected through institutional or judicial intervention, a more likely than not standard introduces unacceptable risks in [...] cases of erroneous analysis of the underlying conflict.[95]

89 LCIA Reference No. UN3490, LCIA Court, 21 October 2005, 27 December 2005, Arb. Int'l 27 (2011), 377-394, 386.
90 LCIA Reference No. 3488, LCIA Court, 11 July 2007, Arb. Int'l 27 (2011), 413-419.
91 *Halliburton Co. v. Chubb Bermuda Ins. Ltd.*, [2020] UKSC 48, Lord Hodge, para. 54.
92 LCIA Reference No. 3488, LCIA Court, 11 July 2007, Arb. Int'l 27 (2011), 413-419. The court referred to Sect. 33(1) EAA and Art. 10.2 LCIA Rules.
93 G. Born, *International Commercial Arbitration*, p. 1911.
94 G. Born, *International Commercial Arbitration*, p. 1912.
95 G. Born, *International Commercial Arbitration*, p. 1912.

The opposing fundamental value of the parties' right to select the arbitrator is protected by requiring more than 5%, 15% or even 30% chance of bias.[96]

The balanced standard of justifiable doubts is especially useful where it is combined with an objective-subjective perspective (see above chapter 6.1.1). "Doubts" provide enough flexibility to be applicable in different scenarios of potential grounds for finding dependence and partiality, while also providing clarity through the objective-subjective perspective. Further, the doubts being "justifiable", means that the threshold of partiality and dependence is not too low and the parties' initial choice for the tribunal is not quickly annulled. "Doubts" do not require proof of certainty or likelihood of partiality.[97] It is a reasonable mixture of objective and subjective elements, balancing both parties' interests and meeting the needs of the dual nature of arbitration.[98] It is practically possible for the party alleging an arbitrator's lack of independence and impartiality to demonstrate that justifiable doubts exist, safeguarding its interest in an independent and impartial arbitrator and the integrity of the proceedings. At the same time, the standard does not undermine the opposing party's interest in having its chosen candidate act as arbitrator.

6.1.2.5 Impression of Dependence and Partiality

The impression of dependence and partiality is close to a real possibility and a definite risk of dependence and partiality, and the approaches may arguably be merged with the justifiable doubts standard. Particularly, case law from the United States applies this standard, using the wording of "apparent bias".[99] The frequent use of this standard in the United States stems from the controversial interpretation of *Commonwealth Coatings Corp. v. Continental Casualty Co. et al.* The U.S. Supreme Court's plurality opinion was written by Justice Black who held that "any tribunal permitted by law to try cases and controversies not only must be unbiased but also must avoid even the appearance of bias".[100] Justice Black relied on the fact that the same standard applies to arbitrators and judges. Deviating from this, Justice White, while joining Justice Black in the opinion, made some

96 G. Born, *International Commercial Arbitration*, p. 1912. Following this approach, Born criticises the approach in General Standard 2(c) IBA Guidelines 2014. The "likelihood that an arbitrator 'may' be 'influenced' by factors other than the merits of the parties' cases would, if taken literally, disqualify most arbitrators in most cases", p. 1976. He refers to influences through legal training, philosophical approaches, cultural and national characteristics that are always present. Therefore, the analysis of independence and impartiality should "focus [...] on the risk that an arbitrator will in fact base his or her conclusion on considerations other than an independent evaluation of the evidentiary record and the applicable law".

97 G. Born, *International Commercial Arbitration*, p. 1911 et seq.

98 See also, N. Voser/E. Fischer, *The Arbitral Tribunal*, pp. 63-64, on the Swiss approach to a balanced mixture. See above chapter 1.3, on the dual nature of arbitration.

99 *Cristina Blouse Corp. v. International Ladies Garment Workers Union, Local 162*, 492 F.Supp. 508 (S.D. New York 1980); *International Produce, Inc. v. A/S Rosshavet*, 504 F.Supp. 736 (S.D. New York 1980).

100 *Commonwealth Coatings Co. v. Continental Casualty Co. et al.*, 89 S.Ct. 337 (1968), 340.

"additional remarks" and was later interpreted to apply a different standard of dependence and partiality.[101] Justice White held that

> [t]he Court does not decide today that arbitrators are to be held to the standards of judicial decorum of Article III judges, or indeed of any judges. It is often because they are men of affairs, not apart from but of the marketplace, that they are effective in their adjudicatory function.[102]

He established the criteria of "triviality" for measuring whether the threshold of dependence and partiality was crossed. Only non-trivial relationships could lead to the annulment of arbitral awards. Relying on his concurring opinion, other courts ruled that "[t]o vacate an arbitration award where nothing more than an appearance of bias is alleged would be 'automatically to disqualify the best informed and most capable potential arbitrators'".[103] Other courts additionally criticised the appearance of bias standard by, first, arguing that it does not fit the wording of Section 10 FAA; in fact, it is "contrary to the statutory language".[104] Second, it is within the nature of arbitration that arbitrators may be less independent and impartial.[105] Third, the standard for annulment of an award cannot be as low as "appearance of bias".[106] On the other hand, other courts favoured Justice Black's opinion and interpreted the standard of *Commonwealth Coatings Corp. v. Continental Casualty Co. et al.* to be a "reasonable impression of bias".[107] Commentators concluded on *Commonwealth Coatings Corp. v. Continental Casualty Co. et al.* that the "lack of a clear five-justice majority subscribing to an appearance of bias standard has led to federal and state courts adopting inconsistent standards".[108]

---

101 Only *Schmitz v. Zilveti*, 20 F.3d 1043 (9th Cir. 1994), tried to interpret both opinions not deviating in the standard for dependence and partiality. However, this decision by the Ninth Circuit was itself highly criticised.

102 *Commonwealth Coatings Co. v. Continental Casualty Co. et al.*, 89 S.Ct. 337 (1968), 340. See also, *Apperson v. Fleet Carrier Co.*, 879 F.2d 1344 (6th Cir. 1989), requesting a higher standard of dependence and partiality applied on arbitrators compared to judges.

103 *International Produce, Inc. v. A/S Rosshavet*, 638 F.2d 548 (2d Cir. 1981).

104 *Mantle v. Upper Deck Co.*, 956 F.Supp. 719 (N.D. Texas 1997).

105 *Mantle v. Upper Deck Co.*, 956 F.Supp. 719 (N.D. Texas 1997). The court applied the same standard for judges and arbitrators.

106 *Thian Lok Tio v. Washington Hosp. Center*, 753 F.Supp.2d 9 (D. Columbia, 2010).

107 *Johnson v. Directory Assistants Inc.*, 797 F.3d 1294 (11th Cir. 2015), however, the court ruled that Johnson failed to investigate the potential dependence and partiality in more detail and denied the action to annul; *Schmitz v. Zilveti*, 20 F.3d 1043 (9th Cir. 1994). See also, *HSM Const. Services, Inc. v. MDC Systems, Inc.*, 239 Fed.Appx. 748 (3d Cir. 2007), applying this standard as an alternative line of argumentation.

108 J. Bailey, *The Search to Clarify an Elusive Standard: What Relationships Between Arbitrator and Party Demonstrate Evident Partiality?, ANR Coal Co. v. Cogentrix of North Carolina, Inc.*, J. Disp. Resol. (2000), 153-163, 156.

In the United Kingdom too, some courts apply the standard of a mere impression of dependence and partiality or appearance of bias.[109] For crossing the threshold of dependence and partiality, "there must appear to be a real likelihood of bias. Surmise or conjecture is not enough".[110] The standard is rather a "real danger" than a "real likelihood" of bias, to ensure that the court is thinking in terms of possibility rather than probability of bias.[111] Analysing the decisions applying this standard, one has to conclude that although the wording refers to a low standard, the application itself is higher. Additionally, the most recent case law from the U.K. Supreme Court clarified that "appearance of bias" and "justifiable doubts" require the same test.[112]

Such varying standard of "appearance of bias" has also been applied by some courts in Germany,[113] Switzerland,[114] and some ICSID Tribunals.[115]

> [P]roof of bias or dependence must almost always rest on "appearances," that is, on circumstantial evidence. Proving a person's actual bias, dependence, or prejudice is practically impossible, absent an admission or declaration from the person himself. There is simply no way for ordinary people to scrutinize or fathom the operations of a human mind.[116]

6.1.2.6 Potential Dependence and Partiality

Theoretically, the standard for finding dependence and partiality could rely on a purely potential dependence and partiality. However, even though some case law can be interpreted as espousing this view,[117] most case law does not apply such a standard. Also, further

109 *H v. L and M*, [2017] EWHC 137 (Comm); *Cofely Ltd. v. Anthony Bingham and Knowles Ltd.*, [2016] EWHC 240 (Comm); *Sierra Fishing Co. v. Farran*, [2015] EWHC 140 (Comm), 51; *Halliburton Co. v. Chubb Bermuda Ins. Ltd.*, [2018] EWCA Civ 817, upheld by *Halliburton Co. v. Chubb Bermuda Ins. Ltd.*, [2020] UKSC 48; *AMEC Capital Projects Ltd. v. Whitefriars City Estates Ltd.*, [2004] EWCA Civ 1418. In *Halliburton Co. v. Chubb Bermuda Ins. Ltd.*, [2018] EWCA Civ 817, the court differentiated "apparent bias" from "legitimate concerns", the latter being below the former.

110 *Metropolitan Properties Co. (F.G.C.) Ltd. v. Lannon*, [1969] 1 QB 577.

111 *Sphere Drake Ins. v. American Reliable Ins. Co.*, [2004] EWHC 796 (Comm).

112 *Halliburton Co. v. Chubb Bermuda Ins. Ltd.*, [2020] UKSC 48, Lord Hodge, para. 54. See also, chapter 6.1.2.4.

113 OLG München, 17 November 2016, 34 SchH 13/16, NJOZ 2018, 437-439. See also, A. Rojahn/C. Jerger, *Richterliche Unparteilichkeit und Anabhängigkeit im Zeitalter sozialer Netzwerke*, NJW 2014, 1147-1150, 1147.

114 In German: "*Anschein der Befangenheit*", BGer, 29 October 2010, BGE 136 III 605; BGer, 30 October 2008, 9C_836/2008, para. E 4.1; BGer, 7 January 2004, 4P.196/2003 /ech, para. C 3.1.

115 *RSM Production Corp. v. Saint Lucia*, ICSID Tribunal, 23 October 2014, ARB/12/10.

116 *RSM Production Corp. v. Saint Lucia*, ICSID Tribunal, 23 October 2014, ARB/12/10, para. 66, citing *Blue Bank International & Trust (Barbados) Ltd. v. Bolivarian Republic of Venezuela*, ICSID Tribunal, 12 November 2013, ICSID Case No. ARB/12/20. It should be noted that these difficulties are not exclusive to independence and impartiality but are attached to any subjective legal requirement.

117 E.g., *Gianelli Money Purchase Plan and Trust v. ADM Investor Services Inc.*, 146 F.3d 1309 (11th Cir. 1998).

arguments demand rejecting such a low standard – the fact that the parties themselves appointed the arbitrators, the general high threshold for non-enforcement and annulment of an award under the New York Convention and the UNCITRAL Model Law, and the need to balance the dualistic nature of arbitration in the standard for finding dependence and partiality.

6.1.3 *Evaluation and Comparison*

Most authorities apply and suggest a standard of justifiable doubts. It is difficult to differentiate among the "real possibility", "impression of", and "justifiable doubts" standards convincingly, and one may speak of the development towards a unified standard of independence and impartiality using either of these terms.[118] However, certain differences remain.

The questions arises whether a uniform standard is at all desirable when evaluating the different approaches applied in arbitration laws, institutional rules, and guidelines. In light of the objectives of the New York Convention and UNCITRAL Model Law, i.e., to promote uniform treatment in international arbitration, a uniform standard appears preferable.[119] Additionally, "[c]ourts need a clear standard to evaluate arbitrators' independence and impartiality and arbitrators need to know when to investigate or disclose potential conflicts of interest before agreeing to sit on a case and throughout its administration".[120]

At the same time, one may question the need for a uniform standard. Without an international standard, institutions and arbitral seats compete with each other. Parties may deliberately choose their favoured standard of independence and impartiality by choosing the arbitral institution and seat suiting their needs. Such competition exists between the arbitral institutions and, to some extent, between arbitral seats. In addition, having some degree of competition ensures development. However, even if the latter line of argumentation may have some merit at first sight, these competitive features should focus on rather non-fundamental issues, e.g., differences in costs, procedural rules of using an emergency arbitrator, or allowing tribunal secretaries. The principles of independence and impartiality are of fundamental nature to the arbitral proceedings.[121] There should

118 Or of an "organic development of autonomous international standards of independence and impartiality" in arbitration, G. Born, *International Commercial Arbitration*, p. 1927. See also, B. Berger/F. Kellerhals, *International and Domestic Arbitration in Switzerland*, para. 795.

119 G. Born, *International Commercial Arbitration*, p. 1927.

120 B. Fuller, *Arbitrary Standards for Arbitrator Conflicts of Interest: Understanding the "Evident Partiality" Standard*, PIABA Bar J. 20 (2013), 59-66, 59.

121 See above Introduction, on the fundamentality of the principle.

not be a competition on divergent approaches to principles of fundamental nature. Hence, following the approach of the New York Convention and UNCITRAL Model Law, it is to be welcomed to have an international, unified standard of independence and impartiality.

6.1.3.1 Evaluation of Different Standards

The criteria for concretising the most useful standard for determining dependence and partiality are the balance of the dualistic nature of arbitration, i.e., contractual and judicial, and diverse aspects of the efficiency of the proceedings – proof, time, and costs.[122] The balance of the dualistic nature of arbitration includes various elements. It requires safeguarding the parties' autonomy, and especially the parties' right to appoint their preferred arbitrator, and at the same time judicial requirements of due process, e.g., equal treatment of the parties.[123]

The "impression of bias" standard provides a high degree of the parties' protection of their trust in the judiciary and the arbitrators. In line with the approach in some English case law that justice needs to be seen to be done, such a low standard of finding dependence and partiality compensates the limited judicial control of arbitral awards. Usually, the parties cannot appeal the arbitral award. On the other hand, the limited judicial control is deliberately chosen by the New York Convention and the UNCITRAL Model Law and their general pro-arbitration approaches. As such, and commenting on the FAA, a "stringent standard for vacating awards is a necessary corollary to the federal policy favouring arbitration".[124] This policy could be eroded by a standard for finding dependence and partiality that is extremely low. Additionally, the contractual nature of arbitration may demand a higher standard. If arbitrators can be disqualified too often, the appointing party's right to choose the arbitrator is weakened.[125] Also, efficiency requires a more balanced approach. Any low standard for finding dependence and partiality may invite challenges of the arbitrator or award.

> If a supposed neutral arbitrator is biased, the quality of the arbitration proceeding begins to degenerate rapidly. However, the goals of arbitration, such as quick resolution and minimal costs, are also defeated if a party is allowed

---

122 See also, K. El Chazli, *L'impartialité de l'arbitre*, para. 28, on efficiency when evaluating the applicable standard of method for evaluating impartiality.

123 See above chapter 1.3, on the dual nature of arbitration in general.

124 B. Ostranger/M. Viskocil, *Modern Reinsurance Law and Practice*, p. 598, cited in *Certain Underwriting Members of Lloyds of London v. Florida*, 2018 WL 2727492 (2d Cir.).

125 *Morelite Construction Co. v. New York City District Council Carpenters Benefit Funds*, 748 F.2d 79 (2d Cir. 1984).

to bring claims of arbitrator partiality because the standard is so low that almost any evidence of relationships with the opposing party is considered bias.[126]

On the other hand, and in favour of a "real possibility of bias" standard, a high threshold of dependence and partiality safeguards the efficiency of arbitration as a dispute resolution mechanism. The arbitral process is not easily disturbed, and the arbitral award not easily annulled. Efficiency regarding time and cost is upheld. However, the interests of the party challenging the arbitrator or award are less focused by this standard. It is more difficult for that party to prove a "real possibility of bias" than an "impression of bias".

The dual nature of arbitration requires a standard in between the appearance of bias and proof of actual bias.[127] It must balance objective and subjective elements, to ensure that both parties' interests, the parties' autonomy, and especially the parties' right to appoint their preferred arbitrator are equally secured and fairly balanced. At the same time, this intermediate standard must ensure the essential judicial requirements of due process. The analysis demonstrates that the standard of "justifiable doubts" lies between the appearance of bias and proof of actual bias, even though some courts refer to this intermediate standard as an "impression of bias" or a "real possibility of bias". The label of any applied standard should not matter. It is the substance of the standard that matters. The question can be raised whether it is at all useful to provide a label for the applicable standard. Critical voices can argue that using such empty shells does not provide practical guidance or any legal security. A purely case-by-case approach is the only practical method to address the "infinite number of possibilities of claims for some connective basis for disqualification".[128] The IBA Guidelines 2014 confront such potential criticism with the compromise of providing general standards in Part I and practical examples in Part II. Even if these and other lists run the "risk of disregarding or obscuring complex or changing circumstances, particular markets or customs, individualized expectations and other factual matters",[129] any standard of independence and impartiality needs criteria of application, i.e., guidance and contextualisation. Since independence and impartiality of the arbitrator protect the decision-making function, the requirements of arbitration as a decision-making mechanism are central: efficiency and the nature of arbitration. The evaluation must consider the

126 J. Bailey, *The Search to Clarify an Elusive Standard: What Relationships Between Arbitrator and Party Demonstrate Evident Partiality?, ANR Coal Co. v. Cogentrix of North Carolina, Inc.*, J. Disp. Resol. (2000), 153-163, 161.

127 *Morelite Construction Co. v. New York City District Council Carpenters Benefit Funds*, 748 F.2d 79 (2d Cir. 1984).

128 *Washburn v. McManus*, 895 F.Supp. 392 (D. Connecticut 1994), citing *U.S. Wrestling Federation v. Wrestling Division of the AAU, Inc.*, 605 F.2d 313 (7th Cir. 1979).

129 G. Born, *International Commercial Arbitration*, p. 1928, not referring to the IBA Guidelines 2014.

"commercial and legal context within which, and the arbitration agreement pursuant to which, any particular arbitrator acts".[130] This guidance and contextualisation can be provided by the applicable institutional rules, arbitration agreement, custom and practice in the industry, and the particular parties' conduct. Any lack of concreteness, however, "hinders the efficiency and economy of arbitration by allowing the loser in a proceeding to extend the dispute through additional months or years of subsequent litigation".[131] In the end, any favoured standard must be both: not too vague, but broad enough to include as many scenarios as possible. A detailed list of scenarios cannot replace a general standard.[132] The harmonised approach provided by the IBA Guidelines 2014 is of paramount importance,[133] even if the Guidelines fall short in specific scenarios. They provide "some assistance to the court on what may constitute an unacceptable conflict of interest and what matters may require disclosure".[134]

6.1.3.2 Comparison with Judges

In substance, the standard of dependence and partiality applied to arbitrators is often compared with that of judges in national judicial systems. The arbitrator's function as a decision maker invites such a comparison. If applicable, a comparison can shed more light on the exact criteria concretising the standard of independence and impartiality and may help in practice by providing additional case law for references.

Although used in many cases,[135] this comparison is not without criticism. Born, for example, opposes the comparison by arguing that the two systems are not alike and any

> equivalence would require the arbitral process to emulate national judicial systems, which runs counter to basic premises of the international arbitral process.[136]

---

130 G. Born, *International Commercial Arbitration*, p. 1929.

131 *Washburn v. McManus*, 895 F.Supp. 392 (D. Connecticut 1994).

132 Therefore, it is useful to have the IBA lists in Part II IBA Guidelines 2014, but not fulfilling in search for a proper standard to be applied. The lists may only serve as an example for applying the general standards.

133 BSK IPRG/W. Peter/C. Brunner, Art. 180 para. 19.

134 *H v. L and M*, [2017] EWHC 137 (Comm).

135 Especially in the United Kingdom, e.g., *Halliburton Co. v. Chubb Bermuda Ins. Ltd.*, [2018] EWCA Civ 817, upheld by *Halliburton Co. v. Chubb Bermuda Ins. Ltd.*, [2020] UKSC 48. German case law: DIS - SV - 217/00, SchiedsVZ 2003, 94-96, 96; but see, OLG Köln, 2 April 2004, 9 SchH 22/03, Beck RS 2012, 10537; OLG München, 5 July 2006, 34 SchH 5/06, BeckRS 2006, 8109, for differentiating between arbitrators and judges. Swiss case law, referring to the constitutional standard of independence and impartiality as a starting point for the analysis: BGer, 6 January 2010, ASA Bull. 2010, 772-775, 774 et seq.; BGer, 29 October 2010, 4A_234/2010, para. C 3.2.1. American case law, comparing but differentiating between arbitrators and judges: *Commonwealth Coatings Co. v. Continental Casualty Co. et al.*, 89 S.Ct. 337 (1968); *Scandinavian Reinsurance Co. Ltd. v. Saint Paul Fire and Marine Ins. Co.*, 668 F.3d 60 (2d Cir. 2012).

136 G. Born, *International Commercial Arbitration*, p. 1925.

Further, Born explains that standards for state court judges are

> designed for, and applied in, defined and comprehensively-regulated domestic contexts, while [arbitral standards] apply in an international context which is defined principally by the parties' agreement and expectations in particular cases.[137]

Overall, he stresses the unique role of arbitrators as chosen experts, i.e., the right to appoint, and by this the contractual nature of arbitration. According to him, parties choose arbitration precisely because of the differences to state court proceedings, i.e., the lack of an appeal mechanism and governmental disclosure obligations, and the overall governmental influence in state courts.[138] Even though this is correct, it does not explain why the comparison of the standards for independence and impartiality is useless. In addition, other authorities refer to the fact that the principles of independence and impartiality serve different purposes: in arbitration only to protect the parties and in state court litigation to protect public interests.[139] All these critical voices can be addressed.

First, any comparison indeed needs to reflect potential differences between arbitration and state court litigation. State court litigation is usually purely judicial while arbitration is of dual nature, judicial and contractual.[140] Parties are free to decide on the procedure, limited by fundamental due process provisions, and are free to choose the applicable law and their arbitrator. Parties may wish to appoint an expert as arbitrator who has business ties to either party due to his or her expertise. The frequency of connections in certain areas may be different than that of judges with counsels or parties before state courts.[141] The standard applied to arbitrators may, thus, be labelled more flexible. The decision-making function of the arbitrator is, however, of a judicial nature, even though

137 G. Born, *International Commercial Arbitration*, p. 1925.

138 G. Born, *International Commercial Arbitration*, p. 1926 et seq. He states, inter alia, that "[i]ndeed, it would frustrate one of the central objectives of the arbitral process to require it – and arbitral tribunals – to function identically to national courts: one of the principal reasons that parties agree to international arbitration is precisely because it is different from national court litigation", p. 1927.

139 BGH, 11 October 2017, I ZB 12/17, SchiedsVZ 2018, 271-275; D. Effer-Uhe, *Schiedsgerichtliche Unabhängigkeit bei wissenschaftlichen Äußerungen*, SchiedsVZ 2018, 75-80, 77; Stein/Jonas/P. Schlosser, § 1036 para. 19.

140 See above chapter 1.3.

141 This difference does not lead to a general modification of the applicable standard due to the vague argument of a "limited pool" of arbitrators, see below chapter 6.5.1.2. On the fact that an arbitrator's conflicts of interest may differ from those of judges, Stein/Jonas/P. Schlosser, § 1036 para. 31; C. Seraglini/J. Ortscheidt, *Droit de l'arbitrage interne et international*, para. 732; C. Müller, *Swiss Case Law in International Arbitration*, Art. 180 para. 1.3.3. See also, P. Mankowski, *Die Ablehnung von Schiedsrichtern*, SchiedsVZ 2004, 304-313, 307, on the importance of the parties' right to appoint in the discussion of diverging standards.

it is based on the arbitration agreement, i.e., the contractual nature of arbitration. This judicial power needs to be regulated. It is regulated, inter alia, by the parties' agreement to arbitrate. As such, the comparison cannot equate arbitration and state court litigation. This is well-put in the Preamble of the AAA/ABA Code of Ethics, providing as follows:

> Arbitrators, like judges, have the power to decide cases. However, unlike full-time judges, arbitrators are usually engaged in other occupations before, during, and after the time that they serve as arbitrators. Often, arbitrators are purposely chosen from the same trade or industry as the parties in order to bring special knowledge to the task of deciding.

Second, the criticism against the comparison with judges cannot diminish the judicial nature of arbitration. Especially in the enforcement stage of any award, the judicial nature is highly relevant. Arbitration is not delocalised or independent from any national legal system.[142] The state's action is required to enforce an arbitral award, often relying on state courts.[143] To justify the functional equalisation of arbitral awards and state court judgments, some standards must be upheld, and the conformity of these standards has to be reviewable.[144] However, the judicial nature of arbitration is not only apparent at the enforcement stage. The initial allowance and approval of national laws to provide party autonomy to the parties to agree on arbitration enables the arbitral system.[145] Arbitration is, to some extent, dependent on national or international jurisdictional power. It is embedded in national legal systems as an enforceable legal dispute resolution mechanism. Thus, arbitration can only be as contractual as provided for by the states accepting it. The standard of independence and impartiality in arbitration has to be in line with the requirements provided for by the states. This does not in itself justify any similar standards for arbitrators and judges on independence and impartiality, but it clarifies that arbitration and state court litigation are not as distinct from each other as argued.

Finally, the purpose of any comparison of standards of independence and impartiality must be considered, and whether this comparison furthers the discussion. On this point, the differentiation and use of a general standard and additional case law might help. Even though the comparison with judges does not further the search for a more concrete general standard, it can provide additional case law and references of scenarios which may constitute

142 See the general introduction on international arbitration and the applicable laws, rules and regulations, above chapters 1 and 2.

143 E.g., Art. III New York Convention.

144 BSK IPRG/S. Pfisterer, Art. 190 paras. 2a, on Swiss arbitration law and clarifying that this review is only on very limited grounds.

145 Whether party autonomy is granted by law or not is irrelevant here.

a conflict of interest. Thus, it broadens the source of guidance and contextualisation. Where necessary, the particularities of arbitration may adjust the analysis in the individual case.

Therefore, the standard applied to state court judges may be used to clarify and implement the standard of arbitrators' independence and impartiality while contextualising the differences. It is not to say that arbitrators are "judicial siblings" of judges.[146] However, the differences are primarily set on a theoretical level. In practice, cases dealing with independence and impartiality of judges may serve as good examples to test the independence and impartiality of arbitrators.

6.2 Same Standards for All Grounds at All Stages in the Proceedings

Especially the ground of non-disclosure has led to diverse case law concerning the use of different standards of independence and impartiality. Generally, it is theoretically possible to have different standards for all sorts of different grounds and also for different stages in the proceedings.

6.2.1 *Different Grounds in General*

The wording of national laws and institutional guidelines is rather broad and does usually not provide for guidance, whether different scenarios require different treatment. This is not surprising, bearing in mind that legislators and institutions often try to use inclusive wording. They aim at including as many grounds for finding dependence and partiality as possible. However, any broad language and terminology needs to be filled with content when applying the applicable standard of independence and impartiality to the case. The question arises whether there is room for diverging standards for different grounds, or whether the differences are merely different tiers within the application of the general standard. Case law from the United States and the United Kingdom on direct financial or proprietary interests and actual bias illustrates this issue.

Some courts in the United States rely on *Commonwealth Coatings Corp. v. Continental Casualty Co. et al.*,[147] to differentiate between financial relations and a remote professional

---

146 See for more details on the criticism of qualifying arbitrator's as judicial siblings of judges C. Rogers, *Regulating International Arbitrators: A Functional Approach to Developing Standards of Conduct*, Stanford J. Int'l L. 41 (2005), 53-121, 59-60.

147 *Commonwealth Coatings Co. v. Continental Casualty Co. et al.*, 89 S.Ct. 337 (1968).

relationship,[148] or other non-financial relations.[149] One may argue that where financial relations are present, the hurdle to demonstrate dependence and partiality is lower than it is for non-financial relations, thus, leading to the conclusion that a different standard of independence and impartiality would be applicable to financial relationships. However, this interpretation is not without alternatives. The U.S. District Court, S.D. New York, explained that the reliance in *Commonwealth Coatings Corp. v. Continental Casualty Co. et al.* on financial relationships was a "function of the frequency with which [financial relationships] occur in a commercial setting and the relative ease with which they can be identified".[150] Hence, the court's differentiation between financial and remote professional relationships is rather a first filter when applying the (general) standard of independence and impartiality. In *International Produce, Inc. v. A/S Rosshavet*, the U.S. Court of Appeals, Second Circuit, reasoned that "only where business and financial dealings are concerned one can equate appearance of bias and evident partiality" and denied annulment since the "assertion of appearance of bias [...] seems to be speculation without substance".[151] Thus, the court in *International Produce* did not apply two different types of standards, but rather analysed whether the scenario fit the applicable standard, filtering the "less intense relationships as speculation without substance". This method is likely to appear with less intense relationships or scenarios where the party relies on allegedly biased conduct.[152]

Also, some English case law provides examples of potentially applying different standards. In 1999, the England and Wales Court of Appeal reasoned that "any direct pecuniary or proprietary interest in the subject matter of a proceeding, however small, operates as an automatic disqualification".[153] Although the court differentiated between different tests as standards for independence and impartiality, this case law, again, may also be interpreted to filter different scenarios within the application of a more general standard. All intermediate standards of independence and impartiality, including justifiable doubts, have the advantage that they cover all scenarios of higher standards as well. Thus, any case of actual bias is covered by the standard of justifiable doubts or the impression of bias. The Court of Appeal itself clarified that the

---

148 *Transmarine Seaways Corp. of Monrovia v. Marc Rich & Co. AG*, 480 F.Supp. 352 (S.D. New York 1979), 358, stating that "commercial relationships in the industry interweave and overlap".

149 *International Produce, Inc. v. A/S Rosshavet*, 638 F.2d 548 (2d Cir. 1981). The previous instance had ruled differently and interpreted *Commonwealth Coatings Corp. v. Continental Casualty Co. et al.* "not as requiring indications of financial dealings, but as requiring strong indications of potential bias of whatever nature", *International Produce, Inc. v. A/S Rosshavet*, 504 F.Supp. 736 (S.D. New York 1980).

150 *International Produce, Inc. v. A/S Rosshavet*, 504 F.Supp. 736 (S.D. New York 1980).

151 *International Produce, Inc. v. A/S Rosshavet*, 638 F.2d 548 (2d Cir. 1981).

152 See also, *WellPoint Health Networks, Inc. v. John Hancock Life Ins. Co.*, 547 F.Supp.2d 899 (N.D. Illinois 2008), on ex parte communication.

153 *Locabail (U.K.) Ltd. v. Bayfield Properties Ltd.*, [2000] QB 451.

> basic rule is not in doubt. Nor is the rationale of the rule: that if a judge has a personal interest in the outcome of an issue which he is to resolve, he is improperly acting as a judge in his own cause; and that such a proceeding would, without more, undermine public confidence in the integrity of the administration of justice.[154]

These examples demonstrate that some case law, applying different standards at first sight, merely provides a detailed description of the analysis of the same standard in different scenarios, i.e., actual bias, direct financial or proprietary interest and apparent bias.[155] These different scenarios do not require application of different standards of independence and impartiality.

6.2.2 *Non-Disclosure as a Special Ground*

While non-disclosure should not be a ground for dependence and partiality in itself,[156] some case law suggests a different standard of independence and impartiality in non-disclosure scenarios. The U.S. Court of Appeals, Ninth Circuit, held in *Schmitz v. Zilveti* that in other scenarios the standard demanded actual bias.

> In a nondisclosure case, the integrity of the process by which arbitrators are chosen is at issue. Showing a "reasonable impression of partiality" is sufficient in a nondisclosure case because the policy of [S]ection 10(a)(2) [FAA] instructs that the parties should choose their arbitrators intelligently.[157]

Such an intelligent choice requires full disclosure. This high standard and the differentiation in standards for non-disclosure cases and other cases is, again, based on *Commonwealth Coatings Corp. v. Continental Casualty Co. et al.*[158]

> In an actual bias case, a court must find actual bias. Finding a "reasonable impression" of partiality is not equivalent to, nor does it imply, a finding of

154 *Locabail (U.K.) Ltd. v. Bayfield Properties Ltd.*, [2000] QB 451.

155 The High Court of Justice clarified that although the wording of Sect. 24(1)(a) EAA might expressly fit the scenario of apparent bias, all scenarios and their detailed description of the analysis can be applied in arbitration, *Laker Airways Inc. v. FLS Aerospace Ltd.*, [1999] CLC 1124, 1128. This clarification is in line with the methodological approach that the lower standard of justifiable doubts includes scenarios fitting a higher standard.

156 See chapter 4.2.1.6.

157 *Schmitz v. Zilveti*, 20 F.3d 1043 (9th Cir. 1994). "[P]arties can choose their arbitrators intelligently only when facts showing potential partiality are disclosed."

158 *Commonwealth Coatings Co. v. Continental Casualty Co. et al.*, 89 S.Ct. 337 (1968).

> actual bias. Otherwise, the Commonwealth Coatings court could not have held that a reasonable impression of partiality was present when no actual bias was shown.[159]

There is a body of case law that supports the approach that the "actual bias" standard does not apply to non-disclosure scenarios.[160] This argumentation relies on the differentiation of actual bias and "reasonable impression of partiality" to be applied in non-disclosure cases. Where, however, the general standard is below actual bias, e.g., justifiable doubts, the differentiation is without substance. Where undisclosed facts create justifiable doubts, the threshold for finding dependence and partiality is met.[161] The parties' right to appoint does not demand any different treatment here. The parties' right to appoint is a cornerstone of the arbitral process, and the applicable standard of independence and impartiality generally must account for this right when balancing different rights and principles in search for the appropriate standard.[162] However, the parties' right to appoint does not require a different standard of independence and impartiality for non-disclosure scenarios. The parties' right to appoint should not modify the standard twice, in the search of the general standard and again when considering whether non-disclosure cases must be treated any differently. It is preferable to provide different consequences for the violation of the obligation to disclose, than to modify the general standard of independence and impartiality.[163]

6.2.3 *Different Stages in the Proceedings*

Besides the differentiation on grounds, some case law and other authorities suggest differentiation of standards for different stages in the arbitral proceedings, especially between the pre- and post-award phases.[164]

---

159 *Schmitz v. Zilveti*, 20 F.3d 1043 (9th Cir. 1994).

160 *Crow Construction v. Jeffrey M. Brown Assoc. Inc.*, 264 F.Supp.2d 217 (E.D. Pennsylvania 2003). See also, *Johnson v. Directory Assistants Inc.*, 797 F.3d 1294 (11th Cir. 2015); *Fowler v. Ritz-Carlton Hotel Co., LLC*, 579 Fed.Appx. 693 (11th Cir. 2014); *University Commons-Urbana, Ltd. v. Universal Constructors Inc.*, 304 F.3d 1331 (11th Cir. 2002).

161 It is the undisclosed fact that need to meet the threshold, see, e.g., *Lucent Technologies Inc. v. Tatung Co.*, 379 F.3d 24 (2d Cir. 2004).

162 See above chapter 6.1.

163 See below chapter 7, for the possible consequences.

164 Or more detailed: pre-arbitration, mid-arbitration, post-arbitration, enforcement proceeding, D. Lawson, *Impartiality and Independence of International Arbitrators, Commentary on the 2004 IBA Guidelines on Conflicts of Interest in International Arbitration*, ASA Bull. 2005, 22-45, 41-42. This differentiation does not include additional requirements for annulment in most national laws.

The FAA stands out in this analysis on differentiation of standards for different stages in the arbitral proceedings. The wording and system of the FAA apply the standard of "evident partiality" with regard to annulment and recognition actions, but do not have such standard with regard to challenges since the FAA does not provide for a challenge mechanism. Therefore, some authors urge caution when applying case law from the United States to the standard of independence and impartiality, and especially in the context of challenges.[165] However, the approach of differentiation is not limited to the FAA. Commenting on English case law, Yu and Shore stipulate that after the award has been rendered any reviewing court "will be less concerned with suspicion or danger than with establishing that bias infected the award".[166] Hence, a lower standard of independence and impartiality exists in the post-award phase.[167] At an earlier stage, a higher standard could be justified with less delay and wasted effort.[168] A standard of actual dependence and partiality for the post-award phase is also favoured by some German scholars.[169]

This approach values the existence of the final award. However, where the wording of the applicable laws and rules does not provide for an explicit differentiation, it is questionable whether the existence of the final award should be honoured by applying different material standards in pre- and post-award stages. Bearing in mind that the applicable standard should balance both parties' interest, as well as the contractual and judicial nature of arbitration, it is apparent that a standard such as that of justifiable doubts provides sufficient room for different arguments. It goes without saying that one argument may be that the correct conduct of one arbitrator during the entire proceedings may weigh against justifiable doubts. Thus, in post-award stages there may be different arguments on the tableau. However, any materially diverging standard would not be in line with the accurate balance of both parties' interest and the needs of the contractual and judicial nature of arbitration.

6.3 Same Standard for All Arbitrators

The general importance of the parties' right to appoint has been frequently addressed in connection with the standard of independence and impartiality. Although highly valuable in arbitration,[170] this right also entails some downsides: especially a heightened risk of

165 Cf. G. Born, *International Commercial Arbitration*, p. 1902.
166 H.-L. Yu/L. Shore, *Independence, Impartiality, and Immunity of Arbitrators: US and English Perspectives*, Int'l & Comp. L.Q. 52 (2003), 935-967, 941.
167 Cf. G. Born, *International Commercial Arbitration*, p. 1954 et seq.
168 G. Born, *International Commercial Arbitration*, p. 1955.
169 Stein/Jonas/P. Schlosser, § 1036 para. 54, Anh. § 1061 para. 359 et seq.
170 See above chapter 1.3.2, addressing the right to appoint as a characteristic of the contractual nature of arbitration.

dependence and partiality towards the nominating party, unconsciously or not. First, it is questionable how much influence the parties may legitimately exercise. Second, it is questionable whether this influence can lead to any general deviation in the standard applicable to party-appointed arbitrators.

The parties' right to appoint is one of the pivotal reasons why parties choose arbitration. The purpose of party nomination is

> to permit a party to ensure that one member of the tribunal will be aware of, and sensitive to, that party's particular legal, cultural and commercial background and its position in the arbitration.[171]

Born even concludes that

> [c]onsidered in their proper international context, party-nominated co-arbitrators are an essential means of ensuring the expert, efficient and internationally-neutral arbitral procedure which is a central object of the parties' agreement to arbitrate.[172]

Additionally, party-appointed arbitrators further other practical objectives, from enhancing the likelihood of cooperation by the parties with the arbitral process to voluntary compliance with the final award, and serve as a means of building confidence.[173] When appointing their chosen arbitrator, parties are free to choose. To ensure a deliberate choice, pre-appointment interviews may be conducted.[174] Parties' influence in the appointment process is, hence, rather high. However, this influence in appointing must be distinguished from any individual control during the arbitral process. Later in the proceedings, ex parte communication and other types of influence are restricted.[175]

Against this background, one has to define the precise application of the standard of independence and impartiality for party-appointed arbitrators.

---

171 G. Born, *International Commercial Arbitration*, p. 1941.

172 G. Born, *International Commercial Arbitration*, p. 1942. In line with this purpose, Born provides a comparison with the Statute of the ICJ and its party-appointed ad hoc judges. The drafting history of the Statute reveals that party appointment was placed to foster parties' confidence in the ICJ. At the same time, the party-nominated ad hoc judges were no representatives of the case of their own country, but should supply local knowledge and a national point of view.

173 G. Born, *International Commercial Arbitration*, p. 1944.

174 Within the limits of the applicable laws and rules, see also, above chapter 4.2.1.1.1.

175 See also, above chapter 4.2.1.1.2.

6.3.1 *Partisan Party-Appointed Arbitrators*

Some case law from the United States explicitly highlights the contractual nature of arbitration and the importance of the parties' right to appoint the arbitrator.[176] According to this case law, parties may choose an arbitrator who is sympathetic to their case, and in the end even partisan.[177]

> Arbitration is essentially a creature of contract, a contract in which the parties themselves charter a private tribunal for the resolution of their disputes. The law does no more than lend its sanction to the agreement of the parties, the court's role being limited to the enforcement of the terms of the contract [...]. In thus enforcing the party's contractual right to designate an arbitrator of his own choice, we implicitly recognize the partisan character of tripartite arbitration. The right to appoint one's own arbitrator [...] would be of little moment [was] it to comprehend solely the choice of a neutral. It becomes a valued right, which parties will bargain for and litigate over, only if it involves a choice of one believed to be sympathetic to his position or favorably disposed to him.[178]

Accepting a different international standard in arbitration, this approach of United States courts is nowadays limited to domestic arbitration.

> Party-appointed arbitrators in international proceedings, including those conducted in the United States, subscribe in principle to essentially the same standards of independence and impartiality as do arbitrators selected by arbitral institutions or by the parties jointly.[179]

---

176 For a historical overview on the development of partisan arbitrators in the United States, see D. Branson, *American Party-Appointed Arbitrators - Not the Three Monkeys*, U. Dayton L. Rev. 30 (2004), 1-62.

177 Cf. *Stef Shipping Corp. v. Norris Grain Co.*, 209 F.Supp. 249 (S.D. New York 1962), 253. See also, D. McLaren, *Party-Appointed vs List-Appointed Arbitrators: A Comparison*, J. Int'l Arb. 20 (2003), 233-245, 235, referring to *Delta Mine Holding Co. v. AFC Coal Properties, Inc.*, 280 F.3d 815 (8th Cir. 2001).

178 *Astoria Medical Group v. Health Ins. Plan of Greater New York*, 11 N.Y.2d 128 (Ct. App. 1962), 132-133. The decision was rendered in domestic arbitration. According to Branson, this decision forms a milestone since it accepted the development from the "quasi-judicial" function of arbitrators to a primarily contractual function of the party-appointed arbitrators, D. Branson, *American Party-Appointed Arbitrators - Not the Three Monkeys*, U. Dayton L. Rev. 30 (2004), 1-62, 20 et seq.

179 J. Carter, *Improving Life with the Party-Appointed Arbitrator: Clearer Conduct Guidelines for "Nonneutrals"*, Am. Rev. Int'l Arb. 11 (2000), 295-305, 295.

In domestic arbitration, the "partisan" or "advocate"[180] party-appointed arbitrator was the presumption under the former AAA Commercial Rules and the ABA/AAA Code of Ethics.[181] According to this approach, the party-appointed arbitrator is "expected to espouse the view or perspective of the appointing party".[182] Therefore, a party-appointed arbitrator who helped prepare party witnesses, participated in a mock arbitration a few days before the hearings, and communicated the neutral arbitrator's draft award to "his" party to obtain comments before again consulting with the neutral arbitrator is not necessarily dependent and partial.[183] In 2004, the AAA/ABA Code of Ethics changed its presumption rule for domestic arbitration to now apply the same standard to all arbitrators.[184] Only where the parties explicitly agree on non-neutral arbitrators, i.e., the Canon X arbitrator, the party-appointed arbitrator may act accordingly.[185] "[This revision…] brings American standards closer to standards accepted in international commercial arbitration."[186] The revision is regarded to reflect a general change of the presumption, no matter if the AAA Commercial Rules apply or not.[187] Therefore, unless agreed explicitly otherwise by the parties, the same standard applies to party-appointed arbitrators.

Although the AAA Commercial Rules and ABA/AAA Code of Ethics undoubtedly changed the presumption and now require an express agreement by the parties to apply different standards, the U.S. Court of Appeals, Second Circuit, applied in 2018 the previous presumption, i.e., that party-appointed arbitrators are expected to act as advocates.[188] The U.S. Court of Appeals, Second Circuit, acted with a general pro-arbitration bias favouring

180 *Petrol Corp. v. Groupement d'Achat des Carburants*, 84 F.Supp. 446 (S.D. New York 1949), 448.

181 In 2004 both sets of regulations were revised.

182 *Certain Underwriting Members of Lloyds of London v. Florida*, 2018 WL 2727492 (2d Cir.). Cf. J. Fellas, *Evident Partiality and the Party-Appointed Arbitrator*, N.Y. L.J. 2018, criticising this ruling as "out of date".

183 *Delta Mine Holding Co. v. AFC Coal Properties, Inc.*, 280 F.3d 815 (8th Cir. 2001). The arbitrator in this case even acknowledged he was trying "to sway the [neutral] arbitrators to rule in Delta Mine's favor". The court ruled that "there was nothing insidious about this process".

184 Canon IX(A) AAA/ABA Code of Ethics 2004. Some authors said that partisan arbitrators have had regrettable effects on the arbitration process, B. Meyerson/J. Townsend, *Revised Code of Ethics for Commercial Arbitrators Explained*, Disp. Res. J. 59 (2004), 10-17, 12-13.

185 The AAA/ABA Code of Ethics 2004 provide an obligation for the party-appointed arbitrator to ascertain whether the parties agreed that he or she serves as a neutral or as non-neutral under Canon X, Canon IX(C) AAA/ABA Code of Ethics 2004.

186 B. Meyerson/J. Townsend, *Revised Code of Ethics for Commercial Arbitrators Explained*, Disp. Res. J. 59 (2004), 10-17, 16. Some authors foresaw this change already before the revision in 2004. In 2000, Carter stated that "the overtly partisan party-appointed arbitrator has been reduced essentially to what one commentator has called an 'American stepsister of dubious integrity'", J. Carter, *Improving Life with the Party-Appointed Arbitrator: Clearer Conduct Guidelines for "Nonneutrals"*, Am. Rev. Int'l Arb. 11 (2000), 295-305, 299.

187 J. Fellas, *Evident Partiality and the Party-Appointed Arbitrator*, N.Y. L.J. 2018 stating that the Code of Ethics "reflects the general practice".

188 *Certain Underwriting Members of Lloyds of London v. Florida*, 2018 WL 2727492 (2d Cir.).

a high standard of dependence and partiality, the high importance of expertise in certain industries, and the contractual nature of arbitration, resulting in a "process of self-governing dispute resolution".[189] The AAA Commercial Rules were not applicable in *Certain Underwriting Members of Lloyds of London v. Florida* and the decision was perceived critically in deviating from the established practice of generally applying the same standard, also in domestic arbitration. Fellas, for example, concluded that the decision's dicta of different standards should be limited in application: "It covers only special cases like ad hoc arbitration in the reinsurance industry, the context in which the case arose, and not arbitrations held under the leading arbitration rules."[190] Hence, and in general, the same standard should apply in international arbitration seated in the United States.

The partisan arbitrator is generally criticised as degrading the party-appointed arbitrator to be a mere "negotiator" instead of a decision maker.[191] The outcome of such a procedure including two negotiators on the tribunal may be an "unjust compromise".[192] The system of partisan party-appointed arbitrators does not respect the judicial nature of arbitration as much as three independent arbitrators do. Therefore, one may conclude in general that

189 *Certain Underwriting Members of Lloyds of London v. Florida*, 2018 WL 2727492 (2d Cir.). The court stated that "[t]he ethos of neutrality that informs the selection of a neutral arbitrator to a tripartite panel does not animate the selection and qualification of arbitrators appointed by the parties [... and requests to] distinguish between party-appointed and neutral arbitrators in considering evident partiality. This distinction is salient in the reinsurance industry, where an arbitrator's professional acuity is valued over stringent impartiality. It also meshes with our case law and takes into account the FAA, which restricts 'evident partiality' as opposed to 'partiality' or 'appearance of bias.' [...] Expecting of party-appointed arbitrators the same level of institutional impartiality applicable to neutrals would impair the process of self-governing dispute resolution".

190 J. Fellas, *Evident Partiality and the Party-Appointed Arbitrator*, N.Y. L.J. 2018, who especially criticised that the clear prerequisites and system of applying different standards under Canon IX AAA/ABA Code of Ethics were not even evaluated.

191 D. Branson, *American Party-Appointed Arbitrators – Not the Three Monkeys*, U. Dayton L. Rev. 30 (2004), 1-62, 57 et seq. Branson, inter alia, cites Harlan Stone who commented on the New York arbitration statute that was passed in 1920 and allowed partisan arbitrators. According to Stone the statute was "a serious impediment to successful arbitration. [...] The practical effect of this procedure is the substitution of a board of negotiation for a judge. [...] The appointment of mere negotiators is likely to result only in an award which is a [mere] compromise disappointing to both sides with consequent distrust of arbitration".

192 D. Branson, *American Party-Appointed Arbitrators – Not the Three Monkeys*, U. Dayton L. Rev. 30 (2004), 1-62, 56. Branson refers to Andreas Lowenfield, who provided the following example: "if the neutral arbitrator said to the two arbitrators that 'his' party was due $300,000, but he had believed 'his party' should, in justice, receive $200,000, it was accepted practice to remain silent and form a majority with the chairman at $300,000: Suppose under the chairman's draft the party that appointed you would be awarded $300,000, while in your own estimation $200,000 would have covered the party's loss. Most arbitrators in that situation would just keep quiet – i.e., go along with the chairman." Branson concludes that this dilemma of an unjust compromise is an "echo over the century". It will not be avoided if parties appoint partisan arbitrators, "because an arbitrator who has a duty to act favoring one side must act accordingly throughout the proceeding", 60.

> [w]hen parties seek what they say they want most in judging – justice – they will seek one to three experienced arbitrators with established reputations from the trade or the law, and instruct them to act with resolute impartiality.[193]

In this regard, partisan arbitrators do not appear practical, except where the parties explicitly contracted for partisan party-appointed arbitrators.

6.3.2 *Sympathetic Party-Appointed Arbitrators*

Slightly less extreme is the position in some English case law, which also upholds the importance of the parties' right to appoint. Concerning the applicable standard of independence and impartiality of party-appointed arbitrators, the England and Wales High Court of Justice positions itself somewhere between a partisan arbitrator and three neutrals. On the one hand, a party-appointed arbitrator may be "sympathetic".[194] On the other hand, any general argument that the party-appointed arbitrator is not expected to comply with the principles of independence and impartiality is "offensive to the international arbitration community in general".[195] Hence, the general standard of being independent and impartial applies to the party-appointed arbitrator. Losing trust and confidence in "one's" party-appointed arbitrator is explicitly no ground for a challenge.[196]

In Germany, some case law and scholars favour a sympathetic party-appointed arbitrator as well.[197] The German legislator deliberately refrained from settling the issue when reforming the arbitration laws in 1996. According to the legislator, individual questions such as whether the same requirements concerning independence and impartiality apply to the party-appointed arbitrators cannot be solved by law.[198] Authorities favouring to differentiate between presiding and party-appointed arbitrators occasionally refer to § 40(1) German RiG, applicable for state court judges, stating that

193 D. Branson, *American Party-Appointed Arbitrators – Not the Three Monkeys*, U. Dayton L. Rev. 30 (2004), 1-62, 62.

194 D. Branson, *American Party-Appointed Arbitrators – Not the Three Monkeys*, U. Dayton L. Rev. 30 (2004), 1-62, 55 et seq. However, Branson concludes that the "sympathetic" arbitrator can be compared with the "partisan" arbitrator in American case law.

195 *H v. L and M*, [2017] EWHC 137 (Comm).

196 *Laker Airways Inc. v. FLS Aerospace Ltd.*, [1999] CLC 1124.

197 E.g., P. Mankowski, *Die Ablehnung von Schiedsrichtern*, SchiedsVZ 2004, 304-313, 309. Against differentiating the standard of party-appointed arbitrators: S. Albers, *Der parteibestellte Schiedsrichter im schiedsgerichtlichen Verfahren der ZPO und das Gebot überparteilicher Rechtspflege*, p. 189. See also, Zöller/ R. Geimer, § 1036 para. 7, for an overview.

198 BT-Drucks. 13/5274, p. 40 et seq.

> [a] judge may only be granted permission to act additionally as an arbitrator or give an expert opinion in arbitration proceedings where the parties to the arbitration agreement appoint him jointly or where he is nominated by an institution that is not a party to the proceedings.[199]

The fact that judges are only allowed to act as arbitrators if appointed by both parties shows some resentment towards party appointments.[200] However, concluding that this generally leads to different standards would over expand the purpose of this provision. The purpose of § 40 German RiG is to protect the status of state court judges and to prevent even the slightest impression of bias.[201] This purpose serves the public interest of state court proceedings. Although the standard of judges is, to some extent, comparable to arbitrators, it is questionable whether the national provision of § 40(1) German RiG can be used to argue in favour of differentiated standards for party-appointed arbitrators, also in international arbitration.

6.3.3 *Three Independent and Impartial Arbitrators*

Much case law from Germany, and some from the United Kingdom and the United States, requires all three arbitrators to be independent and impartial.[202] Without explicitly stating that there is a difference between the party-appointed and presiding arbitrator, this case law applies the elaborated standard of independence and impartiality. Additionally, most rules and laws, including the UNCITRAL Model Law, do not distinguish in their wording between the party-appointed and presiding arbitrators.

In Switzerland, case law and authorities have argued in both directions: for and against the differentiation between the presiding and party-appointed arbitrators. Since 2010, case law, however, disfavours the distinction in the applicable standard explicitly. Previously, the Swiss *Bundesgericht* ruled that a higher degree of independence and impartiality is

199 In German: "*Eine Nebentätigkeit als Schiedsrichter oder Schiedsgutachter darf dem Richter nur genehmigt werden, wenn die Parteien des Schiedsvertrags ihn gemeinsam beauftragen oder wenn er von einer unbeteiligten Stelle benannt ist.*" The German RiG regulates the status of judges in Germany.

200 P. Mankowski, *Die Ablehnung von Schiedsrichtern*, SchiedsVZ 2004, 304-313, 309. See also, D. Effer-Uhe, *Schiedsgerichtliche Unabhängigkeit bei wissenschaftlichen Äußerungen*, SchiedsVZ 2018, 75-80, 78-80.

201 C. Armbrüster/V. Wächter, *Ablehnung von Schiedsrichtern wegen Befangenheit im Verfahren*, SchiedsVZ 2017, 213-223, 215.

202 E.g., OLG Frankfurt a.M., 28 March 2011, 26 SchH 2/11, SchiedsVZ 2011, 342-344; *Sierra Fishing Co. v. Farran*, [2015] EWHC 140 (Comm); *Dealer Computer Services, Inc. v. Michael Motor Co., Inc.*, 761 F.Supp.2d 459 (S.D. Texas 2010). See also, MünchKomm/J. Münch, § 1036 para. 31; Zöller/R. Geimer, § 1036 para. 2.

required for the presiding arbitrator.[203] The court based its argumentation on the wording of Article 180(1)(c) Swiss IPRG, only referring to independence and not impartiality.[204] By referring only to independence, the Swiss legislator intended to approach international arbitration with some realism and flexibility.[205] However, this interpretation of the wording of the Swiss IPRG rests merely on the differentiation between independence and impartiality, which is outdated and not practical.[206] In line with the generic term of independence and impartiality, the Swiss *Bundesgericht* overturned its previous case law in 2010.[207] The court ruled that the same legal standard applies to all arbitrators. It held that the general need for credibility and transparency of arbitration requires that the guarantees of independence and impartiality must apply to all arbitrators irrespective of who appointed them.

French case law is even stronger in its wording to ensure the application of the general standard of independence and impartiality to party-appointed arbitrators. French authors highlight the judicial function of the arbitrator and the need for equal treatment of the parties.[208] French courts apply an absolute and strict requirement of independence and impartiality and do not differentiate between the presiding arbitrator and the party-appointed arbitrators.[209]

Particularly where the wording of the applicable standard does not provide any leeway, the same standard should apply to all three arbitrators. This ensures that the whole tribunal complies with its judicial function, i.e., decision-making. Additionally, with regard to the judicial nature of the arbitrator's role, the following factors demand the application of the same standard: the need for credibility and transparency of arbitration as a decision-making system, and, purely dogmatically, the lack of statutory grounds for differentiating between the arbitrators' standards. In addition, the contractual relationship between the parties

---

203 BGer, 30 June 1994, 4P.292/1993, ASA Bull. 1997, 99-107, 104; BGer, 9 February 1998, ASA Bull. 1998, 634-652, 644 et seq. In other decisions, the Swiss *Bundesgericht* deliberately did not decide whether the same or a different standard applied: BGer, 27 May 2003, BGE 129 III 445; BGer, 18 August 1992, BGE 118 II 359. Some lower instances, however, already applied the same standard to all arbitrators in the 1990s, BezGer Affoltern am Albis, 26 May 1994, ASA Bull. 1997, 262-273, 268.

204 BGer, 9 February 1998, ASA Bull. 1998, 634-652, 644.

205 N. Voser/E. Fischer, *The Arbitral Tribunal*, pp. 63-64.

206 See above chapter 3.3, on the changes of the Swiss IPRG, and the Introduction on differentiating between independence and impartiality in general.

207 BGer, 29 October 2010, BGE 136 III 605, 608 et seq. See also, B. Berger/F. Kellerhals, *International and Domestic Arbitration in Switzerland*, para. 788, clarifying that there is no difference between the party-appointed and presiding arbitrator.

208 C. Seraglini/J. Ortscheidt, *Droit de l'arbitrage interne et international*, para. 729.

209 CA Paris, 10 March 2011, 09/28537, ASA Bull. 2013, 443-447. See also, CA Paris, 12 February 2009, Rev. de l'Arb. 2009, 186-190, and CA Paris, 9 September 2010, ASA Bull. 2011, 187-192.

and the arbitrators is the same for all three arbitrators.[210] Thus, there is no need for differentiating. Much more, the paramount role of independence and impartiality, being a fundamental principle,[211] leaves no room for different standards.[212]

To conclude, where the applicable law does not explicitly provide differently, there is a tendency in international arbitration to apply the same standard of independence and impartiality to all arbitrators within the tribunal.

6.4 Same Standard for Unconscious Bias

A particular category of bias includes biases that are unconscious, cultural, implicit, or psychological. The terminology is diverse in this regard. Some prefer to use the term "blinders" in order to circumvent the negative connotation of bias. Others stick to bias but clarify through the addition "unconscious",[213] cultural, implicit, or psychological that this type of bias is to be differentiated. It is uncertain whether the elaborated standard can be applied to these biases. In fact, it is questionable whether this category may constitute a conflict of interest at all. This category includes "blinders" that are "simply human nature".[214] The fact that an arbitrator as a human being is predisposed in itself does not constitute a lack of independence and impartiality. "[P]arties do not choose blank slates or empty vessels, but experienced practitioners, whose views and experience are strengths of the arbitral process, not grounds for challenge."[215]

A conflict of interest based on unconscious bias may be demonstrated by the arbitrator's conduct.[216] However, the conduct always needs to meet the threshold of constituting a conflict of interest.[217] Justifiable doubts as to independence and impartiality exist only where there are concrete predispositions towards one of the parties or counsels. Even though this category of bias does not often qualify as a conflict of interest, arbitrators

210 MünchKomm/J. Münch, § 1036 para. 31.
211 See above the Introduction.
212 Zöller/R. Geimer, § 1036 para. 2.
213 Often used in English case law, e.g., *Interprods Ltd. v. De La Rue International Ltd.*, [2014] EWHC 68 (Comm); *A v. B*, [2011] EWHC 2345 (Comm); *AT & T Corp. & Anor v. Saudi Cable Co.*, [2000] CLC 220.
214 E. Sussman, *Arbitrator Decision Making – Unconscious Psychological Influences and What You Can Do About Them*, YB Int'l Arb. IV (2015), 70-96, 71.
215 G. Born, *International Commercial Arbitration*, p. 1897.
216 *Cofely Ltd. v. Anthony Bingham and Knowles Ltd.*, [2016] EWHC 240 (Comm). The arbitrator's lack of awareness of his conduct being inappropriate demonstrated a lack of objectivity and an increased risk of unconscious bias, paras. 110-114.
217 See examples in chapter 4.2.

should actively work on de-biasing and tackle their blinders.[218] Irrespective of the terminology, unconscious bias may constitute a conflict of interest, and constitute a ground for finding dependence and partiality. Neither a conflict of interest nor grounds for finding dependence and partiality require any voluntary element.

English case law provides some guidance on the question of whether this category fits the general standard of independence and impartiality. Generally, it affirms the application of the same standard.[219] Since the general standard of independence and impartiality is initially rather broad, any other approach would be unpractical and may lead to legal insecurity. The applicable standard is high enough to filter the inherent unconscious bias that is due to human nature and should not lead to a lack of independence and impartiality.

6.5 PARTIES' POSSIBILITY TO MODIFY THE STANDARD

For the question of whether parties may modify the standard of dependence and partiality, the balance of the dualistic nature of arbitration becomes again decisive. Bearing in mind that United States case law and rules provide explicitly for the possibility of the parties to agree on a non-neutral party-appointed arbitrator, it is not surprising that case law modifies the standard applied in these scenarios.

> Where an agreement entitles the parties to select interested arbitrators, "evident partiality" cannot serve as a basis for vacating an award under [Section] 10(a)(2) [FAA] absent a showing of prejudice.[220]

Again, this case law highlights the importance of the contractual nature of arbitration[221] and the paramount role of the parties' right to appoint an arbitrator. The task of judging an arbitrator's independence and impartiality is "best consigned to the parties, who are the architects of their own arbitration process, and are far better informed of prevailing ethical standards and reputations within their business".[222] The question arises to what

218 E. Sussman, *Arbitrator Decision Making – Unconscious Psychological Influences and What You Can Do About Them*, YB Int'l Arb. IV (2015), 70-96, 88-91; E. Sussman, *The Arbitrator Survey, Practices, Preferences and Changes on the Horizon*, Am. Rev. Int'l Arb. 26 (2015), 517-538.

219 *A v. B*, [2011] EWHC 2345 (Comm); *Lawal v. Northern Spirit*, [2003] UKHL 35; *AT & T Corp. & Anor v. Saudi Cable Co.*, [2000] CLC 220.

220 *Winfrey v. Simmons Foods, Inc.*, 495 F.3d 549 (8th Cir. 2007).

221 In *Winfrey v. Simmons Foods, Inc.*, the court argued that parties to an arbitration choose their method of dispute resolution, and can ask no more impartiality than inheres in the method they have chosen.

222 *Commonwealth Coatings Co. v. Continental Casualty Co. et al.*, 89 S.Ct. 337 (1968), 151, Justice White.

extent the fundamental principle of independence and impartiality[223] calls for a concrete standard of independence and impartiality, and whether parties may derogate from the standard laid out in the applicable arbitration laws and rules. On the one hand, one may generally affirm the possibility to modify the standard of independence and impartiality and conclude that "the choice to have more or less independence, or even more or less impartiality, belongs to [the parties]".[224] This argumentation might even result in the statement that there cannot be an absolute standard of independence and impartiality apart from the nature of the parties' agreement.[225] A practical advantage of focusing on the contractual nature is that it "allows differentiations to emerge naturally from the practices that have given rise to the several forms of international adjudication, and it integrates the consensual feature that they share".[226] This approach is, however, limited by the mandatory provisions of the applicable laws and rules. The parties' consent cannot deviate from these. Usually, the most fundamental rules of procedure are mandatory. Therefore, any modified lower or higher standard needs to be in line with the mandatory character of potentially conflicting procedural provision.

Possible ways of modifying the standard are directly changing the standard to be applied through an additional agreement, naming new grounds for challenge or annulment and by this heightening the standard, or explicitly excluding specific scenarios from resulting in a conflict of interest. It is questionable whether such modification can proceed under the applicable arbitration laws and rules.

6.5.1 *Agreeing on a Lower Standard of Independence and Impartiality*

Agreeing on a lower standard of independence and impartiality changes the balance between the contractual and judicial nature of arbitration as well as both parties' interests and rights that lead to the standard of justifiable doubts.[227] A lower standard requires more than justifiable doubts to challenge an arbitrator. A conflict of interest will be less likely to be found. Parties may either bilaterally agree on a lower standard, or the individual circumstances may demand applying such a deviated standard.

---

223 See above the Introduction.

224 F. Gélinas, *The Independence of International Arbitrators and Judges: Tampered With or Well Tempered?*, N.Y. Int'l Rev. 24 (2011), 1-48, 38.

225 F. Gélinas, *The Independence of International Arbitrators and Judges: Tampered With or Well Tempered?*, N.Y. Int'l Rev. 24 (2011), 1-48, 39. However, Gélinas criticises this view being limited to ad hoc tribunals "where self-help is the last resort for implementation".

226 F. Gélinas, *The Independence of International Arbitrators and Judges: Tampered With or Well Tempered?*, N.Y. Int'l Rev. 24 (2011), 1-48, 42.

227 See above chapter 6.1.3.1.

6.5.1.1 Agreement

Parties may agree on a lower standard of independence and impartiality in different forms and intensities. For example, the parties may add the following terms to their arbitration agreement: that arbitrators are not required to be independent and impartial; that the standard for finding dependence and partiality is definite dependence and partiality;[228] they could name a specific person to act as arbitrator who is not independent and impartial; or they could exclude the possibility to challenge an arbitrator in general. In every scenario, it is questionable whether the mandatory requirements of the applicable laws would allow the deviation.

United States case law provides examples of favouring the contractual nature of arbitration and allowing deviations for finding dependence and partiality. The U.S. Court of Appeals, Seventh Circuit, states that parties are free to choose the binding character of Section 10(a)(2) FAA.[229] This approach is in line with the possibility of agreeing on a non-neutral arbitrator in U.S. domestic arbitration, and may be compared with the possibility of agreeing on non-neutral arbitrators to English umpires and ICJ ad hoc judges.[230] According to Born, these approaches affirm the more general

> substantial presumptive force to the position that parties should generally be free to agree upon predisposed arbitrators, provided that this is done transparently and that the parties are treated equally.[231]

Additionally, Articles II and V(1)(d) New York Convention, and national arbitration laws uphold party autonomy. Article II(1), (3) New York Convention mandates Contracting States to recognise valid arbitration agreements.[232] This raises the question of whether the deviation to the applicable standard of independence and impartiality renders the arbitration agreement invalid. This will be a question answered by the applicable law and rules. The U.S. Court of Appeals, Seventh Circuit, explicitly ruled that the parties' deviations were

---

228 For this standard, see chapter 6.1.2.1.

229 *Sphere Drake Ins. Ltd. v. All American Life Ins. Co.*, 307 F.3d 617 (7th Cir. 2002).

230 G. Born, *International Commercial Arbitration*, p. 1948.

231 G. Born, *International Commercial Arbitration*, p. 1948.

232 Art. II(1), (3) New York Convention read: "1. Each Contracting State shall recognize an agreement in writing under which the parties undertake to submit to arbitration all or any differences which have arisen or which may arise between them in respect of a defined legal relationship, whether contractual or not, concerning a subject matter capable of settlement by arbitration. [...] 3. The court of a Contracting State, when seized of an action in a matter in respect of which the parties have made an agreement within the meaning of this article, shall, at the request of one of the parties, refer the parties to arbitration, unless it finds that the said agreement is null and void, inoperative or incapable of being performed."

limited by the applicable rules.[233] These rules only allowed non-neutral arbitrators to communicate ex parte "until the case is taken under advisement" and required them to be "impartial adjudicators" thereafter.[234] Thus, these were the applicable limitations.

The opposite position is to exclusively highlight the judicial function of arbitration, and prohibit deviations due to the fundamental role of independence and impartiality.

First, the EAA serves as an example here. Section 1(a) EAA highlights the adjudicatory function of an impartial tribunal. It reads:

> [t]he provisions of this Part are founded on the following principles, and shall be construed accordingly – the object of arbitration is to obtain the fair resolution of disputes by an impartial tribunal without unnecessary delay or expense.

Positioning the principle of impartiality that prominently as a "General principle" may favour an imbalance towards the judicial nature. Additionally, Sections 4(1) and 33(1)(a) EAA require all arbitrators to act fairly and impartially "notwithstanding any agreement to the contrary".[235]

Second, the French concept of the international *ordre public* may serve as an additional argument: since the arbitrator's mission is to judge, he or she must pay attention to the presence of justice,[236] potentially including independence and impartiality. However, the concept of the international *ordre public* is limited in its application.[237] It is uncertain whether independence and impartiality, even as a part of the international *ordre public*, prohibit every modification. Additionally, French arbitration law also upholds party autonomy.[238] Thus, there is more flexibility.

233 ARIAS U.S. Rules.

234 *Sphere Drake Ins. Ltd. v. All American Life Ins. Co.*, 307 F.3d 617 (7th Cir. 2002).

235 In fact, Sect. 4 EAA refers to Schedule 1, naming all mandatory provisions. Schedule 1 includes Sects. 24, 33, 67 and 68, providing the picture that independence and impartiality may not be deviated from in total. However, the application of English courts shows, that this cannot be equated with justifiable doubts in all cases.

236 C. Seraglini/J. Ortscheidt, *Droit de l'arbitrage interne et international*, para. 895.

237 C. Seraglini/J. Ortscheidt, *Droit de l'arbitrage interne et international*, para. 896.

238 E.g., in regard to challenge procedures C. Seraglini/J. Ortscheidt, *Droit de l'arbitrage interne et international*, para. 740, also relying on Art. 13 UNCITRAL Model Law, although the French arbitration law did not adopt the Model Law.

Similarly, the German and Swiss approaches provide for some flexibility. The Swiss approach does not permit alterations in the standard of dependence and partiality for the challenge procedure.[239] Even though party autonomy is of paramount importance, the standard of justifiable doubts in Article 180(1)(c) Swiss IPRG cannot be deviated from by parties.[240] Parties may, however, exclude any review at all, and therefore exclude setting aside procedures where the seat of arbitration is Switzerland.[241] German cases differentiate according to the point in time of agreeing on the modification: where the parties modify after the dispute already arose, courts grant the parties more discretion to deviate.[242] At this point in time, the parties are aware of their need of (independent and impartial) adjudicators. At the point in time when the parties agree on their initial contract and the arbitration agreement, they usually lack this awareness.[243] This mediated approach provides enough flexibility while ensuring compliance with the fundamental principles.[244] Some scholars also favour a flexible approach: while highlighting the importance of a general minimal standard of independence and impartiality, parties should be free to agree on sympathetic or even partisan party-appointed arbitrators.[245]

In conclusion, under the FAA, French, German, and Swiss arbitration law there is some room for modifying the applicable standard of independence and impartiality, while adhering to a minimal standard. The exact nuances of parties' discretion differ. In practice, parties are well advised to use "clear, unambiguous language" when deviating from the applicable standard of independence and impartiality.[246]

6.5.1.2 Modification Due to Limited Pool of Arbitrators

Besides explicitly agreeing on modifying the standard, case law from different jurisdictions uses the fact that arbitration, either in general or in specific industries, merely provides a limited pool of arbitrators, and thus needs to apply a lower standard of independence and

---

239 It allows, however, deviations regarding the procedure, cf. BSK IPRG/W. Peter/C. Brunner, Art. 180 para. 29 et seq.

240 BSK IPRG/W. Peter/C. Brunner, Art. 180 para. 31. E.g., where the parties' named an arbitrator in their agreement who is not independent and impartial, the award cannot be enforced according to Art. V(2)(b) New York Convention, BezGer Affoltern am Albis, 26 May 1994, ASA Bull. 1997, 262-273, 268.

241 Art. 192 Swiss IPRG.

242 BGH, 11 October 2017, I ZB 12/17, SchiedsVZ 2018, 271-275. See also, BGH, 2 May 2017, I ZB 1/16, SchiedsVZ 2017, 317-323. Although this case primarily deals with the challenge of experts, it applies a general concept of § 1036 German ZPO, applying to arbitrators.

243 Additionally, under the German ZPO, parties cannot waive their right to challenge in advance, Stein/Jonas/P. Schlosser, § 1036 para. 51.

244 Both in Germany and Switzerland the constitutional prerequisites demand adherence to the fundamental principles and a minimal standard of independence and impartiality. On German law: Zöller/R. Geimer, § 1035 para. 3.

245 G. Born, *International Commercial Arbitration*, p. 1950 et seq.; Stein/Jonas/P. Schlosser, § 1036 para. 51.

246 G. Born, *International Commercial Arbitration*, p. 2058, n. 1642.

impartiality.[247] Alternatively, some courts refer to the trade-off between expertise and partiality, lowering the standard of independence and impartiality.[248] Arbitration is a procedure "overseen not by professional judges, who are trained to preserve a neutral appearance, but by ordinary businessman".[249] Where parties opt for arbitrators vested

> with specialized experience in a certain field, the available number of arbitrators will be limited, and, relatedly, specialized arbitrators are more likely to have come into contact with the parties operating in their field.[250]

The vague argument that a limited pool shall modify the standard of independence and impartiality is unconvincing. Where the parties explicitly agree on a specific arbitrator, or a specifically framed standard or set of rules, the parties define the standard. The interpretation of the mere fact that the parties' choice for arbitration impliedly includes a deviation of the standard for independence and impartiality would circumvent the analysis of the applicable standard. This argument would be a back door for a different applicable standard. The balanced nature of arbitration, however, does not tolerate such additional implied deviation. In any case, the very premise of this argument may be rightfully criticised, as in international arbitration there is usually not a limited pool of arbitrators.[251]

6.5.2 *Agreeing on a Higher Standard of Independence and Impartiality*

Raising the standard of finding independence and impartiality is less problematic, and can be agreed upon by the parties.[252] The parties' right to appoint their chosen arbitrator and the principle of party autonomy in general justify this approach. Additionally, the judicial requirements of the dual nature of arbitration welcome such an approach. The integrity of the arbitral proceedings may be better protected where the parties agree that the mere

---

247 E.g., BGer, 4 August 2006, 4P.105/2006/fun, para. C 4; BGer, 27 May 2003, BGE 129 III 445, 449-465; BGer, 9 February 1998, ASA Bull. 1998, 634-652, 645. Also acknowledging such a limited pool, but using this argument to explain the rising number of challenges, M. Baker/L. Greenwood, *Are Challenges Overused in International Arbitration?*, 2 J. Int'l Arb. 30 (2013), 101-112, 102-106.

248 E.g., *Certain Underwriting Members of Lloyds of London v. Florida*, 2018 WL 2727492 (2d Cir.); *LGC Holdings, Inc. v. Julius Klein Diamonds, LLC*, 238 F.Supp.3d 452 (S.D. New York 2017); *National Indemnity Co. v. IRB Brasil Resseguros SA*, 164 F.Supp.3d 457 (S.D. New York 2016); *Morelite Construction Co. v. New York City District Council Carpenters Benefit Funds*, 748 F.2d 79 (2d Cir. 1984).

249 *First Interregional Equity Corp. v. Haughton*, 842 F.Supp. 105 (S.D. New York 1994).

250 *National Indemnity Co. v. IRB Brasil Resseguros SA*, 164 F.Supp.3d 457 (S.D. New York 2016).

251 Cf. H.-L. Yu/L. Shore, *Independence, Impartiality, and Immunity of Arbitrators: US and English Perspectives*, Int'l & Comp. L.Q. 52 (2003), 935-967, 943.

252 G. Born, *International Commercial Arbitration*, p. 1948.

impression of or potential dependence and partiality satisfies a challenge.[253] Thus, in case of a heightened standard of independence and impartiality, the contractual and judicial nature are appropriately balanced. Examples for agreeing on a higher standard of independence and impartiality may be that the parties include additional grounds for challenging an arbitrator or lower the procedural requirements of a challenge.[254]

6.6 STANDARD FOR EXPERTS

The established applicable standard of independence and impartiality primarily applies to arbitrators as the decision makers. If experts are enrolled in the arbitral process, their dependence and partiality may be questioned as well.[255] The first question is, therefore, whether the arbitrator's standard of independence and impartiality applies to experts. The arbitral process may rely on tribunal-appointed experts or party-appointed experts. Party-appointed experts are individually appointed and paid for by the parties. Thus, and secondly, it is questionable whether tribunal-appointed and party-appointed experts are treated alike.

First, courts reviewing arbitral proceedings in France, Germany, and Switzerland generally answer the first questions in the affirmative: applying the obligation to act independently and impartially of arbitrators and judges to experts,[256] and using the same standards.[257] Moreover, the CIArb Guideline on Experts requires "impartial and objective" expert

253 See above chapters 6.1.2.5 and 6.1.2.6, on the standards of the impression of or potential dependence and partiality.

254 OLG Frankfurt a.M., 15 October 2018, 26 SchH 3/18, NJOZ 2019, 1127-1130, on additional grounds for challenge in the chosen arbitration rules; Stein/Jonas/P. Schlosser, § 1036 para. 52 et seq., on additional qualifications of the arbitrator listed in the arbitration agreement

255 See also, chapter 4.1.5, for expert's relationships and, not directly on experts, *AMEC Civil Engineering Ltd. v. Secretary of State for Transport*, [2005] EWCA Civ 291. The dispute arose under clause 66 ICE conditions, providing for referral of a dispute between an engineer and the contractor to the engineer. The Court of Appeal held that "[t]he rules of natural justice are formalised requirements of those who act judicially. Compliance with them is required of judges and arbitrators and those in equivalent positions, but not of an Engineer giving a decision under clause 66 of the ICE conditions".

256 See also, above chapter 4.1.5.

257 BGH, 2 May 2017, I ZB 1/16, SchiedsVZ 2017, 317-323; Cass civ 2ème, 21 January 2010, 09-10144; Cass civ 2ème, 5 December 2002, 01-00224, on applying the provisions applicable to state court judges to court-appointed experts; BGer, 28 April 2000, BGE 126 III 249, 253-256. Either the provisions for arbitrators apply directly, e.g., in France, see C. Chanais/F. Ferrand/S. Guinchard, *Procédure civile*, para. 689, n. 1949; *mutatis mutandis*, e.g., in Germany: § 1049(3) German ZPO, or by analogy, e.g., in Switzerland, see ZK IPRG-Oetiker, Art. 180 para. 10 et seq.

opinions,[258] and the Prague Rules require the appointment of an "independent expert".[259] Similar to the Prague Rules, the IBA Rules 2020 require the expert's independence.[260]

Second,[261] party-appointed experts are comparable to witnesses and their relationships with the party appointing them usually will not create a conflict of interest. The use of tribunal-appointed experts, on the other hand, may create conflicts of interest. Thus, it is necessary to differentiate in their applicable standard.[262] Many provisions only address the requirement of being independent and impartial regarding the tribunal-appointed expert.[263] However, even on these provisions, some authors demand the arbitral tribunal "to safeguard a certain standard by conducting proper briefings or requesting confirmation that that expert witness is impartial and has no prior involvement in the respective dispute".[264] As long as the party-appointed expert's evidence should be as useful as any other evidence, they should be independent and impartial. The practical differentiation between tribunal-appointed and party-appointed arbitrators would risk the uselessness of the latter. The party-appointed expert is particularly useful where the parties are more familiar with specific industries and know the relevant experts. Accepting that the independence and impartiality of arbitrators as decision makers is a fundamental principle of arbitration,[265] there is a need to safeguard that their chosen assistance is objective and neutral as well.

To conclude, party-appointed experts are not required to be independent and impartial, but their independence and impartiality strengthens their evidence. Parties are well advised to appoint an independent and impartial expert or to even make a joint proposal.

---

258 Art. 4.1 CIArb Protocol on Use of Experts: "An expert's opinion shall be impartial and objective." According to Art. 4.2 this applies even to party-appointed experts: "Payment by the appointing Party of the expert's reasonable professional fees for the work done in giving such evidence shall not, of itself, vitiate the expert's impartiality." Likewise, comment to Art. 3 CIArb Guideline on Experts, p. 7 enumerates the qualities of tribunal-appointed experts: the "arbitrators should be satisfied that the expert (1) has the relevant qualifications and expertise; (2) is independent and impartial; (3) is able to devote sufficient time to the arbitral proceedings and to complete their report in an efficient and timely manner; and (4) is available to attend pre-hearing meetings and hearings. For these purposes, arbitrators should require expert candidate(s) to provide, prior to accepting their appointment, a declaration of independence and impartiality and a statement of their availability as well as a copy of their resume. All such information should be disclosed to the parties and they should be given an opportunity to provide any comments within a specified time limit".

259 Art. 6.1 Prague Rules.

260 Art. 5(2)(c), 6(1) IBA Rules 2020.

261 See in more detail, above chapter 4.1.5.2.

262 J.-F. Poudret/S. Besson, *Comparative Law of International Arbitration*, para. 419. See also, *Glencot Development and Design Co. Ltd. v. Ben Barrett & Son (Contractors) Ltd.*, [2001] EWHC 15, dealing, primarily, with adjudicators and only marginally addresses that experts are less independent and impartial.

263 For example, Art. 28.3 DIS Rules; Art. 25.5 HKIAC Rules; Art. 6(1) IBA Rules 2020, although the party-appointed expert shall submit a statement of independence, Art. Art. 5(2)(c) IBA Rules 2020.

264 DIS Commentary/R. Trittmann/R. Schardt, Art. 28 para. 55.

265 See above the Introduction.

6.7 Standard for Tribunal Secretaries

Tribunal secretaries have to be independent and impartial.[266] Where the applicable rules or guidelines provide accordingly, there is not much debate.[267] Even if the need for independence and impartiality is not explicitly provided for, the tribunal secretaries' role as an assistant to the tribunal generally requires independence and impartiality.[268]

Arguably, the standard applicable to tribunal secretaries could depend on the role performed by the secretary. Independence and impartiality primarily serve the integrity of the arbitral process as a process of decision-making. Therefore, where the tribunal secretary is merely tasked with administrative matters, there appears to be no need for a medium standard of dependence and partiality, i.e., justifiable doubts. The higher standard of actual bias could suffice. Only if the secretary's role is closer to the decision-making process, the same standard as that for arbitrators would apply, i.e., justifiable doubts. In line with this approach, Swiss case law applies the needs of independence and impartiality, under Article 30 Swiss BV, to secretaries of tribunals and Swiss *Gerichtsschreiber* that are involved in decision-making.[269]

One may also argue that the tribunal secretary is less important than the tribunal itself,[270] and may easily be exchanged. This differentiation potentially allows a lower standard applicable to tribunal secretaries. Additionally, the secretary is often not chosen by the parties, but by the tribunal. Therefore, the parties' right to appoint their arbitrator is not at stake when challenging a tribunal secretary. Thus, evaluating what standard applies to tribunal secretaries does not need to take the parties' right to appoint as much into consideration. All these arguments could result in a different standard applicable to secretaries.

On the other hand, the tribunal secretaries' work and conduct influence the arbitrator. It is striking that the most recent revisions of the ICC and LCIA Rules favour the approach to align the standard and challenging mechanism applied to tribunal secretaries to that of

266 T. Clay, *Le secretaire arbitral*, Rev. de l'Arb. 2005, 931-957, 947.

267 For example, Art. 13.4 HKIAC Rules; Art. 14A LCIA Rules; Art. 15(5) Swiss Rules; General Standard 5(b) IBA Guidelines 2014; ICC Note, para. 219; UNCITRAL, Notes on Organizing Arbitral Proceedings, para. 37.

268 See also, above chapter 4.1.3.

269 BSK BV/J. Reich, Art. 30 paras. 7-8. According to KuKo ZPO/R. Kiener, Art. 47 para. 7, Art. 30 Swiss BV only applies directly if the *Gerichtsschreiber* participates in decision-making.

270 O. Jensen, *Tribunal Secretaries in International Arbitration*, para. 7.33 et seq.

arbitrators.[271] The reason may be a practical one. Where the tribunal secretaries' relationships or conduct creates a conflict of interest,[272] it is less harmful to the proceedings to challenge the secretary and not the arbitrator. Though this is no argument on differentiating between the applicable standards, it outlines the practicability. An argument in favour of applying the same material standard to arbitrators and tribunal secretaries is the tribunal secretaries' potential influence on the arbitrator. When researching legal issues or outlining the relevant procedural history, the tribunal secretary undertakes tasks that are the groundwork for decision-making. Additionally, even the tribunal secretary, who performs administrative tasks, could theoretically violate the parties' right to be heard. Although independence and impartiality primarily serve the integrity of the arbitral process as a process of decision-making, the integrity of the arbitral process includes the parties' right to be heard.[273]

This leads to no differentiation of the material standard of independence and impartiality based on the secretaries' role. Applying different standards would be practically not useful: it is not a clear line where the involvement in decision-making commences, and disclosure of the involvement of tribunal secretaries is not required by all rules yet.[274] The analysis of whether issues of independence and impartiality exist would, first, include the evaluation of the role of the secretary and, second, that of whether a conflict of interest exists. Additionally, the role performed by the secretary is one of the aspects evaluated at the stage of conflicts of interest.[275] It does not need to change the material standard of independence and impartiality. Therefore, the same standard should be applied to all types of tribunal secretaries.

6.8 CONCLUDING REMARKS

In conclusion, the detailed analysis of applicable standards for independence and impartiality provides the theoretical background to the casuistic in chapters 4 and 5. A balanced approach to the dual nature of arbitration leads to, first, a mixed objective-subjective perspective for evaluating the applicable standard, second, a standard that is best described as justifiable doubts, and third, some discretion for arguments based on the application of different grounds, different arbitrators, and the parties' agreement.

---

271 Art. 14A LCIA Rules; ICC Note, para. 219. See also, Art. 15(5) Swiss Rules; General Standard 5(b) IBA Guidelines 2014.

272 See above chapters 4.1.3 and 4.2.3.

273 The tribunal secretary may especially risk the parties' right to be heard through his or her conduct.

274 See above chapter 4.1.3.1, for more details.

275 See above chapter 4.1.3.2.

Although different wording may be used for the favourable intermediate standard for independence and impartiality, "justifiable doubts" allows a sufficiently inclusive interpretation. It thus leaves room for potential deviations when different grounds or stages in the proceedings are at issue.

Parties can modify the applicable standard. Without doubt, they may agree on a higher standard for independence and impartiality. More crucial is the question of whether parties can agree on a lower standard. The analysed case law is not consistent in this regard. United States case law serves as an example for allowing more leeway on modifications, whereas the wording of the EAA and case law from Germany and Switzerland is more restrictive.

Finally, the standard applied to (tribunal-appointed) experts and tribunal secretaries does not deviate from the generally applicable standard. Where experts or tribunal secretaries assist and support the tribunal in their decision-making function, they have to be measured by the same yardstick.

7 Consequences

The applicable standard of independence and impartiality affects different stages of the arbitration proceedings including: the arbitrator's selection, appointment, almost any procedural action, and the enforcement stage. The most obvious consequence of the requirement to be independent and impartial is the potential challenge of the arbitrator or the annulment of the award. Many national arbitration laws and rules grant the parties both procedural actions;[1] however, they often name different grounds and procedural prerequisites for challenge or annulment.[2] Regarding challenge procedures, for example, arbitration laws and rules differ on who decides the challenge[3] and on the effects of the challenge.[4] Challenge and annulment procedures are not applicable in parallel but sometimes cumulatively.[5] Besides these particularities, the central issue for challenge and annulment actions are the grounds to challenge or annul, e.g., a ground of finding dependence and partiality. These grounds are addressed in chapters 4 and 5. Additional

1 See above chapter 3, for an overview on some national arbitration laws. With regard to arbitration rules, e.g., Art. 14(3) ICC Rules referring to the ICC Court of Arbitration, and Art. 10.1 LCIA Rules referring to the LCIA Court are worth mentioning. The decision rendered by institutions can usually not be reviewed by state courts, cf. Art. 13(3) UNCITRAL Model Law.

2 With regard to independence and impartiality, some authors favour different standards of independence and impartiality for challenge and annulment, see above chapter 6.2.3. Also, the German arbitration law provides for the additional requirement of "having had an effect on the arbitration award", in § 1059(2)(1)(d) German ZPO, where the award is to be annulled due to an incorrect formation of the arbitral tribunal. Different procedural prerequisites are in particular different time frames for challenges and annulment actions.

3 The decision may be rendered by an institution, if there is any, the arbitral tribunal or a national court. E.g., under the rules of the HKIAC, ICC, LCIA, SCC and SIAC the tribunal will not decide on the challenge.

4 Under French arbitration law, the proceedings are usually not suspended while the challenge is pending, C. Seraglini/J. Ortscheidt, *Droit de l'arbitrage interne et international*, para. 744. This is, however, subject to the parties' agreement or the arbitrator's order, according to Art. 1472 French CPC. The same applies under German law, § 1037(3) German ZPO. See also, OLG Frankfurt a.M., 4 October 2007, 26 Sch 8/07, SchiedsVZ 2008, 96-102. Under Swiss law, the tribunal may continue with the challenged arbitrator, subject to opposing agreement by the parties, and render an award even including the challenged arbitrator, Art. 180a(3) Swiss IPRG.

5 In particular where additional and new grounds for annulment arise, the annulment action may proceed after an unsuccessful action for challenge. In general, the annulment action cannot circumvent the failure to properly challenge an arbitrator, C. Seraglini/J. Ortscheidt, *Droit de l'arbitrage interne et international*, para. 739, on French arbitration law. If the tribunal renders an award before the challenge is decided, the parties may proceed with an annulment action, B. Berger/F. Kellerhals, *International and Domestic Arbitration in Switzerland*, para. 833, on Swiss arbitration law. See also, below chapter 7.2, on the requirement to object and the concept of waiver. Interestingly, the requirement of timely objection and the concept of waiver apply also in the United States although there is no possibility to challenge an arbitrator.

grounds and issues of procedure will not be addressed in more detail in this book.[6] Rather, this chapter focuses on disclosure, objection and waiver, and possible ways to circumvent the challenge of an arbitrator.

The obligation to disclose is closely connected but must be distinguished from the obligation to be independent and impartial (7.1). The relation of the standard of independence and impartiality and the scope of disclosure are often conflated in case law. To clarify the difference, the role of the obligation to disclose as a consequence of the principles of independence and impartiality will be addressed in the following.

Furthermore, the parties do not enjoy independence and impartiality without procedural limits. Parties need to object to violations of independence and impartiality. Otherwise, they waive their right to rely on the violation (7.2). At the end of this chapter, some practical approaches on circumventing a challenge will be addressed (7.3), before concluding with final remarks (7.4).

7.1 Disclosure

Disclosure is the parties' protection against "prejudices, biases, or the appearance thereof".[7] The obligation to disclose is necessary in support of independence and impartiality as it contributes to the parties' confidence in the appointed arbitrator.[8] Before appointing an arbitrator, disclosure enables both parties to assess the suitability of the arbitrator in question. Only when informed sufficiently in regard to the arbitrator's independence and impartiality may the parties use their full party autonomy when appointing the arbitral tribunal. At the same time, one party's interest in being informed about a potential

6 Detailed literature on challenges can be found in: B. Spiegelfeld/S. Wurzer/H. Preidt, *Chapter II, The Arbitrator and the Arbitration Procedure – Challenge of Arbitrators: Procedural Requirements*, Austrian YB Int'l Arb. 2010, 45-77 (for an overview on procedural prerequisites); on Swiss law, see N. Jaisli Kull/A. Roth, *Chapter II, The Arbitrator and the Arbitration Procedure, Challenging Arbitrators for Lack of Independence or Impartiality: Procedural Pitfalls from a Swiss Perspective*, Austrian YB Int'l Arb. 2019, 223-248; on German law, P. Mankowski, *Die Ablehnung von Schiedsrichtern*, SchiedsVZ 2004, 304-313; on institutional rules, L. Pfister, *Who Decides Arbitrator Challenges?, A Comparative Analysis of Institutional Approaches*, SchiedsVZ 2017, 164-171; on investment arbitration, F. Cristani, *Challenge and Disqualification of Arbitrators in International Investment Arbitration*, L. & Prac. Int'l Cts. & Trib. 13 (2014), 153-177. Detailed literature on annulment, on English law, D. Sutton/J. Gill/M. Gearing, *Russel on Arbitration*, Chap. 8, Sect. 6(a); on German law, Zöller/R. Geimer, § 1059 para. 32 et seq.; MünchKomm ZPO/J. Münch, § 1059 para. 22 et seq.

7 C. Palo, *Bias of Arbitrator as Ground for Vacatur of Arbitration Award*, Sect. 12.

8 M. Henry, *Note – Cour d'appel de Paris, 14 octobre 2014, SA Auto Guadeloupe Investissements v. société Columbus Acquisitions Inc. et autres*, Rev. de l'Arb. 2015, 156-182, 164.

arbitrator, and this party's right to object to the appointment, may run up against the appointing party's fear that too much disclosure may affect its right to appoint.

Furthermore, disclosure enables the parties' right to challenge.[9] The right to challenge ensures that the parties can claim their rights with regard to an independent and impartial tribunal during the proceedings. The obligation to disclose is usually not limited to the point in time before appointment, but continues throughout the proceedings.[10]

Disclosure is "a means of maintaining the integrity of international arbitration".[11] As a means, it should not be confused with the need to guarantee the integrity of international arbitration itself, as a precondition of justice and as part of the judicial nature of arbitration.[12] The practical meaning of disclosure as an important element to implement independence and impartiality in arbitration, is regarded divergently. In particular, the exact scope and legal nature, consequences of a violation of the obligation to disclose, the relationship of the obligation and the standard of independence and impartiality, and whether there is even an obligation to investigate are treated differently.

7.1.1 Scope of Disclosure – What Needs to Be Disclosed

Different approaches regarding the scope of disclosure exist within case law and scholarly writings, as well as arbitration laws and rules. Possible scopes vary from requiring full disclosure, i.e., the need to disclose any fact that may be of interest to the parties, to minor and limited disclosure, i.e., the need to disclose only facts that also fulfil the applicable standard of independence and impartiality.

7.1.1.1 Broad Scope of Disclosure

The broadest approach to disclosure is to require the arbitrator to disclose anything he or she may be aware of that, from the parties' point of view, may be of any interest. In practice, it would be difficult to operate with such broad scope and usually the apologists of a broad approach apply nuances.

---

9 C. Seraglini/J. Ortscheidt, *Droit de l'arbitrage interne et international*, para. 737.

10 E.g., Art. 9.6 DIS Rules; Art. 11(3) ICC Rules; Art. 5.5 LCIA Rules; Art. 9(2) sentence 2 Swiss Rules.

11 *Halliburton Co. v. Chubb Bermuda Ins. Ltd.*, [2020] UKSC 48, Lord Hodge, para. 69.

12 Cf. M. Henry, *Note – Cour d'appel de Paris, 14 octobre 2014, SA Auto Guadeloupe Investissements v. société Columbus Acquisitions Inc. et autres*, Rev. de l'Arb. 2015, 156-182, 159. See above chapter 1.3, on the judicial and contractual nature of arbitration.

The IBA Guidelines 2014 include a broad obligation for the arbitrator to disclose, that is, close to the broadest approach.[13] The obligation to disclose "rests on the principle that the parties have an interest in being fully informed of any facts or circumstances that may be relevant in their view".[14] The IBA Guidelines 2014 repeatedly underline that the act of disclosing demonstrates that the arbitrator considers himself or herself to be independent and impartial.[15] The purpose of disclosure is additionally "to allow the parties to judge whether they agree with the evaluation of the arbitrator and, if they so wish, to explore the situation further".[16] In line with this purpose, the Guidelines encourage disclosure in any case of doubts. The lists in Part II IBA Guidelines 2014 name many scenarios that need to be disclosed, i.e., both the Red and Orange Lists. Although these lists provide a useful guideline and checklist for arbitrators, it can be difficult to differentiate between disclosure and other consequences of a violation of the obligation to be independent and impartial when applying the lists.[17]

The Guidelines address the arbitrator's disclosure to the parties, the arbitration institution or another appointing authority, and the co-arbitrators.[18] Although the wording of the scope of disclosure in the IBA Guidelines 2014 is similar to that applicable for the standard of independence and impartiality, i.e., justifiable doubts, the application of the obligation to disclose in the lists of Part II is broader. Thus, more scenarios call for disclosure. The perspective of evaluating the scope of necessary disclosure is through the "eyes of the parties". This is a purely subjective standard, and deviates from the applicable standard of independence and impartiality under the IBA Guidelines 2014.[19] Depending on the context

13 Part. I, General Standard 3(a) states: "If facts or circumstances exist that may, in the eyes of the parties, give rise to doubts as to the arbitrator's impartiality or independence, the arbitrator shall disclose such facts or circumstances to the parties, the arbitration institution or other appointing authority (if any, and if so required by the applicable institutional rules) and the co-arbitrators, if any, prior to accepting his or her appointment or, if thereafter, as soon as he or she learns of them." General Standard 3(b) adds: "An advance declaration or waiver in relation to possible conflicts of interest arising from facts and circumstances that may arise in the future does not discharge the arbitrator's ongoing duty of disclosure under General Standard 3(a)." And General Standard 3(d) clarifies: "Any doubt as to whether an arbitrator should disclose certain facts or circumstances should be resolved in favour of disclosure."

14 Part I, Explanation General Standard 3(a) IBA Guidelines 2014. The Explanation adds that the obligation of disclosure under General Standard 3(a) is ongoing in nature.

15 Part I, General Standard 3(c) and Explanation to General Standard 3(c) IBA Guidelines 2014. See also, above chapter 4.2.1.6, on the issue of non-disclosure as a ground for dependence and partiality.

16 Part I, Explanation General Standard 3(c) IBA Guidelines 2014.

17 E.g., Born criticises that "in the absence of textual guidance, application of the Guidelines has in practice tended to blur the distinction between disclosure and disqualification, a dynamic that is exacerbated by the structure and drafting of the Orange List", G. Born, *International Commercial Arbitration*, p. 1983. See also, above chapter 2.1, on this criticism.

18 Part I, General Standard 3(a) IBA Guidelines 2014.

19 I.e., "a reasonable third person having knowledge of the relevant facts and circumstances", Part I, General Standard 2(b) IBA Guidelines 2014.

in which the parties are situated, the subjective perspective applied to disclosure may broaden the list of circumstances that require disclosure. The approach in the IBA Guidelines 2014 is comparable to the one expressed in the CIArb Code of Conduct. Rule 2 in Part II requires CIArb members to disclose "all interests, relationships and matters likely to affect the member's independence or impartiality or which might reasonably be perceived as likely to do so". The England and Wales High Court of Justice concluded that this broad scope demands disclosure of any involvement, however remote.[20] The wording "reasonably be perceived as likely to do so" can be interpreted as an objective or objective-subjective perspective. The perception may either be that of a reasonable third person or a reasonable third person in the shoes of the parties, the latter being an objective-subjective perspective. More direct in regard to the applicable perspective is the approach in the ICC Rules and the ICC Note, favouring a subjective perspective and requesting the arbitrator to

> assess what circumstances, if any, are such as to call into question his or her independence in the eyes of the parties or give rise to reasonable doubts as to his or her impartiality

and to disclose accordingly.[21] Both the ICC Rules and the ICC Note use the same wording for the material scope of disclosure.

> The prospective arbitrator shall disclose in writing to the Secretariat any facts or circumstances which might be of such a nature as to call into question the arbitrator's independence in the eyes of the parties, as well as any circumstances that could give rise to reasonable doubts as to the arbitrator's impartiality.[22]

The scope of disclosure is thus broader than those grounds for finding dependence and partiality, similar to the approach taken by the IBA Guidelines 2014. Article 14(1) ICC Rules merely refers to a "lack of impartiality or independence" as a potential ground for a challenge.

Similarly, the AAA Rules require disclosure much broader than their standard of independence and impartiality, particularly in conjunction with the AAA/ABA Code of Ethics.[23] The AAA Rules oblige not only the arbitrator to disclose to the AAA, but also the

20 *Cofely Ltd. v. Anthony Bingham and Knowles Ltd.*, [2016] EWHC 240 (Comm).

21 ICC Note, para. 27. The ICC Note provides some guidance on what kind of relationships may be disclosed.

22 Art. 11(2) sentence 2 ICC Rules and ICC Note, para. 25.

23 R-17 AAA Rules requests disclosure of "any circumstances likely to give rise to justifiable doubt as to the arbitrator's impartiality or independence". The discrepancy with the standard of independence and impartiality is apparent: R-18(a)(i) requires "partiality or lack of independence".

parties and the representatives.[24] The AAA/ABA Code of Ethics for arbitrators provides in Canon II: "An arbitrator should disclose any interest or relationship likely to affect impartiality or which might create an appearance of partiality." Additionally, Canon II A(2) addresses the standard to be applied, i.e., "the eyes of any of the parties". Again, this subjective standard broadens the evaluation of the obligation. Canon II D further provides: "Any doubt as to whether or not disclosure is to be made should be resolved in favour of disclosure." The disclosure obligation is thus similarly broad as the one under the IBA Guidelines 2014. Finally, Canon II E provides that disclosure should be made to the parties and the other arbitrators.

United States case law is diverse in its scope of disclosure. Some case law applies a broad scope of disclosure, in line with the approach in the AAA/ABA Code of Ethics.[25] According to these cases, the purpose of broad disclosure is, first, to uphold the parties' right to object to the arbitrators. "The parties are the best judge of bias and in order to be able to choose intelligently they must be made aware of all the facts showing potential partiality."[26] The same argument holds true for the parties' right to challenge an arbitrator. Second, a broad scope of disclosure enables more transparency of arbitrators, who are "within the world of commerce".[27] The scope of disclosure in this case law is, however, not without limits. Generally, not every former social or financial relationship has to be disclosed – in particular, no trivial relationships have to be disclosed.[28]

French authors and case law offer another broad understanding of disclosure. Some scholars interpret Article 1456(2) French CPC to oblige arbitrators to disclose as broadly as necessary to inform the parties of existing interactions.[29] According to Clay, statements of

24 R-17(a) AAA Rules.

25 E.g., in *Commonwealth Coatings Co. v. Continental Casualty Co. et al.*, 89 S.Ct. 337 (1968); *Merit Ins. Co. v. Leatherby Ins. Co.*, 714 F.2d 673 (7th Cir. 1983). However, neither case applied the AAA/ABA Code of Ethics.

26 *Crow Construction v. Jeffrey M. Brown Assoc. Inc.*, 264 F.Supp.2d 217 (E.D. Pennsylvania 2003). Or in the words of Justice White in *Commonwealth Coatings Co. v. Continental Casualty Co. et al.*, 89 S.Ct. 337 (1968): "the judiciary should minimize its role in arbitration as judge of the arbitrator's impartiality. That role is best consigned to the parties, who are the architects of their own arbitration process, and are far better informed of the prevailing ethical standards and reputations within their business."

27 H.-L. Yu/L. Shore, *Independence, Impartiality, and Immunity of Arbitrators: US and English Perspectives*, Int'l & Comp. L.Q. 52 (2003), 935-967, 950, not addressing disclosure, but generally independence and impartiality.

28 *Merit Ins. Co. v. Leatherby Ins. Co.*, 714 F.2d 673 (7th Cir. 1983); citing *Commonwealth Coatings Co. v. Continental Casualty Co. et al.*, 89 S.Ct. 337 (1968).

29 Clay/Cadiet/T. Clay, Art. 1456 paras. 69-70. Art. 1456(2) French CPC reads: "*Il appartient à l'arbitre, avant d'accepter sa mission, de révéler toute circonstance susceptible d'affecter son indépendance ou son impartialité. Il lui est également fait obligation de révéler sans délai toute circonstance de même nature qui pourrait naître après l'acceptation de sa mission.*" The wording of the German arbitration law, § 1036(1) German ZPO, is

independence and impartiality should be mandatory, even if nothing is to be disclosed.[30] Similarly, the *cour d'appel de* Paris ruled regularly for some years that the arbitrator has the obligation to disclose all facts that are interesting to the parties.[31] The sentence often referred to, and provided by the French *cour de cassation* in 1999, is that the scope of disclosure encompasses "any circumstances affecting the judgment of [the arbitrator] and causing a reasonable doubt in the minds of the parties".[32] Similar to United States case law, the French *cour de cassation* reasoned that the arbitrator was required to disclose fully in order to enable the party to exercise its right of objection.[33] Additionally, Seraglini and Orthscheidt clarify that the scope of disclosure is not limited to facts listed in Article 341 French CPC and Article L. 111-6 French COJ, i.e., the grounds for challenging a French judge.[34] The authors stress that full disclosure enables the parties to evaluate the arbitrator's suitability.[35] However, in the end, these authors also advocate for limiting the scope of disclosure to circumstances affecting the arbitrator's judgment and provoking reasonable doubts in the minds of the parties regarding independence and impartiality or facts that may legitimately raise doubts among the parties.[36] Finally, both authors refer to the potential downside of full disclosure: it may enable delaying tactics.[37]

With regard to the wording of § 1036(1) German ZPO, some German case law can be interpreted to fit the category of full disclosure as well. Differing from

---

similar: "A person asked to serve as an arbitral judge is to disclose any and all circumstances that might give rise to doubts as to his impartiality. An arbitral judge is under obligation to disclose such circumstances to the parties without undue delay, also after his appointment and until the close of the arbitration proceedings, if he has failed to so inform them previously." However, German case law demonstrates that in practice this provision is interpreted narrowly, leading to an intermediate scope of disclosure, see below chapter 7.1.1.3.2.

30 Clay/Cadiet/T. Clay, Art. 1456 para. 70. This is in line with the practice in most institutions. The statement of independence and impartiality provides for the possibility to disclose nothing. The value of such statement is as high as the value of a positive statement.

31 See Clay/Cadiet/T. Clay, Art. 1456 para. 70. This may even lead to an obligation to investigate on the arbitrator's side, see below chapter 7.1.5.2.

32 Cass civ 1ère, 16 March 1999, 96-12748. The same wording is used by, e.g., CA Paris, 2 April 2003, Rev. de l'Arb. 2003, 1232-1236, 1235. In French: "*toute circonstance de nature à affecter le jugement de [l'arbitre] et provoquer, dans l'esprit des parties, un doute raisonnable.*" Another wording requires even more: "*l'arbitre doit révéler totalement*", i.e., total disclosure, CA Reims, 2 November 2011, Rev. de l'Arb. 2012, 112-119. This decision was, however, overruled by CA Paris, 12 April 2016, Rev. de l'Arb. 2017, 234-240, requiring only relevant facts to be disclosed.

33 Cass civ 1ère, 20 October 2010, 09-68131. The right of objection is linked to the right to appoint, it appears to be the counterpart of it.

34 C. Seraglini/J. Ortscheidt, *Droit de l'arbitrage interne et international*, para. 230, citing, inter alia, CA Paris, 9 September 2010, ASA Bull. 2011, 187-192.

35 C. Seraglini/J. Ortscheidt, *Droit de l'arbitrage interne et international*, paras. 735-737. The authors refer to CA Paris, 10 March 2011, 09/28537, ASA Bull. 2013, 443-447.

36 C. Seraglini/J. Ortscheidt, *Droit de l'arbitrage interne et international*, para. 230.

37 C. Seraglini/J. Ortscheidt, *Droit de l'arbitrage interne et international*, paras. 735-737.

§ 1036(2) sentence 1 German ZPO, i.e., the ground for challenging the arbitrator, § 1036(1) sentence 1 German ZPO merely requires arbitrators to disclose "any circumstances that may cast doubt on their impartiality or independence".[38] The standard of independence and impartiality for challenging an arbitrator requires that the circumstances "give rise to justifiable doubts as to his impartiality or independence".[39] Substantially, many more circumstances "may cast doubt" than "give rise to justifiable doubts". Similar to other jurisdictions, German case law highlights the function of disclosure to enable the parties' right to appoint and object: "Such circumstances must also be disclosed which were already decisive for the selection of the arbitrator."[40] The *Oberlandesgericht* Frankfurt a.M. additionally emphasised that disclosure aims at filling the gap in arbitral proceedings that exists compared to state court proceedings, where parties have a tribunal that is in line with the constitutional prerequisites on independence and impartiality.[41] Parties must be enabled to verify the arbitrator's independence and impartiality.

The information provided to the parties is of paramount importance in evaluating the advantages of a broad scope of disclosure. Disclosure is closely connected to the parties' right to appoint the arbitrators in arbitral proceedings and to object to their appointment. Disclosure fosters party autonomy in arbitration since it allows the parties to judge the suitability of the arbitrators.[42] The parties, as the "gatekeepers" of independence and impartiality,[43] have a high demand of information. A broad scope of the requirement to disclose satisfies this demand. Also, some authorities suggest that disclosing itself demonstrates that the arbitrator considers himself or herself to be independent and impartial.[44] Additionally, a broad scope may be seen as an efficient approach to waiver: full disclosure enables parties to waive their right to challenge the arbitrator with regard to the disclosed circumstances, limiting later challenges.[45] Following these advantages of a broad scope, the above cited ample case law and scholars suggest disclosure in case of

---

38 In German: "*alle Umstände offen zu legen, die Zweifel an ihrer Unparteilichkeit oder Unabhängigkeit wecken können.*"

39 In German: "*die berechtigte Zweifel an seiner Unparteilichkeit oder Unabhängigkeit aufkommen lassen.*"

40 OLG Frankfurt a.M., 24 January 2019, 26 SchH 2/18, BeckRS 2019, 848, para. 80.

41 Referring to Art. 101(1) sentence 2 German GG, requiring, inter alia, a judgment by an independent and neutral judge in line with Arts. 92, 97 German GG.

42 This may even lead to a modified standard of independence and impartiality where the parties refrain from objecting after a full disclosure including grounds for dependence and partiality. This concept is also enshrined in the Waivable Red List in Part I, IBA Guidelines 2014.

43 *Positive Software Solutions, Inc. v. New Century Mortg. Corp.*, 476 F.3d 278 (5th Cir. 2007), Concurring Op., Justice Wiener.

44 See above n. 15 in this chapter, for references on the IBA Guidelines.

45 See below chapter 7.2, on waiver.

doubt: whenever the person required to disclose is insecure whether to disclose or not, he or she should disclose.[46]

Finally, full disclosure, in particular, but also disclosure in general, raises the question of whether confidentiality may limit the scope of disclosure. Contractual obligations with other parties in parallel proceedings or statutes may require confidentiality.[47] Although different concepts of confidentiality apply in international arbitration,[48] one may either argue that where disclosure is required by law or in the interest of justice, confidentiality cannot restrict disclosure.[49] Thus, the scope of disclosure in the context of independence and impartiality cannot be limited by issues of confidentiality.[50] Alternatively, and where the obligation to disclose does not trump the obligation to maintain confidentiality, the person requested to disclose would be restricted to decline the nomination.[51]

7.1.1.2 Limited Scope of Disclosure

Alternatively, disclosure can be limited to those facts known to the person disclosing and only relevant from his or her point of view, or from a purely objective point of view.

A limited scope of disclosure can be found in some case law from jurisdictions not addressing the obligation to disclose in their arbitration laws. This case law demonstrates a tendency to compare the scope of the disclosure requirement for arbitrators with that of judges. Unlike the arguments in favour of broad disclosure, the obligation to disclose applicable to judges does not aim at informing the parties in order to enable them to make an appointment or to object. Thus, the purpose of both obligations to disclose may vary. English law provides an example of such a limited scope. While the EAA does not address disclosure at all, case law provides that courts

> consider the present position under English law to be that disclosure should be given of facts and circumstances known to the arbitrator which, in the

---

46 OLG Frankfurt a.M., 24 January 2019, 26 SchH 2/18, BeckRS 2019, 848, para. 80; N. Schmidt-Ahrendts/ V. Schneider, „*Gut Ding will Weile haben*“, SchiedsVZ 2020, 35-41, 40.

47 See, e.g., § 43a(2) sentence 1 German BRAO.

48 Different arbitration laws, case law and rules provide different thresholds of confidentiality.

49 M. Hwang/K. Chung/S. Cheng Lim/W. Hui Min, *FS Kaplan*. But see, BSK ZPO/U. Weber-Stecher, Art. 363 para. 12, commenting on Swiss domestic arbitration.

50 The IBA Guidelines 2014 provide in Part I, Explanation to General Standard 3(d) an alternative approach: "In determining which facts should be disclosed, an arbitrator should take into account all circumstances known to him or her. If the arbitrator finds that he or she should make a disclosure, but that professional secrecy rules or other rules of practice or professional conduct prevent such disclosure, he or she should not accept the appointment, or should resign."

51 Stein/Jonas/P. Schlosser, § 1036 para. 66.

> language of Section 24 of the Act, would or might give rise to justifiable doubts as to his impartiality.[52]

English case law on disclosure of both judges and arbitrators does not require an extensive full disclosure: there is "no obligation to disclose circumstances which the informed observer would not regard as raising a real possibility of bias".[53] However, in "borderline" situations

> disclosure should be made because then the judge can consider, having heard the submissions of the parties, whether or not he should withdraw. In other situations disclosure can unnecessarily undermine the litigant's confidence in the judge.[54]

In *Taylor v. Lawrence* the England and Wales Court of Appeal underlined the danger of a broad, extensive disclosure of relationships without a "real possibility of it being regarded by a fair minded and informed observer as raising a possibility of bias". The Court of Appeal reasoned that disclosure may imply that the judge or the arbitrator is biased.[55] Additionally, the U.K. Supreme Court clarified that any later review of the obligation to disclose must take the perspective of the time when the obligation arose and during the period in which the obligation subsisted.[56]

Another example comes from Swiss case law dealing with the old Swiss IPRG, which did not include an obligation to disclose.[57] Before 2021, Swiss scholars generally referred to Article 363 Swiss ZPO, i.e., the obligation to disclose in domestic arbitrations.[58] The scope of Article 363 Swiss ZPO is compared with that of Article 48 Swiss ZPO, the obligation of judges to disclose.[59] Hereunder, the arbitrator is not required to disclose public facts. Facts are public if they are known to the parties or the arbitrator may reasonably assume that

---

52 *Halliburton Co. v. Chubb Bermuda Ins. Ltd.*, [2018] EWCA Civ 817, upheld by *Halliburton Co. v. Chubb Bermuda Ins. Ltd.*, [2020] UKSC 48. This obligation to disclose is derived from the obligation to disclose applied to judges: "Under the common law, judges should disclose facts or circumstances which would or might provide the basis for a reasonable apprehension of lack of impartiality."

53 *H v. L and M*, [2017] EWHC 137 (Comm).

54 *Taylor v. Lawrence*, [2002] EWCA Civ 90, a judgment that is frequently cited by English case law on arbitrators.

55 *Taylor v. Lawrence*, [2002] EWCA Civ 90.

56 "A determination as to whether an arbitrator has failed to perform a duty to disclose can only be made by reference to the circumstances at the time the duty arose and during the period in which the duty subsisted. The question whether there should have been disclosure should not be answered retrospectively by reference to matters known to the fair-minded and informed observer only at a later date." *Halliburton Co. v. Chubb Bermuda Ins. Ltd.*, [2020] UKSC 48, Lord Hodge, para. 119.

57 See below chapter 7.1.1.3.2, for the current approach in Art. 179(6) Swiss IPRG.

58 BSK IPRG/W. Peter/T. Legler/L. Rusch Art. 179 para. 68.

59 BSK ZPO/U. Weber-Stecher, Art. 363 para. 1.

the parties are aware of the facts.[60] The applicable perspective is a mixture of the point of view of the arbitrator and an objective perspective, i.e., a reasonable third person, also with regard to the new Swiss IPRG.[61] This perspective limits the scope of disclosure, compared to full disclosure.[62] In sum, the Swiss approach to an arbitrator's obligation to disclose is nowadays better categorised as an intermediate scope of disclosure.[63] The purpose of disclosure, also in Switzerland, is to inform the parties and to enable them to appoint, object, and challenge. The obligation is either a pre-contractual obligation or derived from the arbitrator's contract with the parties.[64] The arbitrator's obligation to disclose is "based upon the arbitrator's pre-contractual and, after appointment, ancillary contractual duty to take all necessary steps in order to guarantee an orderly and speedy procedure".[65]

In United States case law, some courts merely require that disclosure puts the parties on notice regarding certain potentially critical scenarios.[66] According to this case law, the obligation to disclose encompasses "dealings of which the parties cannot reasonably be expected to be aware".[67] "[W]here the complaining party should have known of the relationship, or could have learned of the relationship 'just as easily before or during the arbitration'", the arbitrator is not required to disclose.[68] Though this position limits disclosure and requires parties to be aware of potential grounds for finding dependence and partiality, disclosure is not obsolete. The arbitrator remains obliged to disclose to put the parties on notice.

60 BGer, 9 October 2012, 4A_110/2012, ASA Bull. 2013, 174-193.

61 BSK IPRG/W. Peter/T. Legler/L. Rusch, Art. 179 para. 68; C. Müller, *Swiss Case Law in International Arbitration*, Art. 180 para. 1.3.7.

62 See BGer, 14 March 1985, BGE 111 Ia 72, 74-76; C. Müller, *Swiss Case Law in International Arbitration*, Art. 180 para. 1.3.7.

63 See below chapter 7.1.1.3.

64 BGer, 14 March 1985, BGE 111 Ia 72; N. Jaisli Kull/A. Roth, *Chapter II, The Arbitrator and the Arbitration Procedure, Challenging Arbitrators for Lack of Independence or Impartiality: Procedural Pitfalls from a Swiss Perspective*, Austrian YB Int'l Arb. 2019, 223-248, 230 et seq.

65 N. Voser/E. Fischer, *The Arbitral Tribunal*, p. 66. See in particular, BGer, 14 March 1985, BGE 111 Ia 72, 74-76, on the nature of the obligation.

66 In U.S. domestic arbitration, the party-appointed arbitrator does not need to disclose unless the parties agree otherwise, R-12(b) AAA Rules.

67 *Andros Compania Maritima, SA v. Marc Rich & Co., AG*, 579 F.2d 691 (2d Cir. 1978). The court ruled that the annulment is untimely where the complaining party delays an objection past the point at which he is deemed on notice of potentially disqualifying circumstances.

68 *Certain Underwriting Members of Lloyds of London v. Florida*, 2018 WL 2727492 (2d Cir.). Similarly, *LGC Holdings, Inc. v. Julius Klein Diamonds, LLC*, 238 F.Supp.3d 452 (S.D. New York 2017), and *Power Services Associates, Inc. v. UNC Metcalf Servicing, Inc.*, 338 F.Supp.2d 1375 (N.D. Georgia 2004) apply the "on notice" scope.

The view by some French authors and case law favouring a broad scope of disclosure is not the only approach to disclosure in France. Regarding Article 1456(2) French CPC,[69] some scholars object the approach laid out above. Jarrosson argues, in contrast to Clay, that this provision addresses a limited scope of disclosure. The provision covers both pre- and post-appointment scenarios and does not differentiate between the two in the scope of disclosure. According to Jarrosson, in post-appointment scenarios the impact of any disclosure in another potentially aligned pre-appointment scenario must be borne in mind when deciding whether to disclose in the pre-appointment scenario.[70] This leads to a generally limited scope of disclosure. The premise is, however, questionable. First, the effect even of the same scenario on two different arbitrations can be different. Even if the circumstance that may require disclosure affects the independence and impartiality of one of the appointment scenarios, e.g., the pre-appointment scenario, it may not affect the independence and impartiality of the post-appointment scenario, i.e., the ongoing arbitration. Second, if there is a real conflict since the circumstance to disclose affects the independence and impartiality of both scenarios, the arbitrator in the pre-appointment stage may indeed be hindered from accepting the appointment. This result, however, will only occur where the conflict created between the two proceedings is one that meets the threshold of a conflict of interest. In the end, however, the fact that only scenarios that may trigger a ground for finding dependence and partiality need to be disclosed limits the scope of disclosure as well. Therefore, only the reason for limitation provided by Jarrosson is questioned here.[71] Finally, some French cases also adopt a limited scope of disclosure. Accordingly, disclosure was not required where the arbitrator participated in a conference with a person presumed hostile to a party, even the day before the hearing; nor was disclosure of a previous political publication required.[72]

---

69 "*Il appartient à l'arbitre, avant d'accepter sa mission, de révéler toute circonstance susceptible d'affecter son indépendance ou son impartialité. Il lui est également fait obligation de révéler sans délai toute circonstance de même nature qui pourrait naître après l'acceptation de sa mission.*" Originally the obligation to disclose was only based on French case law, see with further references to case law C. Seraglini/J. Ortscheidt, *Droit de l'arbitrage interne et international*, para. 229. Interestingly, in international arbitration, parties may derogate from the obligation to disclose according to Art. 1461 French CPC.

70 C. Jarrosson, *A propos de l'obligation de révélation, Une leçon de méthode de la Cour de cassation, Note sous Cass. civ. 1re, 10 octobre 2012*, Rev. de l'Arb. 2013, 130-137, 135. He provides the following example: "A single arbitrator sits in an arbitration between two commercial companies of which one with public capital. One year after being appointed, and while this arbitration is still pending, he is expected to sit as co-arbitrator in another arbitration, relating to a totally separate dispute, with different parties, but one of which is controlled by the same State. The councils of the parties are also different. The only common element is that, through one of the disputing parties, the same State is looming."

71 It should be noted that the difference in argumentation for a limited scope might also lead to different results. E.g., the argument provided by Jarrosson might bar disclosure in rather extreme scenarios.

72 Cass civ 1ère, 4 July 2012, 11-19624 and Cass civ 1ère, 29 June 2011, 09-17346. However, examining the materiality of these two scenarios, they should be categorised as applying an intermediate scope of disclosure.

Evaluating the advantages of a limited scope of disclosure, the high practicability for the person disclosing stands out. It is in that person's interest to evaluate the scope of disclosure from his or her perspective or from an objective perspective. It is convenient not to be obliged to inform the parties of the complete and unexpurgated business biographies. Parties cannot expect such information.[73] Additionally, limiting disclosure to some extent promotes efficiency since disclosure may bear the risk of casting doubts in the minds of the parties.

Another practical limitation often applied is the limitation in time. The IBA Guidelines 2014, for example, require disclosure on repeat appointments from the previous three years.[74] Such restrictions in time are practical for users since they facilitate the assessment of what to disclose. On the other hand, introducing a time restriction for disclosure requires categorising the grounds for finding dependence and partiality. Since such categorisation often depends on the intensity of the relationship or conduct in the individual case,[75] it is difficult to establish general periods of time. Such general periods risk losing flexibility in the individual case.

7.1.1.3 Intermediate Scope of Disclosure

In between both scopes of disclosure, many rules and laws align with the standard of independence and impartiality but are not identical to that standard. Most authors and case law agree that the scope for disclosure is sketched by the standard of independence and impartiality. Even if not identical, the scope for disclosure is dependent on the standard of independence and impartiality.[76] Disclosure is slightly broader than the standard of grounds for finding dependence and partiality. This intermediate scope balances the parties' interest in information to use their right to appoint and challenge, the efficiency of the proceedings not to be delayed by unfounded, potentially tactical, challenges, and the general requirements of independence and impartiality.

---

73 C. Palo, *Bias of Arbitrator as Ground for Vacatur of Arbitration Award*, 3d Am. Juris. Proof of Facts 143, 2014, 12.

74 IBA Guidelines 2014, Part II, para. 3.1.

75 See above chapters 4.1 and 4.2.

76 C. Jarrosson, *A propos de l'obligation de révélation, Une leçon de méthode de la Cour de cassation, Note sous Cass. civ. 1re, 10 octobre 2012*, Rev. de l'Arb. 2013, 130-137, 133-134. Jarrosson, highlights the need to differentiate disclosure and independence (and impartiality), and especially the fact that disclosure does not produce independence.

Under the intermediate scope of disclosure, circumstances that may give rise to justifiable doubts as to independence and impartiality must be disclosed.[77] The arbitrator must disclose all current "relations of interest" with one of the parties and their counsels.[78] Comparing disclosure with independence and impartiality, and having stated that both are inter-related, but not congruent, the question arises which of the two concepts is more extensive. In practice, not every fact has to be disclosed.[79] Also, not every fact that has to be disclosed is a ground for finding dependence and partiality.[80] Therefore, the scope of disclosure is more extensive than the standard of independence and impartiality. This conclusion derives from an evaluation of institutional rules and case law.

7.1.1.3.1 Institutional Rules

The intermediate scope of disclosure can be found in many rules and in the UNCITRAL Model Law. The UNCITRAL Model Law requires an arbitrator to disclose "any circumstances likely to give rise to justifiable doubts as to his impartiality or independence".[81] Although the same wording of "justifiable doubts" is used for evaluating the standard of independence and impartiality, the latter omits the extension by including the word "likely". The addition of the word "likely" broadens the circumstances relevant for the evaluation of disclosure.[82] Similarly, the wording used by the HKIAC Rules provides in Article 11.4 that the arbitrator shall "disclose any circumstances likely to give rise to justifiable doubts as to his or her impartiality or independence".[83]

---

77 Stein/Jonas/P. Schlosser, § 1036 para. 69. Or in other words, used by Clay: disclosure must include "*tout ce qui pourrait être interprété de près ou de loin comme une atteinte à son indépendance*", T. Clay, *L'arbitre*, 2001, p. 335.

78 C. Seraglini/J. Ortscheidt, *Droit de l'arbitrage interne et international*, para. 231. An example for such a "relation of interest" is "*le caractere systematique de la désignation d'une personne donnée par les sociétés d'un même groupe, sa fréquence et sa régularité sur une longue période, dans les contrats comparables, ont créé les conditions d'un courant d'affaires entre cette personne et les sociétés du groupe parties à la procedure*".

79 E.g., *ANR Coal Co., Inc. v. Cogentrix of North Carolina, Inc.*, 173 F.3d 493 (4th Cir. 1999). The court did not require disclosure of the fact that the presiding arbitrator's law firm previously was active for a third company in the same industry which had a contractual relationship with respondent. It interpreted the AAA Rules to only require disclosure of an interest or relationship "likely to affect impartiality". Cf. C. Jarrosson, *A propos de l'obligation de révélation, Une leçon de méthode de la Cour de cassation, Note sous Cass. civ. 1re, 10 octobre 2012*, Rev. de l'Arb. 2013, 130-137, 132.

80 The concept of the IBA Guidelines 2014 indicates that not any disclosed fact may fulfil the standard of dependence and partiality.

81 Art. 12(1) UNCITRAL Model Law. The same wording is used by Art. 11 UNCITRAL Arbitration Rules.

82 The perspective of the evaluation of both standards is not addressed in either the Rules or the Model Law. It is questionable whether one could conclude that the perspective is objective, due to the wording "justifiable doubts", e.g., E. Fontanelli, *The Disclosure Dilemma: Dealing with Arbitrator Issue Conflicts in International Arbitration*, IBA Arb. News 22 (2017), 68-71, 69.

83 Also similar to the UNCITRAL Arbitration Rules and Model Law Art. 11.4 sentence 1 HKIAC Rules does not expressly regulate to whom disclosure needs to be made. Sentence 2, i.e., disclosure during the arbitration proceedings, provides that the parties are addressed.

The ICDR Rules,[84] SCC Rules,[85] SIAC Rules,[86] and the Swiss Rules[87] are comparable in their approaches. Most of these rules require disclosure towards the institution, usually by submitting a statement of independence and impartiality.[88] Once the proceedings commence, disclosure is also required towards the parties and the other arbitrators.[89] Both the UNCITRAL Arbitration Rules and the Model Law expressly require disclosure to the parties only after the arbitrator is appointed. Before appointment, there is no regulation towards whom the arbitrator has to disclose. However, this is no surprise bearing in mind that the UNCITRAL Arbitration Rules and the Model Law are designed to apply to both institutional and ad hoc arbitration. Article 11 sentence 1 UNCITRAL Arbitration Rules and Article 12(1) sentence 1 UNCITRAL Model Law leave room for more specific regulation in the parties' agreement, e.g., applicable institutional rules. The frequent use of statements on availability and disclosure in institutional arbitration, requiring arbitrators to disclose to the institution, fills this gap.

---

84 Art. 13(2) ICDR Rules requires arbitrators to "disclose any circumstances that may give rise to justifiable doubts as to the arbitrator's impartiality or independence and any other relevant facts the arbitrator wishes to bring to the attention of the parties". Similarly to the IBA Guidelines 2014, Art. 13(4) ICDR Rules clarifies that "[d]isclosure by an arbitrator or party does not necessarily indicate belief by the arbitrator or party that the disclosed information gives rise to justifiable doubts as to the arbitrator's impartiality or independence".

85 Art. 18(2) SCC Rules requires arbitrators to disclose "any circumstances that may give rise to justifiable doubts as to the prospective arbitrator's impartiality or independence". In comparison to the standard of independence and impartiality applicable to challenges, the latter requires that "circumstances exist that give rise to justifiable doubts as to the arbitrator's impartiality or independence", Art. 19(1) SCC Rules.

86 Art. 13.4 SIAC Rules states: "A nominated arbitrator shall disclose to the parties and to the Registrar any circumstances that may give rise to justifiable doubts as to his impartiality or independence as soon as reasonably practicable and in any event before his appointment." Additionally, also SIAC provides a Practice Note on Appointment of Arbitrators, Arbitrator's Fees & Financial Management. Para. 9 addresses conflicts of interest and states that "[a]ny potential candidate for appointment must make a full declaration of independence and impartiality and disclose to the parties and to the Registrar any fact, circumstance, or relationship which could give rise to justifiable doubts about his or her independence and impartiality". In comparison, the standard of independence and impartiality in case of a challenge in Art. 14.1 SIAC Rules is that "circumstances exist that give rise to justifiable doubts as to the arbitrator's impartiality or independence". Additionally, the SIAC Code of Ethics exemplifies the scope of disclosure in para. 2.2: "(a) any past or present close personal relationship or business relationship, whether direct or indirect, with any party to the dispute, or any representative of a party, or any person known to be a potentially important witness in the arbitration; (b) the extent of any prior knowledge he may have of the dispute."

87 Art. 9(2) Swiss Rules provides that arbitrators shall disclose "any circumstances likely to give rise to justifiable doubts as to their impartiality or independence". Whereas the standard for challenge due to lack of independence and impartiality in Art. 10(1) Swiss Rules is "circumstances exist that give rise to justifiable doubts as to the arbitrator's impartiality or independence".

88 E.g., Art. 18(3) SCC Rules, para. 9 SIAC Practice Note. The ICDR Rules name it "Notice of Appointment", Art. 13(2) ICDR Rules.

89 E.g., Art. 18(4) SCC Rules; Art. 13.5 SIAC Rules.

Also, the approach taken by the DIS Rules can be categorised as an intermediate scope of disclosure, although it deviates from the above institutional approaches. The DIS Rules provide in Article 9.4 that

> each prospective arbitrator shall disclose any facts or circumstances that could cause a reasonable person in the position of a party to have doubts as to the arbitrator's impartiality and independence.

The use of "doubts" is only applied in the standard of disclosure, and not for that of independence and impartiality.[90] This limitation of using "doubts" in the context of disclosure and not in order to explain the standard of independence and impartiality could be interpreted favouring a broader scope of the need for disclosure than circumstances constituting a positive conflict of interest. Additionally, the perspective is less subjective than other institutional approaches: it is that of a reasonable person in the position of a party, i.e., the mixed subjective-objective perspective.

> In order to avoid too broad disclosures and promote the communication of relevant facts and circumstances, Article 9 introduces the standard of reasonableness, requiring that the prospective arbitrator weighs what information "a reasonable person in the position of a party" could give rise to doubts as to the arbitrator's impartiality and independence.[91]

Taking the purpose of disclosure into consideration, i.e., to enable the parties to make use of their right to appoint, object, and challenge, a broader approach appears again useful. Parties should have all relevant information on the arbitrator in regard to potential issues of independence and impartiality.

7.1.1.3.2 Case Law

Furthermore, case law and statutes in France, Germany, Switzerland, the United Kingdom, and the United States fit the category of an intermediate scope of disclosure. In France, the scope of disclosure is limited by the fact that merely notorious facts do not have to be disclosed.[92] The arbitrator is not obliged to disclose facts that are known to the parties or

90 Art. 9.1 DIS Rules 2018 merely refers to independence and impartiality and refrains from using any additional wording to explain the standard. In contrast to the previous version of the DIS Rules, i.e., the DIS Rules 1998, the new version also refrains from using the "justifiable doubt" standard for challenging an arbitrator, compare Art. 15.1 DIS Rules 2018 and Art. 18.1 DIS Rules 1998.

91 DIS Commentary/A. Meier/L. Gerhardt, Art. 9 para. 2.

92 CA Paris, 2 April 2003, Rev. de l'Arb. 2003, 1232-1236, 1235. "*[L]'obligation d'information qui pèse sur l'arbitre afin de permettre aux parties d'exercer leur droit de récusation doit s'apprécier au regard à la fois de*

facts that cannot reasonably impact the proceedings.[93] For example, if it is publicly known to the parties that an arbitrator is chairman of a professional association in agricultural trade, because both parties operate in agricultural trade, no disclosure is required.[94] Also, trivial relationships, e.g., being "friend" on Facebook, do not need to be disclosed.[95] Hence, the obligation to disclose covers only those circumstances which are likely to affect the judgment, and not those facts that are already known to the parties.[96] However, French case law often evaluates this intermediate scope from the parties' point of view and, thus, broadens the scope.[97]

Similar to the position in French case law, the U.K. Supreme Court excludes trivial relationships.

> To require disclosure of some matter which was trivial and could not materially support a conclusion that there was a real possibility of bias, would be to risk causing the parties unnecessary concerns about an arbitrator's impartiality and also to encourage vexatious challenges by a party to the arbitrator's position.[98]

Generally, "arbitrators have a legal duty to make disclosure of facts and circumstances which would or might reasonably give rise to the appearance of bias", unless the parties to the arbitration otherwise agree.[99]

German case law reveals that the obligation to disclose encompasses all circumstances which are likely to give rise to doubts as to the arbitrator's independence and impartiality.[100]

---

la notoriété de la situation critiquée et de son incidence sur le jugement de l'arbitre." See also, CA Paris, 9 September 2010, ASA Bull. 2011, 187-192, 191.

93 CA Paris, 13 March 2008, 06/12878. According to Henry, the joint participation in a conference is covered by the intermediate scope of disclosure, M. Henry, *Note – Cour d'appel de Paris, 14 octobre 2014, SA Auto Guadeloupe Investissements v. société Columbus Acquisitions Inc. et autres*, Rev. de l'Arb. 2015, 156-182. However, the arbitrator remains obliged to disclose circumstances likely to give rise to justifiable doubts as to independence and impartiality, CA Paris, 18 December 2008, Rev. de l'Arb. 2011, 682-685.

94 CA Paris, 16 December 2010, Rev. de l'Arb. 2011, 710-713.

95 CA Lyon, 11 March 2014, 13/00447. See below chapter 7.1.1.5.4, for details on disclosure in social networking scenarios.

96 M. Henry, *Note – Cour d'appel de Paris, 14 octobre 2014, SA Auto Guadeloupe Investissements v. société Columbus Acquisitions Inc. et autres*, Rev. de l'Arb. 2015, 156-182, 167.

97 See above chapter 7.1.1.1.

98 *Halliburton Co. v. Chubb Bermuda Ins. Ltd.*, [2020] UKSC 48, Lord Hodge, para. 108.

99 *Halliburton Co. v. Chubb Bermuda Ins. Ltd.*, [2020] UKSC 48, Lord Hodge, para. 136.

100 OLG Frankfurt a.M., 10 January 2008, 26 Sch 21/07, SchiedsVZ 2008, 199-200. The court underlines that an arbitrator has to disclose all circumstance which may be relevant for his impartiality and independence. This includes the obligation to disclose professional and social links not only with a party but also with the parties' legal representatives.

Some cases evaluate the likelihood from the parties' point of view[101] and others from the arbitrator's point of view.[102] According to the latter case law, the arbitrator needs to be aware of the scenario potentially constituting justifiable doubts on independence and impartiality in order to establish a real obligation to disclose.[103] The arbitrator is not obliged to disclose information that is public or known to the opposing party.[104] Similarly in Switzerland, the current Article 179(6) Swiss IPRG requires the arbitrator to "disclose any circumstances that may give rise to justifiable doubts as to his or her independence or impartiality". Here, the perspective applied in case law is also that of the arbitrator or an objective one.[105]

Lastly, the approach taken by some courts in the United States can be described as an intermediate scope of disclosure.[106] The FAA does not contain a provision demanding disclosure,[107] but courts have required the arbitrator to disclose.[108] American case law often underlines that disclosure serves to protect the parties' right to appoint[109] and the efficiency of the arbitral proceedings by "encourag[ing] conflicts over arbitrators to be dealt with early in the arbitration process and help[ing] limit the availability of collateral attacks on arbitration awards by a disgruntled party".[110] Arbitrators have a continuing obligation to disclose any financial or personal interest in the outcome of the arbitration, and any existing or past relationship with the parties, attorneys, witnesses, or other arbitrators.[111]

---

101 BGH, 31 January 2019, I ZB 46/18, NZM 2020, 334-336, para. 18.

102 OLG Frankfurt a.M., 13 February 2012, 26 SchH 15/11, BeckRS 2014, 12067.

103 OLG Frankfurt a.M., 13 February 2012, 26 SchH 15/11, BeckRS 2014, 12067.

104 Stein/Jonas/P. Schlosser, § 1036 para. 65.

105 See above chapter 7.1.1.2.

106 E.g., *Republic of Argentina v. AWG Group Ltd.*, 211 F.Supp.3d 335 (D. Columbia, 2016), ruling that the arbitrator has to disclose more than trivial businesses; *Scandinavian Reinsurance Co. Ltd. v. Saint Paul Fire and Marine Ins. Co.*, 668 F.3d 60 (2d Cir. 2012). See also, *Applied Industrial Materials Co. v. Ovalar Makine Ticaret Ve Sanayi, A.S. and Ural Ataman*, Docket No. 06-3297-cv (2d Cir. 9 July 2007), where the court states that disclosure is not onerously applied.

107 However, Sect. 12(a) UAA requests the arbitrator to "disclose to all parties to the agreement to arbitrate and arbitration proceeding and to any other arbitrators any known facts that a reasonable person would consider likely to affect the impartiality of the arbitrator in the arbitration proceeding".

108 *Ario v. Cologne Reinsurance (Barbados), Ltd.*, 2009 WL 3818626 (M.D. Pennsylvania), emphasising the purpose of disclosure to enable the affected party to deal with the issue while the dispute is still before the arbitrators. In addition, the AAA Rules and AAA/ABA Code of Ethics request disclosure. See also, B. Meyerson/J. Townsend, *Revised Code of Ethics for Commercial Arbitrators Explained*, Disp. Res. J. 59 (2004), 10-17, 14-15.

109 *Thomas Kinkade Co. v. Lighthouse Galleries, LLC*, 2010 WL 436604 (E.D. Michigan), affirmed by *Thomas Kinkade Co. v. White*, 711 F.3d 719 (6th Cir. 2013), on domestic arbitration.

110 *Applied Industrial Materials Co. v. Ovalar Makine Ticaret Ve Sanayi, A.S. and Ural Ataman*, Docket No. 06-3297-cv (2d Cir. 9 July 2007), 139.

111 R. Glick/L. Stipanowich, *Arbitrator Disclosure in the Internet Age, Some Guidance Concerning the Obligation to Disclose Internet Activity and Online Relationships*, Disp. Res. J. 67 (2012), 1-7, 2.

7.1.1.3.3 Proposed Perspective

Regarding the perspective to analyse the scope of disclosure, the purpose of disclosure should be highlighted again. Some authors suggest that disclosure provides the parties with an element of confidence in the arbitrators. Only if the arbitrator discloses properly, may the parties decide whether they are confident that the nominated arbitrator is independent and impartial and has the expertise they require to solve their dispute. Therefore, disclosure enables the parties' right to appoint and object. Following this logic, the perspective to analyse what needs to be disclosed should be purely subjective from the parties' point of view. In order for the parties to be able to make an informed choice when appointing the tribunal, the arbitrators should disclose all circumstances potentially interesting for the parties from their point of view. In practice, this would lead to a broad scope of disclosure.[112] Such a "hypertrophy" of disclosure may create more disorder than confidence in the arbitrator.[113] In fact, the purpose of disclosure is not limited to enabling the parties' right to appoint. Disclosure also guarantees independence and impartiality on a more general and objective basis.[114] Disclosure fosters transparency for the sake of all participants and even the arbitral regime. Additionally, practical difficulties are attached to the subjective perspective. It may be difficult for the arbitrator to fully take the position of the party.[115] In order to establish a real obligation for the arbitrator to disclose, he or she must have the possibility to become aware of the scenario potentially constituting justifiable doubts on independence and impartiality. Thus, the arbitrator's "commitment to transparency that would be relevant in the mind of the fair-minded and informed observer" would be sufficient.[116]

A correlate of the purely objective or subjective perspectives is a subjective-objective perspective, i.e., an objective assessment from the parties' point of view.[117] This subjective-objective perspective requires the arbitrator to disclose what may raise a reasonable suspicion in the parties' mind as to the independence and impartiality of the arbitrator, not what the arbitrator thinks is decisive to disclose from his or her point of view. The subjective elements in this perspective do not bear a risk of broadening the

112 See also, above chapter 7.1.1.1.

113 C. Jarrosson, *A propos de l'obligation de révélation, Une leçon de méthode de la Cour de cassation, Note sous Cass. civ. 1re, 10 octobre 2012*, Rev. de l'Arb. 2013, 130-137, 137. Jarrosson's warning is not limited to the scope of disclosure explicitly, but rather general.

114 See also, the approach taken by the U.K. Supreme Court favouring an objective approach, *Halliburton Co. v. Chubb Bermuda Ins. Ltd.*, [2020] UKSC 48.

115 Cf. C. Seraglini/J. Ortscheidt, *Droit de l'arbitrage interne et international*, para. 737.

116 *W Ltd. v. M Sdn Bhd.*, [2016] 1 CLC 437, 438.

117 Such perspective was applied in OLG Naumburg, 19 December 2001, 10 SchH 3/01, SchiedsVZ 2003, 134-142.

grounds for challenges or annulments, since non-disclosure itself is no ground for finding dependence and partiality.[118] Non-disclosure has different consequences.[119]

In conclusion, much case law limits the scope of necessary disclosures to some extent, resulting in an intermediate scope of disclosure. This approach appropriately takes into consideration the purpose of disclosure and provides useful means to the parties to appoint or challenge the arbitrators. The perspective suggested here is that of a reasonable party, i.e., a subjective-objective perspective. This scope of necessary disclosures results in disclosure being slightly broader than the prevalent standard of independence and impartiality.

7.1.1.4 Necessary Specificity of Disclosure

Besides the scope of disclosure, some French authors additionally provide that disclosure needs to be precise enough to enable the parties to challenge.[120] Likewise, it was not sufficient in *Dealer Computer Services, Inc. v. Michael Motor Co., Inc.*, to disclose that the arbitrator was involved in previous arbitral proceedings with claimant.[121] According to the court, the arbitrator should have disclosed that the same contractual provisions were at issue and the same expert witnesses were involved. Such requirement of specific disclosure is in line with the purpose of disclosure to enable the parties' right to appoint, object and challenge.

7.1.1.5 Individual Scenarios

Some individual scenarios regarding disclosure require a more detailed evaluation. With regard to barristers, third-party funders, tribunal secretaries, social networks, and experts it is questionable what kind of scope of disclosure applies to these individual scenarios and what needs to be considered practically.

7.1.1.5.1 Barristers

Though the involvement of barristers does not usually amount to a conflict of interest without additional ties present,[122] different sources call for an early disclosure of the affiliation to a chamber. To avoid any suspicion in this regard, Kendall suggests "full disclosure by the barrister-arbitrator at the earliest possible opportunity", even if the otherwise applicable scope of disclosure is different.[123] The IBA Guidelines 2014 merely

118 See above chapter 7.1.1.3.2, on German case law on the intermediate scope.

119 See below chapter 7.1.4.

120 Cass civ 1ère, 20 October 2010, 09-68131; C. Seraglini/J. Ortscheidt, *Droit de l'arbitrage interne et international*, paras. 228-230.

121 *Dealer Computer Services, Inc. v. Michael Motor Co., Inc.*, 761 F.Supp.2d 459 (S.D. Texas 2010).

122 See above chapter 4.1.1.1.9.

123 J. Kendall, *Barristers, Independence and Disclosure*, Arb. Int'l 8 (1992), 287-299, 299.

call for disclosure of the membership of the same barrister's chambers.[124] The General Council of the Bar of England and Wales does not explicitly suggest another scope of disclosure, but encourages early disclosure.[125] It suggests that barristers should disclose early in the proceedings and that the parties should be asked to identify their legal representatives as soon as possible.[126] The latter suggestion addresses the problematic scenario of a barrister-counsel joining at a later stage of the proceedings. In this scenario, the risk of disrupting the proceedings requires appropriate handling. Additionally, the General Council of the Bar advises that

> [a]t the stage of the first procedural hearing, an Order might be made that the parties notify the arbitrator, and one another, of their current legal teams, and that each party should notify the arbitrator and the other party of any change in the teams, within a set period.[127]

Bearing in mind that the intermediate scope of disclosure is widely recognised and appropriately balances the different purposes of disclosure, "full disclosure" of barristers, as suggested by Kendall, needs more clarification. The intermediate scope is guided by the applicable standard of independence and impartiality, i.e., usually by justifiable doubts. Justifiable doubts on the independence and impartiality of a barrister-arbitrator may exist, where a barrister-counsel is involved in the proceedings from the same chambers and the organisation of the chambers does not guarantee the separation of work. Therefore, a barrister-arbitrator should disclose the name of his or her chambers and some information on the internal structure regarding the separation of work within the chambers.

Finally, a factor to be included in the analysis of a conflict of interest is the particular culture of the Bar in the United Kingdom and the general awareness of how the system operates. Do parties have to be aware of the special arrangements of barristers' chambers?[128] In

124 Part I, General Standard 7(b) IBA Guidelines 2014.

125 The General Council of the Bar, Information Note Regarding Barristers in International Arbitration, para. 34. The Note recalls in the same sentence that barristers should bear in mind their general obligation of confidentiality.

126 The General Council of the Bar, Information Note Regarding Barristers in International Arbitration, para. 34.

127 The General Council of the Bar, Information Note Regarding Barristers in International Arbitration, para. 34. Art. 19.2 JAMS Rules provides for exactly this procedure: any change of counsel needs to be disclosed and even approved by the tribunal.

128 Cf. *PPG Industries Inc. v. Pilkington PLC*, EWHC, 1 November 1989, reported in J. Kendall, *Barristers, Independence and Disclosure*, Arb. Int'l 8 (1992), 287-299, 290-291, denying respondent's request to reject an arbitrator who was barrister in the same chambers as claimant's counsel. The court decided that respondent, being the English party, could not rely on having been unaware of the barristers' organisation. See also, *Hrvatska Elektroprivreda, d.d. v. Republic of Slovenia*, ICSID Tribunal, 6 May 2008, ARB/05/24,

general, to adopt an objective-subjective standard of independence and impartiality, parties must be aware of the special circumstances of the operational system of barristers' chambers.[129] Disclosing the involvement of barristers enables parties to inquire further about the special working arrangements of barristers.[130]

In order to avoid suspicion, the following practical advice may be useful: arbitrators and counsels should adhere to an early and broad disclosure;[131] arrangements should be made to ensure that absolute confidentiality is maintained and that there is no possibility that barristers see correspondence to or from other barristers;[132] the barrister-counsel should advise the solicitor and client of the potential risk of a challenge and any potential risks in relation to the enforceability of the final arbitration award.[133]

7.1.1.5.2 Third-Party Funding

Cases of third-party funding require examination of three potential scopes of disclosure: disclosing the mere presence of the funder, disclosing previously funded cases by the

---

stating that "[f]or an international system like that of ICSID, it seems unacceptable for the solution to reside in the individual national bodies which regulate the work of professional service providers, because that might lead to inconsistent or indeed arbitrary outcomes depending on the attitudes of such bodies, or the content (or lack of relevant content) of their rules", para. 23. The question can be broadened: what role do cultural aspects have when examining conflicts of interest? This question is important in international arbitration. It could be relevant before courts of the country practising the relevant culture or before a court in a third country when enforcing or annulling an arbitral award. An example on the issue of barristers is CA Paris, 29 June 1991, cited in *Laker Airways Inc. v. FLS Aerospace Ltd. & Anor*, [1999] CLC 1124, 1130, where the *cour d'appel* de Paris relied on respondent's submission when explaining the organisation of barristers. The *lex loci arbitri* was French law and claimant requested annulment of the award under that law.

129 Cf. LCIA Reference No. UN97/X11, LCIA Court, 5 June 1997, Arb. Int'l 27 (2011), 320-321, where the objective-subjective standard was not explicitly applied. But claimant's challenge was explicitly denied arguing that claimant and its counsel must have been familiar with the organisation of barristers' chambers in England.

130 However, in *Hrvatska Elektroprivreda, d.d. v. Republic of Slovenia*, ICSID Tribunal, 6 May 2008, ARB/05/24, the respondent did not disclose the involvement of the barrister of the same chamber as one of the arbitrators and claimant was not familiar with the system of English chambers. In this scenario, the tribunal granted an order disqualifying the counsel, i.e., the barrister. See also, J.-P. Bischoff, *Unabhängigkeit und Unparteilichkeit von Schiedsrichtern nach deutschem und englischem Recht*, pp. 151-153. Bischoff clarifies that parties may expressly agree on different treatment of barristers, but if they do not do so, the default rule is to accept the speciality.

131 The General Council of the Bar, Information Note Regarding Barristers in International Arbitration, para. 34. Cf. J. Kendall, *Barristers, Independence and Disclosure*, Arb. Int'l 8 (1992), 287-299, 299, arguing that disclosure is "the best solution", "whatever the strict legal position under the applicable law or institutional rules" is.

132 The General Council of the Bar, Information Note Regarding Barristers in International Arbitration, para. 18, suggesting that separate clerks should be designated to deal with the matter on behalf of the arbitrator and on behalf of the member retained to act as counsel, para. 19.

133 Cf. The General Council of the Bar, Information Note Regarding Barristers in International Arbitration, para. 22.

funder, or even disclosing the funding agreement.[134] The different means of disclosure are: first, disclosure by the arbitrators of all previous connections with third-party funders, i.e., a full disclosure; second, disclosure after being provided with information by the parties of their current interaction with funders; and third, disclosure by the parties or the funder.

Generally, the requirement to disclose the existence of third-party funding is welcomed to accurately assess issues of independence and impartiality and avoid conflicts of interest.[135] Disclosure of the funding agreement itself is often not required.[136] Article 44.1 HKIAC Rules[137] and the Hong Kong AO[138] adopt somewhat limited approaches of disclosure of

134 The regulation of disclosure in the context of third-party funding is crucial. Cf. F. Blavi, *It's About Time To Regulate Third Party Funding.*

135 Most recent, the ICCA Report on Third-Party Funding voted in favour of disclosure, ICCA, Report of the ICCA-Queen Mary Task Force on Third-Party Funding in International Arbitration, p. 83. See also, O. Gayner/A. Croft/K. Hurford, *Third-party Funding for International Arbitration Claims Practical Tips,* on Art. 21 of the new draft ICSID Convention Arbitration Rules. N. Darwazeh/A. Leleu, *Disclosure and Security for Costs or How to Address Imbalances Created by Third-Party Funding,* J. Int'l Arb. 33 (2016), 125-150, 132-133. Requesting institutions to include an obligation to disclose in their rules D. Yeoh, *Third Party Funding in International Arbitration, A Slippery Slope or Levelling the Playing Field?,* J. Int'l Arb. 33 (2016), 115-122, 117-118, 120-121; V. Frignati, *Ethical Implications of Third-party Funding in International Arbitration,* Arb. Int'l 32 (2016), 505-522, 516-517. Also, Art. 8.26(1) Comprehensive and Economic Trade Agreement requires disclosure of the name and address of any third-party funder involved in the proceedings. The definition of third-party funders in the Comprehensive and Economic Trade Agreement is rather broad: Art. 8.1 provides that "third party funding means any funding provided by a natural or legal person who is not a disputing party but who enters into an agreement with a disputing party in order to finance part or all of the cost of the proceedings either through a donation or grant, or in return for remuneration dependent on the outcome of the dispute".

136 Though there may be scenarios where the funding agreement needs to be disclosed to evaluate the control of the funder on the funded party, M. Scherer, *Out in the Open? Third-party Funding in Arbitration.* See also, A. Goldsmith/L. Melchionda, *The ICC's Guidance Note on Disclosure and Third-Party Funding.*

137 Art. 44.1 HKIAC Rules provide: "If a funding agreement is made, the funded party shall communicate a written notice to all other parties, the arbitral tribunal, any emergency arbitrator and HKIAC of: (a) the fact that a funding agreement has been made; and (b) the identity of the third party funder."

138 Sect. 98U Hong Kong AO. It provides that: "(1) If a funding agreement is made, the funded party must give written notice of (a) the fact that a funding agreement has been made; and (b) the name of the third party funder. (2) The notice must be given (a) for a funding agreement made on or before the commencement of the arbitration on the commencement of the arbitration; or(b) for a funding agreement made after the commencement of the arbitration – within 15 days after the funding agreement is made. (3) The notice must be given to (a) each other party to the arbitration; and (b) the arbitration body. (4) For subsection (3)(b), if there is no arbitration body for the arbitration at the time, or at the end of the period, specified in subsection (2) for giving the notice, the notice must in-stead be given to the arbitration body immediately after there is an arbitration body for the arbitration." The Hong Kong AO is comparably detailed and clear on the obligation to disclose. Cf. P. Hirst/M. Yeow, *Comparing Hong Kong Code of Practice for Third Party Funding Arbitration with the Code of Conduct in England & Wales.*

the third-party funder.[139] The funded party must give notice of disclosure to the other party and the "arbitration body," i.e., the arbitral tribunal.[140]

Concerning the means of disclosure, the first approach, i.e., full disclosure, is ineffective and risks misuse as a delaying tactic. An arbitrator's advance disclosure of all his or her previous encounters with any third-party funder would leave too great a possibility for suspicion.

For the second approach, i.e., disclosure after being provided with information by the parties of their current interaction with funders, either the applicable rules or an order from the tribunal may require the parties to disclose. For example, the SIAC Investment Rules 2017 provide the tribunal with the power to

> order the disclosure of the existence of a Party's third - party funding arrangement and/or the identity of the third - party funder and, where appropriate, details of the third - party funder's interest in the outcome of the proceedings, and/or whether or not the third - party funder has committed to undertake adverse costs liability.[141]

Similarly, the SIAC Practice Note, PN – 01/17 grants the tribunal

> the power to conduct such enquiries as may appear to the Tribunal to be necessary or expedient, which shall include ordering the disclosure of the existence of any funding relationship with an External Funder and/or the identity of the External Funder and, where appropriate, details of the External Funder's interest in the outcome of the proceedings, and/or whether or not the External Funder has committed to undertake adverse costs liability.[142]

139 O. Gayner/S. Khouri, *Singapore and Hong Kong: International Arbitration Meets Third Party Funding*, Fordham Int'l L.J. 40 (2017), 1033-1046, 1043, welcome this "sensible" approach of the Hong Kong AO. According to the authors, "the disclosure to the Tribunal and opposing party should be of two discrete points only: first, the existence of funding (including the name and address of the funder), and second, whether the funding agreement contains an agreement to pay any adverse costs".

140 Definition provided in Sect. 98F Hong Kong AO.

141 Rule 24(l) SIAC Investment Arbitration Rules. It is questionable whether this power to order disclosure requires specific regulation or whether it is inherent to the powers of the tribunal. In the following investment arbitration cases the tribunal also ordered disclosure from the parties of the involvement of third-party funders: *South American Silver Ltd. (Bermuda) v. Plurinational State of Bolivia*, PCA Tribunal, 11 January 2016, PCA Case No. 2013-15; *EuroGas Inc. and Belmont Resources Inc. v. Slovak Republic*, ICSID Tribunal, 23 June 2015, ICSID Case No. ARB/14/14; *Muhammet Çap & Sehil Inşaat Endustri ve Ticaret Ltd. Sti. v. Turkmenistan*, ICSID Tribunal, 12 June 2015, ICSID Case No. ARB/12/6.

142 Para. 5, SIAC, Practice Note, PN – 01/17.

This second approach engages both the arbitrators and the parties in the process of disclosing third-party funding. It targets the concrete involvement of funding in the present dispute and is, therefore, not too broad.

Finally, the third approach, i.e., disclosure required by the party and the third-party funder,[143] goes hand in hand with the second approach. After disclosure by the party or third-party funder under the second approach, the arbitrators have to evaluate whether they are obliged to disclose. Article 11(7) ICC Rules follows this approach.[144] The ICC Note specifies the parties' obligation to inform promptly of the existence and identity of a third-party funder.[145] Similarly, the IBA Guidelines 2014 require in General Standard 7(a) that

> [a] party shall inform an arbitrator, the Arbitral Tribunal, the other parties and the arbitration institution or other appointing authority (if any) of any relationship, direct or indirect, between the arbitrator and the party (or another company of the same group of companies, or an individual having a controlling influence on the party in the arbitration), or between the arbitrator and any person or entity with a direct economic interest in, or a duty to indemnify a party for, the award to be rendered in the arbitration. The party shall do so on its own initiative at the earliest opportunity.

This approach was criticised as being too broad and "far beyond present disclosure practices".[146] Von Goeler criticises that by requiring disclosure of "any relationship, direct or indirect", General Standard 7(a) strips the disclosing party of its discretion to reveal or

143 E.g., P. Archer, *Paris Bar Council Indicates Support for Third-party Funding*, requesting counsel to encourage the parties and the funder to disclose.

144 Art. 11(7) ICC Rules states: "In order to assist prospective arbitrators and arbitrators in complying with their duties under Articles 11(2) and 11(3), each party must promptly inform the Secretariat, the arbitral tribunal and the other parties, of the existence and identity of any non-party which has entered into an arrangement for the funding of claims or defences and under which it has an economic interest in the outcome of the arbitration."

145 ICC Note, paras. 20-21 state: "To assist arbitrators and prospective arbitrators in complying with their duty of disclosure (see section III(A)), each party must, pursuant to Article 11(7), promptly inform the Secretariat, the arbitral tribunal and the other parties of the existence and identity of any non-party that has entered into an arrangement for the funding of claims and defences and under which that non-party has an economic interest in the outcome of the arbitration. For example, the non-party is entitled to receive all or part of the proceeds of the award. Subject to any different determination that may be made by the arbitral tribunal in the circumstances of any given case, Article 11(7) would normally not capture (i) inter-company funding within a group of companies, (ii) fee arrangements between a party and its counsel, or (iii) an indirect interest, such as that of a bank having granted a loan to the party in the ordinary course of its ongoing activities rather than specifically for the funding of the arbitration."

146 J. von Goeler, *Third-party Funding*, p. 285.

conceal its funding.[147] However, first, the IBA Guidelines 2014 require merely the disclosure of the funder itself but no further information on the funding agreement. Second, "relationship" is to be interpreted in line with General Standard 6 IBA Guidelines 2014, clarifying in 6(b) that a third-party funder "may" be positioned with the funded party.[148] Even though this does not imply discretion when evaluating the scope of disclosure, it does provide discretion on the previous stage evaluating whether to position the funder at all with the party. If this previous evaluation is positive, i.e., the funder is to be positioned with the party due to the materiality of the relationship, there is no reason to differentiate between the funder and the party in disclosure.

To conclude, disclosure of the concrete existence and identity of the funder through means of requesting the party to provide information on the funding is more practical and effective than the arbitrator's advance disclosure of all his or her previous encounters with any third-party funder. It is practical and effective to support the purposes of disclosure, i.e., inter alia, the parties' right to challenge in case of a conflict of interest, and to ensure the effectiveness of the proceedings.

7.1.1.5.3 Tribunal Secretary

In regard to the use of tribunal secretaries, two issues of disclosure arise: first, whether the mere presence of tribunal secretaries has to be disclosed, and potentially, their concrete tasks, and second, whether the tribunal secretary has to disclose circumstances likely to give rise to justifiable doubts.

While the majority of rules and guidelines do not address the use of a tribunal secretary, those that do often require disclosure.[149] Disclosure of the mere involvement of a tribunal secretary is necessary to inform the parties about who is involved in the administration of the proceedings and potentially close to decision-making tasks.[150] Besides the right to challenge, disclosure of the use of tribunal secretaries is in some rules and guidelines even constitutive to appoint the tribunal secretary.[151] Much more difficult is the question of

---

147 J. von Goeler, *Third-party Funding*, p. 285.

148 Part I, General Standard 6 IBA Guidelines 2014 is titled "Relationships" and provides in 6(b): "If one of the parties is a legal entity, any legal or physical person having a controlling influence on the legal entity, or a direct economic interest in, or a duty to indemnify a party for, the award to be rendered in the arbitration, may be considered to bear the identity of such party."

149 E.g., Art. 1(a), Young ICCA Guide, Young ICCA, *Young ICCA Guide on Arbitral Secretaries*, p. 5; Art. 13.4 HKIAC Rules; ICC Note, para. 220; Arts. 14.9 and 14.14 LCIA Rules; SCC Arbitrator's Guidelines, Sect. 2, p. 8; SIAC, Practice Note, PN – 01/17, paras. 3-4.

150 See O. Jensen, *Tribunal Secretaries in International Arbitration*, para. 5.05 et seq.

151 E.g., in SIAC, Practice Note, PN – 01/17, paras. 3-4, demanding consent of all parties. Also, 76.8% of respondents of the 2013 Survey favoured a requirement that the parties consent to the particular candidate being proposed as arbitral secretary, Young ICCA, *Young ICCA Guide on Arbitral Secretaries*, p. 6.

disclosure in ad hoc arbitration since there are usually no applicable institutional rules demanding disclosure and no institution monitoring the adherence.[152] However, in line with the intermediate scope of disclosure, disclosure is required where the use of a tribunal secretary may give rise to justifiable doubts as to the independence and impartiality of either the tribunal or the secretary.[153] Disclosing the mere involvement of tribunal secretaries does not bear much risk of suspicion and may, hence, not risk delaying the proceedings.[154]

In favour of the general positive approach towards disclosure of the involvement of a tribunal secretary, it is questionable whether the concrete tasks and the level of involvement have to be disclosed as well. Unlike the first question, there may be a slight risk of raising suspicion and potentially misusing the information on the exact tasks performed by the secretaries to delay the proceedings. However, information on the exact tasks performed is crucial to evaluate whether a ground of dependence and partiality exists. Therefore, disclosure should cover an explanation of the secretary's concrete tasks.

Finally, it is questionable whether the tribunal secretary has to disclose circumstances likely to give rise to justifiable doubts as to his or her independence and impartiality. Tribunal secretaries have to be independent and impartial.[155] To implement their independence and impartiality it is important and practically necessary to oblige them to provide information on their previous encounters. Therefore, they have to disclose. Some institutions require statements of independence and impartiality to be submitted by the secretaries themselves.[156] Another approach is to oblige the secretary to disclose to the tribunal and the latter forwards the information to the parties and, if applicable, the institution.[157] Both means of disclosure are appropriate.

152 Even the UNCITRAL, Notes on Organizing Arbitral Proceedings, para. 38, only provide: "If the arbitral tribunal wishes to appoint a secretary, it *would normally* disclose this fact to the parties, along with the identity of the proposed secretary, the nature of the tasks to be performed by the secretary, and the amount and source of any proposed remuneration. The parties may wish to agree on the role and practices to be adopted in respect of the secretaries, as well as on the financial conditions applicable to their services. Institutional guidelines on secretaries may provide useful information to the parties." (Emph. add.)

153 The intermediate scope of disclosure requests disclosure of circumstances that are not necessarily a positive ground for finding dependence and partiality but likely to meet the threshold.

154 The use of tribunal secretaries is widely accepted in international arbitration. Cf. M. Hwang, *Introduction, Musings on International Arbitration*, p. 1 et seq. On the other hand, undisclosed use of tribunal secretaries bears some risk of a breach of confidentiality on the tribunal's side: many institutional rules provide that the hearings and deliberations are to be kept confidential. Introducing a tribunal secretary to either, even if he or she is just to support administratively, may breach the arbitrator's obligation of confidentiality, O. Jensen, *Tribunal Secretaries in International Arbitration*, paras. 4.126-4.127.

155 See above chapter 6.7.

156 E.g., ICC Note, para. 220; JAMS, Guidelines for Use of Clerks and Tribunal Secretaries, point 1; Art. 14.9 LCIA Rules; Sect. 4(2) SCC Guidelines.

157 E.g., ICC Note, para. 220. See also, O. Jensen, *Tribunal Secretaries in International Arbitration*, para. 4.55.

7.1.1.5.4 Social Networks

The scope of disclosure with regard to activities on social networking sites requires its own analysis. For the evaluation of grounds for finding dependence and partiality, the underlying real relationship is decisive, not the one demonstrated on social networks.[158] Therefore, generally, the scope of disclosure encompasses all types of circumstances that may create justifiable doubts regarding independence and impartiality. It is, however, not the fact of a social networking connection that needs to be disclosed but the underlying relationship or conduct.[159]

Some authors and case law suggest a differentiation between professional and social networking sites.[160] Following this differentiation, the scope of disclosure shall be different as well.[161] However, the differentiation is, first of all, difficult to implement since there is no clear line between social and professional networking sites.[162] Second, there is no need to differentiate. Both social and professional ties and conduct in either type of networking sites may create conflicts of interest.[163]

With regard to the French approach to the scope of disclosure and the limitation that notorious facts do not need to be disclosed, one may raise the question of whether relationships and conduct on social networking sites are generally not required to be disclosed since they are in the public domain. Information is notorious when it is public, very easily accessible, and the addressee of the disclosure cannot ignore it.[164] Not all social networking sites are accessible without membership, so it is not necessarily very easy to access the information. Thus, there cannot be a general conclusion to categorise all

158 S. Sanubari, *Arbitrator's Conduct on Social Media*, J. Int'l Disp. Settlement 8 (2017), 483-506, 493. See also, above chapter 4.1.1.1.8.

159 For an opposing view, i.e., that some facts of social networking connections require disclosure, see S. Sanubari, *Arbitrator's Conduct on Social Media*, J. Int'l Disp. Settlement 8 (2017), 483-506, 494.

160 S. Sanubari, *Arbitrator's Conduct on Social Media*, J. Int'l Disp. Settlement 8 (2017), 483-506, 493-494. Although Sanubari is critical on the differentiation, she suggests a distinction based on "whether a social media platform is (i) exclusively used for professional networks or (ii) it can also be used for personal networks".

161 S. Sanubari, *Arbitrator's Conduct on Social Media*, J. Int'l Disp. Settlement 8 (2017), 483-506, 493-494. Sanubari suggests listing professional social networking sites on the Green List of the IBA Guidelines 2014 and general social network sites on the Orange List.

162 In CA Paris, 10 March 2011, 09/28537, ASA Bull. 2013, 443-447, a professional campaign was run on Facebook, a networking site, that may be categorised as social and private.

163 Cf. R. Glick/L. Stipanowich, *Arbitrator Disclosure in the Internet Age, Some Guidance Concerning the Obligation to Disclose Internet Activity and Online Relationships*, Disp. Res. J. 67 (2012), 1-7, 3. Glick and Stipanowich also disfavour the differentiation in the scope of disclosure between social and professional networking sites.

164 M. Henry, *Note – Cour d'appel de Paris, 14 octobre 2014, SA Auto Guadeloupe Investissements v. société Columbus Acquisitions Inc. et autres*, Rev. de l'Arb. 2015, 156-182, 168.

information on social networks as notorious in this manner. The arbitrator remains obliged to disclose those circumstances that may give rise to justifiable doubts.

7.1.2 Personal Scope of the Obligation to Disclose

In addition to the scope of disclosure, it must be determined who bears the obligation to disclose. Generally, and depending on the scenario in question, the arbitrator, an expert, the parties, counsels, a funder, or the tribunal secretary may be obliged to disclose.

7.1.2.1 Arbitrators and Co-Arbitrators

Primarily, arbitrators have to disclose.[165] They are at the centre of independence and impartiality, as the decision makers, and are the persons who have the relevant information on their independence and impartiality.

Much more debated is whether co-arbitrators are obliged to disclose circumstances giving rise to another arbitrator's independence and impartiality.[166] In particular, where the co-arbitrator becomes aware of the circumstance to be disclosed during deliberations, disclosure may conflict with the arbitrator's obligation of confidentiality.[167] However, since the threshold for conflicts of interest based on the conduct of arbitrators during deliberations is comparably high (and the scope of disclosure is sketched by independence and impartiality), this conflict with the obligation of confidentiality is not likely to arise often in practice.[168] Also, where the circumstance that potentially requires disclosure is not one that is connected to the deliberations, e.g., the co-arbitrators become aware of a specific relationship of the other arbitrator as an aside, it is questionable whether the obligation to keep deliberations confidential covers disclosure of this circumstance.[169] Where the scope of the confidentiality obligation is broad, this may be the case.[170] However,

165 E.g., General Standard 3 IBA Guidelines 2014; Canon II AAA/ABA Code of Ethics; Art. 9.4 DIS Rules; Art. 18(2) SCC Rules; Art. 9(2) Swiss Rules.

166 In favour, Musielak/Voit/W. Voit, § 1036 para. 3. See generally, O. Froitzheim, *Die Ablehnung von Schiedsrichtern wegen Befangenheit in der internationalen Schiedsgerichtsbarkeit*, p. 167 et seq.

167 O. Froitzheim, *Die Ablehnung von Schiedsrichtern wegen Befangenheit in der internationalen Schiedsgerichtsbarkeit*, p. 168 et seq. Froitzheim argues that the obligation to keep the deliberations confidential covers these scenarios and generally prohibits disclosure. He construes an exception for the obligation to keep the deliberations confidential. If disclosure is within the interest of due process and the rule of law, it trumps the obligation of confidentiality, p. 172.

168 Cf. Musielak/Voit/W. Voit, § 1036 para. 3. See above chapter 4.2.1.3, on arbitrator's conduct in deliberations.

169 This will depend on the scope of the obligation to keep deliberations confidential. Rule 9 IBA Rules 1987 provides: "The deliberations of the arbitral tribunal, and the contents of the award itself, remain confidential in perpetuity unless the parties release the arbitrators from this obligation."

170 In case of a broad scope of the confidentiality obligation one may argue that the arbitrator is obliged to breach this confidentiality obligation where he or she witnesses a potential ground for finding another

even if the scope is limited and no obligation of confidentiality hinders disclosure, at first sight, it remains questionable whether the co-arbitrators are obliged to disclose.[171] Usually, arbitrators have to disclose circumstances regarding their independence and impartiality.[172] The obligation of arbitrators to disclose information about their co-arbitrator risks conflicts within the tribunal. Therefore, before disclosing for a co-arbitrator, arbitrators should consider alternatives, e.g., exhorting the other arbitrator to disclose or consider joint disclosure.

7.1.2.2 Experts

Not many rules and laws explicitly address the expert's disclosure. The CIArb Guideline on Experts requires the tribunal-appointed expert to disclose to the arbitral tribunal which shall share all information with the parties.[173] Additionally, Article 29(2) sentence 1 UNCITRAL Arbitration Rules requires the expert,

> before accepting appointment, to submit to the arbitral tribunal and to the parties a description of his or her qualifications and a statement of his or her impartiality and independence.

Similarly under the German arbitration law, the tribunal-appointed arbitrator is obliged to disclose.[174] The provision dealing with experts (§ 1049(3) German ZPO), simply refers

---

arbitrator's dependence or partiality, see the argument submitted by the challenging party in OLG München, 10 July 2013, 34 SchH 8/12, NJOZ 2014, 1779-1782.

171 O. Froitzheim, *Die Ablehnung von Schiedsrichtern wegen Befangenheit in der internationalen Schiedsgerichtsbarkeit*, p. 170 et seq. The author deduces the obligation to disclose first from the general principle of independence and impartiality. This is, according to the author, only applicable where the circumstance to be disclosed meets the standard of independence and impartiality. Second, the obligation to disclose may be deduced from the parties' interest to be informed and their procedural rights.

172 E.g., General Standard 3 IBA Guidelines 2014; Art. 9.4 DIS Rules; Art. 18(2) SCC Rules; Art. 9(2) Swiss Rules.

173 Comment on Art. 3, CIArb Guideline on Experts, p. 7. The Protocol on Use of Experts additionally suggests a precise expert declaration: "I understand that my duty in giving evidence in this arbitration is to assist the arbitral tribunal decide the issue or issues in respect of which expert evidence is adduced. I have complied with, and will continue to comply with, that duty. I confirm that this is my own, impartial and objective, opinion. I confirm that all matters upon which I have expressed an opinion are within my area of expertise. I confirm that I have referred to all matters which I regard as relevant to the opinions I have expressed and have drawn to the attention of the arbitral tribunal all matters, of which I am aware, which might adversely affect my opinion. I confirm that, at the time of providing this written opinion, I consider it to be complete and accurate and constitute my true, professional opinion. I confirm that if in the course of this arbitration I consider that this opinion re- quires any correction or modification I will notify the parties and the arbitral tribunal forthwith." Art. 8(a)-(f) Protocol on Use of Experts. Also, LCIA Note for Arbitrators, Sect. 9, para. 84, mentions a statement of independence and impartiality by the expert. Similarly, experts in state court proceedings are obliged to disclose, e.g., Art. 234(3) French CPC, with explanation in C. Chanais/ F. Ferrand/S. Guinchard, *Procédure civile*, para. 689.

174 §§ 1049(3), 1036(1) sentence 1 German ZPO.

to the provision dealing with disclosure and challenge of arbitrators (§ 1036 German ZPO).[175] In line with the German law, and bearing in mind that the same standard of independence and impartiality applies to tribunal-appointed experts and arbitrators,[176] it appears generally useful to apply the same scope of disclosure to experts and to oblige them to disclose as well.

In light of the lack of detailed regulation of the tribunal-appointed expert's disclosure obligation arbitrators should instruct experts on their obligation to disclose thoroughly and in detail.[177] The arbitrators should inform the expert of the kind of relationships and prior conduct the expert is obliged to disclose.[178] This advice is especially useful if the expert is not a lawyer or is a legal expert from another jurisdiction.

7.1.2.3 Parties, Counsels, and Third-Party Funders

Another difficult question is whether the parties, counsels, or funders are obliged to disclose, where the arbitrator's independence and impartiality are at issue – and not their own. These questions are usually not addressed by institutional rules. An exception are the ICDR Rules, obliging the parties to disclose in addition to the arbitrator.[179] Also, Guideline 5 IBA Guidelines 2013 may be interpreted to call for counsel to disclose after the arbitration has commenced and before counsel commences to represent the party. Guideline 5 IBA Guidelines 2013 reads:

> Once the Arbitral Tribunal has been constituted, a person should not accept representation of a Party in the arbitration when a relationship exists between the person and an Arbitrator that would create a conflict of interest, unless none of the Parties objects after proper disclosure.

The purpose of Guideline 5 IBA Guidelines 2013 is to uncover potential conflicts of interest as early as possible.[180] Additionally, the above-mentioned General Standard 7(a) and

175 See above chapter 7.1.1.1, et seq., for references to German law.
176 See above chapter 6.6.
177 N. Schmidt-Ahrendts/V. Schneider, *„Gut Ding will Weile haben"*, SchiedsVZ 2020, 35-41, 40.
178 N. Schmidt-Ahrendts/V. Schneider, *„Gut Ding will Weile haben"*, SchiedsVZ 2020, 35-41, 40.
179 Art. 13(3) ICDR Rules.
180 Where the parties agree on the application of the IBA Guidelines 2013 their counsels are not directly bound by the Guidelines, see C. Rogers, *Context and Institutional Structure in Attorney Regulation: Constructing an Enforcement Regime for International Arbitration*, Stanford J. Int'l L. 39 (2003), 1-58, 34. However, counsels may be obliged to adhere to all the party's obligations. This obligation derives from the contractual relationship of a counsel and the party, see S. Horst, *Das Spannungsverhältnis zwischen Schiedsrichter und Parteivertreter in der internationalen Schiedsgerichtsbarkeit*, p. 195.

(b) IBA Guidelines 2014 place a broad obligation to inform on the parties.[181] General Standard 7(a) IBA Guidelines 2014 encourages the parties to inform the tribunal "on its own initiative at the earliest opportunity". The wording of the provision encompasses any direct or indirect relationship between the arbitrator and the party, another company of the same group of companies, an individual having a controlling influence on the party in the arbitration, or between the arbitrator and a third person with an economic interest in the outcome. The purpose of this provision is to "reduce the risk of an unmeritorious challenge of an arbitrator's impartiality or independence based on information learned after the appointment".[182] There is not much room left for appropriate non-disclosure by the parties.[183] The IBA's broad approach to the scope of disclosure described above, therefore, also applies concerning the group of people obliged to disclose. The wording and purpose of General Standard 7(a) IBA Guidelines 2014 reveal that the parties' obligation to disclose applies after the appointment of the tribunal. Therefore, one may argue that the party does not need to inform the opposing party of any circumstance likely to give rise to justifiable doubts where the tribunal is not yet appointed, but comments are invited by the parties on the proposed arbitrators. However, and following General Standard 7(a) IBA Guidelines 2014, the party would need to disclose the circumstance once the tribunal is appointed. On the one hand, it is questionable whether the circumstance should not be required to be disclosed earlier to inform the opposing party. On the other hand, the procedure limits the risks attached to full disclosure: creating suspicion and the potential of misuse in the form of tactical challenges.

If no rules or guidelines require disclosure of the parties or counsels, there cannot be such an obligation based on the general need for independence and impartiality.[184] First, independence and impartiality are primarily targeted at the arbitrators. They are at the centre of the obligation to disclose. Second, without indication in the applicable set of rules or guidelines that the parties are under an obligation to disclose, requiring parties to disclose

181 The Explanation to General Standard 7(a) IBA Guidelines 2014 reveals that this is also a form of disclosure. There appears to be no difference between the two terms within the IBA Guidelines 2014.

182 Explanation to General Standard 7(a) IBA Guidelines 2014.

183 According to the IBA Guidelines 2014, parties may not tactically hold back circumstances that may create justifiable doubts as to independence and impartiality.

184 The same applies to counsels. The argument that counsels are obliged by bona fides to disclose was rejected in LCIA Reference No. 971X27, LCIA Court, 23 October 1997, Arb. Int'l 27 (2011), 322-324. For an implicit obligation of the counsel towards his or her represented party, see S. Horst, *Das Spannungsverhältnis zwischen Schiedsrichter und Parteivertreter in der internationalen Schiedsgerichtsbarkeit*, p. 195.

would result in shifting the arbitrator's initial obligation to the parties.[185] These issues do not arise, however, where the tribunal orders disclosure.[186]

7.1.3 *Point in Time of Disclosure*

The point in time of disclosure is crucial for the proceedings. A mid-arbitration disclosure may have significant effects on the ongoing arbitral proceedings.[187] Arbitrators are usually obliged to disclose after their nomination and before they are appointed.[188] The obligation to disclose continues during the arbitration.[189] Disclosure needs to be made "timely"[190] or "without delay",[191] i.e., as soon as the arbitrator learns of the circumstance to be disclosed.[192] Again, one of the purposes of disclosure is to inform the parties and to create trust.[193] Prompt disclosure may achieve this purpose.[194] Alternatively, as provided by the England

185 Disfavouring such a shift in regard to the French arbitration law: Clay/Cadiet/T. Clay, Art. 1456 paras. 69-70.

186 This is the favoured approach concerning third-party funders. E.g., ICCA, Report of the ICCA-Queen Mary Task Force on Third-Party Funding in International Arbitration, proposes this approach. Generally, disclosure may be provided by the party or the arbitrator. Cf. for an overview and analysis of the two possibilities J. von Goeler, *Third-party Funding*, pp. 280 et seq.

187 Nevertheless, disclosure needs to be adhered to at any point in time. Explanation to General Standard 3(e) IBA Guidelines 2014 states: "Disclosure or disqualification (as set out in General Standards 2 and 3) should not depend on the particular stage of the arbitration. In order to determine whether the arbitrator should disclose, decline the appointment or refuse to continue to act, the facts and circumstances alone are relevant, not the current stage of the proceedings, or the consequences of the withdrawal. As a practical matter, arbitration institutions may make a distinction depending on the stage of the arbitration. Courts may likewise apply different standards. Nevertheless, no distinction is made by these Guidelines depending on the stage of the arbitral proceedings. While there are practical concerns, if an arbitrator must withdraw after the arbitration has commenced, a distinction based on the stage of the arbitration would be inconsistent with the General Standards."

188 German scholars argue that the obligation to disclose exists before, during and after the arbitration proceedings, Stein/Jonas/P. Schlosser, § 1036 para. 64 et seq.; MünchKomm ZPO/J. Münch, § 1036 paras. 16-18.

189 R-17(a) AAA Rules; Rule 2 CIArb Code of Conduct; Art. 9.6 DIS Rules; Art. 11.4 HKIAC Rules; ICC Note, para. 25; LCIA Notes for Arbitrators, para. 9. On French law, C. Seraglini/J. Ortscheidt, *Droit de l'arbitrage interne et international*, paras. 729-733; CA Paris, 12 February 2009, Rev. de l'Arb. 2009, 186-190. Critical regarding the United States, *National Indemnity Co. v. IRB Brasil Resseguros SA*, 164 F.Supp.3d 457 (S.D. New York 2016). According to the court, the criticism against the full scope of disclosure applies to an extensive ongoing obligation to disclose. "A continuous pre-selection disclosure obligation as envisioned by IRB could easily add up to hundreds of supplemental disclosures, and failure to make any of them would be grounds to vacate any award ultimately issued." But see, Sect. 12(b) UAA.

190 *National Indemnity Co. v. IRB Brasil Resseguros SA*, 164 F.Supp.3d 457 (S.D. New York 2016).

191 C. Brunner, *Note – Federal Supreme Court, 28 April 2000*, ASA Bull. 2000, 566-581, 576, referring to BGer, 28 April 2000, BGE 126 III 249.

192 General Standard 3(a) IBA Guidelines 2014.

193 See above chapter 7.1.

194 Cf. *Halliburton Co. v. Chubb Bermuda Ins. Ltd.*, [2020] UKSC 48, Lord Hodge, para. 70. See also, *Scandinavian Reinsurance Co. Ltd. v. Saint Paul Fire and Marine Ins. Co.*, 668 F.3d 60 (2d Cir. 2012), stating that "disclosure not only enhances the actual and apparent fairness of the arbitral process, but it helps to ensure

and Wales Court of Appeal, the point in time when the circumstance becomes potentially relevant is decisive.[195] Swiss authors argue that disclosure is especially necessary before the next procedural step.[196]

Third-party funding requires early disclosure.[197] Barrington underlines that the risk of disclosure of third-party funding in mid-arbitration would be a potentially dangerous situation.

> How should an arbitrator react for example, if half-way through the case, it transpires that he or she has substantial shareholdings in the insurance company backing the claimant? With the current proliferation of challenges to arbitrators, this is a fire waiting to be ignited.[198]

Finally, arbitrators are well advised to be "particularly mindful of disclosing business activities that occur during the course of the arbitration" if they may give rise to justifiable doubts.[199] "Such mid-arbitration disclosures are particularly important because they occur after the initial selection process and are easier for an arbitrator to hide or sweep under the rug."[200]

7.1.4 Consequences of Non-Disclosure

Having elaborated that arbitrators, parties, counsels, funders, and experts may be obliged to disclose, it is necessary to examine the consequence of breaching this obligation, i.e., non-disclosure. Non-disclosure is in itself usually not sufficient grounds to establish

---

that that process will be final, rather than extended by proceedings like this one. We again reiterate Justice White's observation that it is far better for a potential conflict of interest "'[to] be disclosed at the outset' than for it to 'come to light after the arbitration, when a suspicious or disgruntled party can seize on it as a pretext for invalidating the award'" (Quoting *Commonwealth Coatings Co. v. Continental Casualty Co. et al.*, Supreme Court of the United States, 18 November 1968, 89 S.Ct. 337).

195 *Halliburton Co. v. Chubb Bermuda Ins. Ltd.*, [2018] EWCA Civ 817, upheld by *Halliburton Co. v. Chubb Bermuda Ins. Ltd.*, [2020] UKSC 48. This will usually be the same point in time as the point in time when the arbitrator learns of the circumstance to be disclosed since the circumstance only needs to be disclosed if it is relevant.

196 Sutter-Somm/Hasenböhler/Leuenberger/S. Wullschleger, Art. 48 para. 3; KuKo ZPO/R. Kiener, Art. 48 para. 1, both on judges. See also, *Davidson (AP) v. Scottish Minister* [2004] UKHL 34, Lord Hope of Craighead, para. 54, stating that "the best safeguard against a challenge after the event, when the decision is known to be adverse to the litigant, lies in the opportunity of making a disclosure before the hearing starts. That is the proper time for testing the tribunal's impartiality".

197 L. Barrington, *FS Karrer*, p. 20.

198 L. Barrington, *FS Karrer*, p. 20.

199 C. Palo, *Bias of Arbitrator as Ground for Vacatur of Arbitration Award*, Sect. 12.

200 C. Palo, *Bias of Arbitrator as Ground for Vacatur of Arbitration Award*, Sect. 12.

dependence and partiality.[201] Generally, the standard of independence and impartiality and the scope of disclosure need to be differentiated. Disclosure helps to implement independence and impartiality. Nevertheless, measuring the damage of non-disclosure regarding independence and impartiality proves difficult.

7.1.4.1 Differentiation between Disclosure and the Applicable Standard of Independence and Impartiality

To clarify that the consequences of non-disclosure cannot be the same as for violating the requirement of independence and impartiality, the differences of disclosure and the standard of independence and impartiality need to be elaborated. In 2014, the *cour d'appel de* Paris addressed a claim seeking to sanction the breach of the obligation to disclose.[202] The court did not stop at analysing the consequences of any violation of the obligation to disclose but examined whether the undisclosed circumstance may give rise to justifiable doubts as to the arbitrator's independence and impartiality. Ultimately, the *cour d'appel* sanctioned the lack of independence and impartiality and not the non-disclosure.[203] The obligation to disclose is an instrument that serves and supports the principles of independence and impartiality, but the former is not absorbed by the latter.[204]

Although some decisions mix both concepts,[205] the differentiation established by French case law is to be welcomed. It respects the different purposes of both concepts. Disclosure provides information to the parties and supports their right to appoint or to challenge. Additionally, disclosure may foster the parties' confidence in the arbitral proceedings by providing information.[206] These elements are primarily in the interest of the parties. The need for disclosure must, therefore, include the parties' perspective.[207] Being in the parties'

201 See above chapter 4.2.1.6.

202 CA Paris, 14 October 2014, Rev. de l'Arb. 2015, 151-155.

203 This approach is confirmed in French case law by Cass civ 1ère, 4 May 2017, 15-29 158, Rev. de l'Arb. 2017, 770; Cass civ 1ére, 25 June 2014, 11-16.444, Rev. de l'Arb. 2015, 75-77. See also, Clay/Cadiet/T. Clay, Art. 1456 para. 70.

204 M. Henry, *Note - Cour d'appel de Paris, 14 octobre 2014, SA Auto Guadeloupe Investissements v. société Columbus Acquisitions Inc. et autres*, Rev. de l'Arb. 2015, 156-182, 159. The original wording is: "*[l]'obligation de révélation est un instrumentau service du respect de l'exigence d'indépendance et d'impartialité de l'arbitre et ne l'absorbe pas.*" This French approach is in line with some German case law, e.g., OLG Frankfurt a.M., 24 January 2019, 26 SchH 2/18, BeckRS 2019, 848; OLG München, 10 July 2013, 34 SchH 8/12, NJOZ 2014, 1779-1782.

205 E.g., *HSMV Corp. v. ADI Ltd.*, 72 F.Supp.2d 1122 (C.D. California 1999).

206 O. Froitzheim, *Die Ablehnung von Schiedsrichtern wegen Befangenheit in der internationalen Schiedsgerichtsbarkeit*, p. 148; A. Hoffmann, *Duty of Disclosure and Challenge of Arbitrators*, 3 Arb. Int'l 21 (2005), 427-436, 436.

207 See above chapter 7.1.1.3.3, on the subjective-objective perspective from the parties' point of view.

interest, one may posit that the obligation to disclose resides primarily in the contractual nature of arbitration.[208]

The general principle of independence and impartiality is much broader and ensures the equal treatment of the parties and their right to be heard. Independence and impartiality are preconditions for accepting arbitration as an alternative dispute resolution mechanism.[209] Independence and impartiality guarantee that no external facts and circumstances affect the decision-making process. Disclosure cannot affect the applicable standard of independence and impartiality. It does not enhance the applicable standard of independence and impartiality; it may, however, enhance the perception of independence and impartiality.[210] Following these different purposes and functions, the violation of both concepts cannot be conflated.[211]

7.1.4.2 Non-Disclosure May Hinder Independence and Impartiality

The failure to disclose relevant facts hinders independence and impartiality. It deprives the parties of both a practical means to protect against dependence and partiality,[212] and to appoint a suitable arbitrator.[213] Some authors categorise the obligation to disclose as an "ethical obligation".[214] The legal consequences attached to such an ethical obligation are different than those of the statutory and judicial obligation to be independent and impartial. If any non-disclosure leads to a successful challenge of the arbitrator or annulment of the award, the balance of both parties' interests would be destroyed, and features of the contractual nature of arbitration would be disregarded. Although disclosure ensures a party's right to challenge, the initial right to appoint a trusted and suitable arbitrator of the appointing party must also be respected. Only where the standard of independence and impartiality is not met, may a suitable arbitrator be challenged or the award annulled. Therefore, the legal consequences of challenge and annulment may only come into effect where the scenario in question violates the applicable standard of independence and impartiality.

---

208 See above chapter 1.3.2.

209 See above Introduction, on the fundamentality of independence and impartiality.

210 C. Rogers, *Regulating International Arbitrators: A Functional Approach to Developing Standards of Conduct*, Stanford J. Int'l L. 41 (2005), 53-121, 118. See also, T. Heintz/G. da Costa Cerquiera, *Vers une rationalisation de l'obligation de révélation de l'arbitre en droit français*, ASA Bull. 2013, 448-461, 448-461, who establish that disclosure controls independence and impartiality practically.

211 C. Palo, *Bias of Arbitrator as Ground for Vacatur of Arbitration Award*, Sect. 27. See generally, J.-F. Poudret/S. Besson, *Comparative Law of International Arbitration*, para. 429.

212 C. Palo, *Bias of Arbitrator as Ground for Vacatur of Arbitration Award*, Sect. 12.

213 The arbitrator's role is based on trust by the parties, cf. CA Paris, 18 December 2008, Rev. de l'Arb. 2011, 682-685.

214 E.g., K. Dotseth, *Disqualifying Arbitrators for Failure to Make Complete Disclosures After Scandinavian Re v. St. Paul Re: What Is "Evident Partiality"?*, Def. Coun. J. 79 (2012), 347-354, 352-353.

Concerning non-disclosure of scenarios that do not additionally violate the principles of independence and impartiality, the "self-policing function of each arbitration community"[215] provides for the appropriate consequences. If the parties do not trust an arbitrator, they will most likely not appoint him or her again in future proceedings. Likewise, the counsel in charge will not recommend the appointment of said arbitrator. Since the obligation to disclose contributes to the parties' confidence, and "information is a guarantee of confidence", the natural consequence of any failure to inform is the loss of confidence and, hence, the fact that the arbitrator may not be appointed again in future.[216]

Some scholars suggest that non-disclosure should be "indicative of a lack of independence",[217] and others posit that non-disclosure leads to an inference that the arbitrator needs to prove that no conflict exists.[218] However, both approaches commingle independence and impartiality with disclosure in a way that is not suggested by their different purposes. This becomes evident when evaluating both suggestions in case of non-disclosure of scenarios that do not additionally constitute a ground for finding dependence and partiality. Concluding that such non-disclosure indicates a lack of independence and impartiality bypasses the different standards and perspectives for disclosure on the one hand, and independence and impartiality on the other hand. A frustrated need for information that does not demonstrate the arbitrator's dependence and partiality could constitute a ground for challenge. Additionally, the second suggestion lacks a legal basis and contradicts most approaches calling for the party challenging an arbitrator to demonstrate justifiable doubts as to his or her independence and impartiality.

Finally, the ICC Note provides that

> although failure to disclose is not in itself a ground for disqualification, it will however be considered by the Court in assessing whether an objection to confirmation or a challenge is well founded.[219]

It is to be welcomed that the ICC Note clarifies that non-disclosure is in itself no ground for finding dependence and partiality. However, the second part of the sentence raises

215 K. Dotseth, *Disqualifying Arbitrators for Failure to Make Complete Disclosures After Scandinavian Re v. St. Paul Re: What Is "Evident Partiality"?*, Def. Coun. J. 79 (2012), 347-354, 352-353.

216 M. Henry, *Note - Cour d'appel de Paris, 14 octobre 2014, SA Auto Guadeloupe Investissements v. société Columbus Acquisitions Inc. et autres*, Rev. de l'Arb. 2015, 156-182, 165.

217 D. Hascher, *Independence and Impartiality of Arbitrators*, Am. U. Int'l L. Rev. 27 (2011-2012), 789-806, 800.

218 N. Allen/D. Mallett, *Arbitrator Disclosure*, Asian Int'l Arb. J. 7 (2011), 118-147, 126 et seq.

219 ICC Note, para. 26.

more questions than answers. It remains unclear what kind of role non-disclosure may play in ICC arbitration.[220]

7.1.4.3 Arbitrator's Liability

Finally, in limited scenarios some authors and case law favour more severe consequences for non-disclosure, demanding liability of the arbitrator for the failure to disclose.[221] Some scholars argue that in addition to the arbitrator, the party appointing the arbitrator, who failed to disclose, may be liable.[222] In the following, the arbitrators' liability, its contractual or judicial nature and limitation, and potential damages will be addressed.

7.1.4.3.1 Contractual and Judicial Liability and Its Limitation

French case law serves as an example for the contractual approach to the arbitrators' liability. In the French case *Société Raoul Duval v. V.*, the arbitrator V. failed to disclose. As a consequence of the failure to disclose, two awards rendered by V. were annulled by the *cour d'appel de* Paris.[223] Société Raoul Duval claimed damages including, inter alia, the costs of the arbitration.[224] The *cour d'appel de* Paris upheld the claim.[225] It rejected the argument that V. was protected by immunity, since, according to the court, the arbitrator is not vested with any official function.[226] The court highlighted the contractual nature of arbitration which entails liability.[227]

---

220 It may be arguable that the ICC Court adopts the German approach to grant a challenge where the arbitrator intentionally failed to disclose. See above chapter 4.2.1.6.

221 Particularly, French literature and case law discuss the arbitrator's liability here, see below n. 227 in this chapter. Even though some arguments are based on the application of French statutes, the general idea of holding the arbitrator liable for the failure to disclose may be generalised. As outlined above, the obligation to disclose is present in many different rules and laws, especially in Art. 12(1) UNCITRAL Model Law and Art. 11 UNCITRAL Arbitration Rules. See also, Stein/Jonas/P. Schlosser, § 1036 para. 69.

222 D. Hascher, *Independence and Impartiality of Arbitrators*, Am. U. Int'l L. Rev. 27 (2011-2012), 789-806, 794. "In the case of the non-disclosure of a fact that is known by the arbitrator and a party, shared liability between them could be considered. As between the parties, the other party may claim for a breach of the obligation of loyalty, which flows from the arbitration agreement."

223 CA Paris, 2 July 1992, Rev. de l'Arb. 1996, 411-410.

224 V. on the other hand relied on his alleged immunity and a mere exception of liability in case of gross negligence.

225 TGI Paris, 12 May 1993, Rev. de l'Arb. 1996, 410-411.

226 On the limits of immunity under French arbitration law, see also, C. Seraglini/J. Ortscheidt, *Droit de l'arbitrage interne et international*, para. 750.

227 TGI Paris, 12 May 1993, Rev. de l'Arb. 1996, 410-411, applying Art. 1142 French CC (*"Toute obligation de faire ou de ne pas faire se résout en dommages et intérêts en cas d'inexécution de la part du débiteur."*). The decision was affirmed on appeal, CA Paris, 12 October 1995, Rev. de l'Arb. 1999, 324-326. Also, the final attempt before the French *cour de cassation* to annul the decision was not successful, Cass civ 1ère, 16 December 1997, Rev. de l'Arb. 1999, 253. The decision is also welcomed by P. Fouchard, *Note - Cour d'appel de Paris (1re Ch. C) 12 octobre 1995 - V. v. société Raoul Duval*, Rev. de l'Arb. 1999, 327-328, 327. See generally on the arbitrator's liability, A. Salahuddin, *Should Arbitrators Be Immune from Liability?*, Arb. Int'l 33 (2017), 571-581, who favours a contractual liability.

Other French case law deals with the more general question of whether an arbitrator is liable for certain non-performances, and answers this question affirmatively.[228] However, these cases address situations where the parties explicitly agreed on the respective obligation in their arbitration agreement. For example, if the parties explicitly agree on the arbitrator's obligation to render an award in a certain period of time in the arbitration agreement, the violation of this obligation may entail liability of the arbitrator.[229]

Alternative to this French approach, i.e., basing liability on the contractual nature of arbitration, liability may arise from the judicial nature of arbitration. Qualifying the arbitrator as a "quasi-judicial officer"[230] one may apply those liability provisions applicable to judges to arbitrators. In line with this argument, some German scholars suggest determining liability based on Article 34 German GG, the provision applicable to judges.[231] However, following the approach that the obligation to disclose roots in the contractual nature of arbitration,[232] liability for non-disclosure should be contractual as well.[233] Other German scholars differentiate between a potential pre-contractual liability in the event the arbitrator fails to disclose before his or her appointment.[234] This approach resembles the argument suggested by Swiss scholars to treat the obligation to disclose as a pre-contractual obligation.[235]

Another question that may arise is that of limited liability and immunity.[236] Only few arbitration laws but many institutional rules directly address limitations in liability and

228 Cass civ 1ère, 6 December 2005, Rev. de l'Arb. 2006, 126-127. See generally, C. Jarrosson, *Note - Cour de cassation (1re Ch. civ.), 6 decembre 2005*, Rev. de l'Arb. 2006, 127-138.

229 Cass civ 1ère, 6 December 2005, Rev. de l'Arb. 2006, 126-127. The decision led to a discussion in literature on the nature of the arbitrator's obligation towards the parties. See generally, C. Jarrosson, *Note - Cour de cassation (1re Ch. civ.), 6 decembre 2005*, Rev. de l'Arb. 2006, 127-138.

230 *Hoosac Tunnel Dock & Elevator v. O'Brien*, 137 Mass 424 (1884), 426.

231 Zöller/R. Geimer, § 1036 para. 17. Art. 34 German GG reads: "*Verletzt jemand in Ausübung eines ihm anvertrauten öffentlichen Amtes die ihm einem Dritten gegenüber obliegende Amtspflicht, so trifft die Verantwortlichkeit grundsätzlich den Staat oder die Körperschaft, in deren Dienst er steht. Bei Vorsatz oder grober Fahrlässigkeit bleibt der Rückgriff vorbehalten. Für den Anspruch auf Schadensersatz und für den Rückgriff darf der ordentliche Rechtsweg nicht ausgeschlossen werden.*" Translation: "If any person, in the exercise of a public office entrusted to him, violates his official duty to a third party, liability shall rest principally with the state or public body that employs him. In the event of intentional wrongdoing or gross negligence, the right of recourse against the individual officer shall be preserved. The ordinary courts shall not be closed to claims for compensation or indemnity."

232 See above chapters 7.1.4.1 and 1.3.2.

233 BeckOK ZPO/C. Wolf/N. Eslami, § 1036 para. 21; MünchKomm ZPO/J. Münch, § 1036 para. 23.

234 Musielak/Voirt/W. Voit, § 1036 para. 3, on *culpa in contrahendo.*

235 See above chapter 7.1.1.1 on Swiss law, and also, N. Voser/E. Fischer, *The Arbitral Tribunal*, p. 66.

236 Generally on immunity, see A. Salahuddin, *Should Arbitrators Be Immune from Liability?*, Arb. Int'l 33 (2017), 571-581.

immunity.[237] An argument in favour of limited liability and immunity applicable to arbitrators is that exposing arbitrators to liability in damages would undermine their impartiality and independence[238] in decision-making. Thus, the judicial nature of arbitration may include the arbitrator's immunity or limited liability. It is debatable whether this conclusion calls for implicit limited liability or immunity where no provision or agreement requires it. The primarily contractual nature of disclosure does not favour an implicit limited liability or immunity of arbitrators. Judges' immunity is, inter alia, rooted in the idea that their work is in the public interest and their independence and impartiality require institutional protection. These two ideas do not apply to the same extent to arbitrators. To the contrary, the parties' interest in protecting their confidence and trust in their chosen arbitrator may demand unlimited liability where this trust and confidence is frustrated. Therefore, in the event no explicit limitation of liability or immunity applies, the contractual nature of disclosure may call for an unlimited liability.

7.1.4.3.2 Damages

The French case *Société Raoul Duval v. V.* addressed only the issue of additional consequences where non-disclosure is material, i.e., the undisclosed scenario violates independence and impartiality. In this case, if the award is annulled, the resulting damages may include the costs of the arbitration[239] and damages caused by delay.[240] Where the party requesting damages is aware of the undisclosed circumstance, a claim for damages will usually lack causality.[241] Regarding the purpose of disclosure, inter alia, to inform the parties and to establish confidence and trust in the arbitrators, one may question whether immaterial damages are recoverable. Likewise, a party may argue that the mere frustration of its right to appoint constitutes a damage. The recoverability of these immaterial damages depends on the applicable law. However, there may be difficulties regarding causality. The argument that the party relying on the violation of disclosure would have objected to or

---

237 E.g., Sect. 98W Hong Kong AO, which provides: "(1) A failure to comply with this Division does not, of itself, render any person liable to any judicial or other proceedings. (2) However, any compliance, or failure to comply, with this Division may be taken into account by any court or arbitral tribunal if it is relevant to a question being decided by the court or arbitral tribunal." See also, Sect. 29 EAA and Sect. 14 UAA; Art. 46.1 HKIAC Rules; Art. 41 ICC Rules; Art. 38 ICDR Rules; Art. 31.1 LCIA Rules; Art. 52 SCC Rules; Art. 38.1 SIAC Rules; Art. 45(1) Swiss Rules.

238 *Malik v. Ruttenberg*, 398 N.J. Super. 489 (N.J. Super. Ct. App. Div. 2008), 496, stating that the doctrine of immunity "is supported by a long-settled understanding that the independent and impartial exercise of judgment vital to the judiciary might be impaired by exposure to potential damages liability", with further references.

239 Stein/Jonas/P. Schlosser, § 1036 paras. 69, 72. According to Schlosser, the liability limitation of § 839(2) German BGB, applicable to judges, does not apply to arbitrators.

240 Musielak/Voit/W. Voit, § 1036 para. 3. Additional difficulties of calculating damages are outlined in C. Jarrosson, *A propos de l'obligation de révélation*, Rev. de l'Arb. 2013, 130-137, 133-134.

241 Musielak/Voit/W. Voit, § 1036 para. 3.

challenged the arbitrator in question – if the arbitrator had disclosed – and that the objection or challenge would have led to excluding the arbitrator will be difficult on a factual and legal basis.

Where non-disclosure is not material and does not lead to a successful challenge or annulment, it will be difficult to demonstrate any damages.

7.1.5 *The Obligation to Investigate*

Finally, some case law and authors suggest that there is not only an obligation to disclose, but additionally an obligation to investigate. Theoretically, there may be an obligation to investigate for the arbitrator, the parties, and probably even any involved institution.[242]

Corresponding to the arbitrator's obligation to disclose, it is arguable that the parties bear an obligation to investigate. Following the French approach of the scope of disclosure excluding "notorious" information, or United States case law merely requiring the arbitrator to put the parties "on notice", the parties have an obligation to perform due diligence,[243] i.e., to at least conduct a cursory internet search on the arbitrators' names.[244] In the words of two Swiss authors, who favour requiring an obligation to investigate, "[o]nly justifiable reliance is worthy of protection".[245]

The potential arbitrator's obligation to investigate may be a consequence, or specification, of the obligation to disclose. The arbitrator may have both, the obligation to investigate and the obligation to disclose "his reasons for believing there might be a conflict and [even] his intention not to investigate".[246] Such an obligation may derive from the need for trust

242 Depending on the applicable laws and rules. Any potential obligation to investigate of institutions will not be addressed here.

243 R. Glick/L. Stipanowich, *Arbitrator Disclosure in the Internet Age, Some Guidance Concerning the Obligation to Disclose Internet Activity and Online Relationships*, Disp. Res. J. 67 (2012), 1-7, 6.

244 M. Henry, *Note – Cour d'appel de Paris, 14 octobre 2014, SA Auto Guadeloupe Investissements v. société Columbus Acquisitions Inc. et autres*, Rev. de l'Arb. 2015, 156-182, 168, however, stating that this would not amount in "a duty to deeply investigate". ("*Les diligences attendues des parties sont des diligences mineures ('googlisation', consultation du site du cabinet) mais ne sauraient couvrir des recherches approfondies sauf à vider l'obligation de révélation de son contenu : les parties n'ont pas à se transformer en détectives.*") In the same direction *Power Services Associates, Inc. v. UNC Metcalf Servicing, Inc.*, 338 F.Supp.2d 1375 (N.D. Georgia 2004).

245 B. Berger/F. Kellerhals, *International and Domestic Arbitration in Switzerland*, para. 814.

246 C. Palo, *Bias of Arbitrator as Ground for Vacatur of Arbitration Award*, Sect. 15, concluding that "[w]hile the mere failure to investigate is not, by itself, sufficient to vacate an arbitration award, when an arbitrator knows of a potential conflict, a failure to either investigate or disclose an intention not to investigate is

between the parties and the arbitrators, similar to the purpose of the obligation to disclose.[247] Thus, some scholars suggest that the IBA Guidelines 2014 should explicitly include such "reasonable attempts to investigate".[248]

7.1.5.1 Parties' Obligation to Investigate

Case law from France, Switzerland, and the United States applies a theoretical approach of an obligation to investigate. French case law does not explicitly refer to an obligation to investigate but positively notes where parties do some research on their arbitrators.[249] Court decisions from the United States welcome parties to research their arbitrators – usually in cases where the parties failed to research, and the prerequisites of a waiver are analysed. For example, parties are required to "dig" for possible annulment grounds during the arbitration and their failure to do so may constitute a waiver.[250] Therefore, awards should not be annulled

> because of undisclosed relationships where the complaining party should have known of the relationship, or could have learned of the relationship "just as easily before or during the arbitration rather than after it lost its case".[251]

In order to preserve "failure-to-disclose-type challenges to an arbitration award, the parties simply need to exercise as much diligence and tenacity in ferreting out potential conflicts ex ante".[252] Swiss case law analyses the obligation to investigate in connection to waiver as well. Under Swiss case law, the time for raising an objection starts to run when the party could have been aware of the objectionable facts.[253] Swiss case law seems to establish an obligation to investigate – "a duty to be suspicious".[254] The relevant point in time for

indicative of evident partiality". *Applied Industrial Materials Co. v. Ovalar Makine Ticaret Ve Sanayi, A.S. and Ural Ataman*, Docket No. 06-3297-cv (2d Cir. 9 July 2007), was cited here.

247 BGer, 9 October 2012, 4A_110/2012, ASA Bull. 2013, 174-193, referring to "*devoir de curiosité*". See also, C. Müller, *Swiss Case Law in International Arbitration*, Art. 180 para. 1.3.8. But see, BGer, 29 October 2010, BGE 136 III 605, 618.

248 N. Allen/D. Mallett, *Arbitrator Disclosure*, Asian Int'l Arb. J. 7 (2011), 118-147, 136 et seq.

249 CA Reims, 2 November 2011, Rev. de l'Arb. 2012, 112-119. The decision was later annulled. However, another French decision, CA Paris, 14 October 2014, Rev. de l'Arb. 2015, 151-155, clarifies that the parties may only reasonably be obliged to research publicly known information before the commencement of the arbitration. In sum, it is far-fetched to speak of a proper obligation to investigate under French law.

250 *Andros Compania Maritima, SA v. Marc Rich & Co., AG*, 579 F.2d 691 (2d Cir. 1978), reasoning that the award-debtor could have been aware of the fact. The wording and the legal consequences remind the reader of negligence.

251 *Certain Underwriting Members of Lloyds of London v. Florida*, 2018 WL 2727492 (2d Cir.), citing *Lucent Technologies Inc. v. Tatung Co.*, 379 F.3d 24 (2d Cir. 2004).

252 *Stone v. Bear, Stearns & Co., Inc.*, 872 F.Supp.2d 435 (E.D. Pennsylvania 2012).

253 BGer, 27 May 2003, BGE 129 III 445, 449-465.

254 BGer, 9 October 2012, 4A_110/2012, ASA Bull. 2013, 174-193.

complying with this obligation to investigate is the nomination of the arbitrator, since the parties have to ensure that the arbitral process is not disturbed later.[255] The legal consequence of failing to comply with the obligation is the waiver of the right to rely on the facts that could have been investigated, but were not.[256] The obligation is based on a concept of good faith.[257]

In sum, there is not much case law constituting a real obligation to investigate. Swiss and United States case law point in the direction of constituting a waiver resulting from the parties' failure to investigate circumstances they could have been aware of. The types of actions and inactions which constitute waiver will be analysed in detail below. Clarifying what kind of circumstances parties may need to investigate, the references to "suspicion" and "failure-to-disclose-type of challenges" in Swiss and United States case law give guidance. These circumstances can only be those that are detectable for the parties, and they should have an idea of the existence of the circumstance. Thus, this case law must be applied in the context of the arbitrator's obligation to put the parties "on notice".[258]

7.1.5.2 Arbitrators' Obligation to Investigate

Some case law arguably suggests an obligation to investigate for the arbitrator. The England and Wales High Court of Justice lauded an arbitrator for carrying out conflict checks and disclosing "where the checks drew matters to his attention".[259] However, the High Court of Justice rejected a request to annul the award arguing that the arbitrator would have disclosed the matter if it had crossed his mind. Interpreting the U.S. Supreme Court's decision in *Commonwealth Coatings Corp. v. Continental Casualty Co. et al.*,[260] the U.S. Court of Appeals, Second Circuit, ruled that "arbitrators must take steps to ensure that the parties are not misled into believing that no nontrivial conflict exist", and, hence, where the arbitrator thinks that a non-trivial conflict may exist he must investigate the conflict or disclose his reasons for believing there may be a conflict, and his intention not to investigate.[261] However, the U.S. Court of Appeals further clarified that this interpretation does not create a "free-standing duty to investigate". Rather, the decision is based on a failure to disclose, adding that the arbitrator should have been aware of the materiality of

255 BGer, 15 October 2001, 4P.188/2001, para. C 2b-2d.
256 B. Berger/F. Kellerhals, *International and Domestic Arbitration in Switzerland*, para. 814.
257 BGer, 21 November 2003, BGE 130 III 66, 75.
258 R. Glick/L. Stipanowich, *Arbitrator Disclosure in the Internet Age, Some Guidance Concerning the Obligation to Disclose Internet Activity and Online Relationships*, Disp. Res. J. 67 (2012), 1-7, 6.
259 *W Ltd. v. M Sdn Bhd.*, [2016] 1 CLC 437, 438.
260 *Commonwealth Coatings Co. v. Continental Casualty Co. et al.*, 89 S.Ct. 337 (1968).
261 In general, *Applied Industrial Materials Co. v. Ovalar Makine Ticaret Ve Sanayi, A.S. and Ural Ataman*, Docket No. 06-3297-cv (2d Cir. 9 July 2007).

the undisclosed facts.[262] Additionally, and according to United States case law, any violation of the obligation to investigate does not by itself allow the annulment of an arbitral award.[263] Therefore, there is no separate obligation to investigate stipulated in case law.[264]

Furthermore, one may deduce an obligation to investigate from General Standard 7(d) IBA Guidelines 2014:

> An arbitrator is under a duty to make reasonable enquiries to identify any conflict of interest, as well as any facts or circumstances that may reasonably give rise to doubts as to his or her impartiality or independence. Failure to disclose a conflict is not excused by lack of knowledge, if the arbitrator does not perform such reasonable enquiries.[265]

It is, however, difficult to clarify what exactly "reasonable enquiries" are, and whether these go beyond the arbitrator's obligation to disclose. When the arbitrator submits a statement of independence and impartiality, he or she will have to go through the past encounters with the parties, counsels, and co-arbitrators involved. Any separate obligation for additional research, e.g., on the parties' group of companies and internal structure, exceeds what is demanded.[266] The interrelation of the obligation to disclose and the need to investigate was exemplified by the U.K. Supreme Court:

> An arbitrator can disclose only what he or she knows and is, as a generality, not required to search for facts or circumstances to disclose. But I do not rule out the possibility of circumstances occurring in which an arbitrator would be under a duty to make reasonable enquiries in order to comply with the duty of disclosure. For example, if a would-be arbitrator had a business relationship

262 Another decision that mixes up the obligation to investigate and the obligation to disclose is *HSMV Corp. v. ADI Ltd.*, 72 F.Supp.2d 1122 (C.D. California 1999). Again, worth mentioning here is *Schmitz v. Zilveti*, 20 F.3d 1043 (9th Cir. 1994), where an applicable provision, NASD Code of Arbitration, Sect. 23(a), (b), required the arbitrator to make an investigation.

263 *Al-Harbi v. Citibank*, 85 F.3d 680 (D.C. Cir. 1996); S. Feldman, *Contract Law and Practice*, Sect. 14:35.

264 Where the parties agree explicitly on an obligation to investigate, the conclusion will be different. Cf. *Gianelli Money Purchase Plan and Trust v. ADM Investor Services Inc.*, 146 F.3d 1309 (11th Cir. 1998), on the importance of the parties' agreement.

265 Similarly, Canon II B AAA/ABA Code of Ethics provides: "Persons who are requested to accept appointment as arbitrators should make a reasonable effort to inform themselves of any interests or relationships described."

266 This may be different in regard to the involvement of third-party funders. Where the favoured approach of disclosing third-party funding through the means of requesting the parties to disclose is accepted, the arbitrator should ask the parties whether they receive funding. See J. von Goeler, *Third-party Funding*, pp. 278-280.

> with a person (A), which, because of a financial interest, would have prevented him from being an arbitrator in a reference in which A was a party, he or she, if offered an appointment in an arbitration in which B was a party, might be under an obligation to make enquiry if he or she had grounds to think that B might a business partner of A.[267]

7.2 RIGHT TO OBJECT AND WAIVER

If the arbitrator or any other involved person discloses prior to appointment, the parties may object to the appointment.[268] If the party fails to object, it may be deemed to have waived its right to rely on the disclosed information and later challenge the arbitrator or other person, or request annulment. Waiver usually requires a certain degree of knowledge, a lapse of a specific period of time and, may additionally require a certain form. For example, the IBA Guidelines 2014 provide as follows:

> If, within 30 days after the receipt of any disclosure by the arbitrator, or after a party otherwise learns of facts or circumstances that could constitute a potential conflict of interest for an arbitrator, a party does not raise an express objection with regard to that arbitrator, subject to paragraphs (b) and (c) of this General Standard, the party is deemed to have waived any potential conflict of interest in respect of the arbitrator based on such facts or circumstances and may not raise any objection based on such facts or circumstances at a later stage.[269]

Parties may not challenge the arbitrator or request annulment of the award on the grounds of previously disclosed facts where the parties did not object to the disclosed facts.[270] The obligation to disclose has, inter alia, the purpose to enable the parties to use their right to challenge.[271] If the parties consciously do not use their right to challenge, i.e., if they refrain from objecting,[272] their silence may be interpreted as an acceptance. Independence and

267 *Halliburton Co. v. Chubb Bermuda Ins. Ltd.*, [2020] UKSC 48, Lord Hodge, para. 107.

268 Practically, a party will not object to the arbitrator it nominated but withdraw the nomination.

269 General Standard 4(a) IBA Guidelines 2014. General Standard 4(b) excludes all circumstances listed on the Non-Waivable Red List in Part II, IBA Guidelines 2014 and General Standard 4(c) clarifies that circumstances listed on the Waivable Red List may not be waived in advance and need to be waived expressly. See also, Art. 32 HKIAC Rules; Art. 40 ICC Rules; Art. 28.1 JAMS Rules; rather limited Art. 32.1 LCIA Rules; Art. 36 SCC Rules; Art. 41.1 SIAC Rules; Art. 30 Swiss Rules.

270 *Washburn v. McManus*, 895 F.Supp. 392 (D. Connecticut 1994); BGer, 28 April 2000, BGE 126 III 249.

271 CA Paris, 9 September 2010, ASA Bull. 2011, 187-192, 191 et seq.

272 Alternatively to refraining from objections, parties may even positively agree on the continuous service of the questioned arbitrator, cf. *Questar Capital Corp. v. Gorter*, 909 F.Supp.2d 789 (W.D. Kentucky 2012).

impartiality in arbitration are also in the parties' interest, and thus, they may waive.[273] The concept of waiver includes the idea that whoever allows a biased arbitrator to rule experiences no injustice.[274] It forbids a "heads we win and tails you lose" position.[275] The concept intends to uphold openness and fair dealing between the parties.[276] Generally, it only applies in cases where an arbitrator disclosed facts, not in cases of non-disclosure.[277]

The extent of any waiver in regard to independence and impartiality is limited by the scope of the disclosure, primarily laid down in the applicable laws, rules, and case law. The arbitrator needs to disclose facts that are likely to raise doubts of his or her independence and impartiality.[278] The following overview addresses different approaches on knowledge of the waived facts and the lack of timely objection. Thereafter, the particular issues of waiver in regard to cumulated grounds and advance waiver will be addressed.

7.2.1 *Knowledge of the Waived Fact*

The first prerequisite of a waiver is that the party waiving its right to challenge or annul was aware of the facts. "Waiver requires properly informed consent, and thus disclosure of the conflict of interest."[279] Usually, full and positive knowledge is required.[280] However, it is questionable whether facts and information that are already public or easily accessible to the parties need to be disclosed. French courts have ruled repeatedly on this issue. According to French case law, "notorious" information may not create a conflict of

273 D. Hascher, *Independence and Impartiality of Arbitrators*, Am. U. Int'l L. Rev. 27 (2011-2012), 789-806, 793.

274 Zöller/R. Geimer, § 1036 para. 6.

275 *ASM Shipping Ltd. of India v. TTMI Ltd. of England*, [2005] EWHC 2238 (Comm), on Sect. 73 EAA. A party cannot remain silent as to perceived or actual partiality or bias and then later object after the panel reaches an unfavourable decision, *Questar Capital Corp. v. Gorter*, 909 F.Supp.2d 789 (W.D. Kentucky 2012).

276 *Dera Commercial Estate v. Derya Inc.*, [2018] EWHC 1673 (Comm).

277 But see, above chapter 7.1.5.1, some approaches on the requirement of the party's investigation.

278 CA Paris, 12 February 2009, Rev. de l'Arb. 2009, 186-190; *Halliburton Co. v. Chubb Bermuda Ins. Ltd.*, [2018] EWCA Civ 817, upheld by *Halliburton Co. v. Chubb Bermuda Ins. Ltd.*, [2020] UKSC 48; C. Seraglini/ J. Ortscheidt, *Droit de l'arbitrage interne et international*, para. 231.

279 *Halliburton Co. v. Chubb Bermuda Ins. Ltd.*, [2020] UKSC 48, Lady Arden, para. 167.

280 OLG Frankfurt a.M., 13 February 2012, 26 SchH 15/11, BeckRS 2014, 12067, para. II. In this regard also *Questar Capital Corp. v. Gorter*, 909 F.Supp.2d 789 (W.D. Kentucky 2012); *Apperson v. Fleet Carrier Co.*, 879 F.2d 1344 (6th Cir. 1989); CA Paris, 18 November 2004, Rev. de l'Arb. 2004, 989; C. Seraglini/ J. Ortscheidt, *Droit de l'arbitrage interne et international*, paras. 735-737.

interest[281] and, hence, does not need to be disclosed.[282] Similarly, Swiss case law asks parties to be "suspicious".[283] The time for raising an objection starts to run when the party could have been aware of the objectionable facts.[284]

United States courts are split, applying two opposing standards to evaluate the knowledge required to constitute a waiver: either the "actual knowledge" standard,[285] i.e., all information has to be disclosed, or the "on notice" standard,[286] i.e., inquiring whether the objecting party was "on notice" and had sufficient information to object.[287] This dispute about the exact standard of knowledge is highly important: does the waiver doctrine apply only when the waiving party had actual knowledge of the facts or is it enough that it was put on notice and should have been aware of the facts? Some English case law favour the "on notice" standard, but they call it "reasonable due diligence".[288]

Applying the "on notice" or "notorious fact" standard, the burden of verifying the arbitrator's ties with the parties and third parties is shifted partly onto the parties' shoulders. The parties are required to react to the information by doing further research.[289] Where the arbitrator appointed by the claimant disclosed that "[he] served on panel [sic] of three arbitrators that considered a dispute between [claimant] and another party", and the respondent failed to inquire further information but acknowledged this disclosure, the latter was put on notice.[290]

Linked to this discussion and like the "on notice" standard, some courts in the United States ruled that a party may have "constructive knowledge" of a fact leading to a waiver.[291]

---

281 CA Paris, 14 October 2014, Rev. de l'Arb. 2015, 151-155, 154. Cf. CA Paris, 12 April 2016, Rev. de l'Arb. 2017, 234-240, the final decision in the so-called "Tecnimont Saga". See also, Arts. 1456(2) and 1466 French Code of Civil Procedure.

282 CA Paris, 13 March 2008, 06/12878; *N. Bouchardie/C. Tran, Arbitration in France*, Practice Note 4-536-9585 (2018).

283 BGer, 9 October 2012, 4A_110/2012.

284 BGer, 27 May 2003, BGE 129 III 445, 449-465.

285 *Positive Software Solutions, Inc. v. New Century Mortg. Corp.*, 476 F.3d 278 (5th Cir. 2007); in this regard also *Middlesex Mut. Ins. Co. v. Levine*, 675 F.2d 1197 (11th Cir. 1982).

286 *Lummus Global Amazonas S.A. v. Aguaytia Energy del Peru SR Ltda.*, 256 F.Supp.2d 594 (S.D. Texas 2002).

287 For a general overview on both, see *Dealer Computer Services, Inc. v. Michael Motor Co., Inc.*, 761 F.Supp.2d 459 (S.D. Texas 2010), in the end in applying the "on notice" standard. The decision was rejected on appeal, *Dealer Computer Services, Inc. v. Michael Motor Co., Inc.*, 485 Fed.Appx. 724 (5th Cir. 2012). Also, in favour of the "on notice" standard, *Stone v. Bear, Stearns & Co., Inc.*, 872 F.Supp.2d 435 (E.D. Pennsylvania 2012).

288 LCIA Reference No. 81224, LCIA Court, 15 March 2010, Arb. Int'l 27 (2011), 461-470.

289 C. Fouchard, *Tecnimont Saga: Episode V – The Paris Court Strikes Back.*

290 *Dealer Computer Services, Inc. v. Michael Motor Co., Inc.*, 485 Fed.Appx. 724 (5th Cir. 2012).

291 *Fidelity Federal Bank, FSB v. Durga Ma Co.*, 386 F.3d 1306 (9th Cir. 2004). Cf. *Schmitz v. Zilveti*, 20 F.3d 1043 (9th Cir. 1994).

The concept of "constructive knowledge" is applied in non-disclosure cases, arguing that the party challenging the arbitrator or requesting annulment of the award had constructive knowledge of the facts and, hence, waived its right to do so. Constructive knowledge is defined as the "[k]nowledge that one using reasonable care or diligence should have, and therefore is attributed by law to a given person".[292] According to the U.S. Court of Appeals, Third Circuit, in *Goldman, Sachs & Co. v. Athena Venture Partners, L.P.*,

> [t]he rationale for applying constructive knowledge in the arbitration context makes good sense. It both encourages parties to conduct adequate due diligence prior to issuance of the award and promotes the arbitration goals of efficiency and finality.[293]

A potential criticism of this term is based on its concrete application: Where is the exact line for constructive knowledge? May the simple fact that the arbitrators agreed to be independent and impartial, and the parties' consent accordingly put both parties on notice for potential conflicts of interest? In *Fidelity Federal Bank, FSB v. Durga Ma Co.*, the U.S. Court of Appeals, Ninth Circuit, ruled that

> [t]here is no charge or evidence of actual bias and no indication that the arbitration award was anything but fair. A rule that places the burden on parties to obtain disclosure statements from arbitrators who were initially party-appointed but later agree to act neutrally is consistent with our policy favoring the finality of arbitration awards.[294]

The most crucial aspect is, however, not to erode the obligation to disclose with the concept of constructive knowledge. The cited case law may be explained in the context of its facts. In *Fidelity Federal Bank, FSB v. Durga Ma Co.*, the parties commenced the domestic arbitration under the AAA Rules in 1999, when the AAA Rules included the default rule of non-neutral party-appointed arbitrators. The parties agreed to have neutral party-appointed arbitrators after the constitution of the tribunal. Hence, the court ruled that the parties initially appointed their arbitrators as non-neutrals. Ties to non-neutral party-appointed arbitrators were common in domestic arbitration in the United States. In *Goldman, Sachs & Co. v. Athena Venture Partners, L.P.*, the institution even informed the parties during the arbitration about the fact that one of the tribunal members was charged with the unauthorised practice of law but neither party requested additional

292 *Goldman, Sachs & Co. v. Athena Venture Partners, L.P.*, 803 F.3d 144 (3d Cir. 2015).
293 *Goldman, Sachs & Co. v. Athena Venture Partners, L.P.*, 803 F.3d 144 (3d Cir. 2015).
294 *Fidelity Federal Bank, FSB v. Durga Ma Co.*, 386 F.3d 1306 (9th Cir. 2004).

information. The facts underpin the impression that the award-debtor did some research to annul the award after it was rendered. Both cases are, therefore, individual and may not be generalised. The possibility to apply and argue constructive knowledge is limited.

7.2.2 *Lack of Timely Objection*

Another prerequisite to constitute a waiver is the failure to make a timely objection. Parties are generally required to object timely, or "as soon as possible".[295] The Swiss *Bundesgericht* clarified that as the arbitration proceeds, the urgency for the obligation to object increases, providing less time to object in a late phase of the arbitration.[296] *Thomas Kinkade Co. v. White* also addressed how to object in the event of late disclosure. According to the court, the underlying issue in case of late disclosure and late objection is that the party challenging risks "offending the neutral" arbitrator with the challenge.[297] The party opposing the disclosure is in a "catch-22 situation": either it objects and bears the risk of offending the arbitrator or it refrains from objecting and appears to "condone a clear conflict".[298] However, the U.S. Court of Appeals, Sixth Circuit, explicitly stated that in this special case the claimant had "good reason to think that [the arbitrator] would resent [claimant] for scuttling it".[299] Thus, whether such a risk exists depends on the concrete facts.

Some rules and laws precisely name the period of time for objecting, especially in regard to the challenge of the arbitrator, e.g., two weeks,[300] ten or fifteen days,[301] thirty days.[302]

---

295 BGer, 28 April 2000, BGE 126 III 249, 253-256; BGer, 9 February 1998, ASA Bull. 1998, 634-652, 646; BGer, 9 April 1998, BGE 124 I 121, 123-126. Not all rules and laws provide for a specific period of time to object. E.g., Art. 180(2) Swiss IPRG; Art. 1466 French CPC; R-41 AAA Rules do not provide a concrete period of time.

296 BGer, 10 June 2003, 4P.263/2002/ech, para. C 4.3-6.1, explaining this rule with the need for efficiency of the proceedings and a special obligation of care of the parties towards the end of the proceedings, obliging them to collaborate in order to make it possible for the award to be rendered in a reasonable time. See also, BGer, 28 April 2000, BGE 126 III 249. According to the decision, 24 months is not timely.

297 *Thomas Kinkade Co. v. White*, 711 F.3d 719 (6th Cir. 2013), on domestic arbitration.

298 *Thomas Kinkade Co. v. White*, 711 F.3d 719 (6th Cir. 2013), on domestic arbitration.

299 *Thomas Kinkade Co. v. White*, 711 F.3d 719 (6th Cir. 2013), on domestic arbitration.

300 E.g., in § 1037(2) German ZPO; Art. 15.2 DIS Rules; Art. 10.2 LCIA Rules (14 days).

301 E.g., Art. 32(1), (3) CIETAC Rules; Art. 11.7 HKIAC Rules.

302 E.g., General Standard 4(a) IBA Guidelines 2014; Art. 14(2) ICC Rules.

Often, the objection needs to be made expressly,[303] i.e., in writing.[304] Finally, all waivers in civil procedure need to be made freely.[305]

7.2.3 *Waiver in Regard to Cumulated Grounds*

Timely and sufficient objection is difficult to analyse where different grounds for challenge or annulment only cumulatively meet the threshold of dependence and partiality.[306] French courts were faced with such a scenario in the so-called "Tecnimont Saga".[307] In five decisions, the two companies Avax and Tecnimont disputed over the annulment of a partial award on liability. Before the award was rendered, Avax filed a challenge before the ICC Court of Arbitration in accordance with Article 14 ICC Rules (Art. 11 ICC Rules previous version). The challenge was based on undisclosed dealings between the presiding arbitrator's law firm and Tecnimont. It was filed after the time limit of thirty days from the date when the party making the challenge was informed of the facts elapsed, according to Article 14(2) ICC Rules.[308] Avax continued to participate, but reserved its right to challenge and annul later. Meanwhile, additional relationships between the presiding arbitrator's law firm and Tecnimont's affiliated companies came to light. Avax, hence, requested annulment, first, before the *cour d'appel de* Paris,[309] second, before the French *cour de cassation*,[310] third, before the *cour d'appel de* Reims,[311] again, before the French *cour de cassation*[312] and finally, before the *cour d'appel de* Paris.[313]

303 E.g., Art. 10 CIETAC Rules; Rule 3.816(a) 2019 California Rules of Court. Criticising the requirement of an express objection, G. Born, *International Commercial Arbitration*, p. 1980. According to Born, there is a risk that formal challenges may be held back and used for delay in the end. However, where no express objection is required, parties may lose their right to challenge too fast. The requirements of an express objection or not must be seen in connection with the scope of disclosure to be applied and the prerequisites of knowledge for constituting a waiver.

304 E.g., R-41 AAA Rules.

305 M. Benedettelli, *Human Rights as a Litigation Tool in International Arbitration*, Arb. Int'l 31 (2015), 631-659, 650.

306 On cumulation of grounds in general, see above chapter 5.6.

307 C. Fouchard, *Tecnimont Saga: Episode V – The Paris Court Strikes Back.*

308 The ICC Court of Arbitration dismissed the challenge. For a good overview of the facts, see CA Reims, 2 November 2011, Rev. de l'Arb. 2012, 112-119, 112-117. This is the third decision of the Tecnimont Saga.

309 CA Paris, 12 February 2009, Rev. de l'Arb. 2009, 186-190. The annulment action was based on irregular composition of the tribunal, now regulated in Art. 1492(2) French CPC. The court annulled the partial award.

310 Cass civ 1ère, 4 November 2010, 09-12716, reversing the previous decision since most grounds raised by Avax were already disclosed prior to initial challenge before the ICC.

311 CA Reims, 2 November 2011, Rev. de l'Arb. 2012, 112-119. The court again annulled the partial award.

312 Cass civ 1ère, 25 June 2014, 11-26529, again reversed the previous decision.

313 CA Paris, 12 April 2016, Rev. de l'Arb. 2017, 234-240.

The main issue was whether Avax adhered to the time limits stipulated in the ICC Rules. Avax argued that even though it may have failed to comply with the time limit regarding its first challenge before the ICC Court of Arbitration, it complied with the time limit regarding the new grounds that came to light later. The French *cour de cassation* held in its second decision that the lower court needed to verify for each individual fact whether the challenge was on time. The *cour d'appel de* Paris, in its second decision, applied this method and concluded that the challenge was not timely since the facts that Avax allegedly discovered after the time limit elapsed were public knowledge and easily accessible. Additionally, the facts discovered after the time limit elapsed did not have the effect of aggravating the doubts on independence and impartiality.[314] The *cour d'appel de* Paris concluded that Avax waived its right to rely on the grounds.

In light of the general approach to allow cumulation of grounds,[315] it is questionable whether the approach of the French *cour de cassation* to calculate the period of time for each ground individually can be generalised. Practically it will often be too late to challenge. The purpose of allowing cumulation of grounds, i.e., to respect the parties' need for confidence in the arbitral tribunal and not accept a tribunal that repeatedly provided small impressions of dependence and partiality, is undermined. However, regarding the Tecnimont Saga, its individual facts need to be considered. The *cour d'appel de* Paris found, first, the other facts were already public and known by Avax, and, second, that they did not have the effect of aggravating the doubts on independence and impartiality. Where either is not the case, the outcome may be different in order to assure the method of cumulating grounds.[316]

7.2.4 *Advance Waiver*

The consequences of a waiver, i.e., acknowledging the concrete circumstances and excluding these circumstances from the list of potential grounds for challenge or annulment, raises the question of whether the person requested to disclose can ask for an advance waiver. Such an advance waiver includes information on circumstances that might later need to be disclosed. The scenario could be, for example, that before his or her appointment, an arbitrator must disclose to the parties any circumstances likely to give rise to justifiable doubts as to his or her impartiality or independence. The presiding arbitrator is a partner

314 Cass civ 1ère, 25 June 2014, 11-26529, also clarifying that the time limits of the chosen procedural rules apply.
315 See above chapter 5.4.
316 Another similar issue is that of reiterated conduct and the relevant point in time to object.

in a global law firm,[317] and one of its offices in another country recently participated in a law firm pitch for one of respondent's sister companies. The pitch concerned legal services unrelated to the dispute. Since there is no significant financial relationship between respondent and its sister company, and it is the firm's office in another country that provided the pitch, the arbitrator is convinced that these circumstances do not create a ground for finding his or her dependence and partiality. The arbitrator discloses the circumstances. Although the sister company had not yet mandated the law firm's office in the other country, the arbitrator asks the parties to waive their right to object and challenge.

The IBA Guidelines 2014 clarify, first, that the arbitrator remains obliged to disclose facts and circumstances once they occur. General Standard 3(b) provides that

> an advance declaration or waiver in relation to possible conflicts of interest arising from facts and circumstances that may arise in the future does not discharge the arbitrator's ongoing duty of disclosure under General Standard 3(a).

Thus, in the above example, the presiding arbitrator would remain obliged to disclose once the sister company mandated the arbitrator's law firm.[318] The wording of General Standard 3(b) does not address the validity or effect at all of the advance waiver. One may interpret the wording to invalidate advance waivers, since otherwise it would not be necessary to disclose the future circumstance again. However, the Explanation to General Standard 3 states that the Guidelines do not

> take a position as to the validity and effect of advance declarations or waivers, because the validity and effect of any advance declaration or waiver must be assessed in view of the specific text of the advance declaration or waiver, the particular circumstances at hand and the applicable law.

317 The issue of advance waiver often arises in connection to larger law firms, D. Girsberger/N. Voser, *International Arbitration*, para. 668.

318 A similar result would apply under the ICC Note. Para. 30 clarifies that "although an advance declaration or waiver in relation to possible conflicts of interest arising from facts and circumstances that may arise in the future may or may not in certain circumstances be taken into account by the Court, such advance declaration or waiver does not discharge an arbitrator from his or her ongoing duty to disclose".

If any advance waiver does not discharge the obligation to disclose, time limits for objecting cannot start to run with the advance waiver.[319] In line with its categorisation of unpermitted circumstances, General Standard 4(b) declares advance waivers of facts or circumstances on the Non-Waivable Red List invalid.[320]

Irrespective of the categorisation of the IBA Guidelines 2014 and the applicable law and rules, the purpose and function of the parties' rights to object and to challenge may shed some light on the treatment of advance waivers. Knowledge of the waived fact is key to a valid objection. Where the party does not know whether a circumstance exists, since the circumstance is potential, it cannot waive. It is questionable whether knowledge of potential and future events is sufficiently concrete to fulfil the prerequisites of waiver.[321] The right to object is the logical consequence of the obligation to disclose. Where the parties have no right to object after an arbitrator disclosed a conflict of interest, the parties do not enjoy their right to appoint that arbitrator fully. The right to challenge carries this thought forward after constitution of the arbitral tribunal. The right to challenge strengthens the parties' right to appoint their chosen arbitrator, which is an essential criterion of the contractual nature of arbitration.[322] Since the right to appoint their chosen arbitrator has this significant role, one may argue that the rights to object and challenge require certain protection as well. Thus, where an advance waiver interferes with this role, it may be questionable whether the advance waiver is valid. On the other hand, the contractual nature of arbitration embraces party autonomy, generally accepted as one of the fundamental principles as well.[323] Where the circumstances disclosed are sufficiently concrete and individual, a limited advance waiver may be in line with the parties' right to appoint. The parties' right to appoint is also at risk in multi-party arbitration and joinder scenarios involving advance waivers.

Finally, the idea of advance waiver can theoretically be reversed: parties may wish to appoint an arbitrator under the condition that he or she will refrain from creating a ground for challenge or annulment. Parties may request the arbitrators to sign an additional declaration

319 O. Froitzheim, *Die Ablehnung von Schiedsrichtern wegen Befangenheit in der internationalen Schiedsgerichtsbarkeit*, p. 161.

320 Part I, General Standard 4(b): "However, if facts or circumstances exist as described in the Non-Waivable Red List, any waiver by a party (including any declaration or advance waiver, such as that contemplated in General Standard 3(b)), or any agreement by the parties to have such a person serve as arbitrator, shall be regarded as invalid."

321 See above chapter 7.2.1.

322 See above chapter 1.3.2.

323 M. Niedermeyer, *Ethics for Arbitrators at the International Level: Who Writes the Rules of the Game?*, Am. Rev. Int'l Arb. 25 (2014), 481-496, 495; B. Oglinda, *Key Criteria in Appointment of Arbitrators in International Arbitration*, Juridical Trib. 5 (2015), 124-131, 125.

in such regard. If a conflict of interest later arises that meets the threshold of a ground for challenge, the party may try to argue that the appointment is void since the arbitrator did not fulfil the condition. Again, it will depend on the applicable law and rules to evaluate the validity and effects of such conditional appointment. However, the presence of provisions addressing challenge and annulment due to any lack of independence and impartiality in most arbitration laws and rules, as well as the legal insecurity of such conditional appointment speak against a conditional appointment.[324] Any reservation made to an appointment risks frustrating the efficiency of the arbitral proceedings. Thus, parties are restricted to challenging the arbitrator in such a scenario or the arbitrator may remove himself or herself.

7.3 CIRCUMVENTING THE ARBITRATOR'S CHALLENGE

Although the parties' right to challenge relies on the parties' right to appoint their chosen arbitrator, i.e., one of the essential criteria of the contractual nature of arbitration,[325] challenges often disrupt the efficiency of the proceedings. Even where the challenge does not suspend the proceedings, challenges may include the risk of delay or even derailing the arbitral proceedings. Thus, practitioners may wonder how to circumvent a challenge.

If the introduction of an expert, witness, or late counsel may create a conflict of interest with one of the arbitrators, the arbitral tribunal may consider excluding that person. These measures severely curtail the rights to be heard and (potentially) be treated equally of the party introducing the expert, witness, or new counsel. Thus, the arbitral tribunal must be empowered to order accordingly, and the individual circumstances will often require a sensitive balance of both parties' rights and an assessment of the real risk of derailing the proceedings. Depending on the applicable law and rules, the arbitral tribunal may function as a gatekeeper.

7.3.1 Exclusion of Party-Appointed Experts

The arbitral tribunal may be faced with a party-appointed expert whose involvement could create a conflict of interest.[326] Even if the standard of independence and impartiality applicable to party-appointed experts may vary from that of tribunal-appointed experts,[327]

---

324 For the same result with regard to German arbitration law, Stein/Jonas/P. Schlosser, § 1036 para. 43 and § 1035 para. 2.

325 See above chapter 1.3, on the dualistic nature of arbitration.

326 See above chapter 4.

327 See above chapter 6.6.

an intensive relationship between a party-appointed expert and one of the arbitrators may result in a challenge of that arbitrator.[328] Hence, the arbitral tribunal being confronted with such a situation, or the opposing party, may wish to exclude that party-appointed expert. It is questionable whether the arbitral tribunal has jurisdiction and the power to exclude an expert or his or her evidence ex officio or upon the other party's request, since the exclusion of the party-appointed expert or the expert evidence curtails the appointing party's right to present its case and to be heard.[329]

Article 9(2)(g) IBA Rules 2020 grants the arbitral tribunal the power to

> exclude from evidence or production any Document, statement, oral testimony or inspection, in whole or in part, for any of the following reasons: [...] considerations of procedural economy, proportionality, fairness or equality of the Parties that the Arbitral Tribunal determines to be compelling.

This rule clarifies that the arbitral tribunal has the power to exclude evidence, and must assess and weigh the procedural economy, proportionality, fairness, or equality of the parties when exercising its power. Whether or not a potential conflict of interest with one of the arbitrators creates a violation of procedural economy remains a case-by-case decision.

The HKIAC, ICDR, and SIAC Rules also explicitly address the tribunal's power to exclude evidence. Article 20(3) ICDR Rules, however, merely grants the tribunal the authority to "exclude cumulative or irrelevant testimony or other evidence", whereas Article 22.3 sentence 2 HKIAC Rules vests the tribunal with "the power to admit or exclude any documents, exhibits or other evidence". Scenarios of conflicts of interest will most often not be classified as "cumulative or irrelevant", and thus will not grant the tribunal the power to exclude an expert under Article 20(3) ICDR Rules. Article 19.4 SIAC Rules uses the same wording as Article 20(3) ICDR Rules.[330]

Many other arbitration rules do not foresee such explicit regulation of the arbitral tribunal's power to exclude an expert or evidence, but generally vest the arbitral tribunal with the

---

328 See concrete examples above chapter 4.1.3. Another possible scenario is misconduct of the expert risking his or her challenge by the opposing party. Where the misconduct relates to the expert's methodology and work, his or her credibility may be at issue and the question arises whether the expert can be challenged on those grounds. See on this issue in investment arbitration M. Hodgson/M. Stewart, *Experts in Investor-State Arbitration: The Tribunal as Gatekeeper*, J. Int'l Disp. Settlement 9 (2018), 453-463, 461 et seq.

329 See also, above chapter 4.1.5.2, for the importance of the party's right to be heard and present its case.

330 Art. 19.4 SIAC Rules states: "The Tribunal may, in its discretion, direct the order of proceedings, bifurcate proceedings, exclude cumulative or irrelevant testimony or other evidence and direct the parties to focus their presentations on issues the decision of which could dispose of all or part of the case."

power to "determine the admissibility, relevance, materiality, and weight of the evidence".[331] Such a provision has, however, less power to circumvent a challenge of an arbitrator who may have a conflict of interest with the party-appointed arbitrator. First, the determination of the evidence's weight may even be detrimental. The party opposing the introduction of a party-appointed expert who potentially creates a conflict of interest will usually fear that the conflicted arbitrator will not objectively weigh the evidence.[332] Thus, for circumventing a challenge it is not helpful that the tribunal may determine the weight of the evidence. Second, the arbitral tribunal has to determine whether the expert evidence potentially creating a conflict of interest is inadmissible. Admissibility of evidence is a matter of procedure and must be determined by the law governing the arbitration.[333] The assessment of admissibility may include public policy considerations.[334] Such public policy considerations may include considerations of procedural economy, proportionality, fairness, or equality of the parties that the arbitral tribunal determines to be compelling, i.e., those grounds referred to in Article 9(2)(g) IBA Rules 2020. Thus, whether or not a potential conflict of interest with one of the arbitrators creates a violation of procedural economy remains, again, a case-by-case decision.

In an investment arbitration under the ICSID Arbitration Rules the arbitral tribunal in *Flughafen Zürich AG v. Venezuela* concluded that it had the power to exclude a party-appointed expert under Rule 34(1) ICSID Rules, including the tribunal's power to determine the admissibility of evidence.[335] However, the issue of that case was not a conflict of interest between the expert and an arbitrator, but potential misconduct of the party appointing the expert.[336]

---

331 Art. 24(2) Swiss Rules. Similar provisions are Art. 19(2) sentence 2 UNCITRAL Model Law; Art. 20(6) ICDR Rules; Art. 22.1(vi) LCIA Rules; Art. 31(1) SCC Rules; Art. 19.2 SIAC Rules; Art. 27(4) UNCITRAL Arbitration Rules.

332 See above chapter 4.1.5.2, for more details on this conflict of interest.

333 J. Lew/L. Mistelis/S. Kröll, *Comparative International Commercial Arbitration*, paras. 22-29.

334 J. Lew/L. Mistelis/S. Kröll, *Comparative International Commercial Arbitration*, paras. 22-32.

335 *Flughafen Zürich AG and Gestión e Ingeniería IDC SA v. Republic of Venezuela*, ICSID Tribunal, 29 August 2012, ICSID Case No. ARB/10/19. Rule 34(1) ICSID Rules states: "The Tribunal shall be the judge of the admissibility of any evidence adduced and of its probative value."

336 See M. Burianski/A. Lang, *"Challenges" to Party-Appointed Experts*, SchiedsVZ 2017, 269-277, 271, providing the facts: The expert was appointed by the respondent after it had already received information related to the case from the claimants, who considered retaining him but eventually decided against it. The claimants challenged the expert on the grounds that he was in possession of allegedly confidential documents, which included the contract, the claimants' business plan and damages calculations, as well as the request for arbitration.

Finally, some arbitration rules empower the tribunal to order the parties to identify potential experts before submitting the evidence.[337] Such a mechanism helps to identify any potential conflict of interest as soon as possible. The consequences remain, however, open.

7.3.2 *Exclusion of Witnesses*

An arbitrator's relationship with one of the witnesses may also create a conflict of interest.[338] Since the right to present witness evidence is covered by the parties' right to be heard and to present their case, exclusion of one party's witnesses curtails that party's rights. Such exclusion requires similar consideration as when assessing the arbitral tribunal's power to exclude an expert. Thus, the party's right to be heard and present its case needs to be balanced with the actual risk of creating a conflict of interest.

7.3.3 *Exclusion of Counsel*

The arbitral tribunal may be faced with a scenario where one party introduces a new counsel during the proceedings. If one of the arbitrator's has a close relationship creating a conflict of interest[339] with that new counsel, the arbitral tribunal or the opposing party may wish to block that counsel to circumvent a potential challenge of the arbitrator. "Counsel's appointment after the constitution of the arbitral tribunal may jeopardize the impartiality and independency of arbitrators."[340]

In these scenarios the parties' right to be represented by their chosen counsel[341] and the legitimacy and integrity of the proceedings demand to be balanced. The right to be represented in legal disputes is part of the right to be heard.[342]

7.3.3.1 Tribunal's Authority to Exclude Counsel

The primary question is again whether the tribunal has jurisdiction and the power to exclude one party's chosen counsel. With regard to the tribunal's jurisdiction, some United

---

337 E.g., Art. 20.2 LCIA Rules; Art. 33(1) SCC Rules; Art. 25.1 SIAC Rules.

338 See above chapter 4.1.1.2.

339 See above chapter 4.1.1.1, for examples of conflicts of interest.

340 M. Benedettelli, *Human Rights as a Litigation Tool in International Arbitration*, Arb. Int'l 31 (2015), 647.

341 Most arbitration laws and rules include this right, e.g., directly addressed in Sect. 36 EAA; Art. 5 sentence 1 UNCITRAL Model Law and Art. 13.6 HKIAC Rules; Art. 16 sentence 1 ICDR Rules; Art. 23.1 SIAC Rules; Art. 15(6) Swiss Rules, or indirectly in other rules such as on costs or the request for arbitration, e.g., Art. 50 SCC Rules and Art. 5.2(ii) DIS Rules.

342 E.g., BGer, 1 July 1991, BGE 117 II 346, 347.

States case law[343] suggests that issues of disqualifying counsel are "substantive matters for the courts and not arbitrators".[344] Under United States case law, public interest and policy may forbid arbitrators from ruling on matters of disqualification, as they involve "interpreting and applying the applicable rules of professional conduct for attorneys".[345] Parties do not expect to derogate from their right to seek judicial review of their counsel's conduct before state courts when agreeing on arbitration – especially, since the arbitrators are not party to the contract between counsel and the party to the arbitration.[346] Thus, only state courts should "monitor the ethics of the legal profession".[347] This case law rests on the premise that the exclusion of counsel in the arbitration proceedings is a matter of counsel's ethical conduct towards its client. The introduction of a new counsel into an ongoing arbitration that creates a conflict of interest is divergent. In this scenario, the exclusion of counsel shall ensure the arbitrator's mandate and the party's right to appoint are protected and enforced.

> Disqualification [...], is primarily an aspect of the decision maker's mandate to resolve disputes – responsive above all to the interest in the proper functioning of the trial process (balancing, for example, concerns of integrity – a fair equality in the presentation of opposing cases – and concerns of efficiency – the minimizing of delay and disruption). Here the interests of the entire legal system outside the hearing room need not be dispositive – need not in fact enter into the matter at all.[348]

It is not an issue of public interest where the individual case does not deal with deontology and professional responsibility, and any need to marginalise the contractual nature of arbitration is absent. Thus, where the tribunal's integrity is at risk the arbitral tribunal should have authority to exclude counsel.[349] Article 17(2) ICC Rules takes a similar position and grants the arbitral tribunal power to

343 See for a good overview A. Rau, *Arbitrators Without Powers? Disqualifying Counsel in Arbitral Proceedings*, Arb. Int'l 30 (2014), 457-512, 482 et seq.

344 *Munich Reinsurance America, Inc. v. ACE Property & Casualty Co.*, 500 F.Supp.2d 272 (S.D. New York 2007).

345 *Dean Witter Reynolds, Inc. v. Clements, O'Neill, Pierce & Nickens, LLP*, 2000 WL 36098499 (S.D. Texas), 5.

346 *Munich Reinsurance America, Inc. v. ACE Property & Casualty Co.*, 500 F.Supp.2d 272 (S.D. New York 2007), 275; *Dean Witter Reynolds, Inc. v. Clements, O'Neill, Pierce & Nickens, LLP*, 2000 WL 36098499 (S.D. Texas), 3 et seq.

347 *Dean Witter Reynolds, Inc. v. Clements, O'Neill, Pierce & Nickens, LLP*, 2000 WL 36098499 (S.D. Texas), 5.

348 A. Rau, *Arbitrators Without Powers? Disqualifying Counsel in Arbitral Proceedings*, Arb. Int'l 30 (2014), 457-512, 486.

349 For the same view A. Rau, *Arbitrators Without Powers? Disqualifying Counsel in Arbitral Proceedings*, Arb. Int'l 30 (2014), 457-512, 495, who also includes scenarios of counsel's misconduct in the tribunal's jurisdiction.

> take any measure necessary to avoid a conflict of interest of an arbitrator arising from a change in party representation, including the exclusion of new party representatives from participating in whole or in part in the arbitral proceedings.[350]

The ICC Note outlines some possible considerations for the arbitral tribunal when deciding to exclude a counsel, including

> (a) the ability of the party that has introduced the new representative to properly submit its case in the absence of that representative, (b) the timing of the addition of such newly introduced party representative, and (c) the disruption to the arbitration that may result from its continuing participation in case of a successful challenge against one or more of the arbitrators.[351]

Lit. a and c especially demonstrate the balance that is at the centre in these cases: the parties' right to be represented on the one hand, and the legitimacy and integrity of the proceedings on the other hand.

Similar to the above United States case law, it is highly disputed in other jurisdictions whether the arbitral tribunal may exclude a counsel. In Germany, some scholars argue that § 1042(2) German ZPO[352] prohibits any limitation in the choice of counsel.[353] Following this view, any contrary party agreement is void. The party's right to be represented by its chosen counsel is to be interpreted broadly, i.e., including the conflict-of-interest scenario. This right is a corollary of the general right to be heard[354] and of utmost importance. Hence, the party's right to be represented by its chosen counsel would trump the legitimacy and integrity of the proceedings in the present scenario. However, other authors argue that

---

350 Art. 17(2) ICC Rules: "The arbitral tribunal may, once constituted and after it has afforded an opportunity to the parties to comment in writing within a suitable period of time, take any measure necessary to avoid a conflict of interest of an arbitrator arising from a change in party representation, including the exclusion of new party representatives from participating in whole or in part in the arbitral proceedings."

351 ICC Note, para. 15.

352 § 1042(2) German ZPO reads in German: "*Rechtsanwälte dürfen als Bevollmächtigte nicht ausgeschlossen werden.*" Translation: "Lawyers may not be excluded as authorised representatives." It is undisputed that § 1042(2) German ZPO is mandatory. Rather, the exact scope of the provision is uncertain.

353 J.-P. Lachmann, *Handbuch für die Schiedsgerichtsbarkeit*, para. 1367. See also, S. Horst, *Das Spannungsverhältnis zwischen Schiedsrichter und Parteivertreter in der internationalen Schiedsgerichtsbarkeit*, pp. 203-213, for a detailed interpretation relying, inter alia, on the wording, history and purpose of the provision.

354 MünchKomm ZPO/J. Münch, § 1042, para. 63.

the arbitral tribunal may exclude a counsel under § 1042(4) German ZPO[355] in exceptional circumstances, e.g., a risk of the integrity of tribunal.[356]

A comparable debate exists under Swiss arbitration law. In domestic arbitration, Article 373(5) Swiss ZPO[357] lays down the parties' right to be represented. This provision is mandatory and, generally, also covers the parties' right to be represented by their chosen counsel.[358] The application of Article 373(5) Swiss ZPO in international arbitration is, however, highly disputed.[359] The dichotomy of domestic and international arbitration under Swiss *lex arbitri* forbids transferral of the applicable principles and rules without a case-by-case analysis.[360] Under Article 182 Swiss IPRG, applicable in international arbitration, parties may, for example, exclude certain groups of people from acting as counsel, which is unnegotiable under Article 373(5) Swiss ZPO.[361] The given scenario of risking a conflict of interest by introducing a new counsel may be another case to differentiate between domestic and international arbitration, especially where the parties chose institutional rules or guidelines that grant the tribunal the power to exclude counsel.[362] Additionally, it is questionable whether even Article 373(5) Swiss ZPO prohibits exclusion of a counsel in the present example.[363]

> In order to ensure the integrity of the arbitral proceedings, the arbitral tribunal should thus be entitled to reserve the right to refuse to permit a new legal representative appointed by a party to appear on behalf of that party subsequent to its constitution.[364]

---

355 § 1042(4) sentence 1 German ZPO reads in German: "*Soweit eine Vereinbarung der Parteien nicht vorliegt und dieses Buch keine Regelung enthält, werden die Verfahrensregeln vom Schiedsgericht nach freiem Ermessen bestimmt.*" Translation: "In the absence of an agreement between the parties and of any provision in this Book, the rules of procedure shall be determined by the arbitral tribunal in its absolute discretion."

356 BeckOK ZPO/S. Wislke/L. Markert, § 1042, para. 16.

357 Art. 373(5) Swiss ZPO reads in German: "*Jede Partei kann sich vertreten lassen.*" Translation: "Each party may be represented."

358 BSK ZPO/P. Habegger, Art. 373 para. 68; B. Berger/F. Kellerhals, *International and Domestic Arbitration in Switzerland*, para. 1171.

359 BSK IPRG/M. Schneider/M. Scherer, Art. 182 para. 82.

360 Cf. ZK IPRG/C. Ötiker, Art. 182 para. 39.

361 BSK IPRG/M. Schneider/M. Scherer, Art. 182 para. 83.

362 E.g., under Art. 17(2) ICC Rules.

363 See BSK ZPO/P. Habegger, Art. 373 para. 68, who argues that temporary or permanent disqualifications of counsel by the arbitral tribunal should be permissible within the tribunal's "police power" when the disqualification is in compliance with the principle of proportionality.

364 B. Berger/F. Kellerhals, *International and Domestic Arbitration in Switzerland*, para. 1154.

Therefore, where the integrity of the tribunal is at risk, the arbitral tribunal should have the authority to exclude counsel.[365] In line with this, the IBA Guidelines 2013 prescribe in Guideline 6 to the arbitral tribunal to consider taking "measures appropriate to safeguard the integrity of the proceedings, including the exclusion of the new Party Representative from participating in all or part of the arbitral proceedings".[366] However, the official Comments to the IBA Guidelines 2013 add that this consideration is under the premise that "compelling circumstances so justify, and where the arbitral tribunal has found that it has the requisite authority".[367] Thus, it is uncertain whether Guideline 6 vests the tribunal with any authority to exclude a counsel.[368]

7.3.3.2 Grounds for Exclusion of Counsel

The possible scenarios giving rise to a party's request or tribunal's order to exclude counsel are multifaceted. They include the risk of a conflict of interest and counsel's misconduct in the arbitration, e.g., disclosure abuses, misstatements, wrongful communications with witnesses, or the failure to adhere to procedural directions.[369]

Two investment arbitrations conducted under the auspices of ICSID serve as examples for both scenarios. In *Hrvatska Elektroprivreda, d.d. v. Republic of Slovenia*, the tribunal ruled that a conflict of interest may be a ground to exclude a counsel.[370] The respondent in that case amended its legal team with a barrister from the same chambers as one of the arbitrators during the arbitral proceedings.[371] The ICSID Tribunal argued that the relationship between the barrister-counsel and the barrister-arbitrator gave rise to "apprehensions of the appearance of impropriety" which, in the interest of the legitimacy of the proceedings, entitled claimant to object to the inclusion of respondent's barrister-counsel.[372] In the tribunal's view, these issues should not be addressed by

365 G. Born, *International Commercial Arbitration*, pp. 3099, 3125.

366 Guideline 6 operates in case of breach of Guideline 5 IBA Guidelines 2013, providing that "once the Arbitral Tribunal has been constituted, a person should not accept representation of a Party in the arbitration when a relationship exists between the person and an Arbitrator that would create a conflict of interest, unless none of the Parties objects after proper disclosure".

367 IBA Guidelines 2013, Comments to Guidelines 4-6.

368 Even if one were to follow the argument that Guideline 6 vests the tribunal with the power to exclude counsel, the nature of the IBA Guidelines 2013, i.e., being soft law, needs to be considered. Thus, any diverging parties' agreement or mandatory *lex arbitri* will supersede the Guidelines. See in detail, G. Schima/ B. Sesser, *Die von Parteivertretern in internationalen Schiedsverfahren zu beachtenden Ethikstandards*, SchiedsVZ 2016, 61-71, 68.

369 G. Born, *International Commercial Arbitration*, p. 3125.

370 *Hrvatska Elektroprivreda, d.d. v. Republic of Slovenia*, ICSID Tribunal, 6 May 2008, ARB/05/24.

371 The presiding arbitrator was door tenant at the same chambers.

372 *Hrvatska Elektroprivreda, d.d. v. Republic of Slovenia*, ICSID Tribunal, 6 May 2008, ARB/05/24, para. 22.

> national bodies which regulate the work of professional service providers, because that might lead to inconsistent or indeed arbitrary outcomes depending on the attitudes of such bodies, or the content (or lack of relevant content) of their rules.[373]

Within its decision to exclude respondent's counsel, the tribunal found that neither the ICSID Rules nor the ICSID Convention explicitly addressed the arbitrator's authority to exclude a counsel,[374] and examined the general principle of the parties' right to choose their counsel.[375] The tribunal balanced this general principle with the highly valued principle of immutability of arbitral tribunals in Article 56(1), (3) ICSID Convention, and concluded that "after a Commission or Tribunal has been constituted and proceedings have begun, its composition shall remain unchanged".[376] In balancing these two principles, the tribunal clarified that although the principle of immutability of the arbitral tribunal was not absolute, the present case was one where one party's action compromised the immutability.

> The present case involves [...] an initiative undertaken by one of the litigants, which only at an extremely late stage has disclosed the involvement of counsel whose presence is for all practical purposes incompatible with the maintenance of the Tribunal in its present proper composition.[377]

The tribunal proceeded in evaluating whether the relationship between the arbitrator and the counsel met the standard of justifiable doubts. After affirming this, it ruled that the procedural interest in maintaining the integrity of the arbitral tribunal prevailed.

Therefore, where the scenario meets the threshold of a conflict of interest, i.e., usually the standard of justifiable doubts,[378] the arbitral tribunal may exclude a counsel if the interest

373 *Hrvatska Elektroprivreda, d.d. v. Republic of Slovenia*, ICSID Tribunal, 6 May 2008, ARB/05/24, para. 23.

374 In the end, the tribunal relied on its "inherent power to take measures to preserve the integrity of its proceedings" based on Art. 44 ICSID Convention and these inherent powers dealt with issues necessary for conducting matters falling within its jurisdiction, *Hrvatska Elektroprivreda, d.d. v. Republic of Slovenia*, ICSID Tribunal, 6 May 2008, ARB/05/24, para. 33.

375 *Hrvatska Elektroprivreda, d.d. v. Republic of Slovenia*, ICSID Tribunal, 6 May 2008, para. 24 et seq. referring to Art. 56(1) ICSID Convention.

376 *Hrvatska Elektroprivreda, d.d. v. Republic of Slovenia*, ICSID Tribunal, 6 May 2008, ARB/05/24, para. 27, also referring to Mr. Aaron Broches who explained on 23 February 1965: "If a party could prevail upon an arbitrator to resign in the course of proceedings without cause he would be able to frustrate or slow down the proceedings", in Memorandum Meeting of the Committee of the Whole, 23 February 1965, Doc. SID/65-6.

377 *Hrvatska Elektroprivreda, d.d. v. Republic of Slovenia*, ICSID Tribunal, 6 May 2008, ARB/05/24, para. 29.

378 See above chapters 6.1.2.4 and 6.1.3.1.

in preserving the integrity of the proceedings[379] outweighs the party's right to be represented by its chosen counsel. The Comments to Guideline 4-6 in the IBA Guidelines 2013 suggest applying the IBA Guidelines 2014 when assessing whether a conflict of interest exists.

The second example is *Fraport AG Frankfurt Airport Services Worldwide v. Republic of the Philippines*, where one counsel's misconduct raised the question of exclusion. Claimant's counsel had not appeared in the original arbitration proceeding, but first appeared on behalf of the claimant when seeking annulment. Respondent's allegation was that counsel had earlier been retained by the Manila International Airport Authority in connection with a related and still pending ICC arbitration.[380] The deciding ad hoc committee concluded that it had authority to decide on the exclusion of counsel, but refrained from doing so. The tribunal's authority to rule on issues of misconduct is even more disputed than the tribunal's authority to do so in regard to conflicts of interest. Prominent scholars conclude that tribunals should have the power to censure counsel[381] or "to disqualify counsel from further representation in arbitration for persistent and grave abuses".[382] According to Born, it is "one of the arbitrators' responsibilities [...] to oversee the arbitral proceedings, including the parties' presentation of their cases".[383]

In the end, regarding both, the risk of a conflict of interest and misconduct, the tribunal's methodology can be described as follows: "The actual decision on disqualification [...] does not follow from the application of a 'rule,' but is closely tailored to address the harm that the tribunal is seeking to prevent."[384] Finally, and in case of doubt over the tribunal's authority to exclude a counsel and the grounds for doing so, parties may consider including both in their arbitration agreement. For example, the following clause could be added:

> To avoid future conflicts of interest after the appointment of members of the Tribunal, the Parties agree that any proposed additions to or changes in their

379 In general, on counsel's integrity, see M. Wittinghofer, *"No Risk, No Fun" – A Counsel's Remarks on Integrity*, SchiedsVZ 2017, 110-113.

380 *Fraport AG Frankfurt Airport Services Worldwide v. Republic of the Philippines*, ICSID ad hoc Committee, 18 September 2008, ICSID Case No. ARB/03/25.

381 E.g., with sanctions for the counsel. This was the case in *Thomas Kinkade v. Lighthouse Galleries, LLC*, where counsel for respondent was accused of undue tactics, obtaining assistance of a former employee of claimant in preparing the cross-examination. Claimant challenged the counsel. The tribunal denied the motion but imposed sanctions, *Thomas Kinkade Co. v. Lighthouse Galleries, LLC*, 2010 WL 436604 (E.D. Michigan), affirmed by *Thomas Kinkade Co. v. White*, 711 F.3d 719 (6th Cir. 2013), on domestic arbitration.

382 G. Born, *International Commercial Arbitration*, p. 3125.

383 G. Born, *International Commercial Arbitration*, p. 3125.

384 A. Rau, *Arbitrators Without Powers? Disqualifying Counsel in Arbitral Proceedings*, Arb. Int'l 30 (2014), 457-512, 496.

> representatives [...] shall be communicated to the Tribunal and shall only take effect if the Tribunal does not object for reasons of conflict of interest.[385]

7.4 Concluding Remarks

In conclusion, the purpose of disclosure is, on the one hand, to foster the parties' confidence in the arbitrators by providing information about the arbitrators and, on the other hand, to enable the parties' rights to appoint, object, and challenge. The general efficiency must be borne in mind when analysing the scope of disclosure. An intermediate scope of disclosure properly balances the interests of the parties. The intermediate scope of disclosure demands disclosure of more circumstances than those meeting the threshold of dependence and partiality.[386] Disclosure functions to support independence and impartiality, but must be distinguished from it. An important difference is that non-disclosure alone cannot be a ground for establishing dependence and partiality. Arbitrators may be required to reasonably inquire about circumstances in order to comply with the obligation to disclose. This is, however, no separate obligation to disclose.

The involvement of barristers, third-party funders, or tribunal secretaries requires special attention. Where barristers are involved, a broad and early disclosure may help to avoid difficulties later. In case of third-party funding, the tribunal and counsels or parties are actively involved in disclosure: the parties should provide information on the funding to enable the arbitrator to disclose any potential conflict. Regarding tribunal secretaries, an arbitrator should disclose the secretary's employment and concrete tasks, while the secretary should also disclose, in line with the scope of disclosure applied to arbitrators.

Opposing one party's right to appoint lies the other's party right to object. The inaction of this right to object may lead to that party's waiver to later rely on the disclosed circumstance. Generally, waiver entails an element of knowledge and a lack of timely objection. Two particular issues may arise in connection to waiver: first, and in case of cumulation of grounds, the question arises when the time to object starts to run; second, arbitrators may ask for advance waiver.

385 *Atlanto-Scandian Herring Arbitration, Denmark in Respect of the Faroe Islands v. European Union*, 15 March 2014, PCA Case No. 2013-30, Rules of Procedure, Art. 3.1.

386 If one applies an obligation to investigate, this obligation must be the broadest in scope since not all circumstances investigated need to be disclosed necessarily. Only if the circumstance investigated fits the intermediate scope of disclosure, it needs to be disclosed.

Finally, where a conflict of interest is not yet present but is at risk, since one party wishes to introduce an expert, witness, or new counsel, the arbitral tribunal may consider excluding that person. Thereby, the arbitral tribunal may circumvent a challenge.

8 Conclusion and Outlook

Independence and impartiality are paramount for any judicial process. The parties' confidence in the judicial process and, in arbitration, particularly in the chosen arbitrator, is central. It "is of fundamental importance that justice should not only be done, but should manifestly and undoubtedly be seen to be done".[1] Although this lodestar is set and applies in international arbitration, its interpretation and application need adjustment to the dual nature of arbitration. This particular nature of arbitration requires a different balancing of interests and may lead to a specific application of independence and impartiality in certain scenarios.

8.1 The Standard of Independence and Impartiality

Regarding the applicable standard of independence and impartiality in international commercial arbitration, a balanced approach to the dual nature of arbitration results in a mixed objective-subjective perspective on the material standard that is best described as justifiable doubts. Case law and its analysis reveal that some particular scenarios require discretion for arguments based on the application of different grounds, different arbitrators, and the parties' agreement. However, the material standard of independence and impartiality remains unchanged.

Non-disclosure does not require a different standard. Although the parties' right to appoint is at issue in case of non-disclosure, it does not require a different standard of independence and impartiality. The parties' right to appoint is sufficiently respected within the general standard of justifiable doubts. Similarly, pre- and post-award phases do not require materially diverging standards of independence and impartiality. In post-award stages there may be different arguments on the tableau, e.g., an arbitrator's previous conduct during the proceedings or efficiency but the material standard should remain unchanged.

Furthermore, where the applicable law does not explicitly provide differently, there is a tendency in international arbitration to apply the same standard of independence and impartiality to all arbitrators within the tribunal. In this regard, partisan arbitrators do not appear practical, except the parties explicitly contracted for partisan party-appointed arbitrators. Thus, parties may, to some extent, modify the applicable standard. No issues

1 Lord Hewart, in *R v. Sussex Justices, Ex p. McCarthy*, [1924] 1 KB 256.

arise in this regard if the parties agree on a higher standard than justifiable doubts. Although parties are well advised to use clear, unambiguous language when deviating from the applicable standard, the mere fact that some industries may have only a few experts available to serve as arbitrators, i.e., there is a limited pool, does not directly lower the applicable standard of independence and impartiality.

Irrespective of the terminology, also unconscious bias may constitute a conflict of interest and constitute a ground for finding dependence and partiality. Grounds for finding dependence and partiality do not require conscious bias.

Finally, the standard applicable to tribunal secretaries is often similar to that of arbitrators, and should not be differentiated based on the secretaries' role. Party-appointed experts, however, are usually not required to be independent and impartial, but their independence and impartiality strengthen their evidence. Contrary to party-appointed experts, tribunal-appointed experts need to be independent and impartial.

8.2 The Obligation to Disclose

Independence and impartiality in international commercial arbitration are supported by the obligation to disclose, the parties' possibility to object, and investigation of the circumstances that may create justifiable doubts. The scope of necessary disclosure is best described as an intermediate one. This scope addresses the purpose of disclosure, namely, to provide information on the arbitrators to the parties, to foster the parties' confidence in the arbitrators, and to enable the parties' right to appoint, object and challenge. Disclosure functions to support independence and impartiality, but must be distinguished from it. Thus, the scope of disclosure demands disclosure of more circumstances than those meeting the threshold of dependence and partiality. Significantly, non-disclosure alone cannot be a ground for establishing dependence and partiality.

With regard to barristers, third-party funders, tribunal secretaries, and social networks it is questionable what kind of scope of disclosure applies to these individual scenarios and what needs to be considered practically. In cases involving a barrister, arbitrators and counsels should adhere to an early and broad disclosure. In case of third-party funding, disclosure of the mere presence of the funder, disclosure of previously funded cases by the funder or even disclosure of the funding agreement is to be differentiated. Practically useful means of disclosure are the arbitrator's disclosure after being provided with information by the parties of their current interaction with funders, combined with disclosure by the parties.

The scope of disclosure with regard to activities on social media networks requires its own analysis. For the evaluation of grounds for finding dependence and partiality, the underlying real relationship is decisive, not the one demonstrated on social networks. Therefore, generally, the scope of disclosure encompasses all types of circumstances that may create justifiable doubts regarding independence and impartiality. It is, however, not the fact of a social networking connection that needs to be disclosed but the underlying relationship or conduct.

Finally, in some scenarios it is questionable who needs to disclose. Co-arbitrators should be cautious on disclosing circumstances relevant for another arbitrator's independence and impartiality. The obligation of arbitrators to disclose information on their co-arbitrator risks conflicts within the tribunal. Before disclosing for a co-arbitrator, arbitrators should consider alternatives, e.g., exhorting the other arbitrator to disclose or consider joint disclosure. Tribunal-appointed experts may be obliged to disclose. However, there is not much guidance on their obligation to disclose, and the tribunal may help to clarify any such obligation.

8.3 The Use of Case Law

Much case law exists on potential grounds for finding dependence and partiality of arbitrators and other decision makers. This case law provides guidance when examining independence and impartiality. Although the standards applied to state court judges may differ, cases dealing with independence and impartiality of judges serve as examples to test the independence and impartiality of arbitrators.

The role of the actor in question will be decisive in determining whether or not there are grounds for dependence and partiality. Decisive for conflicts of interest are, first, the arbitrator's relationships with one of the parties or counsels. Here, much case law demonstrates some more leeway when analysing the relationships between arbitrators and counsels, as both are active in the same field of business. Moreover, the arbitrator's relationship with an expert, a witnesses, another arbitrator, and an arbitral or other involved institution may be relevant. Particularly, relationships with another arbitrator or an institution do not often create a conflict of interest justifying a challenge or annulment. To be differentiated from the arbitrator's direct relationships, are those that exist between his or her law firm and another actor in the arbitral proceedings. Different additional arguments are decisive here to evaluate whether a ground for finding dependence and partiality exists, e.g., the size of the law firm and the internal organisation.

Besides the arbitrator's relationships, those of a tribunal secretary, counsel, and expert may impair the integrity of the proceedings and may, thus, be relevant when evaluating independence and impartiality in international commercial arbitration.

Generally, there is a slight tendency in case law that relationships more often provide for a successful ground for a challenge or an annulment than conduct. Nonetheless, conflicts of interest encompass conduct of the relevant actors, and grounds for finding dependence and partiality may additionally be found or argued based on a previous challenge of the arbitrator in unrelated proceedings or the arbitrator's conviction. Furthermore, certain institutional appointment mechanisms, e.g., arbitrator's lists, may raise allegations of fostering dependence and partiality. Most often, these arguments do not prevail. However, cumulating different grounds may sustain a challenge or annulment, even though the individual grounds are not sufficient.

Again, third-party funding, tribunal secretaries, barristers and social networks deserve particular attention. All these scenarios involve multiple additional connections that arguably create more risks for independence and impartiality. Analysing third-party funding, the decisive question for independence and impartiality is whether the funder is to be positioned with the funded party. In cases involving tribunal secretaries their role is decisive for creating a conflict; and for barristers, decisive is the exact organisation of their chambers. Further, the use of social networks does not affect the analysis of a conflict of interest but offers useful proof.

8.4 Tendencies of Harmonisation

The beginning of this book raised the question of whether there is or will be a harmonised international standard of independence and impartiality in international commercial arbitration.[2] The analyses in chapters 4-7 demonstrate that there are many harmonising tendencies. For example, much case law gathers around the standard of justifiable doubts. Yet, differences remain. Hence, even if there are harmonising tendencies, the application of independence and impartiality in international commercial arbitration remains governed by national courts.[3]

2 See above chapter 2.

3 See also, C. Castres Saint-Martin, *Les conflits d'intérêts en arbitrage commercial international*, p. 435, who requests legislators to clearly define conflicts of interest to be able to deal with issues of independence and impartiality more efficiently.

This is different regarding the use of tribunal secretaries. Current regulatory approaches may be interpreted to oppose harmonisation and the development of an international standard. Institutional guidelines respond divergently to broader concerns about the processes by which secretaries are appointed and the duties performed by them in arbitration proceedings.[4] Though users favour the regulation of the use of tribunal secretaries in arbitration rules,[5] the diverse implementation by arbitral institutions hinders an international standard in this regard. However, the need for an international standard for the use of tribunal secretaries is, at least, questionable. The different regulation on the use of secretaries may as well be seen as an appropriate specialisation of different institutions and a tool of competition with each other.

8.5 Practical Guidance

Finally, the following section provides some short practical guidance to arbitrators, counsels, and the parties when dealing with issues of independence and impartiality in international commercial arbitration. "Arbitrator independence is as much a practical issue as it is a legal requirement."[6] This practical guidance is not an exhaustive checklist, but rather a short practical guide with references to the detailed analysis in this book.

Parties' Choice

When agreeing on arbitration, parties and counsels may consider certain aspects in the context of independence and impartiality:

First, parties should opt for applicable laws and rules that are in accordance with the parties' needs and expectations in regard to independence and impartiality and disclosure.

> Here, both the applicable perspective and the material standard of both the rules and the applicable laws are decisive and should be considered: the perspective may be subjective,

4 E. Shirlow, *The Australian Centre for International Commercial Arbitration's Guideline on the Use of Arbitral Secretaries*. There are no uniform standards in regard to secretaries but different institutional approaches. Differences in the institutional approaches are in particular: the requirement of party consent, the permissible scope of secretaries' tasks, and renumeration.

5 A majority of 70% of respondents favour the regulation of the use of tribunal secretaries in arbitration rules, QMUL/White & Case, *2018 International Arbitration Survey*, Chart 38, p. 34.

6 M. Lavan/S. Smith/L. Kimmelmann/C. Ray/D. MacGrath, *Arbitration of International Commercial Disputes*, Sect. 58:39.

> objective, or mixed objective-subjective; the material standard may be broad, limited, or intermediate (see above chapters 6.1.1, 6.1.2, and 7.1).

Second, in case the parties come from an expert industry with a potentially limited pool of arbitrators, counsels may consider modifying the applicable standard of independence and impartiality, within possible limits, to make use of all available arbitrators (see above chapter 6.5).

Third, parties and counsels may evaluate the risk of excluding evidence or disqualifying counsel under the applicable laws and rules (see above chapter 7.3).

Fourth, the barrister-counsel should advise the party of the potential risk of a challenge based on his or her members in chambers (see above chapters 4.1.1.1.9 and 7.1.1.5.1).

Fifth, parties may wish to control the use of tribunal secretaries and opt for laws and rules accordingly. Once the arbitral proceedings commence, parties may wish to be informed of the exact role a tribunal secretary has (see above chapters 4.1.3, 4.2.3, and 6.7).

Arbitrator's Disclosure

At the outset and during the arbitral proceedings, the arbitrator is obliged to disclose.

First, the arbitrator should disclose all circumstances that constitute a ground for a challenge or annulment under the applicable laws (see above chapters 6.1 and 7.1; see also chapters 4 and 5 for individual scenarios).

Second, the arbitrator should disclose all circumstances that he or she is aware of and, while taking the position of a reasonable party, must assume that the parties have a reasonable interest to know the circumstance (see above chapter 7.1.1.3).

> Here, both the applicable perspective and the material standard of both the rules and the applicable laws are decisive: the perspective may be subjective, objective, or mixed subjective-objective; the material standard may be broad, limited or intermediate (see above chapters 7.1.1.1 et seq.).

Third, the arbitrator is not required to disclose any contact on social networks. The arbitrator is required to disclose those contacts that have an underlying intense connection (see above chapter 7.1.1.5.4).

Fourth, the arbitrator should consider the involvement of third-party funders (above chapters 4.1.1.1.10 and 7.1.1.5.2), tribunal secretaries (above chapters 4.1.3, 4.2.3, 6.7, and 7.1.1.5.3), and experts (above chapters 4.1.3, 4.1.5, and 6.6) and disclose accordingly.

Fifth, a barrister-arbitrator should disclose the name of his or her chambers and some information on the internal structure regarding the separation of work within the chambers (see above chapter 7.1.1.5.1).

Sixth, when evaluating disclosure, the arbitrator may analyse the potential legal consequences of non-disclosure under the applicable law (see above chapter 7.1.4).

Bibliography

G. Aksen, *Chapter 13: The Tribunal's Appointment*, in L. Newman/R. Hill, *The Leading Arbitrator's Guide*, third edition, Juris Publishing Inc.: Huntington 2014, 333-342 (G. Aksen, *The Tribunal's Appointment*).

C. Albanesi, *Unmeritorious Challenges: Is It Time to Say Enough?*, in C. Gonzalez-Bueno, *40 under 40 International Arbitration*, Dykinson, S.L.: Madrid 2018, 23-35 (C. Albanesi, *Unmeritorious Challenges: Is It Time to Say Enough?*).

S. Albers, *Der parteibestellte Schiedsrichter im schiedsgerichtlichen Verfahren der ZPO und das Gebot überparteilicher Rechtspflege*, Peter Lang: Bern 1995 (S. Albers, *Der parteibestellte Schiedsrichter im schiedsgerichtlichen Verfahren der ZPO und das Gebot überparteilicher Rechtspflege*).

N. Allen/D. Mallett, *Arbitrator Disclosure*, Asian Int'l Arb. J. 7 (2011), 118-147.

M. Altenkirch/R. Raheja, *Quo Vadis Party-appointed Experts?*, Global Arbitration News, 18 December 2018, available at https://globalarbitrationnews.com/quo-vadis-party-appointed-experts/ (M. Altenkirch/R. Raheja, *Quo Vadis Party-appointed Experts?*).

American Arbitration Association - American Bar Association, Code of Ethics for Arbitrators in Commercial Disputes, AAA-ABA Code of Ethics, 2004, available at www.adr.org/sites/default/files/document_repository/Commercial_Code_of_Ethics_for_Arbitrators_2010_10_14.pdf (AAA/ABA Code of Ethics).

N. Andrews/J. Landbrecht, *Schiedsverfahren und Mediation in England*, C.H. Beck/Manz/Stämpfli Verlag: München/Wien/Bern 2015 (N. Andrews/J. Landbrecht, *Schiedsverfahren und Mediation in England*).

P. Archer, *Paris Bar Council Indicates Support for Third-party Funding*, Westlaw Note published on 10 May 2017, Thomson Reuter: Toronto (P. Archer, *Paris Bar Council Indicates Support for Third-party Funding*).

C. Armbrüster/V. Wächter, *Ablehnung von Schiedsrichtern wegen Befangenheit im Verfahren*, SchiedsVZ 2017, 213-223.

Association of Litigation Funders' Code of Conduct for Litigation Funders, January 2018, available at associationoflitigationfunders.com/wp-content/uploads/2018/03/Code-Of-Conduct-for-Litigation-Funders-at-Jan-2018-FINAL.pdf (ALF Code of Conduct).

J. Bailey, *The Search to Clarify an Elusive Standard: What Relationships Between Arbitrator and Party Demonstrate Evident Partiality?, ANR Coal Co. v. Cogentrix of North Carolina, Inc.*, J. Disp. Resol. (2000), 153-163.

M. Baker/L. Greenwood, *Are Challenges Overused in International Arbitration?*, 2 J. Int'l Arb. 30 (2013), 101-112.

L. Barrington, *Chapter 3, Third-Party Funding and the International Arbitrator*, in P. Shaughnessy/S. Tung, *The Powers and Duties of an Arbitrator*, FS Pierre A. Karrer, Wolters Kluwer Law International: Alphen aan den Rijn 2017, 15-24 (L. Barrington, *FS Karrer*).

A. Battisson/C. Teo, *The Call to Remove Unilateral Appointments, Seven Years On*, Kluwer Arbitration Blog, 3 July 2017, available at http://arbitrationblog.kluwerarbitration.com/2017/07/03/call-remove-unilateral-appointments-seven-years/ (A. Battisson/C. Teo, *The Call to Remove Unilateral Appointments, Seven Years On*).

N. Beale/J. Lancaster/S. Geesink, *Removing an Arbitrator: Recent Decisions of the English Court on Apparent Bias in International Arbitration*, ASA Bull. 34 (2016), 322-341.

M. Bedjaoui, *The Arbitrator: One Man – Three Roles*, J. Int'l Arb. 5 (1988), 7-20.

A. Bedoya, *Arbitration, Social Media and Networking Technologies, Latent Existing Conflicts*, Kluwer Arbitration Blog, 15 June 2018, available at http://arbitrationblog.kluwerarbitration.com/2018/06/15/arbitration-social-media-networking-technologies-latent-existing-conflicts/ (A. Bedoya, *Arbitration, Social Media and Networking Technologies, Latent Existing Conflicts*).

L. Bench Nieuwveld/V. Shannon Sahani, *Third-party Funding in International Arbitration*, second edition, Wolters Kluwer Law International: Alphen aan den Rijn 2017 (L. Bench Nieuwveld/V. Shannon Sahani, *Third-party Funding in International Arbitration*).

M. Benedettelli, *Human Rights as a Litigation Tool in International Arbitration, Reflecting on the ECHR Experience*, Arb. Int'l 31 (2015), 631-659.

B. Berger/F. Kellerhals, *International and Domestic Arbitration in Switzerland*, third edition, Stämpfli Verlag: Bern 2015 (B. Berger/F. Kellerhals, *International and Domestic Arbitration in Switzerland*).

G. Bermann, *The Yukos Annulment, Answered and Unanswered Questions*, Am. Rev. Int'l Arb. 27 (2016), 1-20.

A.-K. Bertke/H.-P. Schroeder, *Grenzen der Zeugenvorbereitung im staatlichen Zivilprozess und im Schiedsverfahren*, SchiedsVZ 2014, 80-86.

J.-P. Bischoff, *Unabhängigkeit und Unparteilichkeit von Schiedsrichtern nach deutschem und englischem Recht, Unter Berücksichtigung der IBA-Guidelines on Conflicts of Interest in International Arbitration*, Peter Lang: Bern 2013 (J.-P. Bischoff, *Unabhängigkeit und Unparteilichkeit von Schiedsrichtern nach deutschem und englischem Recht*).

N. Blackaby/C. Partasides/A. Redfern, *Redfern and Hunter on International Arbitration*, sixth edition, Oxford University Press: Oxford 2015 (N. Blackaby/C. Partasides/A. Redfern, *Redfern and Hunter*).

F. Blavi, *It's About Time to Regulate Third Party Funding*, Kluwer Arbitration Blog, available at http://arbitrationblog.kluwerarbitration.com/2015/12/17/its-about-time-to-regulate-third-party-funding/ (F. Blavi, *It's About Time to Regulate Third Party Funding*).

K.-H. Böckstiegel/S. Kröll/P. Nacimiento, *Arbitration in Germany, the Model Law in Practice*, second edition, Wolters Kluwer Law International: Alphen aan den Rijn 2015 (K.-H. Böckstiegel/S. Kröll/P. Nacimiento, *Arbitration in Germany*).

G. Born, *International Commercial Arbitration*, third edition, Wolters Kluwer Law International: Alphen aan den Rijn 2021 (G. Born, *International Commercial Arbitration*).

N. Bouchardie/C. Tran, *Arbitration in France*, Thomson Reuters, Practical Law, Practice Note 4-536-9585 (2018) (N. Bouchardie/C. Tran, *Arbitration in France*, Practice Note 4-536-9585 (2018)).

D. Branson, *American Party-Appointed Arbitrators - Not the Three Monkeys*, U. Dayton L. Rev. 30 (2004), 1-62.

S. Brekoulakis, *Chapter 14: Systematic Bias and the Institution of International Arbitration, A New Approach to Arbitral Decision-Making*, in T. Cole, *The Roles of Psychology in*

International Arbitration, Wolters Kluwer Law International: Alphen aan den Rijn 2017, 339-374 (S. Brekoulakis, *Systematic Bias and the Institution of International Arbitration*).

S. Brekoulakis, *Systematic Bias and the Institution of International Arbitration*, J. Int'l Disp. Settlement 4 (2013), 553-585.

C. Brower/S. Melikian/M. Daly, *Tall and Small Tales of a Challenged Arbitrator*, in C. Giorgetti, *Challenges and Recusals of Judges and Arbitrators in International Courts and Tribunals*, Brill Nijhoff: Leiden 2015, 320-336 (C. Brower/S. Melikian/M. Daly, *Tall and Small Tales of a Challenged Arbitrator*).

D. Brown, *Arbitrators, Impartiality and English Law*, J. In'l Arb. 18 (2001), 123-130.

C. Brunner, *Note - Federal Supreme Court, 28 April 2000*, ASA Bull. 2000, 566-581.

M. Burianski/A. Lang, *"Challenges" to Party-Appointed Experts*, SchiedsVZ 2017, 269-277.

BVerfG, Code of Conduct for the Justices of the Federal Constitutional Court, November 2017, available at www.bundesverfassungsgericht.de/EN/Richter/Verhaltensleitlinie/Verhaltensleitlinien_node.html (Code of Conduct for the Justices of the Federal Constitutional Court (Germany)).

O. Byrne, *A New Code of Ethics for Commercial Arbitrators: The Neutrality of Party-Appointed Arbitrators on a Tripartite Panel*, Fordham Urban L. J. 30 (2003), 1815-1847.

J. Carter, *Improving Life with the Party-Appointed Arbitrator: Clearer Conduct Guidelines for "Nonneutrals"*, Am. Rev. Int'l Arb. 11 (2000), 295-305.

J. Carter, *Reaching Consensus on Arbitrator Conflicts*, Disp. Resol. Int'l 17 (2012), 17-35.

C. Castres Saint-Martin, *Les conflits d'intérêts en arbitrage commercial international*, L'Harmattan: Paris impr. 2017 (C. Castres Saint-Martin, *Les conflits d'intérêts en arbitrage commercial international*).

C. Chanais/F. Ferrand/S. Guinchard, *Procédure civile*, thirty-third edition, Dalloz: Paris 2016 (C. Chanais/F. Ferrand/S. Guinchard, *Procédure civile*).

CIArb, Code of Professional and Ethical Conduct for Members, October 2009, available at www.ciarb.org/media/4230/ciarb-code-of-professional-and-ethical-conduct-october-2009.pdf (CIArb Code of Conduct).

CIArb, International Arbitration Practice Guideline, Interviews for Prospective Arbitrators, 2016, available at www.ciarb.org/media/4185/guideline-1-interviews-for-prospective-arbitrators-2015.pdf (CIArb Guideline on Interviews).

CIArb, International Arbitration Practice Guideline, Party-appointed and Tribunal-appointed Experts, including the CIArb Protocol for the Use of Party-Appointed Expert Witnesses in International Arbitration 2016, available at www.ciarb.org/media/4200/guideline-7-party-appointed-and-tribunal-appointed-expert-witnesses-in-international-arbitration-2015.pdf (CIArb Guideline on Experts).

CIETAC Code of Conduct for Arbitrators, 6 May 1994, available at www.cietac.org/index.php?m=Page&a=index&id=113&l=en (CIETAC Code of Conduct).

CIETAC Rules for Evaluating the Behavior of Arbitrators, 1 March 2009, available at www.cietac.org/index.php?m=Page&a=index&id=112&l=en (CIETAC Rules for Evaluating the Behavior of Arbitrators).

J. Clanchy, *Access to Arbitral Justice: Costs for Arbitration, Third Party Funding in Arbitration: Breaking Down Barriers and Building Bridges*, Croatian Arb. YB 23 (2016), 53-69.

T. Clay, *L'arbitre*, Dalloz: Paris 2001 (T. Clay, *L'arbitre*).

T. Clay, *Le secretaire arbitral*, Rev. de l'Arb. 2005, 931-957.

T. Clay/L. Cadiet, *Code de l'arbitrage, commenté*, LexisNexis: Paris 2015 (Clay/Cadiet/Author).

Council of Europe/European Court of Human Rights, Guide on Article 6 of the European Convention on Human Rights, Right to a Fair Trial, civil limb, 31 August 2020, available at www.echr.coe.int/documents/guide_art_6_eng.pdf (ECtHR, Guide on Art. 6 ECHR).

F. Cristani, *Challenge and Disqualification of Arbitrators in International Investment Arbitration, An Overview*, L. & Prac. Int'l Cts. & Trib. 13 (2014), 153-177.

N. Darwazeh/A. Leleu, *Disclosure and Security for Costs or How to Address Imbalances Created by Third-Party Funding*, J. Int'l Arb. 33 (2016), 125-150.

J. De La Jara/J. Olórtegui, *Puma v. Estudio 2000, Three Learned Lessons*, Kluwer Arbitration Blog, 29 May 2017, available at http://arbitrationblog.kluwerarbitration.com/2017/05/29/puma-v-estudio-2000-three-learned-lessons/ (J. De La Jara/J. Olórtegui, *Puma v. Estudio 2000*).

A. Denning, *The Independence and Impartiality of the Judges*, S. African L.J. 71 (1954) 345-358.

Departmental Advisory Committee on Arbitration Law, *DAC Report*, February 1996 (DAC Report).

Deutscher Bundestag, Entwurf eines Gesetzes zur Neuregelung des Schiedsverfahrensrechts, Schiedsverfahrens-Neuregelungsgesetz - SchiedsVfG, 12 July 1996 (BT-Drucks. 13/5274).

DIS, Integrity Principles, available at www.disarb.org/en/about-us/what-matters-to-us/integrity-principles (DIS-Integrity Principles).

M. Donahey, *The Independence and Neutrality of Arbitrators*, J. Int'l Arb. 9 (1992), 31-42.

C. Dos Santos, *Third-party Funding in International Commercial Arbitration, A Wolf in Sheep's Clothing?*, ASA Bull. 2017, 918-936.

K. Dotseth, *Disqualifying Arbitrators for Failure to Make Complete Disclosures After Scandinavian Re v. St. Paul Re: What Is "Evident Partiality"?*, Def. Coun. J. 79 (2012), 347-354.

R. Dunbar, *The Anatomy of Friendship*, Tr. Cog. Sc. 22 (2018), 32-51.

D. Effer-Uhe, *Schiedsgerichtliche Unabhängigkeit bei wissenschaftlichen Äußerungen*, SchiedsVZ 2018, 75-80.

P. Egger, *Die Konstituierung Internationaler Wirtschaftsschiedsgerichte*, neuer wissenschaftlicher Verlag: Wien, Graz 2008 (P. Egger, *Die Konstituierung Internationaler Wirtschaftsschiedsgerichte*).

K. El Chazli, *L'impartialité de l'arbitre, Étude de la mise en oeuvre de l'exigence d'impartialité de l'arbitre*, LGDJ: Paris 2020 (K. El Chazli, *L'impartialité de l'arbitre*).

S. Elsing, *Procedural Efficiency in International Arbitration: Choosing the Best of Both Legal Worlds*, SchiedsVZ 2011, 114-123.

S. Elsing/A. Shchavelev, *Chapter 8, The Role of Party-Appointed Arbitrator*, in P. Shaughnessy/S. Tung, *The Powers and Duties of an Arbitrator*, FS Pierre A. Karrer, Wolters Kluwer Law International: Alphen aan den Rijn 2017, 65-78 (S. Elsing/A. Shchavelev, *FS Karrer*).

S. Feldman, *Contract Law and Practice*, Tennessee Practice Vol. 22, second edition, Thomson Reuters: Eagan 2018 (S. Feldman, *Contract Law and Practice*).

J. Fellas, *Evident Partiality and the Party-Appointed Arbitrator*, N.Y. L.J. 2018, available at www.law.com/newyorklawjournal/2018/06/27/evident-partiality-and-the-party-appointed-arbitrator/ (J. Fellas, *Evident Partiality and the Party-Appointed Arbitrator*, N.Y. L.J. 2018).

G. Flecke-Giammarco/C. Boog/S. Elsing, *et al.*, *The DIS Arbitration Rules - An Article-by-Article Commentary*, Wolters Kluwer Law International: Alphen aan den Rijn 2020 (DIS Commentary/Author).

E. Fontanelli, *The Disclosure Dilemma: Dealing with Arbitrator Issue Conflicts in International Arbitration*, IBA Arb. News 22 (2017), 68-71.

C. Fouchard, *Tecnimont Saga: Episode V – The Paris Court Strikes Back*, Kluwer Arbitration Blog, 2016, available at http://arbitrationblog.kluwerarbitration.com/2016/08/03/tecnimont-saga-episode-v-the-paris-court-strikes-back/ (C. Fouchard, *Tecnimont Saga: Episode V – The Paris Court Strikes Back*).

P. Fouchard, *Note - Cour d'appel de Paris (1re Ch. C) 12 octobre 1995 - V. v. société Raoul Duval*, Rev. de l'Arb. 1999, 327-328.

V. Frignati, *Ethical Implications of Third-party Funding in International Arbitration*, Arb. Int. 32 (2016), 505-522.

O. Froitzheim, *Die Ablehnung von Schiedsrichtern wegen Befangenheit in der internationalen Schiedsgerichtsbarkeit, Internationale Standards und Kasuistik*, Carl Heymanns Verlag:

Köln (2016) (O. Froitzheim, *Die Ablehnung von Schiedsrichtern wegen Befangenheit in der internationalen Schiedsgerichtsbarkeit*).

O. Froitzheim, *Die Kanzleimitgliedschaft und die Ablehnung von Schiedsrichtern in der internationalen Schiedsgerichtsbarkeit*, SchiedsVZ 2017, 172-176.

O. Froitzheim, *Schiedsrichterliche Befangenheit durch Äußerungen zu Rechtsfragen – Eine Antwort auf Effer-Uhe*, SchiedsVZ 2019, 10-16.

B. Fuller, *Arbitrary Standards for Arbitrator Conflicts of Interest: Understanding the "Evident Partiality" Standard*, PIABA Bar J. 20 (2013), 59-66.

O. Gayner/A. Croft/K. Hurford, *Third-party Funding for International Arbitration Claims Practical Tips*, Thomson Reuters, Practical Law, 2018 (O. Gayner/A. Croft/K. Hurford, *Third-party Funding for International Arbitration Claims Practical Tips*).

O. Gayner/S. Khouri, *Singapore and Hong Kong: International Arbitration Meets Third Party Funding*, Fordham Int'l L.J. 40 (2017), 1033-1046.

F. Gélinas, *The Independence of International Arbitrators and Judges: Tampered With or Well Tempered?*, N.Y. Int'l Rev. 24 (2011), 1-48.

D. Girsberger/N. Voser, *International Arbitration Comparative and Swiss Perspectives*, third edition, Schulthess: Zürich 2016 (D. Girsberger/N. Voser, *International Arbitration*).

R. Glick/L. Stipanowich, *Arbitrator Disclosure in the Internet Age, Some Guidance Concerning the Obligation to Disclose Internet Activity and Online Relationships*, Disp. Res. J. 67 (2012), 1-7.

J. von Goeler, *Third-party Funding in International Arbitration and Its Impact on Procedure*, Wolters Kluwer Law International: Alphen aan den Rijn 2016 (J. von Goeler, *Third-party Funding*).

B. Gold/H. Furth, *The Use of Tripartite Boards in Labor, Commercial, and International Arbitration*, Harvard L. Rev. 68 (1954), 293-339.

A. Goldsmith/L. Melchionda, *The ICC's Guidance Note on Disclosure and Third-Party Funding, A Step in the Right Direction*, Kluwer Arbitration Blog, 14 March 2016, available at http://arbitrationblog.kluwerarbitration.com/2016/03/14/the-iccs-guidance-note-on-disclosure-and-third-party-funding-a-step-in-the-right-direction/ (A. Goldsmith/ L. Melchionda, *The ICC's Guidance Note on Disclosure and Third-Party Funding*).

S. Greenberg, *Tackling Guerrilla Challenges Against Arbitrators: Institutional Perspective*, TDM 2 (2010) (S. Greenberg, *Tackling Guerrilla Challenges Against Arbitrators*).

P. Grolimund/L. Loacker/A. Schnyder, *Basler Kommentar, Internationales Privatrecht*, fourth edition, Helbing Lichtenhahn Verlag: Basel 2021 (BSK IPRG/Author).

L. Gross, *Should Parties' Disclosure Requirements For Arbitrators Be Honored by Courts: Positive Software Solutions, Inc. v. New Century Mortgage Corporation*, S. Illinois U.L.J. 33 (2008), 71-93.

W. Habscheid, *Schiedsgerichtsbarkeit und Europäische Menschenrechtskonvention*, in W. Gerhardt/U. Diederichsen/B. Rimmelspacher/J. Costede, *Festschrift für Wolfram Henckel zum 70. Geburtstag am 21. April 1995*, De Gruyter: Berlin 1995, 341-352 (W. Habscheid, *FS Henckel*).

D. Hacking, *Challenges: Theirs Is to Reason Why*, GAR 5 (2006), 26-30.

J. Hamilton/F. Jijon/E. Corzo, *Arbitrator Challenges in Latin America*, in C. Giorgetti, *Challenges and Recusals of Judges and Arbitrators in International Courts and Tribunals*, Brill Nijhoff: Leiden 2015, 407-420 (J. Hamilton/F. Jijon/E. Corzo, *Arbitrator Challenges in Latin America*).

D. Hascher, *A Comparison between the Independence of State Justice and the Independence of Arbitration*, ICC Int. Ct. Arb. Bull., 2007 Special Supplement, 77-89.

D. Hascher, *Independence and Impartiality of Arbitrators*, Am. U. Int'l L. Rev. 27 (2011-2012), 789-806.

D. Hascher, *Les perspectives françaises sur le contrôle de la sentence internationale ou étrangère*, McGill J. Disp. Res. 2 (2015), 1-15.

T. Heintz/G. da Costa Cerquiera, *Vers une rationalisation de l'obligation de révélation de l'arbitre en droit français*, ASA Bull. 2013, 448-461.

G. Helleringer/P. Ayton, *Chapter 2, Bias, Vested Interests and Self-Deception in Judgment and Decision-Making: Challenges to Arbitrator Impartiality*, in T. Cole, *The Roles of*

Psychology in International Arbitration, Kluwer Law International: Alphen aan den Rijn 2017, 21-44 (G. Helleringer/P. Ayton, *Bias, Vested Interests and Self-Deception in Judgment and Decision-Making: Challenges to Arbitrator Impartiality*).

M. Henry, *Le devoir d'independance de l'arbitre*, LGDJ: Paris 2001 (M. Henry, *Le devoir d'independance de l'arbitre*).

M. Henry, *Note - Cour d'appel de Paris, 14 octobre 2014, SA Auto Guadeloupe Investissements v. société Columbus Acquisitions Inc. et autres*, Rev. de l'Arb. 2015, 156-182.

P. Hirst/M. Yeow, *Comparing Hong Kong Code of Practice for Third Party Funding Arbitration with the Code of Conduct in England & Wales*, Kluwer Arbitration Blog, 4 February 2019, available at http://arbitrationblog.kluwerarbitration.com/2019/02/04/comparing-hong-kong-code-of-practice-for-third-party-funding-arbitration-with-the-code-of-conduct-in-england-wales/ (P. Hirst/M. Yeow, *Comparing Hong Kong Code of Practice for Third Party Funding Arbitration with the Code of Conduct in England & Wales*).

HKIAC, Code of Ethical Conduct, available at www.hkiac.org/arbitration/arbitrators/code-of-ethical-conduct (HKIAC Code of Conduct).

HKIAC, Guidelines on the Use of a Secretary to the Arbitral Tribunal, effective 1 June 2014, available at www.hkiac.org/sites/default/files/ck_filebrowser/PDF/services/HKIAC%20Guidelines%20on%20Use%20of%20Secretary%20to%20Arbitral%20Tribunal_R.pdf (HKIAC Secretary Guidelines).

M. Hodgson/M. Stewart, *Experts in Investor-State Arbitration: The Tribunal as Gatekeeper*, J. Int'l Disp. Settlement 9 (2018), 453-463.

S. Hofbauer, *History of Arbitration*, in M. Arroyo, *Arbitration in Switzerland, the Practitioner's Guide*, second edition, Kluwer Law International: Alphen aan den Rijn 2018, 3-16 (S. Hofbauer, *History of Arbitration*).

A. Hoffmann, *Duty of Disclosure and Challenge of Arbitrators*, 3 Arb. Int'l 21 (2005), 427-436.

S. Horst, *Das Spannungsverhältnis zwischen Schiedsrichter und Parteivertreter in der internationalen Schiedsgerichtsbarkeit*, Mohr Siebeck: Tübingen 2017 (S. Horst, *Das Spannungsverhältnis zwischen Schiedsrichter und Parteivertreter in der internationalen Schiedsgerichtsbarkeit*).

A. Hosang, *Obstructionist Behavior in International Commercial Arbitration*, Eleven International Publishing: Den Haag 2014 (A. Hosang, *Obstructionist Behavior in International Commercial Arbitration*).

M. Hwang, *Arbitrators and Barristers in the Same Chambers – An Unsuccessful Challenge*, Bus. L. Int'l 6 (2005), 236-257.

M. Hwang, *Introduction, Musings on International Arbitration*, in M. Hwang, *Selected Essays on International Arbitration*, Academy Publishing: Singapore 2013, 1-19 (M. Hwang, *Introduction, Musings on International Arbitration*).

M. Hwang/L. Lee, *Chapter 18, Standard of Proof for Challenge Against Arbitrators: Giving Them the Benefit of the Doubt*, in P. Shaughnessy/S. Tung, *The Powers and Duties of an Arbitrator*, FS Pierre A. Karrer, Wolters Kluwer Law International: Alphen aan den Rijn 2017, 169-186 (M. Hwang/L. Lee, *FS Karrer*).

M. Hwang/K. Chung/S. Cheng Lim/W. Hui Min, *Chapter 2, Defining the Indefinable: Practical Problems of Confidentiality in Arbitration*, in Hong Kong International Arbitration Centre, *Issues, Perspectives and Practice*, FS Neil Kaplan, International Arbitration, Wolters Kluwer Law International: Alphen aan den Rijn 2018 (M. Hwang/K. Chung/S. Cheng Lim/W. Hui Min, *FS Kaplan*).

IBA Guidelines on Conflicts of Interest in International Arbitration, 2014, available at www.ibanet.org/Document/Default.aspx?DocumentUid=E2FE5E72-EB14-4BBA-B10D-D33DAFEE8918 (IBA Guidelines 2014).

IBA Guidelines on Party Representation in International Arbitration, 2013, available at www.ibanet.org/Document/Default.aspx?DocumentUid=6F0C57D7-E7A0-43AF-B76E-714D9FE74D7F (IBA Guidelines 2013).

IBA Rules of Ethics for International Arbitrators, 1987, available at www.trans-lex.org/701100/_/iba-rules-of-ethics-for-international-arbitrators-1987/ (IBA Rules 1987).

IBA Rules on the Taking of Evidence in International Arbitration, 2020, available at https://iaa-network.com/wp-content/uploads/2021/03/2020-IBA-Rules-on-Taking-Evidence-in-Int-Arbitration.pdf (IBA Rules 2020).

ICC, Note to Parties and Arbitral Tribunals on the Conduct of the Arbitration under the ICC Rules of Arbitration, 1 January 2021, available at https://iccwbo.org/content/uploads/sites/3/2020/12/icc-note-to-parties-and-arbitral-tribunals-on-the-conduct-of-arbitration-english-2021.pdf (ICC Note).

ICCA, Report of the ICCA-Queen Mary Task Force on Third-Party Funding in International Arbitration, April 2018, available at https://cdn.arbitration-icca.org/s3fs-public/document/media_document/Third-Party-Funding-Report%20.pdf (ICCA, Report of the ICCA-Queen Mary Task Force on Third-Party Funding in International Arbitration).

International Law Association, Study Group on the Practice and Procedure of International Courts and Tribunals, in association with the Project on International Courts and Tribunal, The Burgh House Principles On The Independence Of The International Judiciary, available at www.ucl.ac.uk/international-courts/sites/international-courts/files/burgh_final_21204.pdf (Burgh House Principles).

N. Jaisli Kull/A. Roth, *Chapter II, The Arbitrator and the Arbitration Procedure, Challenging Arbitrators for Lack of Independence or Impartiality: Procedural Pitfalls from a Swiss Perspective*, Austrian YB Int'l Arb. 2019, 223-248.

JAMS, Guidelines for Use of Clerks and Tribunal Secretaries in Arbitrations, available at www.jamsadr.com/files/Uploads/Documents/JAMS-International-Guidelines-for-Use-of-Clerks-and-Tribunal-Secretaries-in-Arbitrations.pdf (JAMS, Guidelines for Use of Clerks and Tribunal Secretaries).

C. Jarrosson, *Note - Cour de cassation (1re Ch. civ.), 6 decembre 2005*, Rev. de l'Arb. 2006, 127-138.

C. Jarrosson, *A propos de l'obligation de révélation, Une leçon de méthode de la Cour de cassation, Note sous Cass. civ. 1re, 10 octobre 2012*, Rev. de l'Arb. 2013, 130-137.

O. Jensen, *Tribunal Secretaries in International Arbitration*, Oxford University Press: Oxford 2019 (O. Jensen, *Tribunal Secretaries in International Arbitration*).

B. Jolley/O. Cook, *Revised ICC Note to Parties and Tribunals: Will Publication of Awards Become the New Normal?*, Kluwer Arbitration Blog, 7 March 2019, available at http://arbitrationblog.kluwerarbitration.com/2019/03/07/revised-icc-note-to-parties-and-tribunals-will-publication-of-awards-become-the-new-normal/ (B. Jolley/O. Cook, *Revised ICC Note to Parties and Tribunals*).

J. Kalicki, *Social Media and Arbitration Conflicts of Interest: A Challenge for the 21st Century*, Kluwer Arbitration Blog, 23 April 2012, available at http://arbitrationblog.kluwerarbitration.com/2012/04/23/social-media-and-arbitration-conflicts-of-interest-a-challenge-for-the-21st-century/ (J. Kalicki, *Social Media and Arbitration Conflicts of Interest: A Challenge for the 21st Century*).

A. Kaplan/M. Haenlein, *Users of the World, Unite!, The Challenges and Opportunities of Social Media*, Bus. Horiz. 53 (2010), 59-68.

J. Kendall, *Barristers, Independence and Disclosure*, Arb. Int'l 8 (1992), 287-299.

J. Kendall, *Barristers, Independence and Disclosure Revisited*, Arb. Int'l 16 (2000), 343-351.

R. Kiener, *Richterliche Unabhängigkeit, Verfassungsrechtliche Anforderungen an Richter und Gerichte*, Stämpfli: Bern 2001 (R. Kiener, *Richterliche Unabhängigkeit*).

D. Kozlowska-Rautiainen, *The Right to a Public Hearing in Arbitration in Light of ECtHR Judgments*, Stockholm Arb. YB 2020, 137-166.

W. Krüger/T. Rauscher, *Münchener Kommentar zur Zivilprozessordnung: ZPO*, seventh, sixth edition, C.H. Beck: München 2017, 2020 (MünchKomm ZPO/Author).

D. Kühner, *Das neue französische Schiedsrecht*, SchiedsVZ 2011, 125-131.

J.-P. Lachmann, *Handbuch für die Schiedsgerichtsbarkeit*, third edition, Verlag Dr. Otto Schmidt: Köln 2008 (J.-P. Lachmann, *Handbuch für die Schiedsgerichtsbarkeit*).

M. Lavan/S. Smith/L. Kimmelmann/C. Ray/D. MacGrath, *Chapter 58, Arbitration of International Commercial Disputes*, in R. Haig, *Successful Partnering Between Inside and Outside Counsel*, Westlaw, Thomson Reuters: Eagan 2018 (M. Lavan/S. Smith/L. Kimmelmann/C. Ray/D. MacGrath, *Arbitration of International Commercial Disputes*).

D. Lawson, *Impartiality and Independence of International Arbitrators, Commentary on the 2004 IBA Guidelines on Conflicts of Interest in International Arbitration*, ASA Bull. 2005, 22-45.

LCIA, Notes for Arbitrators, latest version dated 26 October 2017 and references the LCIA Rules (2014), available at www.lcia.org/adr-services/lcia-notes-for-arbitrators.aspx (LCIA Notes for Arbitrators).

LCIA, Notes for Parties, latest version dated 18 August 2017, available at www.lcia.org/adr-services/lcia-notes-for-parties.aspx (LCIA Notes for Parties).

L. Lévy, *The Chairman's Roles in the Arbitral Tribunal's Dynamics*, in B. Hanotiau/A. Mourre, *Dossier IX: Players' Interaction in International Arbitration*, Dossiers of the ICC Institute of World Business Law: Paris 2012, 67-85 (L. Lévy, *The Chairman's Roles in the Arbitral Tribunal's Dynamics*).

J. Lew/L. Mistelis/S. Kröll, *Comparative International Commercial Arbitration*, Kluwer Law International: Alphen aan den Rijn 2003 (J. Lew/L. Mistelis/S. Kröll, *Comparative International Commercial Arbitration*).

N. Lindström, *Challenges to Arbitrators – Decisions by the SCC Board during 2008 – 2010*, available at https://sccinstitute.com/media/93825/challenges-to-arbitrators-decisions-by-the-scc-board-during-2008.pdf (N. Lindström, *Decisions by the SCC Board during 2008 – 2010*).

S. Luttrell, *Bias Challenges in International Commercial Arbitration: The Need for a "Real Danger" Test*, Kluwer Law International: Alphen aan den Rijn 2009 (S. Luttrell, *Bias Challenges in International Commercial Arbitration*).

P. Mankowski, *Die Ablehnung von Schiedsrichtern*, SchiedsVZ 2004, 304-313.

D. McLaren, *Party-Appointed vs List-Appointed Arbitrators: A Comparison*, J. Int'l Arb. 20 (2003), 233-245.

J. Menz, *The Fourth Arbitrator?, Die Rolle des Administrativen Secretary im Scheidsverfahren*, SchiedsVZ 2015, 210-218.

J. Menz/A. George, *How Much Assistance Is Permissible?, A Note on the Swiss Supreme Court's Decision on Arbitral Secretaries and Consultants*, J. Int'l Arb. 33 (2016), 311-324.

B. Meyerson/J. Townsend, *Revised Code of Ethics for Commercial Arbitrators Explained*, Disp. Res. J. 59 (2004), 10-17.

M. Moses, *The Role of the IBA Guidelines on Conflicts of Interest in Arbitrator Challenges*, Kluwer Arbitration Blog, 23 November 2017, available at http://arbitrationblog.kluwerarbitration.com/2017/11/23/role-iba-guidelines-conflicts-interest-arbitrator-challenges/ (M. Moses, *The Role of the IBA Guidelines on Conflicts of Interest in Arbitrator Challenges*).

A. Mourre, *Are Unilateral Appointments Defensible? On Jan Paulsson's Moral Hazard in International Arbitration*, Kluwer Arbitration Blog, 5 October 2010, available at http://arbitrationblog.kluwerarbitration.com/2010/10/05/are-unilateral-appointments-defensible-on-jan-paulssons-moral-hazard-in-international-arbitration/ (A. Mourre, *Are Unilateral Appointments Defensible? On Jan Paulsson's Moral Hazard in International Arbitration*).

A. Mourre, *Chapter 25: About Procedural Soft Law, the IBA Guidelines on Party Representation and the Future of Arbitration*, in P. Shaughnessy/S. Tung, *The Powers and Duties of an Arbitrator*, FS Pierre A. Karrer, Wolters Kluwer Law International: Alphen aan den Rijn 2017, 239-250 (A. Mourre, *FS Karrer*).

A. Mourre/E. Zuleta, *The IBA Guidelines on Party Representation in International Arbitration*, Disp. Resol. Int'l 7 (2013), 135-158.

C. Müller, *Swiss Case Law in International Arbitration*, second edition, Schulthess: Zürich 2010 (C. Müller, *Swiss Case Law in International Arbitration*).

M. Müller-Chen/C. Widmer Lüchinger, *Zürcher Kommentar zum IPRG*, third edition, Schulthess: Zürich 2018 (ZK IPRG/Author).

H.-J. Musielak/W. Voit, *ZPO, Zivilprozessordnung*, eighteenth edition, Vahlen: München 2019 (Musielak/Voit/Author).

G. Nicholas/C. Partasides, *LCIA Court Decisions on Challenges to Arbitrators: A Proposal to Publish*, Arb. Int'l 23 (2007), 1-41.

M. Niedermeyer, *Ethics for Arbitrators at the International Level: Who Writes the Rules of the Game?*, Am. Rev. Int'l Arb. 25 (2014), 481-496.

P. Oberhammer/T. Domej/U. Haas, *ZPO, Schweizerische Zivilprozessordnung Kurzkommentar*, second edition, Helbing Lichtenhahn Verlag: Basel 2014 (KuKo ZPO/Author).

B. Oglinda, *Key Criteria in Appointment of Arbitrators in International Arbitration*, Juridical Trib. 5 (2015), 124-131.

A. Okekeifere, *Appointment and Challenge of Arbitrators Under the UNCITRAL Model Law: Part 2: Challenge*, Int'l Arb. L. Rev. 3 (2000), 13-18.

B. Ostranger/M. Viskocil, *Modern Reinsurance Law and Practice*, third edition, Glasser LegalWorks: New Jersey 2014 (B. Ostranger/M. Viskocil, *Modern Reinsurance Law and Practice*).

C. Palo, *Bias of Arbitrator as Ground for Vacatur of Arbitration Award*, 143 American Jurisprudence Proof of Facts 3d, Thomson Reuters: Eagan 2014, 335 (C. Palo, *Bias of Arbitrator as Ground for Vacatur of Arbitration Award*).

W. Park, *Arbitrator Integrity: The Transit and the Permanent*, San Diego L. Rev. 46 (2009), 629-704.

W. Park, *Rectitude in International Arbitration*, Arb. Int'l 27 (2011), 473-526.

C. Partasides, *Chapter 7, Secretaries to Arbitral Tribunals*, in B. Hanotiau/A. Mourre, *Players' Interaction in International Arbitration*, 2012, 84-88 (C. Partasides, *Secretaries to Arbitral Tribunals*).

C. Partasides, *The Fourth Arbitrator?*, Arb. Int'l 18 (2002), 147-161.

C. Partasides/N. Bassiri/U. Gantenberg/L. Bruton/A. Riccio, *Arbitral Secretaries*, in J. van den Berg, *International Arbitration*, 17 ICCA Congress Series 2013, 327-368 (C. Partasides/N. Bassiri/U. Gantenberg/L. Bruton/A. Riccio, *Arbitral Secretaries*).

J. Paulsson, *Are Unilateral Appointments Defensible?*, Kluwer Arbitration Blog, 2 April 2009, available at http://arbitrationblog.kluwerarbitration.com/2009/04/02/are-unilateral-appointments-defensible/ (J. Paulsson, *Are Unilateral Appointments Defensible?*).

A. Perry/J. Valencia, *Draft Model BIT Abandons Party-Appointed Arbitrators*, Global Arbitration News, 19 June 2018, available at https://globalarbitrationnews.com/the-netherlands-draft-model-bit-abandons-party-appointed-arbitrators/ (A. Perry/J. Valencia, *Draft Model BIT Abandons Party-Appointed Arbitrators*).

L. Peterson, *Citing the Need for Independence and Impartiality for all Arbitrators, Tribunal Frowns on BIT's Provision that Each Party Should Fund Its Own Arbitrator, Similar BIT Wording Led to Unpublicized Reversal of Costs Ruling in Eureko v. Poland Case*, Investment Arbitration Reporter, 19 February 2019, available at www.iareporter.com/

articles/citing-need-for-independence-and-impartiality-of-all-arbitrators-tribunal-frowns-on-bits-provision-that-each-party-should-fund-its-own-arbitrator-similar-bit-wording-led-to-unpublicized-reversal-o/ (L. Peterson, *Citing the Need for Independence and Impartiality for all Arbitrators*).

L. Pfister, *Who Decides Arbitrator Challenges?, A Comparative Analysis of Institutional Approaches*, SchiedsVZ 2017, 164-171.

M. Polkinghorne/C. Rosenberg, *The Role of the Tribunal Secretary in International Arbitration*, Disp. Res. Int'l 8 (2014), 107-128.

J.-F. Poudret/S. Besson, *Comparative Law of International Arbitration*, second edition, Sweet & Maxwell: London 2007 (J.-F. Poudret/S. Besson, *Comparative Law of International Arbitration*).

QMUL/White & Case, *2012 International Arbitration Survey, Current and Preferred Practices in the Arbitral Process*, 2012, available at www.arbitration.qmul.ac.uk/media/arbitration/docs/2012_International_Arbitration_Survey.pdf (QMUL/White & Case, *2012 International Arbitration Survey*).

QMUL/White & Case, *2015 International Arbitration Survey, Improvements and Innovations in International Arbitration*, 2015, available at www.arbitration.qmul.ac.uk/media/arbitration/docs/2015_International_Arbitration_Survey.pdf (QMUL/White & Case, *2015 International Arbitration Survey*).

QMUL/White & Case, *2018 International Arbitration Survey, The Evolution of International Arbitration*, 2018, available at www.arbitration.qmul.ac.uk/media/arbitration/docs/2018-International-Arbitration-Survey---The-Evolution-of-International-Arbitration-(2).PDF (QMUL/White & Case, *2018 International Arbitration Survey*).

H. Raeschke-Kessler, *The Arbitrator as Settlement Facilitator*, Arb. Int'l 21 (2005), 523-536.

A. Rau, *Arbitrators Without Powers? Disqualifying Counsel in Arbitral Proceedings*, Arb. Int'l 30 (2014), 457-512.

A. Redfern, *The Importance of Being Independent, Laws of Arbitration, Rules, Guidelines - and a Disastrous Award*, IJAL 6 (2017), 9-23.

C. Rogers, *Context and Institutional Structure in Attorney Regulation: Constructing an Enforcement Regime for International Arbitration*, Stanford J. Int'l L. 39 (2003), 1-58.

C. Rogers, *Ethics in International Arbitration*, Oxford University Press: Oxford 2014 (C. Rogers, *Ethics in International Arbitration*).

C. Rogers, *Regulating International Arbitrators: A Functional Approach to Developing Standards of Conduct*, Stanford J. Int'l L. 41 (2005), 53-121.

A. Rojahn/C. Jerger, *Richterliche Unparteilichkeit und Unabhängigkeit im Zeitalter sozialer Netzwerke*, NJW 2014, 1147-1150.

A. Ross, *Radical Proposals in Draft Netherlands Model BIT*, GAR - News, 16 May 2018, available at https://globalarbitrationreview.com/article/1169654/radical-proposals-in-draft-netherlands-model-bit (A. Ross, *Radical Proposals in Draft Netherlands Model BIT*).

A. Salahuddin, *Should Arbitrators Be Immune from Liability?*, Arb. Int'l 33 (2017), 571-581.

S. Sanubari, *Arbitrator's Conduct on Social Media*, J. Int'l Disp. Settlement 8 (2017), 483-506.

SCAI Guidelines for Arbitrators, 1 January 2020, available at www.swissarbitration.org/files/36/Guidelines%20for%20Arbitrators/Guidelines%20for%20Arbitrators%20(EN)%20 2020.pdf (SCAI Guidelines for Arbitrators).

SCAI, *Swiss Rules – Selected Case Law, SCAI*, available at www.swissarbitration.org/Arbitration/Case-law (SCAI, *Swiss Rules – Selected Case Law*).

SCC Arbitrator's Guidelines, Stockholm June 2020, available at https://sccinstitute.com/media/1067295/scc-guidelines-for-arbitrators.pdf (SCC Arbitrator's Guidelines).

SCC Policy Appointment of Arbitrators, adopted by the SCC Board on 12 June 2006, amended by the SCC Board on 8 September 2017, available at https://sccinstitute.com/media/220131/scc-policy-appointment-of-arbitrators-2017.pdf (SCC Appointment Policy).

SCC Policy Disclosure of Third Parties with an Interest in the Outcome of the Dispute, adopted by the SCC Board on 11 September 2019, available at https://sccinstitute.com/media/1035074/scc-policy-re-third-party-interests-adopted.pdf (SCC Disclosure Policy).

F. Schäfer, *Institutionelle Schiedsgerichtsbarkeit*, in H. Torggler/F. Mohs/F. Schäfer/ V. Valentina Wong, *Handbuch Schiedsgerichtsbarkeit*, second edition, Nomos/Verlag Österreich/Schulthess: Baden-Baden/Wien/Zürich 2017, 107-121 (F. Schäfer, *Institutionelle Schiedsgerichtsbarkeit*).

M. Scherer, *Out in the Open? Third-party Funding in Arbitration*, CDR News, 26 June 2012, available at iclg.com/cdr/expert-views/out-in-the-open-third-party-funding-in-arbitration (M. Scherer, *Out in the Open? Third-party Funding in Arbitration*).

G. Schima/B. Sesser, *Die von Parteivertretern in internationalen Schiedsverfahren zu beachtenden Ethikstandards*, SchiedsVZ 2016, 61-71.

N. Schmidt-Ahrendts/V. Schneider, *„Gut Ding will Weile haben"*, SchiedsVZ 2020, 35-41.

T. Scholl, *Rechtsschutzversicherung und Prozessfinanzierung, §54*, in B. Heussen/C. Hamm, *Beck'sches Rechtsanwalts-Handbuch*, eleventh edition, C.H. Beck Verlag: München 2016 (T. Scholl, *Rechtsschutzversicherung und Prozessfinanzierung*).

K. Schwab/G. Walter, *Schiedsgerichtsbarkeit*, seventh edition, C.H. Beck Verlag: München 2005 (K. Schwab/G. Walter, *Schiedsgerichtsbarkeit*).

C. Seraglini/J. Ortscheidt, *Droit de l'arbitrage interne et international*, Montchrestien: Paris 2013 (C. Seraglini/J. Ortscheidt, *Droit de l'arbitrage interne et international*).

Y. Shany, *Squaring the Circle?*, Loyola L.A. Int'l & Comp. L. Rev. 30 (2008), 473-490.

E. Shirlow, *The Australian Centre for International Commercial Arbitration's Guideline on the Use of Arbitral Secretaries*, Kluwer Arbitration Blog, 23 February 2017, available at http://arbitrationblog.kluwerarbitration.com/2017/02/23/the-australian-centre-for-international-commercial-arbitrations-guideline-on-the-use-of-arbitral-secretaries/ (E. Shirlow, *The Australian Centre for International Commercial Arbitration's Guideline on the Use of Arbitral Secretaries*).

SIAC, Code of Ethics for an Arbitrator, 2015, available at https://siac.org.sg/images/stories/articles/rules/Code_of_Ethics_Oct2015.pdf (SIAC Code of Ethics).

SIAC, Practice Note on Arbitrator's Conduct in Case of External Funding, 31 March, PN – 01/17, available at www.siac.org.sg/images/stories/articles/rules/Third%20

Party%20Funding%20Practice%20Note%2031%20March%202017.pdf (SIAC, Practice Note, PN – 01/17).

SIAC, Practice Note on the Appointment of Administrative Secretaries, 2 February 2015, available at www.siac.org.sg/images/stories/articles/rules/Practice_Note_for_Tribunal_Secretaries_PN-01-15-January-2015_Final.pdf (SIAC, Practice Note, PN – 01/15).

N. Sievi, *Pre-Appointment Communications with Prospective Arbitrators*, SchiedsVZ 2021, 1-6.

M. Smith, *Impartiality of the Party-Appointed Arbitrator*, Arb. Int'l 6 (1990), 320-342, 339.

Solicitors Regulation Authority, Code of Conduct, 2011, available at www.sra.org.uk/solicitors/standards-regulations/code-conduct-solicitors/ (SRA Code of Conduct).

C. Spalton, *Are Tribunal Secretaries Writing Awards?*, GAR - News, 9 November 2012, available at globalarbitrationreview.com/tribunal-secretaries/are-tribunal-secretaries-writing-awards (C. Spalton, *Are Tribunal Secretaries Writing Awards?*).

C. Spalton, *Tribunal Secretaries, Now SIAC Issues Guidance*, GAR - News, 10 February 2015, available at globalarbitrationreview.com/article/1034062/tribunal-secretaries-now-siac-issues-guidance (C. Spalton, *Tribunal Secretaries*).

B. Spiegelfeld/S. Wurzer/H. Preidt, *Chapter II, The Arbitrator and the Arbitration Procedure - Challenge of Arbitrators: Procedural Requirements*, Austrian YB Int'l Arb. 2010, 45-77.

K. Spühler/H. Aemisegger/A. Dolge/D. Vock, *BGG, Praxiskommentar*, second edition, Dike: Zürich 2013 (BGG PK/Author).

K. Spühler/L. Tenchio/D. Infanger, *Schweizerische Zivilprozessordnung (ZPO), Basler Kommentar*, third edition, Helbing Lichtenhahn Verlag: Basel 2017 (BSK ZPO/Author).

F. Stein/M. Jonas, *Kommentar zur Zivilprozessordnung: ZPO*, twenty-third edition, Mohr Siebeck: Tübingen 2014 (Stein/Jonas/Author).

J. Steyn, *England: The Independence and/or Impartiality of Arbitrators in International Commercial Arbitration*, ICC Int. Ct. Arb. Bull. (2007) Special Supplement, 91-100.

E. Sussman, *Arbitrator Decision Making – Unconscious Psychological Influences and What You Can Do About Them*, YB Int'l Arb. IV (2015), 70-96.

E. Sussman, *The Arbitrator Survey, Practices, Preferences and Changes on the Horizon*, Am. Rev. Int'l Arb. 26 (2015), 517-538.

E. Sussman, *Can Counsel Ethics Beat Guerrilla Tactics?*, Rev. Brasileira Arb. 10 (2013), 98-105.

T. Sutter-Somm/F. Hasenböhler/C. Leuenberger, *Kommentar zur Schweizerischen ZPO*, third edition, Schulthess: Zürich 2016 (Sutter-Somm/Hasenböhler/Leuenberger/Author).

D. Sutton/J. Gill/M. Gearing, *Russel on Arbitration*, twenty-fourth edition, Sweet & Maxwell: London 2015 (D. Sutton/J. Gill/M. Gearing, *Russel on Arbitration*).

P. Tercier, *The Role of the Secretary to the Arbitral Tribunal*, in L. Walker Newman/R. D. Hill, *The Leading Arbitrators' Guide to International Arbitration*, third edition, Juris Publishing Inc.: Huntington/New York 2014, 531-554 (P. Tercier, *The Role of the Secretary to the Arbitral Tribunal*).

The General Council of the Bar, Information Note Regarding Barristers in International Arbitration, 6 July 2015, available at www.barcouncilethics.co.uk/wp-content/uploads/2017/10/bc_information_note_-_perceived_conflicts_in_international_arbitration_-_060715.pdf (The General Council of the Bar, Information Note Regarding Barristers in International Arbitration).

The Russian Federation, Writ of Summons Regarding Veteran Petroleum Ltd., UK 2014.11.2010 Writ VPL and Hodges (served), available at www.private-dispute-resolution.com/uploads/UK%202014.11.10%20Writ%20VPL%20and%20Hodges%20(served).pdf (The Russian Federation, Writ of Summons Regarding Veteran Petroleum Ltd.).

T. Timlin, *The Swiss Supreme Court on the Use of Secretaries and Consultants in the Arbitral Process*, YB Arb. Med. 8 (2016), 268-296.

UNCITRAL, Analytical Commentary on Draft Text of a Model Law on International Commercial Arbitration, 25 March 1985, A/CN.9/264 (UNCITRAL, Analytical Commentary Model Law).

UNCITRAL, Explanatory Note by the UNCITRAL secretariat on the 1985 Model Law on International Commercial Arbitration as amended in 2006, available at https://uncitral.un.org/sites/uncitral.un.org/files/media-documents/uncitral/en/19-09955_e_ebook.pdf (UNCITRAL, Explanatory Note Model Law).

UNCITRAL, Notes on Organizing Arbitral Proceedings, United Nations, New York 2016, available at https://uncitral.un.org/sites/uncitral.un.org/files/media-documents/uncitral/en/arb-notes-e.pdf (UNCITRAL, Notes on Organizing Arbitral Proceedings).

V. Vorwerk/C. Wolf, Beck Online-Kommentar ZPO, fortieth edition, C.H. Beck: München 2021, (BeckOK ZPO/Author).

N. Voser/E. Fischer, *The Arbitral Tribunal*, in E. Geisinger/N. Voser, *International Arbitration in Switzerland, A Handbook for Practitioners*, second edition, Wolters Kluwer Law International: Alphen aan den Rijn 2013, 51-71 (N. Voser/E. Fischer, *The Arbitral Tribunal*).

J. Waincymer, *Reconciling Conflicting Rights in International Arbitration*, Arb. Int'l 26 (2010), 597-624.

J. Waincymer, *Regulatory Developments in the Control of Counsel in International Arbitration*, Arb. Int'l 30 (2014), 513-552.

B. Waldmann/E. Maria Belser/A. Epiney, *Basler Kommentar, Schweizerische Bundesverfassung*, Helbing Lichtenhahn Verlag: Basel 2015 (BSK BV/Author).

R. Williams, *The Selection of a Tripartite Panel: You Get What You Contract For*, Rev. Litig. 36 (2018), 767-785.

S. Wilske/M. Stock, *Rules 3.3.7 IBA Guidelines on Conflicts of Interest in International Arbitration – The Enlargement of the Usual Shortlist?*, ASA Bull. 2005, 45-52.

S. Wilske/T. Fox/C. Krapfl, *Arbitration in Germany*, Thomson Reuters, Practical Law, Practice Note 6-523-9833 (2018) (S. Wilske/T. Fox/C. Krapfl, *Arbitration in Germany*, Practice Note 6-523-9833 (2018)).

S. Wilske/L. Markert/L. Bräuninger, *Entwicklungen in der internationalen Schiedsgerichtsbarkeit im Jahr 2017 und Ausblick auf 2018*, SchiedsVZ 2018, 134-158.

M. Wittinghofer, *"No Risk, No Fun" – A Counsel's Remarks on Integrity*, SchiedsVZ 2017, 110-113.

D. Yeoh, *Third Party Funding in International Arbitration, A Slippery Slope or Levelling the Playing Field?*, J. Int'l Arb. 33 (2016), 115-122.

Young ICCA, *Young ICCA Guide on Arbitral Secretaries*, The ICCA Reports No. 1, 2014, available at https://cdn.arbitration-icca.org/s3fs-public/document/media_document/aa_arbitral_sec_guide_composite_10_feb_2015.pdf (Young ICCA, Young ICCA Guide on Arbitral Secretaries).

H.-L. Yu/L. Shore, *Independence, Impartiality, and Immunity of Arbitrators: US and English Perspectives*, Int'l & Comp. L.Q. 52 (2003), 935-967.

M. Zaremski, *The 'Back Story'*, Alternatives to High Cost Litig. 31 (2013), 107-108.

J. Zekoll, *Comparative Civil Procedure*, in M. Reimann/R. Zimmermann, *The Oxford Handbook of Comparative Law*, Oxford University Press: Oxford 2008, 1328-1362 (J. Zekoll, *Comparative Civil Procedure*).

R. Zöller, *Zivilprozessordnung*; Kommentar, thirty-third edition, Verlag Dr. Otto Schmidt: Köln 2020 (Zöller/Author).

T. Zuberbühler/C. Müller/P. Habegger, *Swiss Rules of International Arbitration – Commentary*, second edition, Schulthess: Zürich 2013 (Swiss Rules Commentary/Author).

K. Zweigert/H. Kötz, *Einführung in die Rechtsvergleichung*, third edition, J.C.B. Mohr: Tübingen 1996 (K. Zweigert/H. Kötz, *Einführung in die Rechtsvergleichung*).

All websites last accessed on 30 March 2021.

Table of Cases

France

Cass civ 1ère, 16 December 1997, Rev. de l'Arb. 1999, 253
Cass civ 1ère, 28 April 1998, 96-11637
Cass civ 1ère, 16 March 1999, 96-12748
Cass civ 1ère, 6 December 2005, Rev. de l'Arb. 2006, 126-127
Cass civ 1ère, 20 October 2010, 09-68131
Cass civ 1ère, 4 November 2010, 09-12716
Cass civ 1ère, 29 June 2011, 09-17346
Cass civ 1ère, 4 July 2012, 11-19624
Cass civ 1ére, 10 October 2012, 11-20.299, Rev. de l'Arb. 2013, 129-130
Cass civ 1ère, 25 June 2014, 11-26529
Cass civ 1ére, 25 June 2014, 11-16.444, Rev. de l'Arb. 2015, 75-77
Cass civ 1ère, 4 May 2017, 15-29 158, Rev. de l'Arb. 2017, 770

Cass civ 2ème, 5 December 2002, 01-00224
Cass civ 2ème, 4 December 2003, 01-16420
Cass civ 2ème, 13 July 2005, 04-19962
Cass civ 2ème, 13 October 2005, 04-10834
Cass civ 2ème, 21 January 2010, 09-10144
Cass civ 2ème, 5 January 2017, 16-12394

Cass com, 7 January 1992, YB Com. Arb. XVIII (1993), 140-142
Cass com, 3 November 1992, 90-16751
Cass com, 16 March 1993, 91-10314

CA Lyon, 11 March 2014, 13/00447

CA Paris, 29 June 1991, cited in *Laker Airways Inc v. FLS Aerospace Ltd & Anor*, [1999] CLC 1124, 1130
CA Paris, 2 July 1992, Rev. de l'Arb. 1996, 411-410
CA Paris, 12 October 1995, Rev. de l'Arb. 1999, 324-326
CA Paris, 12 January 1999, Rev. de l'Arb. 1999, 381-384
CA Paris, 2 April 2003, Rev. de l'Arb. 2003, 1232-1236
CA Paris, 10 June 2004, YB Com. Arb. XXX (2005), 499-504

CA Paris, 18 November 2004, Rev. Arb. 2004, 989
CA Paris, 13 March 2008, 06/12878
CA Paris, 18 December 2008, Rev. de l'Arb. 2011, 682-685
CA Paris, 12 February 2009, Rev. de l'Arb. 2009, 186-190
CA Paris, 9 September 2010, ASA Bull. 2011, 187-192
CA Paris, 16 December 2010, Rev. de l'Arb. 2011, 710-713
CA Paris, 10 March 2011, 09/28537, ASA Bull. 2013, 443-447
CA Paris, 1 July 2011, Rev. de l'Arb. 2011, 761-765
CA Paris, 21 February 2012, Rev. de l'Arb. 2012, 587-595
CA Paris, 14 October 2014, Rev. de l'Arb. 2015, 151-155
CA Paris, 12 April 2016, Rev. de l'Arb. 2017, 234-240
CA Paris, 24 May 2016, Rev. de l'Arb. 2017, 533-538

CA Reims, 2 November 2011, Rev. de l'Arb. 2012, 112-119

TGI Paris, 13 January 1986, Rev. de l'Arb. 1987, 63-66
TGI Paris, 12 May 1993, Rev. de l'Arb. 1996, 410-411

Germany

BVerfG, 8 February 1967, 2 BvR 235/64, NJW 1967, 1123–1124

BGH, 3 July 1975, III ZR 78/73, NJW 1976, 109-111
BGH, 4 March 1999, III ZR 72/98, NJW 1999, 2370-2372
BGH, 1 February 2001, III ZR 332/99, NJW-RR 2001, 1059-1061
BGH, 14 May 2002, XI ZR 388/01, NJW 2002, 2396-2397
BGH, 6 April 2006, V ZB 194/05, NJW 2006, 2492-2495
BGH, 28 March 2012, III ZB 63/10, NJW 2012, 1811-1812
BGH, 12 January 2016, 3 StR 482/15, NStZ 2016, 218-219
BGH, 13 January 2016, VII ZR 36/14, NJW 2016, 1022-1025
BGH, 19 September 2016, IX ZA 37/15, BeckRS 2016, 18053
BGH, 2 March 2017, I ZB 42/16, SchiedsVZ 2017, 200-202
BGH, 2 May 2017, I ZB 1/16, SchiedsVZ 2017, 317-323
BGH, 10 November 2017, I ZB 12/17, SchiedsVZ 2018, 271-275
BGH, 31 January 2019, I ZB 46/18, NZM 2020, 334-336
BGH, 10 December 2019, II ZB 14/19, NJW 2020, 1680-1681

KG Berlin, 7 June 2010, 20 SchH 2/10, SchiedsVZ 2010, 225-227
KG Berlin, 12 February 2018, 13 SchH 2/17, NJ 2018, 206-208

OLG Dresden, 27 January 2005,11 SchH 02/04, SchiedsVZ 2005, 159-163
OLG Dresden, 12 December 2008, 11 SchH 7/08, OLGR Dresden 2009, 924

OLG Frankfurt a.M. 27 April 2006, 26 SchH 1/06, SchiedsVZ 329-331
OLG Frankfurt a.M., 4 October 2007, 26 Sch 8/07, SchiedsVZ 2008, 96-102
OLG Frankfurt a.M., 10 January 2008, 26 Sch 21/07, SchiedsVZ 2008, 199-200
OLG Frankfurt a.M., 26 June 2008, 26 SchH 2/08, BeckRS 2008, 13980
OLG Frankfurt a.M., 29 October 2009, 26 Sch 12/09, SchiedsVZ 2010, 52-56
OLG Frankfurt a.M., 28 March 2011, 26 SchH 2/11, SchiedsVZ 2011, 342-344
OLG Frankfurt a.M., 13 February 2012, 26 SchH 15/11, BeckRS 2014, 12067
OLG Frankfurt a.M., 15 October 2018, 26 SchH 3/18, NJOZ 2019, 1127-1130
OLG Frankfurt a.M., 24 January 2019, 26 SchH 2/18, BeckRS 2019, 848

OLG Hamburg, 9 July 2015, 6 SchH 1/14

OLG Karlsruhe, 14 July 2006, 10 Sch 1/06, BeckRS 2006, 19851

OLG Köln, 2 April 2004, 9 SchH 22/03, Beck RS 2012, 10537
OLG Köln, 28 June 2011, 19 Sch 11/10, SchiedsVZ 2012, 161-168

OLG München, 5 July 2006, 34 SchH 5/06, BeckRS 2006, 8109
OLG München, 10 January 2007, 34 SchH 7/06, BeckRS 2007, 00709
OLG München, 3 January 2008, 34 SchH 3/07, SchiedsVZ 2008, 102-104
OLG München, 1 July 2009, 34 SchH 4/09, BeckRS 2011, 7079
OLG München, 10 May 2012, 23 U 4635/11, BeckRS 2012, 10669
OLG München, 10 July 2013, 34 SchH 8/12, NJOZ 2014, 1779-1782
OLG München, 3 January 2014, 34 SchH 7/13, SchiedsVZ 2014, 45-48
OLG München, 18 December 2014, 34 SchH 3/14, NJOZ, 893-896
OLG München, 31 March 2015, 15 U 2227/14, NJW-RR 2015, 1333-1338
OLG München, 17 November 2016, 34 SchH 13/16, NJOZ 2018, 437-439

OLG Naumburg, 19 December 2001, 10 SchH 3/01, SchiedsVZ 2003, 134-142

LG Berlin, 14 July 2014, 33 O 494/13, BeckRS 2015, 2546

LG Duisburg, 6 October 1981, 15 O 173/81, ZIP 1982, 229

Netherlands

Russian Federation v. Veteran Petroleum, Ltd., Yukos Universal Ltd. and Hulley Enterprises, Ltd., RB Den Haag, 20 April 2016, C/09/477160 / HA ZA 15-1, C/09/477162 / HA ZA 15-2, and C/09/481619 / HA ZA 15-112

Switzerland

BGer, 12 February 1958, BGE 84 I 39
BGer, 26 October 1966, BGE 92 I 271
BGer, 25 January 1967, BGE 93 I 49
BGer, 17 February 1982, BGE 108 Ia 48
BGer, 14 March 1985, BGE 111 Ia 72
BGer, 20 December 1989, BGE 115 Ia 400
BGer, 15 February 1990, BGE 116 Ia 14
BGer, 1 July 1991, BGE 117 II 346
BGer, 11 May 1992, ASA Bull. 1992, 381-401
BGer, 18 August 1992, BGE 118 II 359
BGer, 15 March 1993, BGE 119 II 271
BGer, 30 June 1994, 4P.292/1993, ASA Bull. 1997, 99-107
BGer, 9 February 1998, ASA Bull. 1998, 634-652.
BGer, 9 April 1998, BGE 124 I 121
BGer, 17 February 2000, 4P.168/1999, ASA Bull. 2001, 781-786
BGer, 28 April 2000, BGE 126 III 249
BGer, 15 October 2001, 4P.188/2001
BGer, 10 January 2002, 4P.272/2001
BGer, 27 May 2003, BGE 129 III 445
BGer, 10 June 2003, 4P.263/2002/ech
BGer, 21 November 2003, BGE 130 III 66
BGer, 7 January 2004, 4P.196/2003/ech
BGer, 10 December 2004, BGE 131 I 223
BGer, 14 December 2004, 4P.208/2004/lma
BGer, 4 August 2006, 4P.105/2006/fun
BGer, 7 November 2006, BGE 133 I 89
BGer, 7 December 2006, BGE 133 I 1
BGer, 20 March 2008, 4A_506/2007
BGer, 28 April 2008, BGE 134 I 238
BGer, 30 October 2008, 9C_836/2008
BGer, 19 February 2009, 4A_539/2008

BGer, 12 June 2009, 4A_586/2008
BGer, 6 January 2010, 4A_348/2009, ASA Bull. 2010, 772-775
BGer, 10 June 2010, 4A_458/2009 ASA Bull. 2010, 520-539
BGer, 29 October 2010, BGE 136 III 605
BGer, 4 May 2011, BGE 137 I 227
BGer, 7 June 2011, BGE 137 III 289
BGer, 9 October 2012, BGE 138 I 406
BGer, 9 October 2012, 4A_110/2012, ASA Bull. 2013, 174-193
BGer, 27 August 2013, BGE 139 III 433
BGer, 13 November 2013, BGE 139 III 511
BGer, 20 May 2014, BGE 140 III 221
BGer, 22 August 2014, BGE 140 I 271
BGer, 4 January 2015, 4A_598/2014
BGer, 22 January 2015, 2C_814/2014
BGer, 27 April 2015, BGE 141 IV 178
BGer, 21 May 2015, 4A_709/2014
BGer, 24 November 2017, 4A_236/2017
BGer, 14 May 2018, 5A_701/2017
BGer, 4 July 2018, 4A_505/2017
BGer 6 August 2019, 4A_62/2019
BGer, 16 October 2019, 4A_292/2019

KGer Graubünden, 30 January 1996, ASA Bull. 1996, 264-267

BezGer Affoltern am Albis, 26 May 1994, ASA Bull. 1997, 262–273

United Kingdom

A v. B, [2011] EWHC 2345 (Comm)
Aldcroft v. International Cotton Association Ltd., [2017] EWHC 642 (Comm)
AMEC Capital Projects Ltd. v. Whitefriars City Estates Ltd., [2004] EWCA Civ 1418
AMEC Civil Engineering Ltd. v. Secretary of State for Transport, [2005] EWCA Civ 291
ASM Shipping Ltd. v. Harris & Ors., [2007] EWHC 1513 (Comm)
ASM Shipping Ltd. of India v. TTMI Ltd. of England, [2005] EWHC 2238 (Comm)
ASM Shipping Ltd. of India v. TTMI Ltd. of England, [2007] EWHC 927
AT & T Corp. & Anor v. Saudi Cable Co., [2000] CLC 220

Beumer Group U.K. Ltd. v. Vinci Construction U.K. Ltd., [2016] EWHC 2283 (TCC)
Bubbles & Wine Limited v. Reshat Lusha, [2018] EWCA Civ 468

Cofely Ltd. v. Anthony Bingham and Knowles Ltd., [2016] EWHC 240 (Comm)

Dera Commercial Estate v. Derya Inc., [2018] EWHC 1673 (Comm)
Director General of Fair Trading v. Proprietary Association of Great Britain and Proprietary Articles Trade Association, [2001] EWCA Civ 1217

El Farargy v. El Farargy and others, [2007] EWCA Civ 1149

Glencot Development and Design Co. Ltd. v. Ben Barrett & Son (Contractors) Ltd., [2001] EWHC 15

H v. L and M, [2017] EWHC 137 (Comm)
Halliburton Co. v. Chubb Bermuda Ins. Ltd., [2018] EWCA Civ 817
Halliburton Co. v. Chubb Bermuda Ins. Ltd., [2020] UKSC 48
Harb v. Aziz, [2016] EWCA Civ 556
Hays Specialist Recruitment (Holdings) Ltd., Hays Specialist Recruitment Ltd. v. Mark Ions, Exclusive Human Resources Ltd., [2008] EWHC 745 (Ch)
Helow v. Advocate General for Scotland, [2008] UKHL 62

Interprods Ltd. v. De La Rue International Ltd., [2014] EWHC 68 (Comm)

K/S Norjarl A/S v. Hyundai Heavy Industries Co. Ltd., 1991 WL 838002

Laker Airways Inc. v. FLS Aerospace Ltd., [1999] CLC 1124
Lawal v. Northern Spirit, [2003] UKHL 35
Liverpool Roman Catholic Archdiocesan Trustees Incorporated v. David Goldberg Q.C., [2002] TCLR 4
Locabail (U.K.) Ltd. v. Bayfield Properties Ltd., [2000] QB 451

Magill v. Porter, [2001] UKHL 67
Metropolitan Properties Co. (F.G.C.) Ltd. v. Lannon, [1969] 1 QB 577

Nye Saunders and Partners v. Alan E Bristow, (1987) 37 BLR 92

P v. Q, R, S, U, [2017] EWHC 194 (Comm)
PPG Industries Inc. v. Pilkington PLC, EWHC, 1 November 1989, reported in J. Kendall, *Barristers, Independence and Disclosure*, Arb. Int'l 8 (1992), 287-299, 290-291
Primary Health Investment Properties Ltd., Primary Health Properties PLC, Dr N.B. Turnbull, Dr V.L. Beveridge, Dr R.A. Elder, Dr I.M. Wheatley v. The Secretary of State for Health &

others, The National Health Service Litigation Authority Family Health Services Appeal Unit, [2009] EWHC 519 (Admin)
Prince Jefri Bolkiah v. State of Brunei Darussalam, [2007] UKPC 62

R v. Camborne Justices, Ex p. Pearce, [1955] 1 QB 41
R v. Gough (Robert), [1993] AC 646 (HL)
R v. Sussex Justices, Ex p. McCarthy, [1924] 1 KB 256

Sierra Fishing Co. v. Farran, [2015] EWHC 140 (Comm)
Sphere Drake Ins. v. American Reliable Ins. Co., [2004] EWHC 796 (Comm)
Stretford v. Football Association Ltd., [2007] EWCA Civ 238

Taylor v. Lawrence, [2002] EWCA Civ 90

W Ltd. v. M Sdn Bhd., [2016] 1 CLC 437

United States

Federal

Al-Harbi v. Citibank, 85 F.3d 680 (D.C. Cir. 1996)
Amerisure Mut. Ins. Co. v. Everest Reinsurance Co., 109 F.Supp.3d 969 (E.D. Michigan 2015)
Anderson, Inc. v. Horton Farms, Inc., 166 F.3d 308 (6th Cir. 1998)
Andros Compania Maritima, SA v. Marc Rich & Co., AG, 579 F.2d 691 (2d Cir. 1978)
ANR Coal Co., Inc. v. Cogentrix of North Carolina, Inc., 173 F.3d 493 (4th Cir. 1999)
Apperson v. Fleet Carrier Co., 879 F.2d 1344 (6th Cir. 1989)
Applied Industrial Materials Co. v. Ovalar Makine Ticaret Ve Sanayi, A.S. and Ural Ataman, Docket No. 06-3297-cv (2d Cir. 9 July 2007)
Apusento Garden (Guam) Inc. v. Superior Court of Guam, 94 F.3d 1346 (9th Cir. 1996)
Ario v. Cologne Reinsurance (Barbados), Ltd., 2009 WL 3818626 (M.D. Pennsylvania)

Ballantine Books, Inc. v. Capital Distributing Co., 302 F.2d 17 (2d Cir. 1962)
Bernstein Seawell & Kove v. Bosarge, 813 F.2d 726 (5th Cir. 1987)
Blackwell v. Merrill Lynch, Pierce, Fenner & Smith Inc., 22 F.Supp.3d 565 (W.D. North Carolina 2014)
British Ins. Co. of Cayman v. Water Street Ins. Co., Ltd., 93 F.Supp.2d 506 (S.D. New York 2000)
Brown v. Brown-Thill, 762 F.3d 814 (8th Cir. 2014)

Certain Underwriting Members of Lloyds of London v. Florida, 2018 WL 2727492 (2d Cir.)
Commonwealth Coatings Co. v. Continental Casualty Co. et al., 89 S.Ct. 337 (1968)
Continental Cas. Co. v. Staffing Concepts, Inc., 2011 WL 7459781 (M.D. Florida)
Cooper v. WestEnd Capital Management, LLC, 832 F.3d 534, (5th Cir. 2016)
Cristina Blouse Corp. v. International Ladies Garment Workers Union, Local 162, 492 F.Supp. 508 (S.D. New York 1980)
Crow Construction v. Jeffrey M. Brown Assoc. Inc., 264 F.Supp.2d 217 (E.D. Pennsylvania 2003)

Dealer Computer Services, Inc. v. Michael Motor Co., Inc., 761 F.Supp.2d 459 (S.D. Texas 2010)
Dealer Computer Services, Inc. v. Michael Motor Co., Inc., 485 Fed.Appx. 724 (5th Cir. 2012)
Dean Witter Reynolds, Inc. v. Clements, O'Neill, Pierce & Nickens, LLP, 2000 WL 36098499 (S.D. Texas)
Delta Mine Holding Co. v. AFC Coal Properties, Inc., 280 F.3d 815 (8th Cir. 2001)
Dow Corning Corp. v. Safety National Cas. Corp., 335 F.3d 742 (8th Cir. 2003)

Erving v. Virginia Squires Basketball Club, 349 F.Supp. 716 (E.D. New York 1972)

Fairchild Corp. v. Alcoa, Inc., 510 F.Supp.2d 280 (S.D. New York 2007)
Federal Vending, Inc. v. Steak & Ale of Florida, Inc., 71 F.Supp.2d 1245 (S.D. Florida 1999)
Fidelity Federal Bank, FSB v. Durga Ma Co., 386 F.3d 1306 (9th Cir. 2004)
First Interregional Equity Corp. v. Haughton, 842 F.Supp. 105 (S.D. New York 1994)
Fowler v. Ritz-Carlton Hotel Co., LLC, 579 Fed.Appx. 693 (11th Cir. 2014)

Gianelli Money Purchase Plan and Trust v. ADM Investor Services Inc., 146 F.3d 1309 (11th Cir. 1998)
Goldman, Sachs & Co. v. Athena Venture Partners, L.P., 803 F.3d 144 (3d Cir. 2015)

HSM Const. Services, Inc. v. MDC Systems, Inc., 239 Fed.Appx. 748 (3d Cir. 2007)
HSMV Corp. v. ADI Ltd., 72 F.Supp.2d 1122 (C.D. California 1999)

In re Sussex, 781 F.3d 1065 (9th Cir. 2015)
International Produce, Inc. v. A/S Rosshavet, 504 F.Supp. 736 (S.D. New York 1980)
International Produce, Inc. v. A/S Rosshavet, 638 F.2d 548 (2d Cir. 1981)

Johnson v. Directory Assistants Inc., 797 F.3d 1294 (11th Cir. 2015)

Kolel Beth Yechiel Mechil of Tartikov, Inc. v. YLL Irrevocable Trust, 878 F.Supp.2d 459 (S.D. New York 2012)
Kolel Beth Yechiel Mechil of Tartikov, Inc. v. YLL Irrevocable Trust, 729 F.3d 99 (2d Cir. 2013)

LGC Holdings, Inc. v. Julius Klein Diamonds, LLC, 238 F.Supp.3d 452 (S.D. New York 2017)
Lucent Technologies Inc. v. Tatung Co., 379 F.3d 24 (2d Cir. 2004)
Lummus Global Amazonas S.A. v. Aguaytia Energy del Peru SR Ltda., 256 F.Supp.2d 594 (S.D. Texas 2002)

Mantle v. Upper Deck Co., 956 F.Supp. 719 (N.D. Texas 1997)
Merck & Co., Inc. v. Pericor Therapeutics, Inc., 2016 WL 4491441 (S.D. New York)
Merit Ins. Co. v. Leatherby Ins. Co., 714 F.2d 673 (7th Cir. 1983)
Metropolitan Property and Cas. Ins. Co. v. J.C. Penney Casualty Ins. Co., 780 F.Supp. 885 (D. Connecticut 1991)
Middlesex Mut. Ins. Co. v. Levine, 675 F.2d 1197 (11th Cir. 1982)
Midwest Generation EME, LLC v. Continuum Chemical Corp., 768 F.Supp.2d 939 (N.D. Illinois 2010)
Morelite Construction Co. v. New York City District Council Carpenters Benefit Funds, 748 F.2d 79 (2d Cir. 1984)
Munich Reinsurance America, Inc. v. ACE Property & Casualty Co., 500 F.Supp.2d 272 (S.D. New York 2007)

National Indemnity Co. v. IRB Brasil Resseguros SA, 164 F.Supp.3d 457 (S.D. New York 2016)
Nationwide Mut. Ins. Co. v. First St. Ins. Co., 213 F.Supp.2d 10 (D. Massachusetts 2002).
Nationwide Mutual Ins. Co. v. Home Ins. Co., 429 F.3d 640 (6th Cir. 2005)
Nationwide Mutual Ins. Co. v. Home Ins. Co., 90 F.Supp.2d 893 (S.D. Ohio 2000)
NGC Network Asia, LLC v. PAC Pacific Group Intern., Inc., 511 Fed.Appx. 86 (2d Cir. 2013)

Olson v. Merrill Lynch, Pierce, Fenner & Smith, Inc., 51 F.3d 157 (8th Cir. 1995)
Oracle Corp. v. Wilson, 276 F.Supp.3d 22 (S.D. New York 2017)
Ortiz-Espinosa v. BBVA Securities of Puerto Rico, Inc., 852 F.3d 36 (5th Cir. 2017)
Ostrom v. Worldventures Marketing, LLC, 60 F.Supp.3d 942 (M.D. Louisiana 2016)

Peoples Sec. Life Ins. Co. v. Monumental Life Ins. Co., 991 F.2d 141 (4th Cir. 1993)
Petrol Corp. v. Groupement d'Achat des Carburants, 84 F.Supp. 446 (S.D. New York 1949)
Pitta v. Hotel Ass'n of New York City, Inc., 806 F.2d 419 (2d Cir. 1986)
Ploetz for Laudine L. Ploetz, 1985 Trust v. Morgan Stanley Smith Barney LLC, 2018 WL 3213877 (8th Cir.)
Positive Software Solutions, Inc. v. New Century Mortg. Corp., 476 F.3d 278 (5th Cir. 2007)
Power Services Associates, Inc. v. UNC Metcalf Servicing, Inc., 338 F.Supp.2d 1375 (N.D. Georgia 2004)

Questar Capital Corp. v. Gorter, 909 F.Supp.2d 789 (W.D. Kentucky 2012)

Rai v. Barclays Capital Inc., 739 F.Supp.2d 364 (S.D. New York 2010)
Ray v. Chafetz, 236 F.Supp.3d 66 (D. Columbia 2017)
Republic of Argentina v. AWG Group Ltd., 211 F.Supp.3d 335 (D. Columbia 2016)

Savers Property and Cas. Ins. Co. v. National Union Fire Ins. Comp., 748 F.3d 708 (6th Cir. 2014)
Scandinavian Reinsurance Co. Ltd. v. Saint Paul Fire and Marine Ins. Co., 668 F.3d 60 (2d Cir. 2012)
Schmitz v. Zilveti, 20 F.3d 1043 (9th Cir. 1994)
Sodexo Management, Inc. v. Detroit Public Schools, 200 F.Supp.3d 679 (E.D. Michigan 2016)
Sphere Drake Ins. Ltd. v. All American Life Ins. Co., 307 F.3d 617 (7th Cir. 2002)
Standard Tankers (Bahamas) Co., Ltd. v. Motor Tank Vessel, AKTI, 438 F. Supp. 153 (E.D. North Carolina 1977)
Stef Shipping Corp. v. Norris Grain Co., 209 F.Supp. 249 (S.D. New York 1962)
Stone v. Bear, Stearns & Co., Inc., 872 F.Supp.2d 435 (E.D. Pennsylvania 2012)
Sunkist Soft Drinks, Inc. v. Sunkist Growers, Inc., 10 F.3d 753 (11th Cir. 1993)
Sunoco Overseas, Inc. v. Texaco Intern. Trader, Inc., 69 F.Supp.2d 502 (S.D. New York 1999)

Tamari v. Bache Halsey Stuart Inc., 619 F.2d 1196 (7th Cir. 1980)
Thian Lok Tio v. Washington Hosp. Center, 753 F.Supp.2d 9 (D. Columbia 2010)
Thomas Kinkade Co. v. Lighthouse Galleries, LLC, 2010 WL 436604 (E.D. Michigan)
Thomas Kinkade Co. v. White, 711 F.3d 719 (6th Cir. 2013)
Transmarine Seaways Corp. of Monrovia v. Marc Rich & Co. AG, 480 F.Supp. 352 (S.D. New York 1979)

United Transp. Union v. Gateway Western Ry. Co., 284 F.3d 710 (7th Cir. 2002)
University Commons-Urbana, Ltd. v. Universal Constructors Inc., 304 F.3d 1331 (11th Cir. 2002)
U.S. Wrestling Federation v. Wrestling Division of the AAU, Inc., 605 F.2d 313 (7th Cir. 1979)

Washburn v. McManus, 895 F.Supp. 392 (D. Connecticut 1994)
WellPoint Health Networks, Inc. v. John Hancock Life Ins. Co., 547 F.Supp.2d 899 (N.D. Illinois 2008)
Winfrey v. Simmons Foods, Inc., 495 F.3d 549 (8th Cir. 2007)

States

American Eagle Fire Ins. Co. v. New Jersey Ins. Co., 240 N.Y. 398 (Ct. App. 1925)
Astoria Medical Group v. Health Ins. Plan of Greater New York, 11 N.Y.2d 128 (Ct. App. 1962)
Hodges Intern. Inc. v. Rembrandt Fabrics, Ltd., 353 N.Y.S.2d 462 (1st Dep't 1974)
Hoosac Tunnel Dock & Elevator v. O'Brien, 137 Mass 424 (1884)
Malik v. Ruttenberg, 398 N.J. Super. 489 (N.J. Super. Ct. App. Div. 2008)

European Courts

ECJ

Allianz SpA, Generali Assicurazioni Generali SpA v. West Tankers Inc., ECJ, 10 February 2009, C-185/07
Slovak Republic v. Achmea BV, ECJ, 6 March 2018, C-284/16

ECtHR

Bramelid and Malmström v. Sweden, ECtHR, 12 October 1982, Nos. 8588/79 and 8589/79
McGonnell v. United Kingdom, ECtHR, 8 February 2000, 28488/95
Mutu/Pechstein v. Switzerland, ECtHR, 2 October 2018, Nos. 40575/10 and 67474/10
Steck-Risch and others v. Liechtenstein, ECtHR, 19 May 2005, 63151/00
Suovaniemi and others v. Finland, ECtHR, 23 February 1999, 31737/96
Wettstein v. Switzerland, ECtHR, 21 December 2000, 33958/96

Arbitral Decisions

DIS

DIS - SV - 217/00, SchiedsVZ 2003, 94-96

ICSID

Blue Bank International & Trust (Barbados) Ltd. v. Bolivarian Republic of Venezuela, ICSID Tribunal, 12 November 2013, ICSID Case No. ARB/12/20
Bridgestone Licensing Services, Inc. and Bridgestone Americas, Inc. v. Republic of Panama, ICSID Tribunal, 13 December 2018, ARB/16/34
EuroGas Inc. and Belmont Resources Inc. v. Slovak Republic, ICSID Tribunal, 23 June 2015, ICSID Case No. ARB/14/14
Flughafen Zürich AG and Gestión e Ingeniería IDC SA v. Republic of Venezuela, ICSID Tribunal, 29 August 2012, ICSID Case No. ARB/10/19
Fraport AG Frankfurt Airport Services Worldwide v. Republic of the Philippines, ICSID ad hoc Committee, 18 September 2008, ICSID Case No. ARB/03/25
Hrvatska Elektroprivreda, d.d. v. Republic of Slovenia, ICSID Tribunal, 6 May 2008, ARB/05/24
Hrvatska Elektroprivreda d.d. v. Republic of Slovenia, ICSID Tribunal, 17 December 2015, ARB/05/24
Muhammet Çap & Sehil Inşaat Endustri ve Ticaret Ltd. Sti. v. Turkmenistan, ICSID Tribunal, 12 June 2015, ICSID Case No. ARB/12/6
RSM Production Corp. v. Saint Lucia, ICSID Tribunal, 23 October 2014, ARB/12/10
Suez, Sociedad General de Aguas de Barcelona SA, and others v. The Argentine Republic, ICSID Tribunal, 12 May 2008, ICSID Case Nos. ARB/03/19 and ARB/03/17
Víctor Pey Casado and Foundation President Allende v. Republic of Chile, ICSID Tribunal, 18 May 2014, ICSID Case No. ARB/98/2
Víctor Pey Casado and Foundation President Allende v. Republic of Chile, ICSID Tribunal, 21 February 2017, ICSID Case No. ARB/98/2

Iran-U.S. Claims Tribunal

Sedco Inc. v. Iranian National Oil Co. and the Islamic Republic of Iran, Iran-U.S. Claims Tribunal, Award, 2 July 1987 - No. 309-129-3

LCIA

PCA

SCC

SCC Arbitration 2015/064, SCC Practice Note, p. 9

SCC Arbitration V (137/2008), N. Lindström, *Decisions by the SCC Board during 2008 - 2010*, p. 7

Index

International Commerce and Arbitration (Series editor: Ingeborg Schwenzer)

Volume 1: Mariel Dimsey, The Resolution of International Investment Disputes: Challenges and Practical Solutions, ISBN 978-90-77596-52-4
Volume 2: Sarah E. Hilmer, Mediation in the People's Republic of China and Hong Kong (SAR), ISBN 978-90-77596-74-6
Volume 3: Christina Knahr, Christian Koller, Walter Rechberger and August Reinisch (eds.), Investment and Commercial Arbitration - Similarities and Divergences, ISBN 978-90-77596-81-4
Volume 4: Markus Jäger, Reimbursement for Attorney's Fees, ISBN 978-90-77596-98-2
Volume 5: Olivier Luc Mosimann, Anti-Suit Injunctions in International Commercial Arbitration, ISBN 978-90-77596-99-9
Volume 6: Edgardo Munoz, Modern Law of Contracts and Sales in Latin America, Spain and Portugal, ISBN 978-94-90947-03-3
Volume 7: Pascal Hachem, Agreed Sums Payable upon Breach of an Obligation, ISBN 978-94-90947-04-0
Volume 8: Ingeborg Schwenzer and Lisa Spagnolo (eds.), Towards Uniformity, ISBN 978-94-90947-10-1
Volume 9: Natia Lapiashvili, Modern Law of Contracts and Sales in Eastern Europe and Central Asia, ISBN 978-94-90947-20-0
Volume 10: Lara Pair, Consolidation in International Commercial Arbitration - The ICC and Swiss Rules, ISBN 978-94-90947-27-9
Volume 11: Ingeborg Schwenzer and Lisa Spagnolo (eds.), State of Play, ISBN 978-94-90947-46-0
Volume 12: Ingeborg Schwenzer and Lisa Spagnolo (eds.), Globalization versus Regionalization, ISBN 978-94-6236-020-4
Volume 13: Marie-Camille Pitton, Le rôle du jugement étranger dans l'interprétation du droit conventionnel uniforme, ISBN 978-94-90947-81-1
Volume 14: Andreas F. Müller, Protecting the Integrity of a Written Agreement, ISBN 978-94-6236-073-0
Volume 15: Ingeborg Schwenzer, Yeşim M. Atamer and Petra Butler (eds.), Current Issues in the CISG and Arbitration, ISBN 978-94-6236-097-6
Volume 16: Alain Hosang, Obstructionist Behavior in International Commercial Arbitration: Legal Analysis and Measures Available to the Arbitral Tribunal, ISBN 978-94-6236-100-3
Volume 17: Alissa Palumbo, Modern Law of Sales in the United States, ISBN 978-94-6236-439-4
Volume 18: Ingeborg Schwenzer and Lisa Spagnolo (eds.), Boundaries and Intersections, ISBN 978-94-6236-441-7
Volume 19: Ingeborg Schwenzer (ed.), 35 Years CISG and Beyond, ISBN 978-94-6236-624-4

Volume 20: Marçal Justen Filho, Cesar Pereira and Maria Augusta Rost (eds.), Brazil Infrastructure Law, ISBN 978-94-6236-640-4

Volume 21: Ingeborg Schwenzer, Cesar Pereira and Leandro Tripodi (eds.), CISG and Latin America: Regional and Global Perspectives, ISBN 978-94-6236-653-4

Volume 22: Ingeborg Schwenzer and Lisa Spagnolo (eds.), Growing the CISG, ISBN 978-94-6236-667-1

Volume 23: Ingeborg Schwenzer (ed.), The CISG Advisory Council Opinions, ISBN 978-94-6236-719-7

Volume 24: Ingeborg Schwenzer and Lisa Spagnolo (eds.), The Electronic CISG, ISBN 978-94-6236-751-7

Volume 25: Lina Thieme, Damages for breach of the obligation to arbitrate, ISBN 978-94-6236-791-3

Volume 26: Miquel dels Sants Mirambell Fargas, The Seller's Right to Cure under Article 48 CISG, ISBN 978-94-6236-830-9

Volume 27: Gustavo Moser, Rethinking Choice of Law in Cross-Border Sales, ISBN 978-94-6236-846-0

Volume 28: Michael Bridge, Ulrich Schroeter and Ingeborg Schwenzer (eds.), The CISG Advisory Council Opinions, second edition, ISBN 978-94-6236-200-0

Volume 29: Ilka Hanna Beimel, Independence and Impartiality in International Commercial Arbitration, ISBN 978-94-6236-207-9

www.ingramcontent.com/pod-product-compliance
Ingram Content Group UK Ltd.
Pitfield, Milton Keynes, MK11 3LW, UK
UKHW051310180926
15262UKWH00004B/24

9 789462 362079